MASSACHUSETTS POLITICS
AND PUBLIC POLICY

MASSACHUSETTS

POLITICS

AND

PUBLIC POLICY

STUDIES IN POWER
AND LEADERSHIP

RICHARD A. HOGARTY

UNIVERSITY OF MASSACHUSETTS PRESS

AMHERST AND BOSTON

Copyright © 2002 by University of Massachusetts Press
Printed in the United States of America

LC 2001008415
ISBN 1-55849-351-4 (library cloth ed.); 1-55849-362-X (paper)

Designed by Milenda Nan Ok Lee
Set in Copperplate and Adobe Minion
Printed and bound by Maple-Vail Book Manufacturing Group

Library of Congress Cataloging-in-Publication Data

Hogarty, Richard A.
Massachusetts politics and public policy : studies in power and
leadership / Richard A. Hogarty.
   p.   cm.
Includes bibliographical references and index.
ISBN 1-55849-351-4 (lib. cloth ed. : alk. paper)—ISBN 1-55849-362-X
(pbk. : alk. paper)
   1. Political planning—Massachusetts. 2. Massachusetts—Politics
and government—1951– I. Title.
JK3149.P64 H64 2002
320.9744—dc21   2001008415

British Library Cataloguing in Publication data are available.

This book is published with the support and cooperation of the John W.
McCormack Institute of Public Affairs, University of Massachusetts Boston.

To the cherished memory of my parents,
James and Marie Hogarty

CONTENTS

PREFACE

Properly conceived, the basic task of public policy analysis is to deal in a timely and practical fashion with pressing public issues of the day. The focus typically is on hot-button political issues and topics that are ripe for public debate and scrutiny. That is clearly the central theme of this book. Most of these essays focus primarily on state politics, policy innovation, program development, administrative practice, and organizational change in entities that are generally mandated to provide public services for various constituencies and clientele groups. Consideration is also given to the policy environment in which such organizations operate. Another objective is to understand the shifting problems of accountability that arise when public services are provided by a variety of political actors and types of organizations. Still another objective is to identify the implicit and explicit political struggles that are at the heart of policy issues and the delivery of public services.

Politics is a very human and unpredictable enterprise. In the Bay State it is commonly referred to as a "blood sport" that is fought with risks and uncertainties. Politicians constitute a special breed of individuals who seek to advance by establishing a favorable record and by trying to be all things to all people. Most successful politicians engage in bargaining and compromise, building coalitions, brokering deals, and achieving consensus, while placating as many constituents as possible and avoiding their wrath. In conducting the public business, they display human weaknesses and foibles that dismay us. Occasionally inept and evasive, sometimes even venal and corrupt, but more often than not well-intentioned and unsung, they are never free from the most direct, unremitting pressure and intense public scrutiny. Much of their labor is mundane, repetitive, time-consuming, and lackluster. Yet, without their hard work and valiant efforts, a huge and diverse society would splinter into its myriad warring parts. At their best, they serve to soften our harsh judgments and combat the cynicism to which we are all too prone. Politics for some does not come easily. In an increasingly invasive journalistic culture, the media intrude into their fishbowl existence and private lives.

This book is based on the fundamental assumption that ordinary citizens can learn a great deal about the political character of a state by studying actual events that involve the many participants who influence and shape its public policy and programs. Astonishingly, there are too few studies that examine the exercise of political power and leadership in Massachusetts, which is, after all, a state with a lively and liberal politics. Over the years I have written a series of studies that deal with Bay State politics and the operations of the state government, including the legislative branch and the various executive departments and agencies. These areas have been very much neglected, and this book fills some of the glaring gaps in the literature.

More specifically, these essays examine the process of policymaking and implementation—how, in fact, policy is initiated and carried out—identifying the participants and their roles and strategies. They chronicle actual power situations that are entangled in an intricate web of legislative, executive, and judicial relationships. All provide valuable lessons in public management. There is, of course, some repetition, but that is unavoidable because some of the episodes involve the same cast of characters and cover the same time frame.

Initially published individually, these essays gain strength and coherence, I believe, when put together as a collection of readings. With this goal in mind, I have attempted to fit them into a coherent framework. The essays reflect my convictions that analyses of state politics will be enriched by the integration of theory and practice. Thus, they are intended to convey a sense of the political reality involved in the shaping of desired outcomes. In this context, they describe as accurately as possible the inner workings of both the political and bureaucratic systems. They also shed light on the styles and methods of contemporary public figures.

Anticipating the consequences of any policy is always difficult at best. New ideas are not easily translated into policy. Policymakers usually land in trouble if they do not identify correctly the nature of a problem and the viable options for its resolution. Playing the devil's advocate role for the moment, one needs to ask why apparently well designed, carefully researched public policy so often seems to fail, to produce unintended results, or to dissatisfy the people whom it is intended to benefit.

Two contemporary illustrations come readily to mind. Take, for example, the Massachusetts Comprehensive Assessment System (MCAS) examination, which is mandated as a graduation requirement for high school students. It has provoked a storm of controversy in the Bay State. This standardized test is supposedly designed to spur schools to attain higher academic standards, not just to test basic skills. Yet this high-stakes test has divided parents, students, and educators who disagree on whether a single test should determine if students get a high school diploma.

Another case in point is the controversial dirty-needle exchange program. It is designed to reduce the spread of blood-borne diseases, such as HIV and hepatitis C, by steering drug users toward clean syringes and hypodermic needles. Advocates, such as the AIDS Action Committee of Massachusetts, argue that the program prevents transmission of these diseases while encouraging drug users to enter treatment. Not everyone, however, believes that this program is beneficial. For instance, the Citizens Action Network (CANE) in the city of Springfield exerted political pressure on its officials to terminate a needle exchange program. Nevertheless, a statewide poll conducted by the McCormack Institute at the University of Massachusetts in Boston revealed that 62 percent of those polled support the needle exchange program.

The major emphasis of this book is on political power and how it is amassed, used, and abused in the context of state and local situations. Some of the theoretical selections offer various analytical approaches, while others assess particular government problems. Special attention is focused on issues involving an ethics code, the delivery of mental health services, urban transportation, environmental protection, public safety, corrections, the death penalty, public welfare, and public higher education.

Nearly all of the information for these essays comes from a rich array of public documents, government reports, memoranda, newspapers, and interviews conducted with the major participants in the episodes. These sources provide us with valuable insights into the concerns and perceptions of those who were involved. As with most scholarly studies, the impossibility of screening all relevant facts and the need to rely on what participants choose to reveal means that some critical data are often overlooked. Participant-observers may miss certain details as well. Even so, this approach at least takes into account the different ways in which the central actors saw each episode and their roles in it. Although my sources are far too numerous to mention here, I owe all of them my gratitude. Without their help and cooperation, these essays could not have been written.

By way of acknowledgment, I wish to thank Padraig O'Malley, editor of the *New England Journal of Public Policy*, for permission to use four of my previously published essays. Robert Keough, editor of *Common Wealth Magazine*, gave permission to use portions of an essay that I had written for his journal. I also wish to acknowledge the late Richard A. Manley, with whom I co-authored a McCormack Institute occasional paper on the subject of lawmaking by outside budget sections. Duane Lockard, John E. Mc-Donough, and Robert C. Wood read and critiqued various chapters. They have contributed in many ways too numerous to detail. Much credit goes to Paul Wright, editor at the University of Massachusetts Press, who was receptive to the idea of this book and nurtured its publication. Similarly, Amanda Heller did a superb job of editing and saved me from untold pitfalls. All of them in one way or another helped to make this book much better than the original manuscript.

Finally, the person most instrumental in helping me produce this volume has also been the most important person in my life for the past forty-five years—my wife, Ann. She deserves special mention for her patience, her kindness, and her unstinting support during the long months of research and writing. She has been a loving partner, a dear friend, and a constructive critic. The same spirit of cooperation prevailed among our six children, who are all adults. Not only have they been a source of inspiration and encouragement, but also they have understood and put up with the onerous demands and innumerable sacrifices of academic life. Their support is likewise appreciated.

RICHARD A. HOGARTY

MASSACHUSETTS POLITICS
AND PUBLIC POLICY

1

UNDERSTANDING
POWER IN
MASSACHUSETTS

Power to rule and direct the affairs of state implies that
deference is given to those who exercise political power.
This authority legitimizes the role of the governors and
the public objectives that they seek when they utilize
power. A political culture may be highly democratic
but lack agreement on the uses of power and the qualifications of the powerful.

Edgar Litt, *The Political Cultures of Massachusetts*

THE BAY STATE'S PEOPLE AND POLITICAL ECONOMY

Massachusetts is a relatively small state with a net land area of 7,838 square
miles. An intensely political state, it has a population of over 6 million
people, who live in its 351 cities and towns of varying wealth and demographics, where multiple cultures and diverse traditions abound. They are
represented in the state legislature by 160 representatives and 40 senators.
From the mid-nineteenth century on, as its society became more urban
and more industrial, its economy depended mainly on textile mills, leather
tanneries, shoe factories, family-owned farms, and the fishing fleets that
once defined its coastal communities. But those industries either have gone
south or else have seen natural resources and open space depleted. A 2001
study shows that five major industries drive the Massachusetts economy
today. These industries, which account for more than half of the jobs in
the greater Boston metropolitan region, include financial services, health
care, high technology, education and consulting, and tourism. Their combined employment grew substantially between 1997 and 2000, creating more
than 78,000 new jobs. The high technology industry accounted for nearly
half of these new jobs.[1]

More than half the people of the Bay State live in the greater Boston
area, although a substantial number reside in the outlying cities of Lowell,

New Bedford, Worcester, and Springfield. The rural western part of Massachusetts, nestled in the Berkshire Mountains, is sparsely populated. The state measures 190 miles east to west, and 110 miles north to south. According to the 2000 census, the total population of 6,355,568 represents a 5.5 percent increase from 1990. A racial breakdown reveals that 81.9 percent of the populace is white, 5.0 percent black, 6.8 percent Latino, 0.2 percent American Indian, and 3.7 percent Asian. Asians, who experienced a 68 percent population increase, are the fastest-growing minority group in the state. In recent years there has been a large influx of immigrants and refugees from Southeast Asia, Central America, the Caribbean islands, and the former Soviet Union. They have come seeking the same economic opportunities that earlier generations of immigrants sought.

An analysis of the census figures shows that Boston, once known as a racially segregated city, is becoming more integrated as Latinos and Asians move into neighborhoods that previously had been nearly all black or all white. Even places such as historically white South Boston saw an influx of minorities. For the first time Boston is now a "majority minority city," as the white population declined to 49.5 percent. These census figures confirm the pattern of population shifts that Barry Bluestone and Mary Stevenson documented in their book *The Boston Renaissance*. They make the case that Boston's revival is attributable to its rapid economic transition from "mill-based to mind-based industries," to the spatial pattern of its growth, and to its transformation from a racially polarized city into a multicultural community.[2] Nevertheless, a closer analysis of the census figures reveals that whites and blacks still do not mix significantly in most areas of the city, though nearly all other groups do.[3]

After years of stagnant growth, the population of many smaller cities, such as Chelsea, Revere, Lynn, and Everett, is once again on the rise. The biggest draw for the newcomers is the old and relatively inexpensive housing stock available in those cities—a hidden asset that attracts not only immigrants working in service jobs but also professionals priced out of the housing market in Boston, Cambridge, and Somerville. The cities of Haverhill, Lawrence, Lowell, Peabody, and Salem have experienced similar population gains. After the shoe manufacturing and textile companies moved south in pursuit of cheap nonunion labor, these once potent industrial cities fell on hard times. They are still struggling to find a new identity and to revitalize their economic base. The deserted mills have become a graveyard of American ingenuity.

The Pioneer Valley lies one hundred miles west of Boston, where the land is spacious, the cities are smaller, and the towns are tiny. Fewer than 700,000 people live in the sixty-nine cities and towns spread over Hampden, Hampshire, and Franklin counties. This region is economically mixed and predominantly white, with pockets of growing racial diversity, particularly in Springfield, Holyoke, Northampton, and Greenfield. The westernmost county of Berkshire actually lost population in 2000, while the largest gain of new residents took place in Nantucket County. By all accounts, Cape Cod and the suburban communities lying inside the Interstate 495 belt are the fastest-growing areas in the state. Interstate 495 is 121 miles of concrete and asphalt stretching from Salisbury to Wareham. Suddenly, these once rural towns boomed. With research and high-tech companies sprouting everywhere, they drew tens of thousands of people from the city and beyond. This robust growth can be attributed to suburban office park construction, the expanding technology sector, and the transformation of summer homes into year-round residences.

A SHORT POLITICAL HISTORY

Historically, Massachusetts can legitimately lay claim to many social and political innovations. It was the first state to have a written constitution with a separate Bill of Rights included; the first newspaper, the first public library, the first college, and the first public high school were all founded here. Most of all, it is a state with a dramatically contested past. At various stages in its political history, Massachusetts has been the cradle of liberty, the birthplace of the American Revolution; a hotbed of abolitionism that provoked the Civil War and eventually ended black slavery; a powder keg of working-class discontent that ignited the labor movement; a bastion of isolationism that resisted America's entry into World War II; a seedbed of McCarthyism that spawned a communist witch-hunt; and a crucible of protest that halted the Vietnam War. In the early 1970s its body politic was vehemently opposed to the imperial presidency of Richard Nixon. Here the past is embedded in the present, and the two are invariably mixed in almost every political episode. Plainly, the more history one knows, the better one understands its social divisions and conflicts.

Until the present generation, Massachusetts has been a strong two-party state with a fairly competitive party system. From its antebellum inception in an era before pluralism, the Republican Party gained strength from those people who inhabited the small, predominantly Protestant rural towns rooted in an agricultural past. With abolitionism as their battle cry, Massachusetts Republicans put together a formidable patrician-yeoman coalition that repeatedly won elections and sustained them in power for more than a century. From 1858 to 1958, the Republicans flourished as the dominant party and maintained their numerical superiority and political supremacy. Meanwhile, as Massachusetts became more urban and more industrialized, the large influx of immigrants that poured into the Bay State at the turn of the century signaled a sea change in state politics. These "newer races" came seeking employment and struggled to gain a foothold in America. Immigrant city bosses, who emerged from this multiethnic social milieu, revived a moribund Democratic Party that began to rival its counterpart in the New Deal era. With the changing political order, power shifted inexorably from Republicans to Democrats, but this transformation did not happen overnight. Bucking the incoming political tide, the Republicans retreated and gradually became a minority party. The state legislature has been under Democratic control since 1958, but the governorship remains a competitive office. This situation has frequently led to problems of divided government.

In recent decades Bay State voters have shown a lively interest in issue-oriented politics with a decidedly liberal bent. In 1972, when the country was simmering with opposition to the Vietnam War, Massachusetts stood alone as the only state in the nation to cast its electoral votes for Democrat George McGovern. When President Nixon was impeached, bumper stickers appeared on automobiles which read, "Don't Blame Me, I'm from Massachusetts." In the presidential election of 2000, 60 percent of its voters cast their ballots for Democrat Al Gore, while only 32 percent went for Republican George W. Bush. Figures released after the election by the secretary of state's office show that there are 1.9 million unenrolled, or independent, voters; 1.4 million registered Democrats; 546,333 registered Republicans; and 16,071 registered Libertarians. As Republican governors Paul Cellucci and his predecessor, William Weld, demonstrated, however, successful election campaigns are predicated on more than these numbers. Politics in Massachusetts today is less about traditional party affiliations than about ideas, perceptions, and personality.

CONTRASTING THEORIES OF POWER

This book is a study of political power and leadership in Massachusetts and how it is exercised. The word "power" is not used here with any negative connotation. By using the term, I refer not to something derogatory or petty, but rather to something comprehensive, involving the myriad ways in which men and women can influence others to take desired actions on matters of public policy. Political power takes many forms and is thus multifaceted and multidimensional. It encompasses the personal qualities of political leaders, their formal authority, the political alliances they make, the reputation they acquire, and the sources of rewards or punishments they command. Whether they will prevail in a dispute over policy, or even whether they will become significantly involved, is the result of a subtle combination of factors, not of any single determinant.

For years social scientists have debated the question of power in American society. On the one hand, the so-called *pluralists* see a society with a wide distribution of political and economic power and a multiplicity of organized interests seeking to maximize group objectives. They are not so naïve as to believe that power, wealth, and income are equitably distributed; but it is their contention that any significant group in the society has the capacity to win redress of its grievances if the group feels intensely enough about its problems and demands action. In the typical version of the pluralist model, the "public interest" in America is forged from the convergence of and compromise among special interests in order to build a majority coalition in any given political arena. As the textbook reasoning goes, all three major branches of government, in their distinctive processes, strive to accommodate these interests.

On the other hand, a second set of scholars, commonly referred to as the *power elite* theorists, take a diametrically opposite stand. They are impressed with the way power is concentrated among relatively few groups and individuals. In their view the mass of the American people are pawns in the hands of those who control corporate wealth, the government itself, the military (as a special activity of government), and the communications media. Because these elites interact with one another with some degree of regularity in the discharge of their functions, they are seen as a single elite that is under the control of the "capitalist class." In simplified Marxist terms, this single all-powerful elite is depicted as a national version of a worldwide capitalistic ruling class. The theory of intervening elites is a less grandiose, more refined concept of elitism. Before Rousseau's time few saw anything wrong with rule by elites, and a very large part of classical political theory is concerned with various ways of justifying elite rule.

THE POLITICS OF DEFERENCE VERSUS THE POLITICS OF AFFILIATION

In the early days of the Republic, elections were acts of deference, ratifying rule by the landed gentry and the moneyed aristocracy, who regarded public office as an obligation connected with social standing. Most of the early governors of Massachusetts were aristocrats, conforming to John Adams's criteria of "the rich, the able, and the well-born." By the 1830s, political activists had built mass-based political parties as the politics of affiliation gradually caught on and replaced the politics of deference. The age of Andrew Jackson not only introduced the "common man" theory of government but also produced the problems of patronage and spoils, as well as the principle of rotation in office. Party loyalty assumed a major role in the behavior of the mass electorate, which took its partisan passions seriously. Voters became psychologically attached to their parties and passed party loyalty from fathers to sons. Men dominated politics in those days, and it was strictly a white man's political world. In a slave-owning society, blacks were considered property. Even after they gained their freedom and civil rights at the end of the Civil War, politics for blacks was not the same as politics for other ethnic groups, and it never has been. Few women participated in politics because they were legally denied the right to vote. They remained disenfranchised until 1920, when the Nineteenth Amendment to the Constitution finally gave women the vote. Women organizers were mostly involved in progressive causes including campaigns for social welfare, temperance, suffrage, and birth control.

At some point in the nineteenth century, the idea that a patrician class ought to have the right to govern became so unpopular that no one who believed it would ever say so, unless, like Henry Adams, he could say anything he pleased, having no political ambition. In due course the ideal of democracy became so universally accepted that most people believed participatory democracy was a reality. This was especially true in New England, where the town meeting flourished. People believed as much despite the existence of slavery, political corruption, the exploitation of immigrants, and the exclusively white male domination of political activity.

THE MASSACHUSETTS POLITICAL SYSTEM

In a superficial way, each of these sharply divergent theories of power accurately describes certain aspects of the Massachusetts political system. Where pluralists see openness, wide opportunity for political participation, and a reasonable likelihood that group effort will succeed, the power elite theorists see a system that is closed, collusive, not responsive to the have-nots, leaving an enormous discretionary power in the hands of a relatively few well-placed people.

Whatever their real power and influence, public officials in the Bay State look on its constitution as a central source of power. The Massachusetts constitution, which was adopted in 1780, is the oldest functioning written constitution in the world. Since no national constitution existed at the time, the form of government chosen by each of the states was a matter of utmost importance. James Bowdoin presided as president of the state constitutional convention that met in September 1779 at the First Church in Cambridge, where 250 delegates gathered. Articulate and disciplined in thought and action, John Adams wrote the Massachusetts constitution almost single-handedly.[4] He enshrined in it the doctrine of separation of powers, which created checks and balances among the executive, legislative, and judicial branches of state government. This innovation was intended to provide for stable government and to reduce extreme action by the very fact that powers were scattered and would be brought to bear by one branch against another.

At the core of the concept of separation of powers is the notion that the governor and the legislature would act independently of each other, owing their allegiance to the electorate. An independent judiciary, in exercising its power of judicial review, can declare the acts of the other two branches illegal if such action violates specified provisions of the constitution. By the same token, governors exert control over the judiciary by appointing judges, and the legislature does so by establishing courts and appropriating public funds for their operation.

The power to govern resides with the people. Because such power is derivative, it is predicated on the consent of the governed. The constitution is considered the fundamental legal document. It is the primary source of power in the sense that it prescribes the rules of the political game and it authorizes public officials to exercise certain prerogatives. Besides the governor and lieutenant governor, other constitutional officers include the attorney general, the secretary of state, the treasurer, and the auditor. In addition, there are a host of other major players. They include party leaders, legislators, judges, the bureaucracy, interest groups, lobbyists, and various "publics" that play roles from time to time. Political parties are best understood as organizations that seek to gain power by placing their candidates in public offices. Some public officials play the political game on their own behalf and not necessarily as party leaders. Bureaucrats are those government employees with permanent civil service status who operate governmental entities. They are generally referred to as the professional civil service. In most contests over policy decisions, the bureaucracy is likely to get involved in one way or another.

The more complex and diverse society becomes, the greater the temptation to form interest groups to protect and promote special interests. There is, as the political scientist David Truman suggests, an inevitable tendency for interest groups to turn to government for resolution of their problems.[5] The freedom to organize, however, is not the same thing as the capacity to do so. For instance, a group of people may share common problems, such as poverty, unemployment, poor education, the need for affordable housing, or inadequate health care, but if they are disorganized and not used to dealing with the political system, their efforts to resolve these problems may be in vain. If they lack personal knowledge of politicians, awareness of the way bureaucracy works, or the ability to seek redress in the courts, it may be next to impossible for them to get organized to exert whatever potential clout they might have.

Most people are familiar with the conventional ways in which public sentiment can be expressed and registered. These include elections, petitioning government, writing letters to elected officials, public referenda, and so on. Unconventional ways include protest marches, demonstrations, and even resort to violence. The campus riots against the Vietnam War and the ghetto riots in American cities during the late 1960s had their impact.

Another factor at play in pluralist politics is what one political scientist refers to as the "slack in the system," to use Robert Dahl's felicitous phrase.[6] That is to say, there is always room for participants to exert influence because the political system tends to leave open enough potential power to rectify injustices. This "slack" factor helps to explain, for example, how ordinary citizens who lived in the communities surrounding commercial airports managed to battle the Goliath Massachusetts Port Authority and bring that powerful agency to heel. Through protests and demonstrations, along with coalition building, political activists have succeeded at various times in halting construction of new runways and in getting Massport to reduce noise at Logan International Airport in Boston. These protesters have exploited the slack in the system. But the battle of airport politics continues to be waged, both at Logan and more recently at Hanscom Field in suburban Bedford.

After the terrorist attacks on the Pentagon and the World Trade Center in New York which took place on September 11, 2001, acting governor Jane Swift turned Logan's role in these unthinkable events into a platform for reforming Massport, a patronage-riddled agency responsible for the region's transportation infrastructure. The catastrophe profoundly altered things in Massachusetts and throughout the entire nation. With the shocks to the airline industry, plans for expansion were put on hold. Airport security suddenly became the top priority. On October 2, Swift gave a televised address in which she laid out plans for dealing with the new realities, announced the replacement of Logan's security director, and called for an impartial review of Massport that would overhaul the agency from top to bottom.[7] Under intense pressure for flagrant and continuing lapses in security at Logan, Virginia Buckingham, the airport's executive director, resigned on October 25, six weeks after the horrific terrorist attacks.

When it appears that a massive outpouring of concern is taking place, politicians tend to sit up and take notice. A case in point discussed in this book occurred in May 1970, when ten thousand anti–Vietnam War demonstrators marched on the State House in Boston to protest the killing of four Kent State University students by Ohio National Guardsmen. The extraordinary gathering of demonstrators impressed Governor Frank Sargent, for it provided credible evidence that a large number of people were sufficiently agitated about the moral legitimacy of war to devote themselves to activist politics. The same phenomenon repeated itself in 1972, when an equally large number of angry hard-hats descended on Beacon Hill to protest the lack of construction work in the Boston metropolitan area. Both demonstrations delivered their messages loud and clear. Such protests usually draw public attention and elicit an official response.

The other side of the coin, however, is that mass protests or appeals for policy changes have short active lives. More often than not, they are a momentary phenomenon. Politicians realize that public agitation will eventually simmer down and return to normal. In the meantime, the public may have had some impact on the decisions being contested. Or, at least, that is what the pluralists contend.

THE PLURALIST APPROACH TO POWER

As one who identifies with the pluralist school of thought, I will focus on this approach as a central unifying theme and demonstrate its utility as a way of understanding who benefits from politics in Massachusetts and why. According to the political scientist Harold Lasswell, "The study of politics is the study of influence and the influential."[8] He has posited the central question as "Who gets what, when, and where?" Thus defined, politics is involved in most of what goes on in the governing of society, for people are constantly trying to influence those who make and apply the rules. These efforts take countless forms, ranging from lofty public debates to shady backroom deals.

If the political process is broadly defined as the gaining and use of influence, it is seen to be integrally connected with the process of government. Each concerns itself with essentially the same end product: public policy. Most of the time, policy issues are enacted into law by legislative bodies, are approved by chief executives, and, unless they are found to be unconstitutional by the courts, they are carried out by bureaucrats. This is the conventional way that public policy is made and implemented; but in Massachusetts, policy can also be made through initiative petition, public referendum, executive orders, outside budget sections, bureaucratic rules and regulations, and judicial decisions.

The Massachusetts Supreme Judicial Court, whose origins date back to 1692, has a unique role to play in state government. In addition to adjudicating legal cases on appeal, it oversees the administration of justice and disciplines lawyers and judges. Unlike the other branches of state government, the courts are for the most part insulated from public pressures and from public purview. State judges are appointed by the governor for life, that is, until they reach the mandatory retirement age of seventy. Thus, they are able to make decisions without fear that partisan politics will intrude. For the most part, judges tend to see themselves as impartial guardians of the rule of law, not as policymakers. Yet they often do make policy. For example, while the state constitution prohibits anyone under guardianship from voting in Massachusetts, court decisions have given mentally ill persons under guardianship the right to vote unless they are specifically prohibited from doing so.

How does one look beyond the formal arrangements to the more dynamic features of who manages to get whom to do what and by what means? The answer is found in the exercise of political power. Perceived power, as most political science textbooks tell us, is real power, even if it consists of smoke and mirrors. Ambitious politicians submit to leadership and discipline in anticipation of future rewards. Threats of punishment and the bestowal of rewards can be a potent stimulus for inducing certain kinds of political behavior. The currency of rewards and punishments in the political game is used with varying degrees of subtlety and finesse.

Politicians seeking to stay in office push ideas that are most likely to attract and not alienate voters. They spend much of their time working to solve specific public problems with the expectation of achieving political gain and partisan advantage. Their careers depend in large measure on the successful negotiation of bargains. When confronted with conflicting demands, they help to maintain a viable society by the process of mutual concessions. Their role is a crucial one, because without politicians' espousal and defense, no cause would be adopted or endure. And their special talent, as the political scientist John Kingdon has pointed out, is sensing when an idea's "time has come."[9] No idea, no matter how sensible, can be realized in public action without their judgment.

Political bargaining and compromise lie at the heart of the political process. Mastering the complex role of the politician is not easy these days. Most politicians have very mixed motives, and they are inundated with incessant demands and constant pressures from pluralist subcultures and ethnic groups. In their everyday professional lives, they are preoccupied for the most part with serving their constituents. In short, they are engaged in a host of activities that are very time-consuming. These activities serve to put politicians under considerable stress. Operating in a pressure-cooker environment, most of them accept the inherent messiness of the real world and display a tolerance for chaos and ambiguity.

Compromise is the lubricant that greases the wheels of government and makes them turn. If every politician were adamant and unyielding, the political process could not function, and deadlock would result. Or, to put it differently, if a particular group is so unyielding that it will not consent to deal with the realities of give-and-take politics, the group will find itself frozen out of the political process. As moral absolutes become prominent, compromise becomes an increasingly unacceptable option for political participants. Nevertheless, quite fundamentally, politics means working with different people who have different values, different interests, and different partisan persuasions. Representative Barney Frank put it best when he observed of the United States Congress, "If you're not able to work closely with people you despise, you can't really work here."[10]

AMERICAN FEDERALISM: THE STATE AND THE NATION

To the political actors and major players in the American federal system, each level of government presents a different political arena, with varying advantages and disadvantages for different participants and for the resolution of various public issues. In Washington, D.C., the people of Massachusetts are represented in Congress by ten members of the House of Representatives and two U.S. senators. At the time of writing, all twelve of them are Democrats and all are white males. Only one black has ever represented Massachusetts in Congress: Republican senator Edward W. Brooke, who served from 1967 to 1978. Although there is not much diversity among the state's congressional delegation, it has enjoyed considerable political clout in recent decades.

This clout has flowed from former House Speaker John W. McCormack, Joseph Martin, and Thomas P. ("Tip") O'Neill, who reached the upper echelons of power, through a group of heavyweights that included former congressmen Edward P. Boland, Silvio O. Conte, and Joseph D. Early. The delegation's clout fluctuates from time to time, depending on which party is in control of the legislative branch. "We pool our political strategy," says Congressman Edward J. Markey, "to achieve the common goals that we all share for Massachusetts."[11]

Tip O'Neill was an affable, robust Irish politician with a likeable personality aptly suited for the political arena. He is perhaps best known for "Mrs. O'Brien's" advice for winning votes ("People like to be asked") and for the phrase "All politics is local," an expression handed down from his father, the superintendent of sewers in Cambridge, who steered him down the path to power. After his mother died of tuberculosis when he was an infant, Tip grew up in a single-parent family. He followed his father around Cambridge, watching him dispense jobs and buckets of coal to his working-class constituents. As a senior at Boston College, he came within 229 votes of being elected to the Cambridge City Council. A promising young New Deal Democrat, O'Neill understood the dynamics of depression-era Massachusetts politics—old-style patronage, street-corner rallies, campaigning in Knights of Columbus halls. And therein lay the formula for his future political career. After winning a seat in the state legislature in 1936, he rose through the ranks to become Speaker of the Massachusetts House of Representatives in 1949. At age thirty-seven, he was the second-youngest Speaker in the history of the state, as well as the first Roman Catholic and the first Democrat to hold the position. One reason O'Neill won the job was that his colleagues liked him so much; he was always good for a card game, a story, or a cigar. The other reason was that they respected him for his courage in taking on the followers of McCarthyism who wanted to force public school teachers to swear a loyalty oath. While O'Neill never wore his religion on his sleeve, his biographer John Farrell dispels any doubt that O'Neill's political values were derived from his immersion in Catholicism.[12]

O'Neill was first elected to Congress in 1952, when John F. Kennedy left his Eleventh Congressional District seat to run for the U.S. Senate. He and the Kennedys never had an easy relationship. For one thing, Tip had supported his good friend Michael Neville, a Cambridge city councillor, who ran against JFK for Congress in 1946. So in 1952 Joseph P. Kennedy pumped money into the campaign of state senator Michael LoPresti of East Boston, who was running against Tip in the Democratic primary. (The family patriarch figured that his son had the Irish vote locked up but could use some help with the Italians.) There were few issues in the 1952 campaign, yet it turned out to be a bitter and bruising primary, pitting a prominent Irishman against a prominent Italian. In Farrell's tart description, "It was remembered . . . as the first great tribal war between the Irish, who had ruled the Massachusetts Democratic Party for almost a century, and the Italians who hoped to supplant them."[13] In the end, O'Neill emerged the victor.

During his thirty-two years in Congress, Tip O'Neill proved to be an able politician who could wheel and deal with the best of them. Somewhat curiously, his being on the outs with the rich, handsome, Harvard-educated Kennedys did not hurt him in Congress. On the contrary, House Democratic leader John McCormack, another Massachusetts politician who had problems with the Kennedy family, was a more valuable patron in that setting than any Kennedy. McCormack introduced Tip to Speaker Sam Rayburn's "board of education," an after-hours gathering of House insiders. When McCormack's retirement in 1971 created an opening for a big-city northerner in the House Democratic leadership, O'Neill was appointed party whip. Two years later he was elected majority leader by his fellow Democrats, and four years after that he was elected Speaker in 1977. In both elections the vote was unanimous.

Although very much a loyal party man, O'Neill broke early with President Lyndon B. Johnson over Vietnam. His shift on the war was a dramatic reversal. O'Neill's fondest wish had been to serve as Speaker with a Democratic president. It came true when Jimmy Carter was elected in 1976, but the dream fell far short of reality. Substantively, Carter was not the same kind of Democrat as O'Neill, and Tip did not get along with him. The two men differed philosophically about the role of government. Tip believed in financing programs for the poor and disadvantaged, while Carter was a technocrat who believed in fiscal austerity and government reorganization. Consequently, they did not agree on most issues.

In 1980 Carter lost his bid for reelection to Ronald Reagan, and the Republicans took control of the Senate. Overnight and by default, O'Neill became the most prominent Democrat in the country. He adapted readily to his new role as leader of the opposition, both in the media and in Congress. The Speaker was attacked by a coalition of Republicans and "boll weevil" southern Democrats for being out of touch with the times. In response, O'Neill crafted what Farrell calls a "give him rope" strategy for dealing with Reagan. Knowing that the American people would not turn their backs on Reaganomics until they had seen it fail, he watched patiently as the coalition of Republicans and boll weevils enacted the president's tax and budget cuts.

But O'Neill pounced when Reagan tried to cut Social Security benefits for early retirees and the economy slid into its deepest recession since the 1930s. Far from losing the House in 1982, the Democrats gained twenty-six seats. Rather than losing programs, Farrell argues, O'Neill preserved the New Deal and the Great Society with all their "muscle and bone—and even some flab" intact. Reagan remained personally popular and brought an end to the cold war, but the Reagan revolution was politically dead. These victories made O'Neill an American folk hero. True to his credo, during his sixteen terms in the House, Tip never forgot where he came from and always took care of the voters at home, which had the added benefit of being good politics. A seasoned and savvy backroom politician, he loved the game of politics and played it better than most of his contemporaries. Farrell describes him, warts and all:

> He was no saint. Win or lose, there would be no canonization of Thomas P. O'Neill Jr. In a lifetime in politics he'd gouged eyes, thrown elbows, bent the law and befriended rogues and thieves. He could be mean and small-minded. But at his core there lay a magnificence of spirit, deep compassion and a rock-hard set of beliefs. He had a sense of duty that he refused to abandon for those whom Heaven's grace forgot—and he would sooner die on the floor of the House, or watch his party be vanquished and dispersed, than desert them.[14]

Adhering to these basic values and political beliefs, O'Neill made a real difference in the lives of the working poor and the elderly. That is what made him so beloved by his constituents. Old, rumpled, overweight, and gruff-voiced, the aging warrior retired from public life in 1984 with his reputation intact.

Another reason why Massachusetts has enjoyed such clout in Congress is the towering presence of Democrat Edward M. Kennedy, the state's senior senator. Scion of the most powerful political family in Massachusetts, he was first elected to the U.S. Senate in 1962. Over the years he rose to become the most influential liberal in the country. Whatever Kennedy's failings and flaws, he has been a legislative powerhouse. To be sure, he has kept the liberal flame alive. Adam Clymer, a Washington correspondent for the *New York Times*, argues that Kennedy has accomplished more for his causes and those of the nation than any other legislator of his generation.[15] With his family name and celebrity status, he has been a strong voice for social change.

A notable exception occurred in 1991, when Kennedy's liberal voice fell silent at the Senate confirmation hearings of U.S. Supreme Court Justice Clarence Thomas, partly because of the turmoil that had engulfed him during his nephew William Kennedy Smith's rape trial. During the Clinton years, the senior senator regained his stature and roared back in spirited opposition to right-wing conservatives, and especially to George W. Bush's nomination of John Ashcroft for attorney general in January 2001. Kennedy has consistently championed abortion rights, gun control, civil rights, school desegregation, national health care, education reform, relief for working people, opposition to huge military budget outlays, and a friendly stance toward immigrants. Much of his senatorial effectiveness over time can be attributed to his ability to reach across party lines and to work with people who strongly disagree with him, especially with Republican senators on issues ranging from AIDS to health insurance and the minimum wage, all of which makes him a consummate politician and an indomitable political force.

Another successful politician with national influence was Congressman John Joseph Moakley, dean of the Massachusetts delegation until his death in 2001. A native of South Boston, Joe Moakley grew up in the public housing projects, the son of an Irish father and an Italian mother. During his thirty years in Congress, he became known as more of a workhouse than a show horse. A bread-and-butter Democrat, he was admired for his humor. Never a divisive personality, he had a knack for building coalitions and was respected on both sides of the political aisle.

After serving a stint in the navy during World War II, Moakley began his political career as a member of the Massachusetts House of Representatives, where he served from 1953 to 1963. He was elected to the state Senate in 1964 and served there until 1970, when he lost to Louise Day Hicks in his bid to succeed John McCormack in Congress. Unlike Hicks, he never jumped on the anti-busing bandwagon, an issue that inflamed Boston in the 1970s. Moakley then proved that he was no conventional politician. He abandoned the Democratic Party to run as an independent against Hicks in 1972—his "Hail Mary" pass, as he once told a reporter. Although he lost South Boston, he won the district and was on his way to national leadership.

Moakley remained capable of the boldness that characterized his run against Hicks. Speaker Tip O'Neill recognized a skillful legislator in Moakley and put him on the powerful Rules Committee, where bills could be made or broken by an insider's nod. Moakley became committee chairman in 1989. As chairman, he brought home the bacon. He obtained federal funds for housing in Boston, for cleaning up the badly polluted Boston Harbor, and for rebuilding the Central Artery, the elevated highway running through the city. He told New England Patriots owner Robert Kraft that his South Boston neighborhood wanted no part of a football stadium. He was not afraid to wield his insider's power in pursuit of justice. Upon hearing from Salvadoran refugees in his district that they had been victims of political persecution, he became interested in Central American issues. When a death squad massacred six Jesuits in San Salvador, he headed an investigation to seek the truth about Salvadoran army involvement and succeeded in reducing American aid to the military there.

Moakley remained a loyal son of South Boston, while gaining respect throughout the broader Massachusetts community. As his district moved southward because of population shifts, he retained overwhelming voter support. He influenced the future shape of the Boston waterfront by pushing for construction of the federal courthouse that now bears his name.

THE PROSE OF GOVERNING

Campaigning for public office is very different from governing. Mario Cuomo, former governor of New York, used to make this distinction: "Politics is poetry, but governing is prose." The display of humor is very much a part of the prose in governing the Bay State. Humor can backfire on a politician if used improperly. But properly handled, a sense of humor can be a potent political weapon. It also enables politicians to absorb the cruel blows and political hits that they must inevitably endure in public life. Barney Frank of Massachusetts is a master of political wit and satire. As one reporter says, "Frank is widely regarded as one of the funniest men in state politics, practitioner of a dry, acerbic, and occasionally nasty wit."[16] There is his famous punch line about Boston's Central Artery/Third Harbor Tunnel project, otherwise known as the Big Dig. Given the sheer magnitude and enormous expense of this public works project, Frank quipped, "it would be easier to elevate the city than to depress the artery." As for the importance of having a reliable political base from which power flows, "Your base in politics," he noted, "is made up of the people who are with you even when you are wrong."[17]

The arrival on the scene of Republican William F. Weld was an interesting phenomenon. A mercurial and unpredictable politician, he was like a shooting star that flashed brilliantly and then faded. His political views fit no discernible pattern. Prochoice and pro–gay rights, he was a social liberal but a fiscal conservative. A tall, redheaded, transplanted New Yorker, Weld ran for state attorney general against Frank Bellotti in 1978 and lost badly, carrying only two municipalities. As a consolation prize, he was appointed a U.S. attorney in the Reagan administration, but he quit this post in protest in 1988, when Attorney General Edwin S. Meese refused to resign amid allegations of ethical misconduct. Massachusetts politics, even at the gubernatorial level, is a process of easy in and easy out, and Weld's hasty exit illustrates how fleeting a political career can be. The whimsical former prosecutor was twice elected governor, first in 1990 and again in 1994. (He funded a good part of his first campaign out of his own pocket.) Enjoying high approval ratings as governor, Weld ran for the U.S. Senate against incumbent John F. Kerry in 1996 and lost in a closely contested race. In 1997 he abruptly resigned as governor and tried unsuccessfully to be appointed U.S. ambassador to Mexico.

With his impulsive nature, Weld became one of the most popular governors in the modern era by making politics entertaining. He was known for his self-effacing wit, and frequently poked fun at his own privileged background. "My family has not always had it easy," he would say. "My ancestors arrived here with nothing but the shirt on their backs and a couple of million pounds of gold."[18] During his U.S. Senate race, he showed his lighthearted and impulsive side by diving fully clothed into the Charles River—once among the nation's filthiest—to demonstrate that it was becoming significantly cleaner. As governor, he had just signed into law the state's new Rivers Protection Act. This photo opportunity, of course, made the front pages. When Senator Jesse Helms thwarted his nomination for the Mexican ambassadorship, Weld downplayed the incident by saying, "I needed time to learn Spanish."[19] He then left the state and returned to his native New York. For him state politics was definitely a case of easy come, easy go.

Governor Francis Sargent was equally adept at self-deprecating humor. A liberal Republican and a Yankee blueblood in the finest tradition of integrity and intelligence, Sargent grasped the reins of leadership and became an innovative policy maker. He quickly learned not to take himself or his job too seriously.[20] He was a patrician but easygoing and down-to-earth. A man of multiple talents, Sargent was a master of persuasion while presiding over a divided government. In a predominantly Democratic state, he got skeptical Democrats to support his programs through a combination of political common sense, humor, and a healthy dose of bipartisanship. This proved an effective strategy which enabled him to govern successfully during a trying period in America that evoked deep anxiety.

Like the rest of the nation during the late 1960s, Massachusetts experienced the wrenching upheavals of the Vietnam War, the civil rights crusade, and the countercultural revolution against established authority. Sargent became legendary for the grace and deftness with which he steered the state through these turbulent years of campus unrest and a changing culture. In battling racism in the early 1970s, Sargent walked a difficult but courageous path. The civil rights movement had a terrific impact on him, waking him up to the reality of the way blacks were treated in America—not just in the South, where Jim Crow laws still prevailed, but also in the North, where there was de facto segregation. Issues of race and civil rights were high on Sargent's policy agenda. He appointed blacks to prominent positions in his administration. When racial violence erupted in Boston as a result of the protests against court-ordered school desegregation and the forced busing of students, Massachusetts was suddenly thrust into the national spotlight. In the end, Sargent called out the National Guard to quell the racial disturbances in South Boston.

Frank Sargent's Republican successors would also find themselves in the national news, though in a much less flattering light. Barney Frank's joke about the Big Dig made him look prescient. By the mid-1990s the cost projections had spiraled out of control. Ten years into its construction and five years before its scheduled completion (2005), the mammoth project, about 75 percent complete, had cost much more than anyone ever expected. In April 2000, Governor Paul Cellucci fired the Big Dig management team, including James J. Kerasiotes, chairman of the Massachusetts Turnpike Authority, and project director Patrick J. Moynihan. He replaced Kerasiotes with Andrew Natsios, his secretary of administration and finance. Within a relatively short period of time, Natsios got the project back on track and restored its fiscal credibility. He was seen as an antidote to Kerasiotes.

A year later Robert Cerasoli, the state's inspector general, dropped a political bombshell. He issued a report alleging that federal and state officials had deliberately misled the public about cost overruns, and that there had been a systematic coverup on the part of the Weld and Cellucci administrations. More specifically, Cerasoli charged that they knew as early as 1994 that the price tag of the megaproject was heading toward $14 billion, and so they schemed to hide billions in costs from the public and bond investors. Using deceptive semantics and devious accounting practices, the project managers covered up nearly $6 billion in cost overruns. They did so with the assistance or complicity of local Federal Highway Administration officials and the state's private management consultant, Bechtel, Parsons, Brinckerhoff. Stung by the inspector general's charges, Governor Cellucci denied withholding information related to the Big Dig cost overruns and called the report vindictive. He remarked: "They are making it up. It is pure retaliation because we want to eliminate that office [inspector general]. This being Massachusetts and Massachusetts politics, retaliation is probably what is at the basis of the report. Some of the stuff is just pure fiction."[21] Whether true or not, this kind of charge is a familiar one in the world of Massachusetts politics.

THE CURLEY PHENOMENON

For generations Irish politicians in the Bay State have used the weapons of ethnicity, humor, and intimidation with impunity. When faced with political adversity, the Irish coined the expression "Don't get mad, get even." No one practiced this philosophy better than the flamboyant and colorful James Michael Curley, a charismatic politician who had the indispensable personal traits necessary for leadership and the capacity to inspire intense loyalty among his followers. The son of poor Irish immigrants, he was born in 1874 on the third floor of a cold-water flat on Northampton Street in Roxbury. His father, Michael, an impoverished Irish laborer, died as a result of a burst blood vessel sustained while he was lifting a heavy curbstone. At the time of his father's death, James was ten years of age. To support the family, his mother worked as a cleaning woman, scrubbing floors of downtown office buildings on her hands and knees. A young man with little formal education, Curley spoke the language of his neighbors and shared their grinding poverty, their deep-seated class resentments, and their religious antagonisms.

With a proverbial chip on his shoulder and an axe to grind, Curley came to power at a time when machine politics and political bossism still flourished. He blended traditional Democratic populism with an antagonism toward entrenched interests. He was both a fighter with a taste for battle and a defender of the little guy with contempt for the status quo. In the eyes of Yankee Brahmins, he was a power-hungry politician, a scoundrel, a rogue, and an unscrupulous demagogue. Indeed, Curley was dubbed the "rascal king" by his biographer. Others, like U.S. senator, David I. Walsh, called him the "Mayor of the Poor" because of his genuine empathy for those living on the edge—the destitute, the dispossessed, and the downtrodden. The old-fashioned politics of personal power held sway in his heyday and Curley excelled in projecting an image and in provoking a reaction. He was said to be full of himself and in typical combative style ran roughshod over anyone who dared to get in his way. His biographer Jack Beatty describes him as he appeared on the political stage in his native Boston:

> On that stage he was a giant. The most resourceful, eloquent, energetic, durable political personality of his time and place, he thwarted the ambitions of the generations of politicians who had the bad luck to come of age in the long Curley era. His personal qualities aside, he filled in those years a political space— "urban populist"—which fitted what pluralities and sometimes majorities of Bostonians wanted from their mayor. In point of experience alone, he was better prepared for the job than any mayor in Boston's history. Through the Tammany Club he had dealt in miniature and on an intimate level with problems akin to those he would confront on a larger scale as mayor. His years on the City Council and in Washington had made him aware of the citywide and national contexts of those problems. In his oratory, finally, he had the capacity to speak for the city with a voice, manner, and diction made for leadership— something lacking at nearly every level of office in these ineloquent times.[22]

First elected mayor of Boston in 1914, Curley was an intuitive politician. Politics had been his whole life from the time he emerged as a ward leader at the turn of the century. Few men could match his talents or clout. His power within Boston was sufficient to make him mayor for four terms, U.S. congressman for four terms, and a major force in state politics from 1914 until his death in 1958. Although he ran three times for governor, he won only once, in 1934. He failed to get elected to the U.S. Senate in 1936— he was defeated that year by Henry Cabot Lodge Jr., whom he mockingly referred to as "Little Boy Blue." Curley ranted to the Irish and the working poor about the deprivations and social injustices inflicted on them by their wealthy Republican employers. He also ranted about bigoted groups like the Ku Klux Klan, which never amounted to much in Massachusetts, but the Klan was anti-Catholic and therefore a convenient whipping boy.

Blessed with the common touch and with a mellifluous voice, Curley elevated oratory to an art form. He was a clever politician endowed with that gift for symbolic gesture so beloved in the Irish community. A mischievous sense of humor enhanced his roguish style. As Beatty writes: "James Michael Curley would not be deficient in the ethnic endowment of wit. Indeed, he is remembered today for his one-liners, his comic stunts, his general air of ironic merriment, and his retinue of retainers with their Runyanesque nicknames, their omnipresent cigars, and their funny fedoras."[23] Loved and hated with equal passion and seeking improvement for the downtrodden, Curley was a hard man to beat. He won by allowing his rivals to underestimate him, by stirring ethnic hatreds, and by resorting to threats, intimidation, and blackmail. At times he played the worst sort of politics and engaged in skulduggery and dirty tricks. He unabashedly used public office for private gain. Even two jail sentences and a court order to repay some $42,000 in misused funds did not ruin his political career. By the late 1940s, the solid hold that the Irish had held on political power in Boston and the state was weakening. Although Curley would have one more term as mayor, after his jail sentence in 1949, he was nearing the end of his long career. The once luminous political star had all but faded away.

More fundamental forces were also at work in state politics. The advent first of radio, which FDR had popularized, and then of television in 1952 signaled that old-style house-by-house campaigning and mass rallies, with thousands of people packed into large halls such as Mechanics Hall on Huntington Avenue in Boston, were on the wane. Candidates could not simply rely on rhetoric, as popular as Curley had made it. On the radio and in the television studio, candidates at least had to appear to make sense. Having returned from military service in World War II, Henry Cabot Lodge Jr. defeated incumbent David Walsh for a U.S. Senate seat in 1946. The tradition of campaign debates reappeared to become central by 1960, when the Kennedy-Nixon encounter proved crucial in the presidential election. Charges of ethnic discrimination no longer passed muster with Irish Catholic voters, who were now ready for a different kind of candidate— one who symbolized their success rather than one who exploited their grievances. These changing circumstances of campaign politics meant that candidates had to be knowledgeable on a broad range of issues. New alliances—permanent and temporary, easy and uneasy—came into play in the 1960s.

Following in Curley's footsteps, William Bulger appeared on the political scene in the early 1960s and soon became a major player. He was raised in the Old Harbor public housing project in South Boston. His father died in a railroad yard accident when he was a youngster. Psychologically drawn to politics at an early age, Bulger was steeped in the history of Boston Irish politics, but he recognized that the "Last Hurrah" was just around the corner. Educated in the Jesuit classical tradition, he graduated from Boston College High School, Boston College, and Boston College Law School, credentials that earned him the sobriquet "triple eagle," the common insignia for all three Jesuit institutions. During his last year in law school, Bulger was elected to the Massachusetts House of Representatives, where he served from 1961 to 1971. From there he moved up to the state Senate, where he quickly made a name for himself. His elevation to the Senate presidency in 1978 was an indication of his native intellectual ability and his political skills.

No one could dispute his intellectual firepower. He spent his entire political career in the state legislature, retiring in 1995 to head the University of Massachusetts.

In political parlance, Bulger was known as a hardball politician who often played for keeps. He was as shrewd, as cunning, and as ruthless as they come. For hardball politicians, winning is all-important, whatever the issue or whatever the cost. In doing battle with his political adversaries, Bulger earned a formidable reputation that inevitably forced them either to ignore him or to risk defying him. A reputation for strong leadership, however, depends on more than just personal qualities. Possessing the means to punish or reward is also important, and Bulger did not hesitate to use those resources at his command.

Like the fabled James M. Curley, Bulger threatened and intimidated his opponents. His brilliance lay in fashioning political strategy and tactics, his intuitive grasp of personalities, and his manipulation of men and women to get them to do what they otherwise would not have done. One episode is particularly revealing. He once threatened to reroute a section of the Massachusetts Turnpike through the middle of a Boston Edison plant unless the company stopped polluting the air over South Boston. The company got the message and soon cleaned up its act. No one captured Bulger better than newspaper reporter Scot Lehigh, who wrote in 1995:

> Perhaps no figure in recent Massachusetts history has inspired more contradictory emotions than Senate President William M. Bulger. He is either revered or reviled, with precious little middle ground. To his many fans, the South Boston Democrat is a populist hero, a political scholar who has survived three and a half decades of rough-and-tumble, bloody but unbowed. To his equally numerous detractors, Bulger is nothing but a martinet, an iron-fisted pseudo-intellectual who gets his own way through naked power and intimidation.[24]

Hurt politically by the school busing controversy, Bulger was unable to develop a statewide constituency. Whatever his limitations and shortcomings, he knew how to make the most of his popularity and prestige, whether at an Irish wake or in a public speech. His dramatic oratory flowed in the classical style and was laced with quotations from the ancient orators of Greece and Rome. Humor and song were also part of his repertoire. "The Irish instinct to see life in a comic light," writes Jack Beatty, "never has far to seek for occasions to express itself."[25] In this context, Bulger enjoyed marching in the annual Saint Patrick's Day parade in South Boston and in hosting a convivial breakfast gathering at the Bayside Club, where he entertained his guests by singing Irish folk songs and roasting his fellow politicians. This event is part of the distinctive Massachusetts political culture and its folkways.

THE POLITICAL CULTURE OF MASSACHUSETTS

Conventionally, "political culture" is defined as the predominant way people think, feel, and behave in a political system. In other words, it is a collective psychological orientation toward the structure of government, incumbents in public office, and particular politics, decisions, and the enforcement of those decisions. Daniel Elazar, the preeminent political scientist in the study of American federalism, has defined this elusive term as "the particular pattern of orientation to political action in which each political system is embedded."[26]

Over the years, the Massachusetts political culture has been shaped by bitter partisanship, ethnic and racial conflict, religious antagonism, class hatreds, urban-rural rivalries, and industrial labor-management disputes. As the political scientist Jerome Mileur explains, "Historically, political divisions in the Bay State have been sharp and deep along mutually reinforcing lines of nationality, religion, and class: English, Protestant, upper-class Republicans versus Irish, Catholic, working class Democrats."[27] These forces fueled the simmering class warfare that divided the populace. For more years than most people can remember, the establishment was largely Yankee and largely elite. An unyielding Republican conservatism, dating back to the Civil War, eventually gave way in the late 1930s to a New Deal Democratic liberalism, swayed by ethnic, labor, and religious considerations. These internecine political wars left their battle scars and residual animosities. The politics of Massachusetts has indeed been contentious and tumultuous.

In his 1965 book *The Political Cultures of Massachusetts*, Edgar Litt writes, "The bitter political schisms between Irish and Yankee, Catholic and Protestant, Italo-American and Irish-American burn in the recorded history of Massachusetts politics."[28] He goes on to distinguish four successive political cultures in Bay State politics—patricians, yeomen, workers, and managers—and argues persuasively that their interplay is the dynamic that still drives state politics:

At various points in its historical development, Massachusetts has been dominated by the political ethos of the rural, small-town yeomen, the Brahmin patricians, and the urban workers, especially the Boston Irish community. Today, Massachusetts is part of a post-industrial society that emphasizes technical, clerical, and professional skills to man the burgeoning scientific, defense, educational, and administrative institutions. At the same time, the older industries based on water power, the soil, and unskilled labor are in decline. While the older core cities and small towns have contracted in population and importance, new suburbs of white-collar and professional people have developed.[29]

Since the 1960s, the economic life and social structure of Massachusetts have been changing significantly. Shifts in population tell the story of a state that is being transformed both demographically and economically. Social change constantly alters the circumstances of the political game, and the shrewd player must anticipate gradual changes of the rules of the game, the introduction of new and different players, and new strategies that may never have appeared before. Throughout the 1970s and most of the 1980s, a coalition of peace activists, environmentalists, women, and urban minorities disrupted the old alliances and transformed the Democratic Party from one of social conservatism to a party of social liberalism. This was the party of Michael Dukakis. To quote Mileur again:

The Democrats remain strongest where they have always been strongest—in the cities of the Commonwealth, especially those in the eastern part of the state. In 1994, Democratic registration in Boston was 60 percent but was even higher in many of the cities around the Hub: two-thirds in Somerville and Chelsea, over 60 percent in Cambridge and Revere, close to 60 percent in Quincy and Everett. In New Bedford and Fall River to the south of Boston, Democratic registration was 63 and 70 percent, while in the state's second and third largest cities, Worcester and Springfield, it was 54 and 60 percent of registered voters. In 1994 and again in 1996, it was the party's big cities that returned U.S. Senators Edward Kennedy and John Kerry to office, both by more comfortable margins than forecast.

The last remnants of bygone Republican glory are to be found in the small towns south and west of Boston, on Cape Cod and in the Berkshires, as well as along the northern and southern borders of the Commonwealth. Independent voters, however, are spread across the state, but it is in the suburbs surrounding Boston that they have their greatest political impact. Clustered in towns around Route 128, these suburbs grew in the decades after World War II. Peopled by a new college-educated professional class that embraced the anti-war and other movements of the 1960s and 1970s and has taken issues and candidates more seriously than party. These are the switch-hitters in state politics who supported with equal enthusiasm both the managerialism of Michael Dukakis in the 1980s and the libertarianism of William Weld in the 1990s.[30]

WOMEN AND MINORITIES IN MASSACHUSETTS POLITICS

Long before women were allowed to hold public office and participate in party politics, they made significant contributions to the public life of

Massachusetts. Six outstanding women have been honored for their distinguished public service with bronze busts prominently displayed in a portrait gallery at the State House. They are Dorethea Dix, an early advocate for the mentally ill; Florence Luscomb, a suffragist and peace activist; Mary O'Sullivan, a tireless labor activist; Sarah Redmond, a fiery abolitionist; Josephine Ruffin, a journalist and civil rights activist; and Lucy Stone, a leading suffragist and the first woman from Massachusetts to earn a college degree. Stone graduated from Oberlin College in Ohio in 1829 at a time when women were discouraged from pursuing higher education.

It was not until 1920 that American women first won the right to vote and to participate effectively in the political process. Since then, women have made steady progress in Massachusetts politics, but it has been a shamefully slow process. Obtaining power commensurate with their numbers has taken much longer than expected.[31] In January 1923, Sylvia Donaldson of Brockton and Susan W. Fitzgerald of Boston were the first women elected as state representatives. Two years later, in 1925, Edith Nourse Rogers of Lowell became the first Bay State woman to be elected to Congress. She succeeded her husband in office and served there until 1960. Rogers was followed in Congress by Margaret Heckler in 1966 and by Louise Day Hicks in 1970. In 2001, women ran in both the Republican and Democratic primaries to fill the vacant seat in the Ninth Congressional District, the same year Lieutenant Governor Jane Swift stepped in as acting governor on the resignation of Governor Paul Cellucci.

The potency of the women's vote was clearly demonstrated in the U.S. Senate race in 1952, when John F. Kennedy defeated Henry Cabot Lodge Jr. Although many factors contributed to Kennedy's victory, the women's vote was absolutely crucial. During the campaign, Kennedy invited women to attend a series of tea parties, which were organized by volunteers Polly Fitzgerald and Helen Keyes. In the end, the women's vote, which accounted for more than 52 percent of the vote statewide, proved a decisive factor in the outcome of the election.[32]

Women have made great strides in recent years in the executive branch of state government—from Lieutenant Governor Evelyn Murphy to Treasurer Shannon O'Brien to Jane Swift, the first female governor of Massachusetts and the first governor in the nation to give birth while in office. Yet the legislature has remained largely an old boys' club. With the exception of Linda Melconian of Springfield, who became Senate majority leader in 1999, the top leadership in both chambers has been all-male. Patricia McGovern chaired the Senate Ways and Means Committee, but no woman has ever been House Speaker or Senate president. Nor has a female ever been elected U.S. senator.

In 1977, Governor Michael Dukakis appointed Ruth Abrams the first woman justice to the Supreme Judicial Court.[33] Since then, several other women have received judicial appointments. Chief Justice Margaret Marshall, an immigrant from South Africa, is the first woman and the first immigrant to head the state's highest court. For a brief period, Massachusetts was the only state in the nation with a female majority on its high court.[34] But this ended in 2000 with the appointment of Robert J. Cordy, who filled the seat vacated by the mandatory retirement of Ruth Abrams. Cordy was a former lobbyist and power broker who had contributed generously to Republican campaign coffers. He was well connected politically, but he had climbed through the ranks of the criminal justice system from public defender to federal prosecutor, where his mentor in the U.S. attorney's office was William Weld. Cumulatively, even these small discoveries become important in describing the political process, its texture and context, and in forecasting its evolution.

In a state being transformed demographically, one should also note black, Latino, and Asian drives for political equality, especially in cities most resistant to recognizing minority needs and rights. The advent of more women and minority officeholders has displaced the Irish old guard to some extent. Their leadership is being challenged increasingly by those who feel they have been denied the opportunity to advance politically. Given the white male composition of the Massachusetts congressional delegation, these drives have not substantially altered the picture. What has changed dramatically are the rapidly escalating financial requirements of campaigns, a change that has yielded more wealthy candidates running for office. Furthermore, there is now a premium placed on incumbency. Those who are already in public office receive contributions from political action committees by virtue of their seniority in committee assignments. Given the benefits provided by these contributions, incumbents are more likely to stay in office.

Money has always been the "mother's milk" of politics, but many people think that the milk has now turned sour. Money buys access, advertising, and exposure in the print and electronic media. Today there is a growing outrage about the abuse of "soft money" in politics. Many believe that it is corrupting the political system and thereby subverting democracy. Some say that campaign finance is out of control; they argue that there is no longer a level playing field in American politics. The cost of winning a congressional seat keeps going up. According to a nationwide study, in 2000 the price of admission to the U.S. House of Representatives exceeded $1 million.[35] In 1998 the citizens of Massachusetts voted overwhelming to establish an optional system of publicly financed elections, a decision bitterly resisted by powerful leaders of the state legislature. This voter-approved public referendum, known as the Clean Elections Act, would make it easier for qualified citizens to run for office by providing public funds to pay for campaign expenditures and by placing a cap on spending.

THE GOVERNOR AS PARTY AND POLICY LEADER

From John Hancock, the first governor elected under the 1780 constitution, to Paul Cellucci, sixty-eight men served as chief executive of Massachusetts. Jane Swift succeeded Cellucci as acting governor, but she decided not to seek a full four-year term. She bowed out of the 2002 gubernatorial race. Surveying the careers and accomplishments of these sixty-eight men, one is amazed to discover the range and variety of their talents. They have been an incredibly assorted lot. Some were rogues and thieves; some the mere agents of business moguls and party bosses; some were amiable nonentities, adept at platitude and evasion, who served their terms and faded into deserved oblivion. Still others were men of ability and personal distinction who would compare favorably with any group of chiefs of state drawn from a comparable society that developed over three centuries from a collection of a few hundred hardy settlers to a metropolitan state of more than 6 million people. What did they achieve and how did they do it? What kind of leadership did they exercise? Although it is impractical to review all of their careers individually, it is possible to highlight those who made a significant impact.

More than any other political actor in state politics, the governor is the chief initiator of public policy and the energizing force of the state's governing system. He or she shapes the action. The tempo of gubernatorial initiative varies with the disposition of the incumbent, be he passive or active, positive or negative. The governor expresses his or her policy initiative in the State of the State message and in subsequent addresses deals with specific problems or concerns as they may be perceived by the legislature, the Boston political community, the media, and the public at large. Since at least the New Deal era, all these audiences now expect the State of the State address to outline the broad goals of an administration and to be elaborated in specific messages, executive orders, and announcements of gubernatorial appointments.

When a governor is passive, as Edward King (1979–82) seems to have been, the public agenda is light and the pace of public affairs is slow. When a governor is inclined to be active and positive, the pace of the policy process speeds up, and it can suffer from overload. So Frank Sargent found out in his first year as governor, when proposal after proposal appeared on his desk. Nonetheless, the governor's position remains controlling, for the buck stops with him. According to Duane Lockard, who has written extensively on the subject: "Through his formal power as chief executive and his informal power as chief of the party the governor has to be considered the most important single person in making legislative decisions. The governor certainly does not always get his way—not by any means—and yet it is true that all actors in the legislative drama must turn to or contend with the governor throughout legislative struggles on significant bills."[36]

Beyond that, the Massachusetts governor occupies the topmost position in the executive branch, and is thus in charge of the massive state bureaucracy. By any measure, the governorship is an endless job, intensely demanding—nothing like the ceremonial figurehead position of the distant past. Constantly in the media spotlight, the occupant of the office becomes the target of every person, group, or political entity with an agenda to press or with an axe to grind. With an increasingly complex society and the growth of a sprawling bureaucracy, it has become a much more challenging job. This means that governors are shaped both by the historical forces of their time and by the governors who have preceded them. The position gets redefined and recast in almost every term.

THE DEVELOPMENT OF THE OFFICE

The governorship is a much more powerful position today than it was back in 1780. This is due in large part to changing political, social, and economic conditions. At the beginning, the office of governor was a very weak institution.[37] There are historical reasons that explain this phenomenon. Smarting from the imposition of the Stamp Act of 1765, the colonists were angry at King George III for his unfair policies and for what they perceived as "taxation without representation." They mistrusted the royal governors that the king had sent from London and saw them as usurpers. Consequently, the delegates who drafted the state constitution pared down the role of the governor to near irrelevance, if not outright impotence. Although they referred to the governor as the "supreme executive magistrate," they placed severe limits on the office. Denied any meaningful executive authority and elected on an annual basis, the governor was hamstrung by the Governor's Council, an eight-member body that acted as a political check on his power. Strangely enough, this archaic institution, which is a relic of a bygone era, still survives. Today it acts as a major gatekeeper because the governor must obtain its approval in filling over eight hundred major and minor appointments.

In 1780 the diminutive John Hancock, only five feet four, became the first popularly elected chief executive. He served intermittently for a total of eleven annual terms, extending from 1780 to 1785 and again from 1787 to 1793. His length of service set a record that lasted for nearly two hundred years, until 1990, when Michael Dukakis broke it. Hancock was exceedingly fond of ceremony and show. He was replaced in the governor's chair by James Bowdoin in 1786, and by Samuel Adams in 1797. Most of the early governors were lawyers by profession, and most of them had received a college education. Several, like Elbridge Gerry, were known to be men of great wealth, but others, like Samuel Adams, had humbler origins. Adams had begun as a leather tanner and a brewer.

Elbridge Gerry belonged to the so-called "codfish aristocracy" of Marblehead, his father having made a fortune shipping dried cod to Spain and the West Indies. A Harvard graduate, he twice served as governor of Massachusetts from 1810 to 1812. Gerry invented the dubious practice of "gerrymandering," which bears his name today. Redistricting is required after each decennial census in order to reflect population shifts that have taken place since the last census. In reality, it involves the manipulation of legislative districts for the electoral benefit of a specific party or candidate (especially for the protection of incumbents)—a process that is always intricate, contentious, and highly politicized. As fate would have it, Gerry was a Federalist who later became a Jeffersonian Democrat. Under his party leadership, the Democrats, hoping to sustain themselves in power, redistricted the state in 1812. Looking at a map of the reconfigured congressional districts, one newspaperman thought that an Essex County state Senate district resembled a salamander; a fellow reporter dubbed it a "gerrymander." Hence a new term was coined in the lexicon of American politics.

Most nineteenth-century Massachusetts governors failed to grasp the reins of leadership. Typically they were disinclined to act and were deferential to the legislature. Their policy initiatives suffered accordingly. Legislators dominated the political scene: this was the golden era of legislative supremacy. Governors rarely used their authority to veto bills, and unable to organize the state bureaucracy, they did not supervise administrative agencies the way they do today. They were ceremonial figureheads, not dynamic party and policy leaders. As the historian John Wirkkala observed, "The governor in nineteenth-century Massachusetts was an official with a great deal more ceremonial than actual authority."[38] By reading Wirkkala's account, one gains a clearer picture of how the office developed during this period:

> With the local communities originally given the principal responsibility for the administration of laws, the title "chief executive" was largely a misnomer. The prevailing opinion was that the governorship was largely an honorary office to be held by those who had the time and the money to serve. A property qualification remained in effect until 1892.
>
> It was well established that the job was a part-time commitment. A long succession of governors maintained their private business practice while occu-

pying the state's highest elective office. General Nathaniel Banks was the state's first full-time governor (1858–1861). He attained the distinction since he was a full-time politician and had no outside business interest to pursue. His administration proved atypical and set no precedent requiring a full-time attention to public business by future governors.

Then too, there was another consideration working to keep the governorship underdeveloped as an administrative resource. A constitutional requirement for annual elections made frequent turnovers in the office a distinct possibility.

Yet another reason contributing to many legislators' lack of respect for the power of Massachusetts governors was their dependence upon the General Court which often elected them. In the seventy-five years from 1780 to 1855, Massachusetts elections functioned under a majority rule. During this interval, before adoption of the 14th Constitutional amendment, ten governors were elected by the Legislature, the people not having chosen any single candidate by a majority of the popular vote.[39]

From the Civil War on, the governorship was a coming-of-age story. State chief executives began to reflect the most powerful social and political currents of their time. John A. Andrew, who served as governor from 1861 to 1866, proved an exception to the rule of weak governors. He was a formidable personality in his own right. An adroit and clever politician, Andrew soon came to realize that there was no substitute for action. He mobilized public opinion and made appeals for public support. At the time, the governor's power to affect state agencies was almost exclusively appointive. As Wirkkala explains, "A strong governor, such as John Andrew, might also bring personal pressure to bear upon individuals beyond the immediate appointive power; such occurrences, however, were the result of official personality and were not commonplace."[40] Andrew worked to win support for the desegregation of Boston's public schools. He saw this reform as an essential first step in breaking the cycle of discrimination, degradation, and prejudice to which blacks were subjected. His eloquent and rational message on the issue leaped far ahead of its time. While compassion and social justice motivated Andrew, his call for better race relations took courage. Evidence of his success is the fact that he emerged as a popular rather than a hated figure. He was a man much ahead of his time.

A few post–Civil War governors attained considerable power, but their formal role in policymaking remained small, and their informal authority depended on their personality and their party strength. A complex and controversial figure, Governor Benjamin F. Butler was very much a man of his time—the Gilded Age. He believed in competition and laissez-faire economics, but he did not let the business community control him. Instead, he appealed primarily to the deprived urban lower classes and the marginally deprived agricultural yeomanry. Coming to power at the onset of pluralism, he deserted the Republican Party and became a Democrat. In a blatant attempt to win the Irish immigrant vote while running for governor in 1882, Butler attacked the Harvard Medical School for using the corpses of deceased Irish laborers as cadavers for medical research. Although he was denounced as an outrageous demagogue, he nevertheless won the overwhelming support of the Irish political community. The historian Thomas H. O'Connor describes him in these words:

> From the outset, Ben Butler was a thorn in the side of Boston Brahmin politicians, Democrats and Republicans alike. They disliked his combative style of politicking as well as what they considered his vulgar behavior. He was simply not the kind of well-mannered gentleman they liked to see representing the interests of the Bay State. They also resented the way he pandered to the interests of the Irish and shrewdly cultivated the immigrant vote. As a member of the state legislature before the Civil War, Butler led the fight to obtain compensation for the Ursuline convent fire; after the war he supported a congressional appropriation bill on behalf of the Little Sisters of the Poor. Recalling the valiant work of the nuns who aided the sick and wounded Union soldiers on the battlefield, Butler announced he would rather "cut off his right hand" than vote against such an appropriation because of any "religious prejudice against the Catholic faith." Such sentiments were warmly received by the Irish, who continued to view Butler as their champion in the face of nativist attacks.[41]

Arriving on the scene in the antebellum period before pluralism, Butler helped to pave the way for a multiethnic society. As an agent of change, he upset the established order, disrupting the status quo that prevailed in an overly rigid society. In 1884, Butler ran unsuccessfully for president on the Greenback ticket. His career illustrates the rejection of the political type who originally led the urban masses. Nevertheless, he was a forerunner to a type of governor that had not yet appeared on the American political stage.

The safe, comfortable conservatism of the age of industrial expansion was threatened by the Democratic vote at the polls and by the split within the Republican Party when the Bull Moose Progressive element began to make demands and to cause election losses. This split enabled Democrat Eugene Noble Foss to win the governorship for three consecutive terms, extending from 1911 to 1914. A party primary law was passed in 1912 largely as a result of Progressive pressure. That same year Woodrow Wilson became the first Democratic presidential candidate to capture the Bay State's electoral vote. Both Wilson and Foss owed their success to internal discord within the Republican Party.

EMERGENCE OF THE MODERN GOVERNOR

The so-called "modern governor" did not appear on the scene in Massachusetts until the second decade of the twentieth century. Duane Lockard defines this type of governor as one "who shows a certain independence of party organizations; makes the most of his having been popularly elected by appealing for public support; and seeks to maximize his power to govern by increasing his control over governmental administration; and by frankly cultivating a public image."[42] The main job of the modern governor is to engage the public in what he or she is doing. Communication skills are essential for raising the level of public awareness. Modern governors work their staffs prodigiously, and their every move is calculated to further their cause. The will to conquer and to make a difference also comes into play.

Although signs of willingness to use these techniques appeared before 1914, when David Ignatius Walsh became governor, it is apparent that Walsh showed others how to create and make the most of the governor's public image as an honest and fearless public servant. A native of Clinton, a small town in central Massachusetts, Walsh became the first Roman Catholic to occupy the governor's chair. His two consecutive gubernatorial victories (1913 and 1914) ensured that the Irish would constitute not only the main source of strength for the Democratic Party but also its main source of recruiting candidates. From the State House, Walsh went on to the U.S. Senate, where he served with only one interruption from 1919 to 1947. Relatively liberal during his terms as governor, Walsh was a moderate in the Senate on most issues except foreign policy, where his strong isolationism often put him in opposition to the British, a fact that only further cemented his relations with the Boston Irish. He formed an important alliance with Joseph B. Ely, a Yankee Protestant Democrat from Westfield. Walsh fought James Michael Curley within the Democratic Party for decades, but they never ran against each other on the same ticket.

Governor Walsh had the social engineering and scientific management mindset of the Progressive Era. In 1914 and again in 1915, he fought for a constitutional convention to liberalize the framework of state government, but he failed in these efforts. He was replaced in the governor's chair in 1916 by Republican Samuel W. McCall, who joined the fight for a convention and prevailed. The convention met at the State House on June 6, 1917. It continued through 1918 and ended after a short session in August 1919. It was the fourth constitutional convention in state history and provided the first major increase in the governor's formal powers since 1780. As a result, the managerial influence of governors was strengthened in Massachusetts. They were granted control over spending and over the bureaucracy directly. Among other things, the governor was granted an executive budget, the item veto, and the power to recommend the terms under which the Commonwealth could borrow money. At the same time, the administrative system, which had grown in haphazard fashion, was completely reorganized. Over a hundred boards and commissions then existed, and many of them were obscure, independent, and utterly beyond the control of anyone—not subordinate to the governor, the legislature, or anyone else. Under a reorganization plan, all these agencies were concentrated into less than twenty departments. Based on the latest organizational theory available, this was done to give the executive a reasonable span of control. Significantly, the governor's term of office was increased from one to two years.[43]

Republican Calvin Coolidge of Northampton, who presided as governor from 1919 to 1921, was a reluctant politician, more of a public servant. He personified the older America of small towns and villages, of people whose ancestors had arrived long ago. As an inconspicuous chief executive, the transplanted Vermonter embraced the "red scare" that was sweeping the nation in the wake of the Russian Revolution. Against this backdrop, he used state troops to intervene in the Boston police strike of 1919. In a telegram sent to Samuel Gompers, head of the American Federation of Labor, he declared, "There is no right to strike against the public safety by anybody, any time, anywhere." This telegram caught the nation's attention, and he was reelected governor in a landslide. It would be the defining moment for Coolidge. He was now portrayed in the media as a national hero, though organized labor saw him as a strike-breaker. This event catapulted him into the Republican vice presidential nomination in 1920. Three years after Warren G. Harding and he were elected, Harding died in office, and Coolidge, who was known for his reticence, became president. As governor, "Silent Cal" had struggled with executive appointments. "Every time a man makes an appointment," said Coolidge, "he creates one ingrate and a thousand enemies." His landmark achievement was reorganization of the state government on a consolidated, businesslike basis. Years later he confided to a friend, "They say the police strike required executive courage; reorganizing 118 departments into 18 required a good deal more."[44]

In Massachusetts, the Republicans were on a political roll in the 1920s. This was the high-water mark of Yankee hegemony. The conservative mood of the times was partly responsible. Swept into office in 1920, Channing H. Cox, lieutenant governor under Coolidge, was the first governor to serve a two-year term. A graduate of Dartmouth and Harvard Law School, Cox was a lawyer and banker who catered primarily to business interests and reflected the prejudiced Boston elite of the early twentieth century. He defeated Democrat John F. ("Honey Fitz") Fitzgerald by more than 60,000 votes in his bid for reelection in 1922. In heavily Catholic Massachusetts,

Cox sent state troops to protect Ku Klux Klan rallies from any repetition of the violence that had erupted in Worcester in 1923 when nearly three thousand Klansmen gathered to listen to anti-Catholic diatribes by F. Eugene Farnsworth, the King Kleagle of Maine. In April and May 1924 crosses were set afire in over a dozen Massachusetts towns, including Georgetown, near the New Hampshire border, where James M. Curley happened to be speaking. Skeptics surmised that the burning crosses had been lit by Curley's campaign workers. Later on, he admitted as much in his ghostwritten autobiography, which he defiantly titled *I'd Do It Again.*

Republican Alvan T. Fuller, a wealthy car dealer who lived on Beacon Street in Boston, had little trouble defeating Curley for governor in 1924. Like his predecessor, Fuller was a businessman's governor who reflected complacency in the face of social and cultural change. He presided at the State House during the famous murder trial of Nicola Sacco and Bartolomeo Vanzetti. In the eyes of many, the two immigrants were innocent scapegoats, framed, tried in a kangaroo court, and found guilty because they were Italian anarchists. Besieged by pleas for clemency from around the world, the governor adamantly refused to commute their death sentence. Sacco and Vanzetti were executed in the electric chair in 1927. Like Calvin Coolidge, Fuller thought that he could parlay his anti-anarchist and thinly veiled anti-immigrant stance into a bid for the White House, but his hopes were quickly dashed in the presidential preference primary of 1928.

COMING OF THE NEW DEAL

Republican Frank G. Allen, who had served as Senate president and lieutenant governor, was elected governor in 1928. A leather and wool merchant from Lynn, Allen won a narrow victory over his Democratic opponent, Charles H. Cole, a retired army brigadier general who had commanded the famed Yankee Division during World War I. Espousing a short and simple public agenda, Allen was another conservative businessman's governor who was content to perpetuate the status quo. In a stunning upset, Allen was defeated for reelection in 1930 by Joseph Buell Ely. The Democrats had recaptured the governorship for the first time in fifteen years. By this time, the Great Depression had made a devastating impact as soup lines became a common sight. During the heated campaign, Ely took Allen to task for not doing enough to correct America's malfunctioning economy and to solve the problem of hunger and unemployment. He recommended a radical shift to deficit financing and an unbalanced budget. Such a fiscal policy, of course, was considered economic heresy.

In his first term, Ely kept his campaign promise. A firm believer in states' rights, Ely wanted to solve the unemployment problem without depending on the federal government. Discarding the orthodox "pay-as-you-go" fiscal policy, he asked for a $1 million emergency fund and a $20 million bond issue to put men to work clearing the state's forests and repairing its bridges, roads, and public buildings. He was reelected in 1932. Beset by a worsening depression and a rising clamor against mounting debt in his second term, he abandoned his deficit financing and reverted to the more cautious pay-as-you-go policy.[45]

Ely was followed in office by his sworn enemy James M. Curley, the "rascal king" himself. The two men detested each other. In 1934, Curley was denied the gubernatorial nomination at his party's convention, but he did not let this formality stop him. He defeated General Charles Cole in a party primary and became the first Democratic mayor of Boston to be elected governor. During the campaign he had promised—among a plethora of promises—to reinstate the ex-policemen who had been fired in the 1919 strike. He dressed his own state police guard in gold-trimmed military uniforms. Meanwhile, the internecine warfare among Democrats was so debilitating that the New Deal relief programs were slowed in arriving in Massachusetts. Curley signed into law a statute that compelled public school teachers to take a loyalty oath, but he failed to deliver on core issues. His administration was awash in patronage and corruption. As Jack Beatty writes: "No amount of scandal had sufficed to dispel his reputation for competence as mayor of Boston: Curley built Boston, he got things done. Governor Curley got things done too. But his accomplishments were forgotten, buried in the headlines and obliterated in the common memory by things that made the government of Massachusetts ludicrous part of the time, shocking most of the time, and tawdry all of the time."[46]

Curley sought a cabinet post in the Roosevelt administration, but his aspirations were thwarted by FDR, who distrusted him. So Curley abandoned the State House in 1936 to run for the open U.S. Senate seat against Henry Cabot Lodge Jr. He failed in that mission. Charles F. Hurley, another Democrat, was elected governor. Identified with the Walsh-Ely wing of his party, Hurley shared Ely's states' rights outlook and proposed a spate of taxes to shore up the state treasury, but the Republican legislature failed to approve them. The pall of the Great Depression still lingered despite an infusion of federal funds and the stimulus of New Deal pump-priming public works projects.

The Republicans recaptured the governorship in 1938 with former House Speaker Leverett Saltonstall as their candidate. The Democrats were in disarray as the result of a bitter primary battle in which Curley wrested the gubernatorial nomination from Hurley. A moderate-conservative Republican, Saltonstall defeated Curley and proceeded to serve three consecutive terms as governor, from 1939 to 1945. With his craggy features, "Salty" possessed what one newspaper described as "a Back Bay name and a South Boston face." He garnered a large vote in Boston many times, and the fact that he found a Sullivan somewhere in his family tree simply enhanced his popularity.

As governor, Saltonstall carefully avoided criticizing President Roosevelt and even supported his foreign policy in several speeches. He also refrained from being seen as anti-labor, and this posture won him the support of the CIO in 1942. Economic conditions had improved substantially by his second term, mainly because of the war, which increased defense spending and imposed fiscal austerity in state government. He cultivated a popular image and acquitted himself admirably as governor. In 1944, Saltonstall won a special election to fill the U.S. Senate vacancy created by Henry Cabot Lodge's enlistment in the army. As one observer points out, "It was the last time a governor of Massachusetts has been elected to anything but governor."[47]

THE POST–WORLD WAR II ERA

Maurice J. Tobin, a Roxbury Democrat and former Curley protégé, battled his mentor in the 1937 mayoral election and won comfortably. He then went on to capture the governorship in 1944. Tobin faced the problems of providing bonuses, jobs, and education for returning veterans, along with the need for more housing and better working conditions. To finance these programs, he pushed through a series of taxes that did not make him popular. Not unexpectedly, he failed to win reelection in 1946, losing to Republican Robert Bradford, who was a descendant of the original *Mayflower* Pilgrims. In this election Curley deserted Tobin and backed Bradford. Feeling deeply betrayed, Tobin was consoled two years later when President Harry S. Truman appointed him secretary of labor.

Governor Bradford focused on problems of transportation and the deplorable condition of the state's highways, which had been neglected during the depression and the war. He submitted to the legislature a master highway construction plan, requesting a $1 million bond issue to initiate this program, as well as a $13 million bond issue for developing Boston's airport. The legislature rejected his spending requests as well as his anti-labor legislation, but it supported his other programs for public ownership of Boston's elevated railway and the earmarking of gasoline taxes for highway construction. In 1948, Bradford lost the governor's race to Democrat Paul A. Dever, a rotund lawyer who grew up without a father and worked nights in a rubber factory to finance his education. He had previously served three terms in the legislature and was the youngest attorney general in the state's history. That same year the Democrats captured control of the House, and Tip O'Neill was elected Speaker.

Once in office, Dever pushed his progressive agenda through the legislature, fighting for a graduated income tax, compulsory health insurance, $200 million for new highways, and proper care of the mentally ill, and against an MTA fare hike. He won approval of the same $100 million bond issue that the legislature had refused Bradford a year earlier, and the master highway plan became a reality. Having served as the top aide to U.S. senator David Walsh, Dever knew how to use his patronage power to great advantage. Edgar Litt writes, "The strongest and most progressive public policy produced by the Democratic Party since the Walsh-Ely coalition was built on the foundations of politically awarded judgeships, contracts based on favoritism, and financial contributions from patronage-oriented individuals."[48] In 1950, Dever won a resounding reelection victory. In his second term he obtained another $100 million highway bond issue as well as additional millions for the regular road fund. His graduated income tax generated $27 million in new revenues. The old cautious pay-as-you-go financing was gone. The era of big spending had begun.

In 1952, Christian A. Herter beat Dever in an extremely close contest for governor. It was a classic matchup that pitted a Protestant Yankee Republican against an Irish Catholic Democrat. With the popular Dwight Eisenhower heading the Republican ticket, and a new "red scare" gripping the nation, the Republicans recaptured control of the Massachusetts House. The vaunted Dever organization could not overcome the national tide.

Born in Paris in 1895 and educated at Harvard, Herter was a strikingly handsome man who had served as a career foreign service officer before entering politics. His father was an artist who painted the murals that decorate the walls of the State House rotunda. Given his successful first term, Herter had little trouble winning reelection in 1954. Among his more notable accomplishments were reform of the correctional system, a merit rating system for automobile insurance, legislation designed to cope with strikes endangering the public health and safety, and a revamped judiciary. In January 1957, Herter, who suffered from severe arthritis, returned to Washington to become undersecretary of state in the Eisenhower administration. After John Foster Dulles died in 1959, he headed the State Department for the remainder of Eisenhower's second term.

Foster Furcolo, governor from 1957 to 1961, came from East Longmeadow, near Springfield. He was a moderate liberal with the good fortune to have both Italian and Irish ancestors. Educated at Yale and Yale Law School, he had been a boxer during his undergraduate days in college. After serving as a naval officer in World War II, Furcolo was elected to Congress in 1948. As a freshman congressman, he won recognition in *Fortune Magazine* as "one of the nation's ten rising leaders." In an effort to break up the "all-Green" Irish monopoly of the Democratic ticket, Governor Dever appointed him to fill a vacancy as state treasurer in July 1952.

Only forty-five years old at the time he became governor, Furcolo was a man of tremendous energy who worked fourteen-hour days, and often telephoned his staff at six in the morning. But more than long hours were responsible for the success that he achieved as a party leader and as a policy leader. Subjecting himself to a punishing schedule, he was a driving, relentless executive who never let up, who set his goals and pursued them with all the force he could muster. He also wrote several books and plays. Two political scientists, John Mallan and George Blackwood, provided this candid portrait of him:

> It is fair to say that Furcolo has always been one of the more controversial
> figures of Massachusetts politics, a man who has seemed to have many differ-
> ent images. To his friends and supporters, he has seemed warm, intelligent, and
> articulate—with a far greater interest in programs and issues than most Massa-
> chusetts Democrats. But he has also appeared as a non–team player who often
> leaps into a political situation without enough regard for political conse-
> quences. To his opponents, especially in the legislature, he has been criticized
> not only as a poor politician but as a man who "couldn't be worked with,"
> who was not one of the boys. His background separated him from many of the
> Democratic legislators; he was urbane and well educated, with a broad interest
> in national and international issues, while many of them were self-made men—
> small businessmen, lawyers, or insurance salesmen—whose education had
> ended with high school or perhaps with night law school. But more essential
> was the fundamental interest Furcolo had in broad and sweeping programs,
> combined with a determined if not stubborn willingness to push for an idea he
> believed in against the political judgment of his own advisors.[49]

When Furcolo came to the governorship in 1957, one of his first actions was to propose a state sales tax to cover the increasing costs of state government. This he did despite the anti–sales tax pledge of the Democratic platform on which he had been elected. Among those who agreed with his proposal was his Republican predecessor Christian Herter, but the sales tax was soundly defeated by the legislature.[50] Furcolo disdained the mad scramble for patronage and pretty favors that surrounded him. He was a man who thrived on generating ideas. Several of his ideas were adopted into law: a state scholarship program, a network of two-year community colleges, a new state technological institute, new psychiatric clinics around the state, and a program of housing for the elderly. While he did not win all of his battles, he won enough of them to build a reputation as a strong executive.

Furcolo was twice defeated for the U.S. Senate, first in 1954 and again in 1960. The Kennedys did not look with favor on his advancing to the Senate. The JKF-Furcolo rivalry surfaced in 1948 when they served together in Congress. They disliked each other intensely. Their political careers had evolved in parallel fashion. Both were Ivy Leaguers, both served in the navy, and both were elected to Congress. Clashing personalities and ambitions sharpened factional rivalries and divisions. In 1954, JFK bluntly refused to endorse Furcolo in his senatorial race against Republican Leverett Saltonstall. The Kennedys preferred Saltonstall to a Democrat who might upstage JFK. Once Kennedy was elected president, they wanted to keep his Senate seat warm for his youngest brother, Edward. Furcolo planned to appoint himself to the post, but with Republican John Volpe about to assume the governorship, this strategy proved unworkable. Furcolo was thus pressured into appointing Benjamin Smith, mayor of Gloucester, who had roomed with Joseph Kennedy Jr. at Harvard.

Since the governorship of David Walsh, the first three-quarters of the twentieth century had witnessed the ascendancy of the executive. Governors acquired more and more political power because they were the heads of political parties, were publicly visible, and were statewide political leaders. After World War II there were continuing efforts to bring greater rationality to the state bureaucracy. So-called "Little Hoover Commissions" were set up in most states for expressly that purpose. In Massachusetts the "Baby Hoover Commission" put forth a plan to reorganize the bureaucracy, but it was defeated by the legislature.[51] Despite this setback, various reforms continued to strengthen the hand of the governor. A state constitutional amendment, which was adopted in 1964, expanded the governor's term of office from two to four years. At the same time, provision was also made for the governor and lieutenant governor to run as a team on the same ticket. Heretofore they had run independently, which often resulted in a divided executive.

In 1960, John Volpe, a Republican businessman from Wakefield, captured the governorship by beating Democrat John Ward. Realizing that the majority of registered voters were Democrats, Volpe had campaigned on the slogan "Vote the Man." This strategy worked well for him. As a businessman and a firm believer in the gospel of efficiency, Volpe constantly sought administrative improvements. In the divided government that marked his administration from 1960 to 1962, he relied on conciliatory tactics, his capacity to persuade, and the strong position he created for himself in the

Republican Party to achieve his cherished goals. Amid evidence of Democratic corruption, Volpe's honesty carried the day.

In 1962, Democrat Endicott Peabody eked out a slender victory over the Republican incumbent, Volpe. With Ted Kennedy heading the Democratic ticket and a glowing endorsement of Peabody by President Kennedy, victory was assured.[52] A former All-American football player at Harvard, "Chub" Peabody was the first Democratic Protestant Yankee to occupy the governor's suite since Joseph Ely three decades earlier. Although he had little legislative experience, Peabody was successful in engineering his legislative program. But he frequently reneged on promises and made some other serious blunders. He got involved in a bitter battle over the House Speakership and wound up supporting John Thompson, whom he had originally tried to unseat. Worse yet, Peabody was tagged as a loser, and this reputation set him adrift from the Democratic circle of political insiders. His tenure was relatively short-lived: in 1964 he was defeated for renomination by his own lieutenant governor, Frank Bellotti, in a party primary. Peabody had his moment in time. That moment had passed.

The indomitable Volpe made a stunning comeback in 1964 by beating Bellotti. In the words of Edgar Litt, "The Republican governor was viewed as a sincere, honest individual trying to do a businesslike job as chief executive."[53] After a protracted and acrimonious two-year battle, Volpe pushed through a sales tax. In 1966 he became the first governor to be elected to a four-year term. Three years later, in 1969, Volpe left the governor's office to join the cabinet of President Richard Nixon as secretary of transportation. He was succeeded by Frank Sargent, his lieutenant governor. Sargent served the remaining two years of Volpe's term and then was elected to a full four-year term in 1970. A more detailed examination of his two administrations is found in chapter 2.

THE DUKAKIS ERA OF REFORM

The next high-profile governor was Michael S. Dukakis, who defeated Sargent in 1974. Their election contest would bring out the best in both of them. The political fallout from the Watergate scandal contributed heavily to Sargent's defeat. A Greek American, Dukakis was a former legislator who had made his name by sponsoring a "no-fault" automobile insurance law. A relentless campaigner, he was regarded as liberal, intelligent, and aggressive. But the issue now was governing, not campaigning. It was a rough first term (1975–78) for Dukakis, who ran into a combination of political troubles, as well as disaffection among major elements of his party. To begin with, he was a different kind of politician, one who shunned the trappings of office and insisted on riding to work on the MBTA Green Line. Although he had inherited a large fiscal deficit from the Sargent administration, he stubbornly refused to put through a tax increase. Like Foster Furcolo, he disdained patronage and turned over to his staff the task of distributing the petty jobs that his supporters clamored for. This was a reflection of his distaste for spoils and his commitment to a professional civil service. As a "good government" reformer, Dukakis led a crusade to stamp out fraud, waste, and corruption in state government. Toward the end of his first term, he signed legislation creating a state ethics commission. The interplay of politics and personality did not go over well with party regulars. Morally certain of the rectitude of his position and intellectually convinced of its value, Dukakis came across as arrogant, morally self-righteous, and determined to be his own chief policy maker. He seldom reached out for the views of others, and maintained a "hands-on" management style. To offset the fiscal crisis, in an unusual display of gubernatorial prerogative, he applied a "meat cleaver" to the state budget. As a result, he alienated many Democrats, including fellow liberals who had been instrumental in getting him elected. They viewed him as a political ingrate.

Not surprisingly, Edward King, a conservative who courted disaffected Democrats, defeated Dukakis in a party primary in 1978 and then went on to win the general election. King had difficulties in trying to be a modern governor. He had served as executive director of the Massachusetts Port Authority for twelve years, but he was not otherwise experienced in politics. Viewed as a political outsider, he campaigned as a pro-business, pro-growth, anti-government candidate in a very liberal state. King promised to "turn the state around" and do something about its onerous tax burden. Those who worked with him during his tenure as governor attribute some of his difficulties to internal party complications and the intense opposition that came from the *Boston Globe*; but whatever the root cause, he did not excel in asserting personal leadership.

Despite his self-proclaimed image as a "can-do" governor, he wrote off any possible support from environmentalists, consumer advocates, women's groups, good government and civic organizations, planned parenthood groups, state employee unions, welfare advocates, the young, and a host of other constituencies that he tended to see as foes. A purge of non–civil service workers, and generous pay raises for himself and his major appointees in the predawn hours before the legislature adjourned, further eroded his standing with many voters. As one reporter wrote in the *New York Times*, "In the year since his overwhelming election victory, Governor Edward J. King of Massachusetts has managed to incur the enmity of every important local political figure, arouse the anger of most constituent groups and achieve an approval rating in the polls of just around 30 percent."[54]

King did do something about reducing taxes. The reduction was accomplished through increased state aid to localities and a first-time-ever "cap" on local spending increases. The latter came in the form of Proposition 2½, which was passed as an initiative petition. It limited increases in local property taxes to that percentage of fair market value. King's success in tax reduction was overshadowed by the negative reaction to his bulldozer personality that made it possible. He cooperated with the state's banking and industrial interests, which saw him as their representative. Except for conservative working-class voters who supported him, King was distrusted by the political establishment, and the liberal press was outwardly antagonistic toward him. He seemed to go from one debacle to another right from the start. Barney Frank quipped, "The good news is that Ed King is Superman. The bad news is that Massachusetts is made out of kryptonite."[55] In sum, King was unable to overcome these problems as his hard-edged administration stumbled inconclusively to its end.

After a hiatus of four years, which he spent teaching at the Kennedy School of Government at Harvard, Michael Dukakis returned to state politics and made a strong comeback in 1982. It was a critical turning point for him. He seemed wiser, more mature, and willing to acknowledge openly some of his previous mistakes. His next two administrations were dramatic and productive; he caught the public's eye—as he meant to do, since he was aiming for the White House—and in the process dramatized purposeful gubernatorial leadership. He made a point of delegating to his subordinates, but he retained his hands-on managerial style. In his thirst for new ideas, Dukakis surrounded himself with competent people who did a great deal to make him look good. He had one of the best cabinets in the history of the Commonwealth and was therefore able to transform several proposals into operational programs. His long list of accomplishments is impressive, to say the least, especially with regard to achieving a comprehensive transportation system. He also shook up several calcified departments, such as mental health and public works, and got them to operate less dysfunctionally. Some of these adjustments required trial and error as well as the courage to face and learn from mistakes. The office of governor exacted much from him, with its harrowing responsibilities, but Dukakis was up to the task. By any standard he was one of the ablest and most intriguing men ever to serve as governor.

Two factors accounted for his effectiveness. First, on almost every policy front, Dukakis reached out to people for their advice, and was more willing than before to listen to them in trying to build consensus. In a remarkable reversal of form, he now utilized patronage to achieve his ends. Second, he recruited "idea people" like Charles Atkins, Manuel Carballo, Thomas Glenn, Frank Keefe, Evelyn Murphy, Fred Salvucci, and John Sasso into his administration. Sasso, his chief secretary, was a rare commodity in state politics—a reliable, enormously attractive, reassuring, and skillful bridge between politicians and policy experts. In the opinion of two close observers, "Sasso won the respect of legislative leaders, who found him a tough but fair negotiator whose word was reliable. When Sasso bargained, they knew he carried the authority—more than any other administration official—to speak for the governor."[56] In addition, Sasso could tell Dukakis when he was wrong and the governor would listen. Frank Keefe, whom Dukakis named secretary of administration and finance, was a gifted and able administrator. For all practical purposes, Keefe functioned as a deputy governor. The idea for the governor's welfare-to-work program actually came from Tom Glenn, while Fred Salvucci masterminded the massive highway and tunnel project that would reshape the city of Boston. Overall, Dukakis did a much better job of governing during his last two terms (1983–90).

Throughout most of the 1980s, Dukakis was riding the crest of his power and popularity. It was the best of economic times, and he made the most of it. In fact, economic conditions in the Commonwealth were so good that the incumbent Democratic governor parlayed the "Massachusetts Miracle" into his party's presidential nomination. Wounded by corrosive attacks and negative ads (including the infamous "Willie Horton" spot), he failed to counter criticism and lost the presidential election to Republican George Bush.

In all, Dukakis served a record-breaking twelve years, or three terms, as governor, breaking John Hancock's long-standing record. Though he left a lasting legacy, he also left office as an unpopular, even a despised figure. An economic downturn and recession fed a growing cynicism about politics and state government. His party position was almost as weak as King's by the end of his third term. Political scientist Morris Fiorina tells the story of his painful descent:

> By 1990, . . . conditions had deteriorated dramatically. With revenues pouring in during the 1980s there had been little need to set priorities or make hard choices. Moreover, there had been no pressure to address rapidly growing health expenditures. As a result, state expenditures ballooned. Signs of trouble were apparent by the late 1980s, but the exigencies of presidential politics led top state officials to discount bad indicators, accept optimistic forecasts, and otherwise postpone the day of reckoning. By 1990 recession had set in; deficits were growing; taxes had been raised twice; the legislature was paralyzed by the need for yet another, larger increase; and the lame duck Democratic governor had become a political pariah.[57]

The "lame duck" phenomenon accounted for Dukakis's diminished power as well as his ignominious exit. Since he was on the way out and William Weld was on the way in, politicians and the general public read the signs accordingly. Yet even in his decline there was much to admire about Dukakis. He is perhaps best remembered today for his comprehensive transportation policy and his efforts to eliminate corruption. Dukakis could not have been better suited to the task of restoring public faith in the institutions of government.

Republican Paul Cellucci, who had become acting governor on Weld's resignation, barely beat Attorney General Scott Harshbarger for the governorship in 1998. Harshbarger's problems, mostly an issue with political insiders, stemmed mainly from his penchant for headline grabbing and his ill-timed prosecutions of popular Democrats. Cellucci's inability to stem the tide of Republican losses, both statewide and in the legislature, caused him considerable difficulty. Writing in the year 2000, veteran State House reporter Frank Phillips concluded that "the relationship between Governor Paul Cellucci and the small bloc of Republican lawmakers is near a breaking point, with the legislators increasingly rebuffing him and the governor feeling exasperated with what he feels is their coziness with Democrats. It is ironic that the divisions have developed under Cellucci, who, unlike his predecessor William F. Weld, has made it a priority to nurture Republican lawmakers and to rebuild the party organization around the state."[58]

Whatever the quality of Cellucci's advice, his administration could not make an effective transition from broad moral goals to policies that were politically acceptable and programmatically workable. Perhaps the best illustration is the Massachusetts Comprehensive Assessment System (MCAS) examination, a standardized test designed to raise the quality of teaching and learning, not just to measure the mastery of basic reading and math skills. By making a passing grade on this test a high school graduation requirement, the administration provoked a firestorm of controversy. While teachers' unions, nervous parents, and some local school committees opposed the high-stakes test, a group known as Business for Better Schools supported it. Some of Cellucci's other troubles stemmed from the rapidly escalating cost overruns of the Big Dig and from the controversies in which his lieutenant governor, Jane Swift, became embroiled. He did succeed in getting his tax rollback approved by the voters. Upon leaving office after only two years to serve as U.S. ambassador to Canada, Cellucci suggested that he would be remembered mostly as a "tax-cutter" and for driving a stake through the heart of the state's derisive nickname, "Taxachusetts."

As this cursory review of Massachusetts governors suggests, gubernatorial power, much like presidential power, is essentially the power to persuade.

The chief executive is conceived to be the cardinal position in the government, and as such, the initiating and driving force in the policymaking process, assuming responsibility and taking credit for achievements across a broad spectrum of public business. Modern mass communications provide the governor with an unprecedented opportunity to enlist public support. The omnipresence of newspapers, magazines, radio, and television does not mean that all citizens will become concerned about state problems, but it does mean that information can be disseminated more rapidly to those who are concerned. In an informational computer age, this capacity has expanded exponentially. The availability of rapid transportation also increases the governor's opportunities for using personal appearances as a means of persuasion. A four-year term of office gives that person sufficient time for preparing, promoting, and carrying out a program and is plainly much more advantageous than the original one-year term.

One final paradox of gubernatorial power should be noted: the impact of election day. Clearly this forces governors both to insist on certain policies and to evade others. In the course of Massachusetts history, the governor has become an increasingly "representative" official, one who seeks to reflect public desires not only because, ideologically, this is the right thing to do but also because of the expected rewards for doing so. The restraint that the electorate implicitly places on governors, particularly when elections are closely contested, prevents certain kinds of abuse of power, but it also makes for timidity.

THE POLITICAL PARTY AS A SOURCE OF POWER

Over the years, party organizations in Massachusetts have waxed and waned as a source of power. From the Civil War on, the Republicans became extremely powerful because of the intense antislavery feeling in the state and the lukewarm support of the federal government by the Democrats. Since the Republicans had preserved the Union and freed the Negro (the term then in use), many Democrats who had left their party during the war never returned to it. In 1890 the Democrats elected William E. Russell as governor to the first of three one-year terms. Prior to that, they had won the governorship only twice since the Civil War: William Gaston captured the office in 1874, and Benjamin Butler in 1882. Both were one-term governors. Winthrop Murray Crane, a Republican who served from 1900 to 1903, the last governor elected in his own right to come from the Berkshires, was a member of the wealthy Crane paper family. William L. Douglas, another one-term governor, succeeded him in 1904.

Starting in 1910, the Democrats won five consecutive gubernatorial elections, in part because of the splitting off of the Bull Moose Progressives from the Republican Party. Eugene Noble Foss was elected governor in 1910, 1911, and 1912, and David Walsh in 1913 and 1914. These Democratic governors had to contend with Republican-controlled legislatures. Butler and Foss, both of whom were former Republicans, encountered a particularly hostile legislature. Control of the legislature gave the Republicans the power to select the state's two U.S. senators. It should be noted that the direct election of senators did not begin until 1913, when the Seventeenth Amendment was adopted.

By 1928, when New York governor Alfred E. Smith ran for the presidency, the political momentum in Massachusetts began to swing in favor of the Democrats. A cigar-chomping big city party boss with a brown derby hat, Smith stirred the pride of the Irish and other newer immigrant groups. The Democrats continued to make inroads during the next three decades. By 1958 they had become the dominant party in Massachusetts. Their dominance has since reached the point where Republicans allow many seats in the state legislature to go virtually uncontested. The GOP organization pales by comparison to what it was in its glory years. In its present anemic condition, it is a prime candidate for the endangered species list. The decline of the political party and its discipline is one factor; a second is the growing independence and apathy of the voter. Party organization and party discipline were never as strong as current advocates for party resurgence remember. But they were there—an influential factor in nominating or electing a governor. During the twentieth century, the Republicans won the governorship more often than the Democrats.

In fact, the governorship has recently been the most competitive office in state politics. From 1970 to 1998 the two major parties divided the office evenly, each winning four times. In the twenty-five gubernatorial elections prior to 1970, beginning with that of 1919, when Calvin Coolidge won, it changed partisan hands several times, the Republicans winning fifteen times and the Democrats ten. No other statewide office has been more keenly contested or more frequently exchanged between the two major parties.

To varying degrees the modern governors have enjoyed party support because as governor they became party leader. It is worth noting that the governors who have become the most effective leaders have been men of intense ambition and fierce concentration, who pursued their goals relentlessly. This was especially true of Republican governors such as Leverett Saltonstall, Christian Herter, John Volpe, and Frank Sargent. They were more than titular leaders of their party. When they were most successful, they were the party's driving and dominating figures. The same was true of Democratic governors such as Joseph Ely, Paul Dever, Foster Furcolo, and Michael Dukakis. Maurice Tobin, Endicott Peabody, and Edward King did not particularly excel in asserting their personal leadership, and hence they were less effective party chieftains. Not surprisingly, all three were one-term governors.

Equally important to the governor's rise in modern times is the fact that his control over administration has been enlarged by political, legal, and constitutional changes. The enlargement of administrative control has come about partly because the general public has accepted the need for a more hierarchical pattern of state government. Both the public's willingness to accept the propriety of executive control and the constitutional enlargement of gubernatorial authority have become important sources of power.

LEGISLATIVE POWER AND LEADERSHIP

The Massachusetts General Court—the formal name for the state legislature—is a venerable institution that is steeped in history and tradition. The first session of the colonial legislature took place on October 17, 1630. Throughout its 370-year history it has enacted some of the most progressive and pioneering social legislation in the nation. As early as 1676, the General Court passed a law providing for the care of the insane, and subsequently in 1788 it passed another statute that permitted the indefinite imprisonment of lunatics "furiously mad as to be rendered dangerous to the safety of good people." In 1736 the General Court provided funds for the construction of a hospital on Rainsford Island in Boston Harbor. It did likewise for the construction of the old state prison in Charlestown in 1805. Throughout the nineteenth century, it established several poorhouses, industrial schools, and state-run mental hospitals.

During the period between the Civil War and World War I, the legislature passed many new laws affecting public welfare, labor, public health, business corporations, and the regulation of public utilities. The list of firsts included a state board of health, a tuberculosis sanatorium, establishment of a ten-hour workday, a ban against women working at night, a minimum wage law, adoption of the Australian ballot, a civil service law, and a statute requiring free textbooks in public schools. These statutes may seem rather simplistic today, but they were groundbreaking at the time and were often emulated by other states.

Massachusetts has a long and somewhat gruesome history with regard to capital punishment. In 1642 the colony became the first to execute a juvenile, and fifty years later it executed nineteen people in Salem for suspected connections to witchcraft. Two other executions that gained worldwide notoriety were those of Nicola Sacco and Bartolomeo Vanzetti in 1927. Capital punishment, which is the most extreme form of state power, was eventually abolished. The last time the Commonwealth executed a prisoner was in 1947. In recent decades the emotionally charged death penalty issue has been frequently debated in Massachusetts, but the General Court has consistently refused to reinstate capital punishment, although in 1997 the lawmakers came within one vote of approving the death penalty. Social scientists indicate that the state's progressive political culture, its relatively low murder rate, and its preponderance of Roman Catholic residents contribute to its prohibition. The Catholic Church strongly opposes the death penalty as being immoral and unnecessary.

For many of the same reasons why the governor was assigned a limited role in 1780, the framers of the state constitution made the legislature the preeminent power on Beacon Hill. The General Court was conceived as the focal point of representative democracy. Among its enumerated constitutional powers are to enact laws, to appropriate public funds, to establish courts, to prescribe rules for the conduct of elections, to create municipalities, to exercise the right of eminent domain, and to declare martial law. Of these, the "power of the purse" is by far its most potent weapon. Little wonder, then, that the legislature became the premier political institution. To quote Duane Lockard again, writing in 1959:

> Tradition is an important element of any democratic legislative body; habits of procedure once established are durable even beyond the point of utility at times. The traditional elements of Massachusetts legislative life are so ancient and august that one gets the feeling that the institution is even more tradition-oriented than those of other states. The General Court has an air of importance and decorum about it that resembles Congress or the House of Commons more than other state legislatures.[59]

When a legislature works well, there is ample opportunity for its members to discuss, debate, and vote their conscience on the salient issues of the day. In sparse outline, the prescribed way that a bill becomes a law is, first, to have the measure introduced by a member of the legislature or by a citizen through the right of free petition. A public hearing is held, and the measure is voted on by committee and brought to the floor for debate and action. The bill is next sent to the other house, where it goes through essentially the same process. If the bill passes in a different version, it is sent to a conference committee of the two houses, where disagreements are resolved. The statute then goes back to both houses for a final vote. It is finally sent to the governor, who can either sign or veto the measure.

Procedurally, the three main features characterizing the Massachusetts legislature are freedom of petition, public hearings on all bills, and the requirement that all bills be reported out of committees. Like the neighboring states of Connecticut and Maine, it uses a joint House: Senate committee system, thereby avoiding the waste of time involved in duplicate hearings and separate House and Senate committee consideration of each bill.

Representation in the two branches of the Massachusetts legislature is determined by population as prescribed by the U.S. Supreme Court ruling of "one person, one vote." Constitutionally, the membership of the House of Representatives was originally fixed at 379 and the Senate at 40. This made the House membership large and unwieldy. Later on it was reduced to 240. In 1978 a constitutional amendment, sponsored by the League of Women Voters, further reduced the size of the House from 240 to 160 members. The distribution of power in the bicameral legislature is highly centralized. It resides mainly with the Senate president, the Speaker of the House, and the chairs of their respective Ways and Means committees, which are in charge of appropriating money.

The Speaker of the House is a mighty potentate on Beacon Hill, with the power to set the legislative schedule, admit bills to the House floor, recognize legislators during debate, and control the committee assignments of both Republican and Democratic representatives. Many colorful politicians have held this position over the years—eighty-three to be exact. They are far too numerous to list in detail here. Suffice it to say that the Republicans held the post continuously from 1856 to 1948. The last Speaker to be elected governor was Republican Christian Herter in 1952. When the political tide shifted in 1949, Tip O'Neill of Cambridge became the first Democrat to hold the office. He was followed by a succession of other Democratic Speakers. They have included Michael F. Skerry of Medford, John F. Thompson of Ludlow, John F. Davoren of Milford, Robert H. Quinn of Dorchester, David M. Bartley of Holyoke, Thomas W. McGee of Lynn, George Keverian of Everett, Charles Flaherty of Cambridge, and Thomas M. Finneran of Mattapan. Like most politicians who move into the front ranks, these men quickly discovered that the political system within which they had to operate was not only shaping their decisions but also formulating the options from which they could choose.

In the modern era, the Speakership has been dominated by larger-than-life figures. One of the more colorful and flamboyant figures was John Thompson, who was known as the "Iron Duke." He ran things in the House in the heavy-handed and oligarchical fashion of the classic party boss. Thompson fancied himself a "delightful rogue."[60] In 1964 both Speaker Thompson and his predecessor, Charles Gibbons, a Republican from Stoneham, were indicted on charges of bribery and conspiracy. Thompson died of acute alcoholism before his case went to trial, while the charges against former Speaker Gibbons were dismissed.

At age thirty-three, David Bartley was one of the youngest Speakers to preside over the House. Considered brash and overly ambitious, he fought unsuccessfully against the reduction in the size of the House, pushed hard for gun control legislation, and was a strong supporter of the public university. Speaker Thomas McGee, another autocrat, presided for an unprecedented term of ten years. He was the longest-serving Speaker, but his punitive, authoritarian, and domineering style led to a revolt by insurgent reformers. George Keverian, who succeeded McGee, ran for Speaker on a platform of rules reform, since many members thought that McGee had stayed too long and had amassed too much power. A well-liked Everett politician, Keverian allowed genuine debate in the House and permitted committee chairs to run their own show. Undisciplined and occasionally sulky, however, he struggled to respond to a fiscal crisis in the late 1980s. Similarly, Charles Flaherty gave members a voice, led resistance to the death penalty, and pushed liberal causes. Distracted by personal issues, he was forced to resign after pleading guilty to income tax evasion. His successor, Thomas Finneran, has emulated the autocratic, boss-type Speaker. Fancying himself a counterforce to the governor, he delivers his own State of the State message. Although some legislators have chafed under his strong-arm leadership, the House has shown fiscal responsibility, and it is clearly not just reactive or a mere rubber stamp.

Similarly, the Senate presidency is an important leadership position. In 1959 John E. Powers of Boston assumed the office when the Democrats gained control of the upper chamber for the first time. Powers was succeeded by fellow Democrats Maurice Donahue, Kevin Harrington, William Bulger, and Thomas Birmingham. All their careers, except for Donahue's, are detailed elsewhere in this book. Donahue governed the Senate with patience and respect from 1964 to 1970. His calm style cultivated a reservoir of trust on both sides of the aisle. A champion of labor and a strong supporter of the public university, Donahue fought against the enactment of a regressive sales tax, which Governor Volpe advocated in 1964 and again in 1965. This protracted battle was one of the longest and most acrimonious in modern legislative history. Although Donahue lost the sales tax fight, he pushed legislation creating a state medical school in Worcester. In this effort he took on the powerful private medical interests in Boston and beat them at their own political game. In 1970 Donahue won his party's endorsement for governor, but he was defeated in a bitter primary by Boston mayor Kevin White, who in turn lost to Republican Frank Sargent in the general election. The last Senate president to win the governorship was Republican Frank G. Allen in 1928.

THE ECLIPSE OF THE LEGISLATURE

The state legislature is a body that has continuously evolved over three centuries. It breathes the air of the changing political climate, adapting to the social and economic pressure of the time, bending to the habits of its leaders, who strive to accommodate the endless demands of a pluralist society of which it is both a part and a reflection. In its bygone glory days it provided the major impetus for leadership and policymaking in Charles Bulfinch's golden-domed State House in Boston. That earlier prototype was the dominant political agent in the society, far more decisive than the governor, the bureaucracy, or the courts.

For more than a century after 1780, the legislature reigned supreme and remained the central focus of all government. Governors then were not expected to exercise political leadership; policies tended to come from the legislature, not the executive. For all practical purposes, the General Court *was* the state government. It created a host of various boards and commissions and exercised almost complete control over them. John Wirkkala puts this into historical perspective: "It is important to underscore the fact that successive General Courts considered these earliest commissions to be accountable to the legislature. They were independent of the governor and were accountable to the General Court."[61] By marked contrast, the legislature today has only peripheral authority; it shares power with other actors on the political stage and therefore occupies a much less exalted position.

Not all of the General Court's political history has been exemplary. The legislative branch had its share of scoundrels in the nineteenth century. In 1854 the American or "Know-Nothing" Party emerged as a dominant political force throughout most of the nation. It scored its most stunning victory in Massachusetts by capturing all forty seats in the Senate and all but three of the 379 seats in the House, along with the governorship. Anti-Catholic in their orientation and disposition, the Know-Nothings sought to restrict public office to native-born Protestants and to prevent immigrants from voting by extending the naturalization period. As the journalist Cornelius Dalton has pointed out, "The party arose almost by spontaneous combustion during the economic, social and political upheavals of the 1850s, when native-born artisans and manual workers saw the flood of Irish and German immigrants, mostly Catholics, as a threat to their jobs and way of life."[62] The Know-Nothing Party's meteoric rise, however, was matched by an equally sharp decline as it withered away and disappeared within a few years. The Republican Party absorbed most of the Know-Nothings, along with their anti-Catholic biases.

Throughout most of the twentieth century the legislature gradually lost power, while the governor gained power. More accurately, the General

Court became an institution in eclipse. It is a fact of our times that the legislature's prestige, power, and importance are on the wane. The causes for this decline are complex. The rise of technology robbed life and therefore government of the simplicity that had existed in a pre-urban and pre-industrial society. In the post–Civil War era, state legislators were openly bought and sold by corporate interests at a time when patronage seemed to be the paramount concern of state government, and when political machines controlled state government mainly for the vested interests of those machines. They produced the cynical politics of spoils and plunder and bosses who stuffed the ranks of the civil service with officeholders chosen on the basis of family or patronage.

Twentieth-century conditions caused the legislature's further decline, as the complexity of the subjects to be regulated forced the granting of subsidiary rulemaking power to the bureaucracy. Furthermore, a constitutional amendment was adopted in the Bay State in 1917 that provided for initiative and referendum. This was the first formal reduction or limitation of legislative power. It essentially made the citizens partners in the legislative process. The general public was allowed not only to initiate constitutional amendments and laws by petition, but also to challenge acts of the General Court by referendum. Increasingly it was the governor's office that provided the initiative for policy development. In addition, the vast expansion of judicial authority further hemmed in state legislatures across the nation, a development not limited solely to Massachusetts. The U.S. Supreme Court rejected state regulation of commerce and labor in the first four decades of the twentieth century, and subsequently attacked school segregation, legislative reapportionment, the death penalty, and anti-abortion statutes—thereby signaling a further decline in state legislative powers.

Following in the wake of these expansions of executive and judicial authority and the contraction of legislative prerogatives came an increasingly amateurish quality of legislative performance. In the past several decades the legislature has suffered from a series of deleterious scandals. The small loan company scandals in the 1960s, the fraud involving state building contracts in the 1970s, and the acceptance of illegal gratuities in the early 1990s have combined to tarnish the General Court's reputation. One can legitimately debate the harmful effects of such ethical lapses, but they certainly do not enhance political power. In short, the legislature debased itself and fell into disrepute during this period. As a consequence, it has earned the public's disdain.

All of which raises broader questions about legislative power that remain unanswered. Is the modern disregard for the General Court in Massachusetts greater than the disregard for legislative bodies in the other forty-nine states, or is it in reality an artifact of our modern culture? Do the media play a role in shaping a negative perception, in part for their own sensationalistic purposes? For instance, a public opinion poll showed that most people had either read or heard about the raucous late-night "toga party" that took place in the House on April 17, 2000. The same poll, however, showed that only 3 percent of the public knew that the same legislature had passed one of the strongest patient protection bills in the nation.

Despite its shortcomings, the legislature has shown remarkable political resiliency. It performs at least three valuable functions. First, it is the only adequate means yet devised for providing representation and compromise in making law. Whether a particular legislature does its job of representation well or badly, the fact that it is dedicated to this function gives it importance because representation is central to the American democratic ideal. Second, the legislature must approve all new programs in which the state government participates, and it decides which old programs are to be discarded or shifted to another level of government. A third function that the legislature performs is the supervision and oversight of the state's administrative agencies. It not only controls the purse strings of the state but also uses its power of appropriation to influence administrative performance.

Legislators are like birds of passage; their tenure is relatively short, and they come and go with great frequency. Some lawmakers find that because they are paid such meager salaries, one term in office is enough. They do not earn enough money to allow legislating to be their chief occupation. Thus, many capable people are excluded from legislative service because they cannot afford to serve. Except for a few retired or independently wealthy persons, legislators must split their time between legislating and other businesses. This part-time status, along with the tradition of citizen-legislators, contributes to their amateurism. And it has also opened the door to conflicts of interest, some on a grand scale. In sum, Paul Haley, former chair of the House Ways and Means Committee, said it best when he observed, "Everybody loves their legislator, but they hate the Legislature."[63]

THE GOVERNOR AND THE STATE BUREAUCRACY

The state bureaucracy in Massachusetts has grown tremendously in size and scope of activity since its early beginnings. For anyone wanting to effectuate a policy, the dispersal of power to the bureaucracy is a powerfully significant fact. Increasingly it is the governor who is assumed to be the person capable of forcing the bureaucratic apparatus to serve the common good. If something goes wrong in state government, it is usually the governor who catches the blame. From 1919 to 1969, the state bureaucracy mushroomed from 118 to 350 departments and agencies. In 1969 a private management consultant made a study of the executive branch and recommended that it be reorganized. Under a reorganization plan that was implemented in 1971, ten new "super"-agencies were established. The plan also set up a new cabinet as a source of policy initiative. These ten cabinet secretaries serve at the pleasure of the governor, and their staffs are exempt from civil service regulation. In addition, the governor was given greater control over the bureaucracy, and the workings of the system in a managerial sense improved. Such control, however, is not easily asserted.

This is true for several reasons. In the first place, the bureaucracy is large, sprawling, and highly immobile. Most bureaucracies normally move at an incremental pace. Skeptics would probably substitute the word "glacial" for "incremental." The rigid civil service system protects public employees, and thereby insulates them from control while simultaneously safeguarding them from capricious abuse. In short, the merit system exhibits both positive and negative features. Senior civil servants have staying power and thus influence policy just by being there. They have built up personal intelligence and communications networks over many years through dealing with the same organizations, people, and issues. They are in charge of their agency's mission and service delivery.

A governor is assumed to be generally responsible for the whole administrative network. If trouble develops in a prison, even though it may be remote from the governor's direct control, it will be the governor who is blamed in the news media. And any governor who tries to solve the problems, once discovered, may find that it is difficult to remove the personnel who are the source of trouble. In some instances it may be the prison guards. Such was precisely the case in the prison uprisings that occurred in Massachusetts during the early 1970s. Governor Sargent wanted to solve the problem in the prisons, but to do so meant risking his own political future in the turmoil and chaos that ensued. Before regaining control of the prisons, the governor wound up firing his corrections commissioner, John O. Boone, whom he had recruited as a result of national search. The buck in this case stopped with the governor.

Trying to change a big organization that is rigidly set in its bureaucratic ways is an exceedingly difficult task. Governor Weld found out just how hard it can be when a special commission he had appointed concluded that the state had too many mental hospitals for too few patients at too high a cost. It recommended closing three of seven existing state hospitals and a children's psychiatric center. The Department of Mental Health, which had become calcified in the culture of incrementalism, was beset with problems when it sought to implement this hospital reduction strategy and restructure its service delivery system. The biggest obstacle to change was the strong belief within the agency that the sky would fall if DMH did not continue to institutionalize the severely mentally ill. These problems presented a formidable challenge that placed what appeared to be inordinate burdens on the stakeholders involved: patients, their families, providers, and advocates. With their jobs in jeopardy, the hospital employees and their labor unions fiercely resisted the hospital closings. All these factors complicated the policy innovation and organizational change that was then under way. Over the years, Massachusetts has had two runs at hospital closings: the first between 1973 and 1981, when the deinstitutionalization policy flourished, the second between 1991 and 1993, when the privatization policy was initiated. The development of these two policies and the transformation of the state's mental health care system will be examined in much greater detail in chapter 3.

Ironically, the state Civil Service Commission was created as a reform in 1884 to combat the excesses of the spoils system. Since then it has become a bureaucratic albatross.[64] Critics charge that the civil service stifles creativity and promotes inefficiency. From its well-intentioned beginnings, the civil service system has grown in Massachusetts to cover more than 130,000 state, county, and municipal employees. But it has expanded to the point where it now has a stranglehold on the bureaucracy. The five-member commission serves as a quasi-legislative, quasi-judicial body. It functions somewhat akin to a court of appeals. In this context, it reviews the actions of municipalities and state agencies that discipline employees after holding their own hearings. Most of the cases involve police officers, prison guards, and firefighters. The commission also hears cases involving other civil servants, ranging from local school department employees to those who are employed at the Department of Public Works.

In his incisive 2000 critique of the Civil Service Commission, the reporter David Armstrong concludes that it lacks professionalism and renders decisions that disproportionately favor labor unions. He claims that the commission has been plagued by charges of misconduct and union bias. His penetrating analysis shows that an incestuous relationship exists between the members of the commission and the public safety unions. Armstrong goes on to say, "For much of the last decade, the civil service commission has resembled a dysfunctional family. Commissioners have clashed with each other; there has been little, if any, peer review of decisions, and rulings have often been poorly written and lacking in substantive findings of fact."[65]

The stranglehold over the bureaucracy in many areas is a serious problem, and alternatives must be developed to deal with the problem of perpetual incompetence. The bureaucracy and the labor unions are entrenched forces that wield considerable power, to the point where legislators and governors have been reluctant to take them on. Armstrong spells out the conundrum: "In fact, Weld and Cellucci called for abolishing the civil service system during their 1990 campaign. Following their election, they proposed that the commission be replaced with a smaller, less powerful board. But the proposal faded away when the legislature deemed any attempt to alter civil service a 'non-starter.' Today the commission is as entrenched as ever."[66] Future political battles will obviously have to be fought if the power of the bureaucratic fraternity is to be broken.

No governor can possibly keep track of the myriad functions of state government in any more than a superficial manner. There is too much going on to make that feasible, and besides, the governor is too preoccupied with making general policies and settling specific disputes to serve as a supervisor of administrative details. A great deal of what governors do in a day's work is to review and endorse or reject what their staff presents to them. The modern governor is not an overseer of administrative operations so much as a representative of the public, seeking to make policy and to find common ground.

The bureaucracy always has a certain amount of power of its own, thus limiting the governor's control over administrators when he or she deals with them. The clientele groups that support the secretary of human services, or the secretary of environmental affairs, or the corrections commissioner are figuratively at the beck and call of the administrator, and the governor is well aware of it. The capacity to remove subordinates is important as a last resort, but last resorts are what governors seek to avoid.

Because public colleges and universities are creatures of the state, they are accountable to the public and their elected representatives. Their board of trustees is appointed by the governor on the recommendation of civic advisory boards. The budgets and programs of public institutions must be approved not only by the lay boards of trustees but also by the governor and the legislature. Only the public sector is directly responsible to the public for its performance, thus ensuring that its campuses serve the public good. These features make the public higher education system susceptible to political control and manipulation.

An independent state agency such as the former Board of Regents has to concern itself with political realities. If the governor has political power, the agency may "knuckle under" to him or her. If the governor lacks power, the agency will probably turn elsewhere to seek the support it needs to sustain itself in the competitive world of budgets and patronage and the authority to expand operations or to grow in personnel and importance. The lesson that drove home the point was the major battle that erupted in 1986 (discussed in detail in chapter 4), when the Board of Regents ignored the recommendations of its search committee and appointed James Collins, a state legislator and a nonacademic, as its chancellor. In response to these challenges, Governor Michael Dukakis, who felt that the integrity of the search process had been compromised, took a series of actions to correct the problem. These involved firing the chairman of the Board of Regents, packing the board with three new members, removing Collins from office, and replacing him with Franklyn Jenifer, a black educator from New Jersey. It was a classic power struggle in which Collins and his supporters lost. The governor in this episode displayed the will to conquer and to make a difference.

The governor faces many other problems in carrying out any mandate he perceives to be his, but at least one other aspect of his predicament needs to be mentioned. That is, he may have political power and official authority to deal with a given situation, but he may not find out that the problem exists until it has cost him much in the way of adverse publicity. Or, it may be nearly impossible for the governor to use his tools of discipline to exert his control. It should be noted that the public sector bureaucracy in Massachusetts is already expanding again.[67]

Whatever the difficulties of applying the formal authority of a chief executive, it is clear that the character of his or her formal authority is an important determinant of what can be achieved. A governor, after all, deals with problems that most people seldom encounter. Formal authority alone is not sufficient to permit the governor to exert leadership, but in the absence of it, he or she certainly will have great difficulty in being chief executive in fact as well as in name. These and other power relationships will be discussed in the ensuing chapters. The questions now shift from the theoretical to the practical.

2

THE
SARGENT
GOVERNORSHIP

History reminds us that nothing counterfeit has any
staying power, an observation, incidentally, made by
Cicero about 60 B.C. History teaches that character
counts. Character above all.

David McCullough,
commencement address May 30, 1998,
University of Massachusetts, Boston

"SARGE" IN CHARGE

At the height of his power and popularity, Frank Sargent was the most
visible and influential Republican in Massachusetts. A dynamic and visionary party leader, he served as governor during the turbulent and eventful
period extending from 1969 to 1975. A relatively liberal Republican in a state
that was overwhelmingly Democratic, Sargent understood the political
world in which he lived, accepted it for what it was, and moved through it
with a dash and verve rarely seen in state politics in those days. He reached
out for contact and, indeed, for confrontation.

Adept at reading people and in sorting out power relationships, Sargent
was astute at gauging public opinion and in calculating electoral interests.
Relying on his traditional base of Republican support, he crossed party lines
and appealed to liberal Democrats and independent voters, thereby expanding his statewide base. Dealing across party lines was nothing new in
Massachusetts politics and certainly nothing new to Sargent, who was a
seasoned politician and a man of sufficient flexibility to make a little bargaining seem proper. He served twice as governor—first from 1969 to 1970,
when he completed the remaining two years of the unexpired term of his
predecessor, John Volpe; and again from 1971 to 1975, when he was elected
to a full four-year term.

Affectionately known by his nickname, "Sarge," the Yankee reformer first ran for lieutenant governor in 1966 on the same ticket with the incumbent governor, Volpe, a Republican powerhouse, who carried him into office. Plucked from virtual obscurity, Sargent adopted the catchy campaign slogan "Put Sarge in Charge," which caught on with the public and became his rallying cry. Then he got lucky. He was thrust into the governor's office when President Richard Nixon tapped Volpe to become his secretary of transportation in Washington.

In this chapter I undertake to analyze Francis Sargent's style and strategy as a public person. What does his career tell us about the role of character and personality in executive politics and decisionmaking? I also examine his leadership style and his impact on the office of governor. The final sections reflect on the curiously mixed legacy that he left behind.

Evaluating the performance of a single governor is no simple undertaking. To begin with, the sources of power available to a governor are elusive and variable, and the interpretation of the data used to evaluate performance is in part subjective. Whether a governor will prevail in a dispute over policy, or will even become significantly involved, is the result of a subtle combination of factors, not of a single determinant. A governor is first and foremost a politician whose career depends in large measure on the successful negotiation of bargains. When confronted with conflicting demands, he or she helps to maintain a viable society by the process of brokering mutual concessions.

In both style and strategy, Sargent represented a sharp break from his predecessors. Looking on the governorship as a unique position of responsibility, he saw himself as the chief problem solver. Politics for him was a game of risk. Like most elected officials, he kept his advocacy general, positioning himself to take credit for successes and to join the critics in the event of failure. Even this approach involved a modicum of risk that he would be blamed if things went wrong, but he realized it need not be fatal. His politics were hardly cautious.

Dating back to colonial times, there had always been a strong tradition of legislative supremacy in Massachusetts. Elected at large, the governor traditionally served in office for a term of two years, subject to reelection. This short term seriously restricted a governor's ability to get his programs enacted. A handful of governors attained considerable power during the first half of the twentieth century, but the legislature still remained dominant.[1] In marked contrast, Sargent was a prime example of a governor who, both in crisis and in ordinary times, broadened gubernatorial authority. Where he differed most from his predecessors was that he chose to lead rather than simply follow the dictates of the legislature. When he cared intensely about an issue, he reached out for the views of others and responded to ideas capable of garnering support from a coalition of interests. In so doing, he exerted the kind of policy leadership that had rarely been seen in any previous administration.

AN ALTERED POLITICAL AND CULTURAL LANDSCAPE

As a point of departure it is important to acknowledge that Governor Sargent came to power in a tumultuous era. It was a time of great upheaval and revolutionary social change in America. Numerous combustible elements marked the period, including high unemployment, rampant inflation, oil shortages, and economic recession. A series of calamitous events had occurred, including the assassinations of John and Robert Kennedy and of Martin Luther King Jr. These tragedies were coupled with growing protests against the escalating war in Vietnam, civil rights demonstrations, urban riots, prison uprisings, racial violence over school busing, agitation over tenants' rights and welfare rights, and countless other deeply rooted discontents. Cities were beset with seemingly intractable problems. Slums, poverty, street crime, drug abuse, and gang wars were among the social ills that menaced the quality of urban life. There was a general sense of alienation among minorities across the country. Many blacks and Latinos felt marginalized or left out of the political system. Politics for them was not the same as politics for other ethnic groups. The 1965 Voting Rights Act and the black power movement had produced some gains for black Americans, but the underlying racism persisted. The spillover effects of the Vietnam War, which drained the nation's resources to fight the war against poverty at home, poisoned domestic policy. Student protests and campus riots disrupted university life. Dissenting groups marched in the streets, took over public buildings, and shut down colleges in order to protest what they believed to be an unjust war abroad in Southeast Asia and inequalities at home. These societal and economic forces combined to make the forging of gubernatorial policy a hard job.

A state constitutional amendment adopted in 1964 had expanded gubernatorial terms from two to four years. This meant that Frank Sargent would have twenty-two months to complete Volpe's term and consolidate his position before facing the electorate. When he first became acting governor in January 1969, at the age of fifty-four, he was viewed as a political lightweight. After all, he had been a Volpe loyalist and acolyte and was not considered a force in his own right. The transition was fairly coherent in that he picked up where Volpe had left off, but he arrived in office with few ideas in mind and without a clear public agenda. In due course, however, Sargent emerged as an independent chief executive who proved to be quite different from Volpe.

The tempo of gubernatorial initiative varies with the disposition of the incumbent, whether passive or active, positive or negative. Sargent was inclined to be active and positive, and the pace of the policy process increased accordingly. His intention from the outset was to make himself a highly visible governor, a symbol of energy and motion, accepting responsibility for a broad range of public issues, seeking to be innovative on the one hand and reactive on the other. Innovation was more likely when he had to deal with a crisis, though even then he was more reactive than engaged. Eventually he gravitated toward the politics of innovation, although the circumstances were often less than auspicious.

For as long as he was in office, Sargent made the most of his political opportunity, but he had to deal with a legislature controlled by Democrats. This is where his ability to set aside partisanship and to work with those of different persuasions came into play. By the time he finished his second term in 1975, he had achieved significant reforms in urban transportation, public housing, civil rights, environmental protection, mental health, gun control, special education, public welfare, juvenile and adult corrections, social services for children and the elderly, and consumer protection.

The Republicans had been the dominant party in Massachusetts ever since the aftermath of the Civil War, but they were now declining in numerical strength. Although they controlled the governorship from 1964 to 1974, the Democrats had controlled the legislature since 1958. The Republicans were no longer able to mount serious contests for the less visible statewide offices. They were plunging ever deeper into minority party status. By the early 1970s, they were outnumbered in the legislature by almost a 3-to-1 margin. In fact, registered Democrats greatly outnumbered registered Republicans, and the number of independents was on the rise. The Bay State was considered Kennedy territory.

Not surprisingly, Massachusetts voters rejected President Richard Nixon when he ran for reelection in 1972. They voted instead for U.S. Senator George McGovern of South Dakota, who accused Nixon of prolonging the unpopular war in Vietnam. A bastion of liberalism, Massachusetts could claim the distinction of being the only state to go for McGovern—a lesson not lost on its citizens. When the Watergate scandal broke in 1974, bumper stickers soon appeared that sent a subtle but sobering message to the rest of the nation: "Don't Blame Me—I'm from Massachusetts."

Against the onslaughts of this volatile environment, Sargent grappled with the new realities of changing life in America, and dealt in a practical fashion with the pressing public issues of the day. Of the hundreds of bills that he signed into law, three deserve special mention. One was the "anti–snob zoning" law, which mandated location of low-income public housing in the suburbs. This legislation was the first of its kind in the nation. The "no-fault" auto insurance bill eliminated unnecessary litigation and thereby reduced the high costs of automobile insurance. And the so-called Shea bill challenged the legality of the Vietnam War. The last two pieces of legislation were sponsored, respectively, by liberal Democrats Michael Dukakis and James Shea, The Shea bill, which put the state in prominent opposition to the war, was later declared unconstitutional by the courts. Shea tragically ended his life in suicide. Considered a rising star from his earliest days, Dukakis, an ambitious Brookline lawyer, already had his sights set on the governorship.

A NEW KIND OF REPUBLICAN

Sargent was an amalgam of North Shore patrician and hardy Cape Cod fisherman, having lived intermittently in both parts of the state. He was a purebred New England Yankee whose architectural education at MIT signaled a break from the traditional Harvard Law School career path. He thus had a technological capacity, which he used for problem solving and identifying policy alternatives.

Sargent was neither your typical dyed-in-the-wool conservative Republican nor an ideologue. This gave him wide latitude in decisionmaking.[2] Reared in the progressive Yankee reform tradition, he was in some ways a throwback to President Theodore Roosevelt. Like Roosevelt, Sargent was an ardent conservationist, and he sought to save the Massachusetts shoreline. The environment was his passion. He championed issues such as preserving clean air, clean water, and open space. He was an environmentalist before the term came into popular usage and the celebration of "Earth Day" entered the public consciousness. When most of Cape Cod was still relatively unspoiled, Sargent sounded the alarm about the impending danger to its pristine sand dunes and beaches, which were gradually being destroyed by the construction of new housing and large-scale commercial developments. To prevent such a calamity, he spearheaded a crusade to establish what would become the Cape Cod National Seashore.

If Sargent had a political hero, it was New York City's mayor John Lindsay, who had successfully cast aside his traditional base of Republican support and built political alliances that depended heavily on liberal backing. As political actors, Sargent and Lindsay were comfortably matched in ideology and outlook. Both men were liberal Republicans who understood and exploited their positions as popularly elected chief executives. Both exercised their executive powers forcefully and independently, acting as they thought conditions demanded and their conception of the office permitted. Eventually, Lindsay changed his party affiliation and became a Democrat, whereas Sargent remained on the reservation but distanced himself from

Richard Nixon as far as possible, a position that hardly endeared him to the right-wing conservatives who increasingly dominated his party. Simply put, he possessed the intellect, mental toughness, and combativeness that were necessary to survive the nasty political wars at the State House. Secure in his convictions about how the world operated, he was willing to take risks and to push the boundaries of policy leadership. Nothing written about him disputes this interpretation.

PERSONALITY AND POLITICS

The interplay of personality and politics had a lot to do with Sargent's success. Very much the pragmatist, he typically managed to intersperse his comments with good humor, which did a lot to soothe chafed egos. While he delighted in taunting his political adversaries, he also offered them words of kindness and encouragement when life dealt its blows. Democrats who watched him perform conceded that the wit and charm he used with a flourish did not come at the expense of his principles. As former Senate president Kevin Harrington recalled, "He was a physically and mentally tough guy. When he believed in something, nobody could argue him in or out of anything."[3] Sarge was no Puritan and had no difficulty compromising in order to cut deals. Although he frequently "went along to get along," he was determined to lean hard in whichever direction he believed to be right.

Sargent had a knack for sizing up a situation and turning it to his advantage. When sufficiently provoked or frustrated, he could become angry and swear like a trooper, but his self-deprecating wit reassured people that he did not take himself too seriously. He enjoyed the public limelight and the excitement of political life. But he was not unaware of the dark side to it. On one occasion he admitted "When anyone asks me if they should go into politics, I always say, 'Can your marriage stand it?' Politics is demanding, frustrating and doesn't ever stop."[4]

More than one political rival referred to Sargent as "the Marlboro Man." Others referred to him as a "tree hugger." In the words of the political reporter John Powers, "He was the Yankee Republican poster boy (Norman Rockwell actually painted his portrait), spare and angular with sandy hair, a lantern jaw, and the 'S' whistling through his teeth, living out in horse country, growing his own vegetables, and spending not a nickel more than necessary."[5]

Sargent learned how to use his good looks and his resonant voice to his advantage, especially on television. He became adroit at using this medium to mobilize public opinion in support of his programs, even if it meant at times going over the head of the legislature. He fully exploited the public relations potential of the office. His messages to the legislature were consciously addressed to a wider audience. In a 1974 interview Sargent commented, "As a governor, you're not a dictator. You have to be able to persuade the people. One of the problems is getting too far out in front of public opinion."[6] Whatever the inspiration, he had the ability to educate and the capacity to appear concerned while remaining calm and collected in the midst of a political whirlwind. In an era when the word "politician" was becoming increasingly associated with greed, corruption, and venality, he had a reputation for honesty, integrity, and independence.

GLIMPSES OF THE PRIVATE MAN

In 1938, Sargent married well. Jessie Fay was a Yankee of impeccable lineage. Like her husband she enjoyed the outdoors, and she did more than her share of volunteer work in the community. By religion he was a Unitarian, while she was an Episcopalian. Jessie was a liberal Republican who campaigned for her husband and supported social issues such as day care centers, elderly affairs, mental retardation, low-income housing, and juvenile detention centers. She played a leading role in the Women's Political Caucus and co-chaired the state's Commission on Citizen Participation. In her aptly titled book *The Governor's Wife*, Jessie Sargent defined her role:

> As a Governor's wife, I am never in a position to raise a shrill voice. My efforts are often low-keyed and behind the scenes. I have to be aware of "bad press" and behaving in a manner not embarrassing to my husband or the administration. . . . I strongly believe that a wife can be a tremendous campaign asset and the better she is known before the election the more help she can be. If she's been to a neighborhood before, made friends there, helped with local projects and shown concern for their local problems, the candidate's wife can be a major help for gaining endorsement of her husband's policies and candidacy.[7]

In his private life, Sargent was surrounded by close friends and enjoyed the lifestyle that can be afforded only by those of extraordinary wealth. Politically he may have championed the needs of the poor and disadvantaged, but socially he gravitated toward the rich and powerful. Both he and his wife were very private people, Jessie the more private of the two.[8] They had a personal life as well as a public life. They were accessible and yet inaccessible. That was part of their mystique.

In political parlance, Sargent had what is known as the "common touch." Douglas Foy, director of the Conservation Law Foundation, tells a story about Sargent driving up to a tollbooth on the Massachusetts Turnpike, quickly reading the toll collector's name tag, and striking up a friendly conversation. Sargent, of course, had never met the man before, but that was beside the point. Although the toll collector represented a potential vote, the governor interacted with him as both a public and a private man.[9]

Another story is told about Sargent befriending an eleven-year-old boy while attending a World Series baseball game at Fenway Park in October 1967. It was the year of the "Impossible Dream," with the Boston Red Sox playing the Saint Louis Cardinals. The boy's father had purchased two separate tickets from a scalper and was unable to sit with his son, so he planted the boy in a box seat next to the lieutenant governor. Thirty-one years later the youngster, now a grown man, recalled:

> Sargent treated me as if I was the most important guy in the ballpark. It was as if we had gone to the game together. He asked me if I wanted a hot dog, popcorn, peanuts, whatever. I was keeping the box score, and as the game went on Sarge would lean over and say, "What'd he do his last time up?" or, "How many has Lonborg struck out?" The box was swarming with visitors, of course, all looking to shake Sarge's hand or talk a little politics. I still remember that late in the game, Yaz got up and singled cleanly to right. Sarge stood up, applauded, and said, to no one in particular, "That's a damn good hit."[10]

Sargent, an avid sportsman, described himself as being one of the "fin, fur, and feather folks."[11] A hunting companion recalled an incident that took place in the predawn darkness: "We used to hunt together. I remember when he'd show up in the early morning, fire off his shotgun right beneath my bedroom window and yell, 'Get up you lazy bum.' "[12] Subtlety was not his strong suit. As a fisherman, Sargent became acquainted with all kinds of people in a world far removed from Beacon Hill. He told this "shaggy dog" tale about the owner of Thompson's Clam Bar and Wychmere Harbor Club on the Cape:

> I got to know almost everybody on the waterfront. There was a guy who ran a place where you could sell your fish, and he used to drink like a son-of-a-bitch. One day he was stiff and he spotted me as he was going by our house. "Sarge, where the hell have you been?" he called out. "I've been in bed with sciatica," I told him. "Who's she?" he said. Well, Jessie was there and she died laughing.[13]

These episodes provide us with glimpses of the lesser-known Sargent, a man seldom seen in public. His son Bill says that his father "loved doing things that kids loved to do. He was more like a grandfather to us."[14] It is essential to understand the personal element because it was such a vitally important aspect of his political power.

SARGENT'S DECISION-MAKING STYLE

Although Frank Sargent had a fairly clear sense of where he fit on the political spectrum, he had little patience with philosophical discussion and very limited curiosity about issues until they were actually thrust upon him. He craved being at the center of political action and enjoyed dealing with urgent and momentous choices. Sargent's single most important quality was his ability to make bold decisions. He liked to make decisions in a quasi-judicial mode, preferring to let ideas bubble up and then choosing from among alternatives developed and debated by his staff.[15]

As governor, Sargent operated on the principle of centralized management. He assembled a small staff and appointed the best people he could find to head the various executive departments and agencies. They were a mix of old and new faces largely picked by Sargent himself. The inner circle consisted of four men with whom he had worked closely prior to becoming governor. They were Donald Dwight, a mainstream moderate Republican; Albert Kramer, a liberal Democrat and former state representative who came from an urban working-class district in Chelsea; Robert Yasi, a former civil servant who understood the way the state bureaucracy operated; and Jack Flannery, a former newsman who concerned himself with the political stakes and how Sargent was faring with the media. As the pressures of office decended on them, these advisers contended for the governor's mind, and they served him well. Dwight and Kramer were the main policy advocates. Flannery served as a counterweight to Kramer. Steve Teichner and Tom Reardon, another newspaperman, joined this group somewhat later. Both Reardon and Flannery advanced the administration's position with editors and writers.

As Alan Altshuler, an academic at MIT who headed the governor's task force on highways and later became his secretary of transportation and construction, points out, "Sargent's personal inner circle had a high degree of continuity through his six years in office, and it remained dominant, even after the cabinet came into being, on matters that seemed to involve high personal stakes for the governor."[16] The governor sought to avoid being captured by the special interests and clientele groups that abound in public life. He trusted his staff to sort out the arguments put forward by outsiders and to craft his best alternatives.

Sometimes his staff second-guessed his agency and department heads, which became a source of friction and internal squabbles. Martha Weinberg's book *Managing the State*, published in 1977, provides a detailed account of Sargent's relationship as governor with four specific state agencies. According to Weinberg, Sargent tried to exercise some degree of executive control over the Department of Public Works and the Department of Public Welfare, but he did not attempt to do so with regard to the Massachusetts Housing Finance Agency and the Department of Mental Health. The latter provide good examples of his willingness to intervene when he perceived a public or political crisis but to remain relatively unengaged in issues where these imperatives did not exist. Weinberg argues that Sargent remained both crisis-oriented and reactive throughout his tenure, responding to the flow of pressing issues and limiting himself to selecting from among options developed by others.[17]

Sargent embraced an active, involved role for government and accepted the reality of the welfare state. These were trends thoroughly consistent with the governor's temperament and philosophy, although most Republican politicians by instinct and disposition went the other way. Portrayed in the media as a "maverick" governor of a maverick state, Sargent was a leader whose popular appeal transcended party lines.[18] He was the archetype of a new breed of crossover politician—shrewd enough to reach out to Democrats and independents alike. Charles Kenney and Robert Turner, two veteran State House reporters who observed Sargent's battles at close range, described him in these terms: "Though a Republican, he was moderate to liberal on most issues, and he relished the give-and-take that were an essential part of relations with the Democratic legislature. Most important, the voters loved him."[19]

In 1970, Sargent, the incumbent, easily won his party's nomination for governor. He picked Donald Dwight as his running mate. In the general election he ran against Democrat Kevin White, the mayor of Boston. Campaigning throughout the state, Sargent not only energized his Republican base but also appealed to women, blacks, Hispanics, and the elderly. At one point he lost his voice to laryngitis, so his wife and three grown children had to fill in for him as surrogates. When the ballots were finally counted, Sargent had defeated White by 259,354 votes to win his first full term as governor. This amounted to 56.7 percent of the total vote. Much to the chagrin and embarrassment of his opponent, Sargent even carried the city of Boston. After a grueling campaign, he had won the corner office in his own right. No longer was he an accidental governor. The morning after the election, Sargent and White had breakfast together at the Ritz-Carlton Hotel in Boston. As Sargent recalled, "When we were done, Kevin grabbed for the bill [saying] 'I know god damn well you're not going to pay for this.' "[20]

The governor was adept at playing ethnic politics. He enjoyed jousting with Irish Democrats, and, as a Yankee Republican, he made an easy target for them. He was especially fond of attending the annual Saint Patrick's Day brunch at Dorgan's restaurant in South Boston, which was hosted by state senator William Bulger, a stand-up comedian in his own right. Both men enjoyed roasting each other in a good-natured way. This corned beef and cabbage breakfast was a ritual of the Boston Irish political culture. While campaigning in neighborhoods such as Boston's North End, Sargent never failed to mention his Italian grandmother. He also boasted of his membership in the Braintree Lodge of the Sons of Italy, a fact that further cemented his relations with the Italian American population of the state.

Sargent governed more by sheer force of personality than by any grant of formal authority. In many ways his personality matched his politics. He enjoyed marching in parades, slapping backs, pumping hands, and hanging out with the Irish politicians who loved to needle him. Kevin White once commented that Sargent was the best he had ever seen in a parade; that he could make eye contact with every man, woman, and child along the parade route.[21] He was a relatively simple man, not complex or Machiavellian. David Nyhan, one of the most perceptive commentators on the Massachusetts political scene, drew this portrait of him: "What the political community prized most in Frank Sargent was the laughter. No politician of his rank had more fun in office, as often at his own expense as at another's. He was not a complicated man, of twisted psyche, inner turmoil, or desperate ambition. Frank was Frank: a beautiful man, a solid friend, an able leader, an honest public servant. And a million laughs. What's not to prize in such a splendid fellow?"[22]

Who was Governor Frank Sargent? Having risen through the ranks of the fish and game and public works bureaucracies, Sargent brought twenty-two years of experience in government to the task of running the Commonwealth. The only thing he lacked was legislative experience, but this proved to be more of a political asset than a liability. He knew a lot about how government worked and who the key players were. This knowledge and expertise, coupled with his determination to lead rather than follow, made him a different kind of governor.

Looking back at the social and economic conditions that existed in the Bay State during the late 1960s and early 1970s, we can see that the political situation was clearly manipulable from the vantage point of someone like Sargent. He believed that there was no point in holding power unless it could be used effectively. Furthermore, he recognized the social ferment and discontent that were brewing in Massachusetts, and understood the reasons that caused people to press for social change. He used the bully pulpit whenever he thought it necessary, but he seldom preached to people. There is ample evidence to suggest that constituency and leader were attuned to each other's calculations.

Toward the end of his second term, however, Sargent would come to recognize that the magic had gone out of the enterprise. A booming economy had enabled him to create and expand programs without major tax increases until his final year. Then in October 1973 the economy began to falter with the disruption of oil supplies, compounded by rising unemployment and double-digit inflation, or what became known as "stagflation." Sargent's star was sinking fast, and with it any grand hopes for a third term. In his bid for reelection in 1974, he faced a formidable Democratic opponent in Michael Dukakis, who appealed to the same constituencies that Sargent had cultivated.

As the campaign wore on, Sargent seemed to stumble and became preoccupied with falling public opinion polls and day-to-day crises. Not only had he drifted away from his conservative Republican base; he had also antagonized it. A controversy arose over his borrowing $40,000 from his wife in order to finance his campaign, in violation of a recently passed campaign finance law. In typical fashion, Sargent dismissed this disclosure with wry humor. He told the Everett Rotary Club that he was sorry that he had not arrived in time for lunch. "I couldn't come up with the price of the ticket," he said solemnly. "Jessie wouldn't lend me the dough."[23]

As things turned out, it was a hard fought and bitterly contested campaign. On election day, Dukakis garnered 992,284 votes to Sargent's 784,353—53.5 percent of the total. Sargent was defeated by factors beyond his control. The Republicans had held the governorship since 1964. It was time for a change. Sargent shrugged off his defeat, blaming it on "the price of hamburg." As he put it, "I didn't blow my stack at all. I could kind of see it coming."[24] Whether the economy was the substantial cause of his defeat no one can say for certain, but it was surely among the major causes. Racial violence over court-ordered school busing had erupted in Boston in September 1974, just two months prior to the election. Sargent supported the state's Racial Imbalance Act of 1965, and as the chief law enforcement officer, he sent in National Guard troops to quell the civil disturbance.[25] The presence of state troops inflamed passions, especially in South Boston, which became a hotbed of anti-busing fervor. Through the ever-present lens of network television, the nation watched the ugly upheaval unleashed by the desegregation orders of federal judge Arthur Garrity. To top it off, Watergate, the Nixon pardon, oil shock, and the faltering economy all made 1974 a disastrous year for the Republican Party nationally. Sargent ran about as far ahead of the rest of the Republican ticket as he had in winning a comfortable victory four years earlier, but the outcome this time was a crushing defeat.

A POLITICAL APPRENTICESHIP

Francis Sargent was born on July 29, 1915, in the small rural town of Hamilton, Massachusetts, where the North Shore social elite played polo and other equestrian sports. A patrician by birth and disposition, he could lay claim to a sterling Yankee pedigree. Reared a child of privilege, he was a distant cousin to the famous American painter John Singer Sargent. These family credentials gave him sterling native-born, blueblood status. Not much is known about his early childhood except that his father died when Frank was only three years old. His maternal grandfather, George Lee, a former New England amateur boxing and sculling champion, instilled in him the love of the outdoors. Lee also contributed to the future political fortunes of his grandson by marrying an Italian woman, Eva Ballarini.

Sargent and his brother grew up in a family without a father. An Irish nurse helped raise the two boys. This set of circumstances may explain why the future governor was so eager to make friends, and why he later got along so well with Irish American politicians. His mother eventually married Arthur Adams, a direct descendant of President John Quincy Adams. The Adamses were quite conservative, while the Sargents were very liberal, and tensions arose between the two. Young Frank Sargent was sent to the exclusive Noble and Greenough School in Dedham, where he developed his social graces and prepared for college. There he wanted everybody to be his friend, including the teachers and janitors.[26] In 1935 he passed up going to Harvard, a Brahmin preserve, in order to study architecture at MIT.

After graduating in 1939, Sargent joined the prestigious Boston architectural firm of Coolidge, Shepley, Bulfinch, and Abbott, where he apprenticed as a draftsman. For a brief period he worked as a carpenter in order to learn the building trades firsthand. He and an MIT classmate opened a small architect's office. Shortly after the Japanese bombed Pearl Harbor, Sargent enlisted in the U.S. Army. An accomplished skier, he volunteered as a ski trooper and was assigned to the famed Tenth Mountain Division, which trained in Colorado for Alpine combat. Rising in the ranks from private to captain, he fought in Italy, where he was wounded twice, and earned the Purple Heart and Bronze Star. His combat record would later stand him in good stead with veteran's groups.

Upon returning from the war, Sargent devoted himself to his career and to raising a family. The war had changed his outlook on life. He gave up architecture and settled in Orleans on Cape Cod to earn a living doing what he loved most—hunting and fishing. In the fall he worked as a guide for duck hunters; in the winter he fished commercially for lobster and halibut; and in the spring and summer he ran a charter boat out of Rock Harbor. He also operated a successful sporting goods business and opened the Goose Hummock Shop on Route 6A. One of the shop's early bestsellers was a goose decoy that Sargent made out of cork insulation board and the float from a fishnet.

Before long, Sargent grew bored with running his business. His advocacy of fishermen would take him into politics. While chartering a boat out of Rock Harbor, he had heard stories about the illegal netting of striped bass. He investigated the matter and started a crusade to have the abuse stopped. Sargent invited Republican governor Robert Bradford to go out on his boat and see for himself that the current laws were not working properly. In 1947 Bradford asked Sargent to become the state's director of marine fisheries. Sargent at first agreed to take the job just for the winter, but he stayed in the post for almost ten years.

Commercial fishermen were upset by the appointment of a man whom they considered a dilettante, but Sargent surprised them by shipping out with the Boston trawler fleet and working as one of the crew on the Grand Banks. He also devoted considerable time speaking to rod-and-gun clubs, garden clubs, Audubon groups, and other conservationists about the dangers of pollution. In Sargent's own words, "I used to be kind of a voice in the wilderness, railing against pollution of our tidal waters and marshes. Some hunters and fishermen listened, but others were more interested in how many trout you were going to stock in Round Pond, even though a developer might pollute the pond."[27] (Interestingly, this occurred before Rachel Carlson published her pioneering book *Silent Spring* in 1962.)

From 1959 to 1962, Sargent served in Washington as executive director of a temporary federal commission on recreational open-space resources. In this capacity he formed a unique partnership to save the Cape Cod shoreline by creating a new park. It was an auspicious time for such a venture. Alarmed by urban sprawl and the proliferation of housing subdivisions that threatened to change forever the pristine shoreline, Sargent took a lead position in promoting this audacious project. The idea was anathema to many local real estate agents and businessmen, who objected on the grounds that they would be hurt financially. Others worried that a park would bring a rush of tourists, spoiling the habitat and overrunning their quiet communities. Enlisting the support of U.S. senators John F. Kennedy and Leverett Saltonstall, along with the philanthropist Paul Mellon, Sargent overcame fierce, short-sighted local opposition by taking a novel approach to the problem of land protection. Previous national parks had been created by federal land purchases and private funding. To these techniques they added a zoning agreement among the six affected localities to set aside the land and limit development. To minimize political opposition, private landowners were allowed to retain ownership of their land for a period of ninety-nine years, but they had to agree not to develop it. On August 7, 1961, President Kennedy signed the law creating the Cape Cod National Seashore, which set aside 44,600 acres of land, including forty miles of shoreline on the Great Beach and ten miles flanking Cape Cod Bay.

On returning to Massachusetts in 1962, Sargent ran unsuccessfully for state senator in Barnstable County. He lost in a Republican primary, mainly because of lack of time and poor organization, but he learned from his mistakes. In 1963 he accepted an appointment from Democratic governor Endicott Peabody to serve as an associate commissioner of the Department of Public Works. The DPW had just been reorganized after a major scandal, so this was a fairly visible reform appointment. While undertaking this assignment, Sargent met Al Kramer, who helped him clean up the mess in the scandal-ridden department.

When Republican John Volpe became governor again in 1965, he named Sargent chair of the commission, which meant that he served as head of the department. The conservationist had now become a public road builder. In his DPW role, Sargent was responsible for planning and design work on interstate expressway projects, and he led a successful effort to secure legislation eliminating local authority to veto state highway projects. In 1966 Volpe picked Sargent as his running mate. The rest, as they say, is history.

A MAVERICK PARTY LEADER

Sargent was the chief spokesman of the liberal wing of the state Republican Party. The governor, by virtue of his office, was the leader of his party, sometimes beholden to it, sometimes able to bend it to his own vision. Party organization and party discipline were never as strong as some observers remember, but they were an influential factor in nominating or electing a governor. Still, the links were not strong. Sargent's views frequently clashed with those of right-wing conservative Republicans. As the years went by, the chasm between them became wide and deep. A more serious and potentially more damaging chasm opened among members of the Republican State Committee. As Martha Weinberg observed:

> The Republican state committee regarded [Sargent] with suspicion because of his liberal policies, his appointment of many Democrats to positions in his administration, his refusal to back unilaterally all party candidates, and his lukewarm response to the candidacy of Richard Nixon and Spiro Agnew. Sargent, in turn, did not rely heavily on the state Republican party organization but instead built "Governor Sargent Committees" in each county in the state. Although several times he attempted to purge the Republican State Committee of his opponents, he relied on his own organization to attract the Independents and Democrats whom he needed to survive in Massachusetts, where a large majority of registered voters are Democrats and Independents.[28]

Sargent possessed an inner ballast that was absolutely immovable. He got along better with Democratic legislative leaders than he did with some members of his own party. This group included House Speaker David Bartley and two consecutive Senate presidents, first Maurice Donahue and then Kevin Harrington. Their power relationships reflected a partial truce in the cultural wars that had long pitted the Irish against the Yankees in Massachusetts.

For the moment, however, Sargent had little time for such considerations. At the beginning, their relations were untested. To break the ice, the governor put a sign on his desk that read "Don't Ask Me, I Didn't Go to Harvard," and he set about wooing enough Democratic lawmakers to allow him to function. By his own admission, "I pissed off some Republicans, but there was no other way to get anything done."[29] His wooing of Democrats made for prudent politics because it enabled him to get most of his legislative program enacted. He essentially led a coalition government.

HALTING THE CONSTRUCTION OF BOSTON EXPRESSWAYS

Immediately upon taking office in January 1969, Sargent was confronted by neighborhood and environmental activists seeking to stop five interstate expressway projects scheduled for completion in the greater Boston metropolitan region. These included the so-called Inner Belt, I-95, I-93, the Southwest Expressway, and the Route 2 extension. The extension of Interstate 95 would have cut through Roxbury, the Back Bay, Cambridge, Somerville, and Charlestown and would have required the demolition of about 3,800 homes. It would also have damaged a natural wildlife and conservation area, known as Fowl Meadow, in the Canton-Milton woods. The homes of many low-income families had already been taken by eminent domain and bulldozed for clearance purposes.[30] With some buildings partially demolished and others completely reduced to rubble, the Southwest Corridor looked very much like a bombed city in Germany during World War II.

Community organizers had mobilized the working poor and urban minorities, who marched on the State House. Their demands could hardly be ignored. The protest movement was quite successful, given the redistributive objectives that the protesters were pursuing. Day by day, week by week, media-savvy community groups dominated the public discussion, framing the issues in their favor and putting the Massachusetts Department of Public Works on the defensive.

Cross-pressured, Sargent was cautious in his initial response. After four months, however, in September 1969, he announced that he would appoint a special task force to review pending highway plans for the Boston region. As chair of the task force he named Alan Altshuler, a professor of political science at MIT, who had written on the politics of transportation and planning. The task force included a mix of business leaders, academics, and independent professionals but no one who had taken a public position on the disputed projects.

In January 1970, Altshuler informed the governor that the task force would recommend a moratorium on the controversial expressways and urge the development of a new, environmentally sensitive plan for a major highway and mass transit facilities in the Boston area. At the time, no American governor had ever halted work on an interstate expressway. The task force's recommendations touched off an intense month-long debate, which the governor structured with his inner circle of advisers. Donald Dwight opposed the moratorium, while Al Kramer favored it. Altshuler took a middle-ground position. He wanted to kill some of the proposed expressways but not all of them, and build the remainder on a reduced scale. As Altshuler recalled, "Sargent confided privately that he thought I was very likely right technically, but he did not see who would support my middle-ground position. The pro-highway and anti-highway forces were so polarized that he felt compelled to choose one or the other in clear-cut fashion."[31]

Sargent benefited from the highly politicized context in which policy was being formulated. Soon to face the electorate, he was searching for issues, allies, and liberal credentials. Sargent, who had previously been pro-highway, came down squarely on the side of the environmentalists and neighborhood groups. His intuition favored the bold stroke. The solution, he decided, was to call a halt to construction.

On February 11, 1970, Sargent appeared on television to announce his decision. The governor endorsed the task force's recommendations and declared a moratorium on the five expressway projects. His message was simple and compelling. Taking note of his own role as former DPW commissioner, he told his viewing audience, "Nearly everyone was sure highways were the only answer to transportation problems for years to come. But we were wrong."[32] In making such a dramatic turnabout, Sargent took a giant step in defining his public image, emphasizing that he cared about the soft side of politics. His critics accused him of manipulating the issue for votes.

Sargent had no money to carry out the recommended planning study, which was a necessity if he was to replace the discarded plan with a new one. The task force had estimated a need for $3.5 million, which the Democratic, pro-highway legislature was not about to provide. The Federal Highway Administration was certain to be hostile. Frank Turner, the federal highway administrator, soon forecast publicly that Boston would "strangle" on its traffic unless the proposed expressways were built.

Sargent's only hope was that John Volpe, now Nixon's secretary of transportation, might be persuaded to overrule his subordinates. But such persuasion would be very difficult. As governor, Volpe had fully supported the projects now to be halted. Sargent had put off informing Volpe of his decision until an hour before he went on television, not wanting to offer him an opening to argue the issue. A few days later, Sargent, along with Altshuler and MBTA chairman Robert Wood, went to Washington to meet with Volpe in the vice president's office. There was every indication that this meeting would be sensitive. Volpe marched in with his entourage and immediately started lecturing Sargent. He told him that he was listening to the wrong people and then pointed directly at Altshuler. Fortunately, Volpe had his own "in-house" liberal assistant, Joseph Bosco, whose views were shifting in this peak year of environmentalism. Sargent would get the funding he needed.

Sargent won reelection and moved ahead with the Boston Transportation Planning Review in 1971. Although it ultimately resulted in the cancellation of every major highway project proposed for the Boston metropolitan area, the BTPR process was not intended to achieve such a result. Rather it was an effort to assess the relative costs and benefits of a variety of strategies for addressing the region's transportation needs.[33] It soon became clear that some projects could not be built without enormous disruption. These included the Inner Belt and the Route 2 extension. Consequently, in December 1971 Sargent dropped both plans from further consideration.[34]

The moratorium would turn out to be the act that most defined Sargent's governorship. Afterwards, Altshuler was asked by what authority the governor had acted in this situation. He replied, "by his own authority," for Sargent would have to sign any enabling legislation.[35] It was a bold move on the governor's part and a dramatic departure from his previous position. Evidence of the wisdom of his policy decision lies in the fact that his moratorium still stands today.

CALMING AN ANTIWAR PROTEST

As the Vietnam War and resistance to it escalated, it became increasingly difficult to keep the peace at home. Antiwar demonstrations and protests were common occurrences. When the young rebelled against the accustomed norms, the reaction was often severe. Older generations of Americans, especially those who had served in World War II and Korea, were outraged by what they perceived as the rejection of patriotism. Most governors in America responded to these crises by sending anti-riot squads into the streets, often using tear gas and billy clubs. With a Republican president in the White House, Sargent was the first Republican governor to come out against the war.[36] Nevertheless, in response to a request from

Harvard president Nathan Pusey, the governor ordered state police to break up an anti-ROTC demonstration and the occupation of University Hall by student protesters, in April 1969. Several students were arrested and sent to jail.

By the time Ohio national guardsmen shot four students at Kent State University in 1970, unrest was boiling over on campuses across the country. In Boston, thousands of angry students descended on the State House to hold an antiwar rally. One of their speakers demanded that the American flag be lowered to half mast as a tribute to those slain at Kent State. Shouts of "Lower the flag!" rippled through the surging crowd. Two frightened capitol policemen stood guard at the flagpole.

The stage was set for what followed. Looking out the window of his corner office, Sargent wondered aloud what would happen to the police officers if the flag was not lowered.[37] He realized that they would probably be injured. The students, he decided, were only asking for respect, so he ordered Donald Dwight to lower the flag. This statesmanlike gesture averted a riot and saved the policemen from possible harm. The political task was truly one of keeping the peace. No one can measure all the results of the simplest act performed under such circumstances, but in this case Sargent's order had a calming effect. The crowd gradually dispersed. As Al Kramer later recalled, "Sargent responded not to the anger, but to the idealism and hope of those times."[38]

Many observers saw the flag incident as more of a political statement and publicity stunt than a genuine peace offering. The Democratic "hawks" in the legislature urged Senate president Maurice Donahue to blast Sargent publicly for having caved in to the students' demands. At the time, Donahue was seeking the Democratic nomination for governor. Fully aware of Sargent's distinguished military combat record in World War II, he refused to criticize him.

CREATING A NEW CABINET SYSTEM

Sargent's administrative style evolved considerably between his first term and his second. During the first term, he and his staff confronted a bureaucracy consisting of more than 350 state agencies. They were able to do little more than patch over crises, set a few initiatives in motion, and nurture Sargent's personal image with the media and electorate. In the first year of Sargent's second term, however, a state cabinet system was created.[39] The legislature had adopted the cabinet system in 1969, deferring its effective date to 1971, on the assumption that a Democrat would win the governorship in 1970. Maurice Donahue was not about to place ten "patronage plums" at Sargent's disposal. After Sargent prevailed in 1970, the legislature balked for several months at funding the cabinet offices, but finally relented after Sargent mounted an effective media campaign.

The reorganization plan established ten new executive "super" agencies. The cabinet secretaries served at the pleasure of the governor, and their staffs were exempt from civil service regulations. Moreover, their appointments did not require legislative confirmation. They had little statutory authority, but the governor had broad discretion to delegate agency oversight authority to the secretaries. Sargent used this authority to the fullest. He also specified that in those matters in which the law required him to act personally, he wanted to be advised by the secretaries rather than by their agencies.

Sargent appointed well-qualified people to the top positions in his administration. Among them were Peter Goldmark, secretary of human services; Charles H. Foster, secretary of environmental affairs; Steven Minter, commissioner of public welfare; Thomas Atkins, commissioner of housing; David Liederman, director of the Office of Children; and Jack Leff, secretary of elder affairs, to mention a few. As it turned out, some of these appointees were Democrats. This did not sit well with hard-line Republicans.

Steven Minter was recruited from Ohio, where he had been director of the welfare department of Cuyahoga County. Sargent wanted him to straighten out the mess that had resulted when the state took over the welfare system from the localities in July 1968. No longer were the 351 cities and towns in Massachusetts responsible for welfare. But the central office was in shambles. There was no standardized payment system for recipients. Each local office functioned according to the standards of its own director, and there were large discrepancies in records. Saddling the department with the additional task of administering the new Medicaid program simply added to the disarray.

Politicians, depending on their ideological persuasion, wanted to know why recipients were not being paid promptly, why the welfare rolls were increasing, and why vendors of medical services were not being reimbursed. The National Welfare Rights Organization staged several demonstrations to demand increased benefits. Against this background, Minter tried his best to maintain the current level of support and services. He restructured welfare in Massachusetts, and the workings of the system, in a managerial sense, improved. Martha Weinberg concludes:

> On most management issues in welfare, the governor was unable to dictate the behavior of the agency or to ensure that it act as he wanted it to act. For the governor and his staff, managing welfare seldom offered the possibility of clear rewards. There was little room for dramatic policy initiation or for intervention

that would capture the public imagination. Instead, Sargent faced constraints on his ability to control the department accompanied by constant potential for crisis. This was positive incentive for him to ignore the department whenever possible.[40]

On another front, Sargent appointed a political scientist, Robert Wood, as chairman of the Massachusetts Bay Transportation Authority. It seemed a natural appointment. In his 1956 book *Suburbia*, Wood had written that "transportation is the central reality of the metropolitan community."[41] He had just returned from Washington, where he had served first as undersecretary and then secretary of Housing and Urban Development in the Lyndon Johnson administration. After his tenure at HUD, he got a chance to put his ideas into action locally. On assuming his new post, Wood inquired about the MBTA's equal opportunity office (the agency had a history of discriminating against minorities), but to his dismay found that no such office existed, a situation he brought to Sargent's attention and took steps to remedy. Wood also oversaw the extension of both the Orange Line and the Red Line, dramatically transforming communities such as Somerville and Quincy. Because of the Red Line extension, Davis Square was given a new life, which helped Tufts University in nearby Medford to prosper and allowed graduate students from Harvard and other universities to settle in Somerville. A similar revitalization happened in Quincy.[42]

DEINSTITUTIONALIZATION OF MENTAL PATIENTS

Sargent named Peter Goldmark, a twenty-nine-year-old whiz kid, as his secretary of human services. Goldmark had previously served in the Lindsay administration in New York City. One of his policy objectives, shared by Sargent, was to move as many people as possible out of the large state mental institutions and into smaller community facilities. Goldmark's strategy relied on forcing bureaucratic agencies to act by applying pressure from constituency groups at the grassroots level.

Whatever its merits, Goldmark's strategy of citizen participation was staunchly resisted by mental health commissioner Milton Greenblatt, who did not favor the concept of deinstitutionalization. This reform, fueled by federal money, was designed to place mental patients in community residences and halfway houses as an alternative to warehousing them in large custodial institutions. Under fire from a citizens' task force on children in state institutions known as "children out of school," Greenblatt stonewalled their efforts to monitor the implementation of Chapter 750, which called for the delivery of mental health and educational services to emotionally disturbed youngsters who were at risk. The commissioner also came under attack from a legislative commission that had investigated the deaths of four mentally retarded clients at the Belchertown State School. Although an internal probe conducted by the Department of Mental Health absolved Greenblatt of any negligence in the matter, an investigative commission found him partially responsible and called for his resignation. These events led to his forced departure in December 1972.

After a six-month nationwide search, Sargent replaced Greenblatt with William Goldman, a San Francisco psychiatrist. Goldman set a new direction for the department by allowing citizen area boards to participate in the budgetary process and by refusing to curry favor with the medical establishment, which had been viewed as sacrosanct. He saw the doctors as stubborn resisters of change and impediments to the implementation of new policies. Furthermore, he infuriated them by refusing to fund psychiatric residencies at many university-affiliated hospitals and clinics. Goldman became the original architect of the plan for closing the state mental hospitals. Over the years these institutions had suffered from benign neglect, and the quality of treatment for patients had steadily deteriorated. Under Goldman's direction, three state mental hospitals (Grafton, Gardner, and Foxborough) were closed within a span of three years.[43]

CLOSING JUVENILE JAILS

In October 1969, Sargent appointed Jerome Miller commissioner of the Department of Youth Services (DYS), which oversaw the Massachusetts juvenile corrections agency. A native of South Dakota, Miller grew up in Minnesota and attended college in the Midwest. He then entered a Roman Catholic seminary to study for the priesthood, but soon left, joined the U.S. Air Force, and attained a doctorate in social work. While stationed in England as a psychiatric social worker, he developed a community treatment program for troubled children of air force personnel.[44]

But Miller was hardly prepared for what he found in Massachusetts. The state's century-old reform schools had become nightmarish outposts of neglect and abuse, where callous state workers meted out punishment destined only to reinforce the antisocial behavior that landed young offenders there in the first place. These institutions were described in the press as "barbaric relics of an embarrassing past." Grim stories of physical and sexual abuse abounded. At the Shirley Industrial School, the punishment for misbehavior was to scrub the floors with a toothbrush. More serious transgressions landed youths in a section known as the Tombs, where juveniles could spend weeks or even months in isolation, not even allowed to speak. Miller's secretary showed him files documenting the punishment for trying to escape from the Tombs. The infraction resulted in having one's finger broken. The rule had its intended deterrent effect. For several years there had been no escapes.

Miller struggled without success to turn these institutions into decent, caring places. But the entrenched employees at these facilities, who owed their jobs to political patronage, were openly hostile to his efforts. He concluded that even incremental change would be impossible. So he decided on a radically different approach, and began closing the institutions in the fall of 1971.

Fearful of resistance, Miller moved so quickly that some closures were carried out virtually overnight and without the governor's being informed. At the Lyman School for Boys in Westborough—which, fittingly, Charles Dickens had once visited—the shutdown was announced on a Thursday, and the facility was closed by the following Tuesday. When Miller shut down the institute for Juvenile Guidance at Bridgewater, he removed the brass locks from the isolation rooms and mounted them on small stands. He gave the first one to Governor Sargent, who grew tearful. "And, by God, from then on," said Miller, "that lock stood on his desk, and it was a great thing because it told us where the governor stood."[45]

By mid-January 1972, Miller had closed all but one of the institutions, and the remaining one—Lancaster—housed a substantially reduced population. He replaced the reform schools with a highly decentralized system of community-based group homes and other mentor programs designed to create a "positive peer culture," to use his gracious phrase. Miller contracted with private nonprofit agencies to operate many of the new DYS programs. These programs, which were federally funded, made Massachusetts the first state to eliminate juvenile detention centers. They attracted the attention of penologists across the nation. The department spent the remainder of 1972 attempting to cope with the consequences of the closings, to consolidate the new directions for treatment of delinquency, and to ward off mounting opposition from the legislature.

DYS was subjected to intensive legislative investigation and public hearings. This powerful oversight was led by Westfield Democrat Robert McGinn, a former police officer, who engaged in a bitter feud with Miller. After a shouting match at the State House, McGinn yelled to reporters, "I'll bury Miller. He's a nut. He's insane. He belongs in an insane asylum."[46] Despite these attacks, Miller had strong allies in House Speaker David Bartley and State Representative John McGlynn of Medford. Better yet, he had the support of Jessie Sargent, who had a keen interest in the issue and was a strong public advocate for closing the reform schools. He also had the support of the *Boston Globe*. Miller would never have been able to accomplish what he did without the help of these allies.

Miller resigned as commissioner of DYS in January 1973. He left Massachusetts to become director of children's services agencies first in Illinois, then in Pennsylvania. His departure met with reactions as varied as those he had aroused throughout his thirty-nine months in office. The governor accepted his resignation with much regret; the *Boston Globe* offered effusive praise; the House Speaker lamented the administrative chaos he had left behind; and the legislature began yet another investigation. In 1990, Miller recounted his Massachusetts experience in a book aptly titled *Last One Over the Wall*, which won an award from the American Society of Criminology. He was an extraordinary agent for change who made an indelible mark both in the Bay State and nationally.

PARK PLAZA URBAN RENEWAL PROJECT

In early 1971 the Boston Redevelopment Authority proposed the construction of a $266 million urban renewal project in downtown Boston. Situated adjacent to the Boston Public Gardens, the Park Plaza project contained some of the most valuable real estate in the city.[47] This economic development project, which was viewed by the news media as Mayor Kevin White's baby, was to be privately financed, without any federal aid. One of the two private developers involved in the project was the real estate tycoon Mortimer Zuckerman, who was a close friend of the mayor.

Under state law, local urban renewal projects required the approval of the Department of Community Affairs. On May 4, 1972, Sargent appointed Miles Mahoney commissioner of DCA. Mahoney had previously served as the director of the Philadelphia Housing Authority. A month later, on June 9, the new commissioner turned down the Park Plaza project on the grounds that the site, which included portions of the tawdry "Combat Zone," did not meet the "blight" criterion of the law. Mahoney's finding sparked a heated controversy. His opponents derisively commented that the existing blight was apparently not the "right blight."

Then came the public outcry. Mayor White vigorously objected and filed home rule legislation designed to circumvent the need for state approval. At the time, Sargent was in the process of killing the plan for expanding the major highways around Boston. In a period of inflation and high unemployment, he could ill afford to stop all development projects. The administration desperately needed a political trophy. Disagreements and disappointments were initially papered over. Al Kramer tried his best to resolve the dispute, but to no avail. Negotiations came to a standstill.

On resubmission of a revised proposal, Mahoney once again rejected it. He remained resolute in his opposition and refused to back down. But there were repercussions. Both the business community and organized labor got into the act. Some ten thousand angry construction workers marched on the State House to voice their protests. The battle took on a momentum of its own and grew in intensity, reflecting the stresses and strains fracturing the administration.

On November 29, 1972, Sargent decided to overrule his DCA commissioner and to push ahead with the project. Soon afterward, the governor fired Mahoney for being too parochial and rigid. He appointed Louis Crampton to replace him. A special irony lay in the fact that the Park Plaza project fizzled and was never built. Instead, the state constructed the huge Transportation Building on the site.

HIRING AND FIRING A CORRECTIONS COMMISSIONER

The subject of prison reform aroused considerable public attention and controversy in Massachusetts in December 1971. The prison uprising in Attica, New York, and its brutal suppression by excessive police force had shocked the nation. It was a rude awakening that sparked a similar prison uprising at Walpole. As a consequence of this disturbance, Massachusetts corrections commissioner John Fitzpatrick resigned. The Sargent administration conducted an extensive search for a new commissioner committed to prison reform and community-based correctional programs. They were looking for someone who could bridge the gap between inmates and the community at large. From a list of twenty names the selection committee chose three finalists. Sargent interviewed each of them and picked John O. Boone.[48]

A career civil servant, Boone was a forty-nine-year-old black man from Atlanta. He had been the warden of the federal penitentiary at Lorton, Virginia. Although his southern origins put him at a considerable disadvantage in parochial Boston, his race proved even more of an impediment in a department that was almost entirely white. Sargent and Goldmark did not set out to look for a black commissioner, but when they found a likely candidate who was black, they believed that this might be an advantage in relating to inmates, a large percentage of whom were black. Long persuaded that the Department of Corrections (DOC) was an ossified and intransigent bureaucracy, they wanted someone who would shake things up. The governor told Boone that he would have "two good years" to implement his programs. "I knew very well, when I appointed him, there was going to be hell to pay," Sargent said. "And there sure was."[49]

The prison world was a complex and brutal one. Murders, robberies, rapes, and other forms of brutality were committed by inmates on other inmates and staff, and by staff on inmates. Upon taking office, Boone promptly removed the prison superintendents at Walpole and Norfolk and replaced them with wardens recruited from outside the state. DOC personnel were very unhappy that he had recruited from outside the system. Obviously Boone hoped to improve conditions within the prisons and to reduce the inmate population, but he seriously underestimated the countervailing power of the guards and their labor union.

To the outrage of prison guards, Boone allowed inmates the right to organize and to participate in some aspects of prison management. As a result of these actions, the guards saw themselves in grave physical danger. They were infuriated by what they perceived as a loss of discipline and control of the prisoners. From their perspective, they had been stripped of their authority and relegated to merely opening and closing the cell gates.

The appointment of Boone stirred emotions on all sides. As the leading figure of prison reform, Boone was out in front on the issue and hence a lightning rod for criticism. The *Boston Herald* launched a concerted campaign to discredit him. Articles appeared each week that detailed the chaos and disorder that prevailed in the prisons. These stories were advanced so vigorously that the governor's press secretary, Tom Reardon, openly questioned their fairness and accuracy. The political fallout from the stories had the immediate effect of putting Boone on notice that his job was in jeopardy. It also generated a barrage of criticism from legislators, who were being pressured by the guards. Alarmed by the disorder, Senate president Kevin Harrington felt that the situation had gotten dangerously out of hand. Editorials soon appeared calling for Boone's dismissal.

Under intense fire, Boone had to manage a different and more demanding organizational change. While he had his detractors, he also had his defenders. A coalition of interests, which included prison reform advocates, leaders in the black community, ex-offender groups, and several liberal legislators, staunchly defended him. Democratic state senator Jack Backman of Brookline was among his most ardent supporters. As far as they were concerned, Boone was doing what needed to be done. The governor showed him steadfast loyalty and declared as much in the press.

Tensions at Walpole remained high. Violence among the inmates erupted again. On March 17, 1972, the prison exploded in another major riot that resulted in considerable damage. Responding to what became known as the Saint Patrick's Day Riot, Boone announced a new training program for the guards and asserted that it would take $1.3 million to turn the corrections system around. Shortly after this outburst of violence, another riot occurred, this time at the women's prison in Framingham. Boone dismissed its new superintendent, only to reinstate her when the guards threatened a walkout. Protected by civil service rules, she could not be fired without adequate cause.

Meanwhile, Sargent filed his Omnibus Correctional Reform bill on February 9, 1972, calling it one of his most important pieces of legislation for that session. Its central provisions were logical and linked: halfway houses, work and education release, furloughs, prison industries, setting county jail standards, making ex-offenders eligible for correction jobs, and so on. Sargent contributed to the reform effort by placing the prestige of his office behind it and by utilizing his talents in public relations to overcome political obstacles. The omnibus bill was passed in July 1972, due in large measure to the cooperation of Speaker David Bartley, who quietly slipped the bill through the House without much debate.

Nevertheless, a series of dreadful events combined to dramatize the dangerous situation in the prisons and to seal the commissioner's fate. First, two prison guards were killed by a Norfolk inmate; then another inmate killed himself when his homemade bomb accidentally exploded; the inmates at Concord doused the prison chaplain with gasoline, although state police came to the rescue before they could immolate him; and a convicted murderer killed again while out on furlough. The guards were traumatized by these horrific events, especially the murders of their fellow guards. They staged a one-day sickout in protest. Sargent attended the funerals, where he received a hostile reception. The guards publicly branded him a murderer. Not accustomed to such abusive treatment, he was deeply shaken. He later recalled how it felt

> to go to a funeral and as far as you can see, a line on either side of the church, of corrections officers in uniform from around our state and from surrounding states, from Rhode Island and elsewhere. And to walk into the church and you get the rumble of a boo. And I tried to shake hands with a couple and I got "Go on, F——k you!," and all that kind of stuff, outside the church. It was a little unnerving to go in and sit in the front pew with the casket and a woman comes over to beat your brains in, that gets to be tough. Also you have the television cameras noting that and that doesn't play very well on the news.[50]

In the meantime, the savage attacks on Boone continued. Cumulatively, these attacks made his firing almost inevitable. For Sargent, the situation was deteriorating fast. He was under tremendous pressure, especially with his reelection less than a year away. By the spring of 1973, the governor's staff and Goldmark realized that Boone had to go. They were now convinced that he was a weak administrator, and that his continued presence jeopardized the entire reform program. Goldmark felt that if Boone was going down, there was no point in wasting any more political currency on him. Despite his public pronouncements, Sargent was not disposed to tolerate further chaos. A reckoning was due. As he explained:

The main reason the whole corrections thing became very tough wasn't merely the fact we had some violence, somebody killed, the fact we had a strike and all that sort of stuff. It was the day-to-day pressure from the newspapers. When you're in public life and you get a few bad headlines it isn't all that much fun, but when you get them day after day after day and week after week after week, then it gets rugged and you have to do something about it.[51]

In the end, Sargent capitulated. But it was not an easy choice for him. He had great respect for Boone and knew how much the commissioner had suffered during the long ordeal. Once Sargent decided to fire him, the question then became how to do it without appearing to surrender to the anti-Boone forces.

On the evening of June 20, 1973, the governor went on television and announced his decision. The tone of his speech was conciliatory. He felt it was important to praise Boone and his cause, even as he fired him. The stormy Boone era was over. Ultimately the governor replaced Boone with Frank A. Hall, who was deputy commissioner of the Department of Prisons in North Carolina. Before long, Hall restored peace to Walpole and the other prisons. He succeeded in keeping the prisons relatively safe and orderly while cautiously implementing Sargent's package of reforms.

SARGENT VERSUS DUKAKIS

It is interesting to compare Frank Sargent with his successor, Michael Dukakis. In many respects they were the antithesis of each other, offering a vivid contrast between the pragmatist and the idealist, the affable honest broker and the detached policy wonk. When they first met, they took an instant dislike to each other. The two governors differed sharply in style as well as personality. Sargent was friendlier and less driven than Dukakis. Whereas Dukakis was cold, aloof, and arrogant, Sargent displayed warmth, charm, and a remarkable lack of arrogance; whereas Dukakis was stiff, self-righteous, a paragon of virtue, Sargent was relaxed, outgoing, and profane; whereas Dukakis was viewed as a technocrat and a "know-it-all," Sargent was perceived as a good listener who reached out for the views of others. Dukakis was almost devoid of a sense of humor, and therefore was unable to empathize and soothe chafed egos the way Sargent did. About the only thing the two men had in common was their personal frugality.

While Sargent had his strengths, he also had his weaknesses. He hated to fire people. The most painful failure was his firing of John Boone. He also had difficulty relating to blacks. As a public manager, Sargent did not focus on details and had a short attention span. Nor did he get absorbed in economic development. He was bored by fiscal and administrative issues. He recognized their importance in principle and appointed excellent managers to handle them, but he assigned them little priority and preferred not to hear much about them personally. Hence, he chose not to heed the Cassandra-like warnings of his budget director, and thus left his successor a large deficit estimated to be somewhere around $200 million.

Sargent's executive style was the opposite of that of his nemesis. His preference for centralized management ran directly counter to Dukakis's "hands-on" managerial style. As Alan Altshuler puts it: "Sargent felt comfortable delegating, and he had no apparent sense of competitiveness with his appointees. He viewed himself as a conductor rather than star soloist and delighted in surrounding himself with talent."[52] Dukakis, by contrast, found it difficult to delegate. Advised of his shortcomings, the "Duke" attempted to change his image with a makeover. After losing the governorship to Edward King in 1978, he won it back in 1982 by convincing voters that he was a new, humble, more mellow figure ready to listen. There are many styles of leadership. I do not mean to suggest that one style is better than the other, but there were significant differences between the two men.

With due adjustment for differences in their style, character, and personality, there was another final dissimilarity. Sargent was not an ideologue, and this gave him a broader range in decisionmaking. He was oriented toward making decisions case by case. In the style of a classic manager, he retained the facts long enough to reach a decision, and then purged his mind of them. He emerged over time as a governor who consistently protected the weak, the underdog, and the environment, acting in ways that kept him in tune with the populace in general. Did Sargent change in any important sense the way governors make their decisions? Close observers of gubernatorial policy conclude that he did. As Altshuler sums up:

> Sargent, in short, was a man of politics and concrete decisions. While resistant to ideology in the abstract, his decisions expressed a consistent set of liberal values. His interest in management was confined, in general, to selecting key personnel and inspiring their loyalty. He was a reactive decision-maker in most circumstances, one who responded to crises and chose from among the options brought to him by staff. But he also gave the highest priority to recruiting a diverse and talented staff; he could be extremely patient when they needed time to generate fresh options; and he was willing to take major risks on behalf of policies about which he cared deeply. He had his blind spots, most notably in those areas where fiscal and administrative detail count for a lot. But he led an exciting administration with unfailing decency, compassion, and integrity.[53]

THE SARGENT LEGACY

Sargent was respected and admired on Beacon Hill, where he earned a reputation for objectivity and wise judgment. To this day, Democrats and Republicans still speak fondly of him. Reflecting on his own experience, former House Speaker David Bartley remarked, "Frank Sargent was one of the finest human beings I've ever met, and certainly the best governor I've served under."[54] Former Senate president Kevin Harrington put it somewhat differently: "Sargent had great instincts. He had a political piano tuner's ear; he had perfect pitch. He could smell whether an idea was good, great, or bad."[55]

To his credit, Sargent took more "stand-up" positions on legislation than most of his predecessors, and he received in his six years the highest percentage of bipartisan support in the history of his office. Add to the legislative record the policy innovations introduced through executive orders, gubernatorial memoranda, and rules and regulations, and the record is even more impressive. He was the first governor to address the manifold problems of urban life. His cabinet plan followed the best organizational theory of the decade. No other Republican leader in Massachusetts had so consciously and successfully developed a strategy for involving experts and academics in the various stages of policymaking. Many of his appointments were bold and courageous.

As historians struggle with the Sargent legacy, they will no doubt remember him for his comprehensive transportation policy and his policy of deinstitutionalization. Whatever the verdict on specific initiatives, he will be remembered most of all as an environmental visionary. He did more for the cause of the environment than any of his predecessors—or indeed any of his successors.

But Sargent was not an original thinker. He relied on Al Kramer, Robert Yasi, and others to feed him ideas. They were a dependable policy source. His wife, Jessie, was the driving force behind Jerome Miller and his efforts to improve the Department of Mental Health. Of the many participants who influenced policy and programs, the governor's staff and the *Boston Globe* played an invaluable role. Sargent had a good working relationship with the publishers of the *Globe* as well as with other media allies.

In his book *Leadership without Easy Answers*, Ronald Heifetz distinguishes between leaders who presume that their responsibility is to make decisions and leaders who help others to confront problems. Sargent clearly falls into the latter category. He believed in participatory democracy and sought to develop ways of getting ordinary people involved in making critical decisions that deeply affected their lives. Such a phenomenon was something entirely new in state politics. Until Sargent came along, the question of empowering nonestablishment groups remained largely unexplored and undefined.

One of Sargent's most important legacies was the extent to which he reshaped the state's judiciary. He filled ninety-seven judgeships, at both the district and superior court levels. (This large number of vacancies was due mainly to a new law that required judges to retire at age seventy.) William Young, the governor's legal counsel, was largely responsible for coordinating this effort. While patronage considerations were taken into account in appointing district court judges, the same was not true with regard to superior court judges. They were picked strictly on merit. Since there were only a few blacks on the bench, diversity was also a factor. Sargent appointed David Nelson, a highly respected black lawyer, to the superior court. Nelson later became a federal district court judge. Overall, Sargent's judicial appointments were of the highest rank.

Frank Sargent died on October 22, 1998, at the age of eighty-three. At the time of his death, the *Boston Globe* published an editorial that captured both his political and personal legacy. It is worth quoting at length:

Francis W. Sargent always acted as if his six years as governor were the most enjoyable accident that could befall a man. "I got a hell of a big kick out of it," he told the Globe's John Powers this summer.

The sentiment was mutual. Nearly everyone at the State House from 1969 to 1975 drew on Sargent's infectious sense of enjoyment. This included his top lieutenants as well as the Democratic leaders in the Legislature. If he had an afternoon meeting with House Speaker David Bartley, Sargent said, he would put out a press release in the morning blasting him for something or other just so the meeting would start off on the right foot.

But he did not see politics as a game of tricks requiring deception and guile. He was a most straightforward political executive, taking on issues with boldness and, often, vision. He presided during a period of significant transition, when the state was implementing its takeover of welfare from the cities and towns and was also taking more responsibility for funding local education and school construction.

One of his most memorable actions was stopping construction of the planned Inner Belt of highways. His appointments were superior; his Cabinet is widely viewed as the best of the modern era, with the possible exception of the Cabinet in Michael Dukakis's third term.

Sargent, an architect by training and a fisherman by choice, would laugh at attempts to list his accomplishments, but they were considerable. The fact that he made the state feel good in the process is a legacy to be treasured, and remembered.[56]

Frank Sargent made substantial progress in solving the problems that the citizens of Massachusetts faced, a goal that had eluded his predecessors. Single-minded and secure in his convictions, he responded effectively to contentious social issues. Several decades later, such issues still generate controversy. He made his share of mistakes, but he also made adjustments and moved on. Despite the fact that his career ended in defeat, he made a significant impact on the governorship itself. By seizing the policy initiative and exercising vigorous leadership, he broke the mold and turned the governor's office into an instrument for social change. That is his most enduring legacy.

3

TRANSFORMING THE MENTAL HEALTH CARE SYSTEM

Fifty years ago, mentally ill people in Massachusetts were locked away in "insane asylums." Today, in one of the great overlooked success stories of modern medicine, most state-run mental hospitals are shuttered— and the mentally ill are living in the community. Although as a group they still die too young and don't get all the help they need, most are substantially better off than in the era of the asylum.

Larry Tye, *Boston Globe*, April 17, 2001

THE CONTENDING FORCES

Public service bureaucracies like the Massachusetts Department of Mental Health (DMH) are notoriously cumbersome and inefficient. They often have to contend with powerful and well-organized public service employee unions, which drive up costs and complicate policy innovation and organizational change. Perhaps there is no better illustration of this phenomenon than the downsizing of the mental health care system. Between 1991 and 1993, Massachusetts closed three of its seven existing mental hospitals and the only public psychiatric treatment facility for children with serious emotional problems. Over the years the quality of treatment at these four institutions had steadily deteriorated. To be sure, the deliverers of mental health services had become unduly burdened by political and contractual obligations to organized groups. Mental health advocates and labor unions denounced these plans as schemes to destroy the social safety net for patients. Although the results of these changes were not altogether beneficial, they at least provided an alternative approach to the traditional way of doing things. This innovation, if still extremely controversial, broke the stranglehold of power that the contending forces maintained over the system.

Mental illnesses are among the most devastating illnesses in our society. Severe mental disorders such as schizophrenia and bipolar disorder (otherwise known as manic-depressive disorder) are incurable, incapacitating, and extremely difficult to treat. They cause incalculable suffering for patients and wreak havoc on their families. Those afflicted lose touch with reality. "After all," as one observer notes poignantly, "mental illnesses by their nature involve a person's ability to think clearly and rationally. The mood, or affective disorders, such as bipolar, may produce extreme emotional states. The thought disorders, such as schizophrenia and other psychoses, may produce hallucinations and delusions."[1] During a psychiatric breakdown or full-blown psychosis, a person's whole world falls apart. Sometimes it tragically ends in suicide. Others become dysfunctional and thus unemployable. They also become homeless.

Few social problems are more perplexing, obdurate, and intractable. Given the erratic and often unpredictable course of mental illness, the problems that accompany it do not lend themselves to simple solutions. Many families with a troubled member find their lives disrupted, even torn asunder. They wind up in dire straits. Older parents particularly feel the effects of their own aging in their desire to see a mentally ill son or daughter restored to stability and living independently. It is essential to recognize that although mental illness can be treated, there is no cure. During the acute phase of illness, most patients require short-term intensive services in secure settings, usually locked hospital wards. This involves either voluntary or involuntary commitment. The latter means that the person has to be taken into police custody, or "pink-slipped."

In Massachusetts, with a population of more than 6 million people, an estimated 44,730 adults are diagnosed with serious mental illness. With an annual budget of $624 million for fiscal year 2002, the DMH service system was designed to accommodate 80,000 clients. This beleaguered department has been a recurring managerial nightmare for Republican and Democratic administrations alike. Indeed, the agency has always been regarded as complicated to manage. Buffeted by changing social demographics and the competition for scarce resources, the state's mental health system has been vulnerable to underfunding and inadequate staffing for as long as anyone can remember. In the 1950s there were more than 23,000 patients in the custody of state-operated mental hospitals scattered around the Commonwealth. As a result of restructuring policies that were implemented during the early 1990s, by 2001 DMH had 1,222 inpatient beds in four state hospitals, five community mental health centers, and contracted adolescent units in public and private hospitals.

In the early nineteenth century, Massachusetts led the nation in building a network of public asylums whose spacious outdoor campuses provided fresh air and a serene environment for the mentally ill. In their prime, these large congregate hospitals functioned best as an extended system. They responded to the needs of the insane, the aged infirm, the poor and disabled, and the dispossessed who could not afford proper medical care. With the passage of time, these facilities have become increasingly obsolete, outdated relics of a bygone era. Contributing to their obsolescence were the dramatic changes in psychiatry and community mental health programs that have taken place in recent decades.

On closer inspection, mental health care can be classified as a latent issue. A taboo topic that no one wants to talk about, it is the opposite of a hot-button issue. Mental hospitals are out of sight, and therefore out of the public mind. From time to time hot-button events do occur, but for the most part the problem receives little attention. Nobody wants to deal with it. Too often it falls prey to the politics of evasion.

There are essentially four contending forces at play here. First, mental health is a social problem whose complexities are routinely ignored. Without more knowledge about how to cure such illnesses, there may be no immediate resolution. Second, mental health care involves a changing technology that seeks to stabilize people, but because of the adverse side effects of mind-altering drugs, this new technology is not fully understood. Nor are the "miracle drugs" user-friendly, for they have potential benefits and risks. In handling this technology, doctors have sometimes been naïve about releasing patients from hospitals. Some who are deemed well enough to live in the community have proved to be a danger to themselves and others. This social disruption, plus the lack of tolerance for deviance in the larger society, explains why it takes so long for new programs to develop. Third, the bureaucracy and labor unions are entrenched forces that wield considerable power so that legislators and governors have been reluctant to take them on. Fourth, mental health advocates have made a significant impact on policy development. Activists such as Ben Ricci, who first challenged the system in the early 1970s, have made their presence felt in Massachusetts. The primary mission of those who have engaged in the politics of public advocacy in order to combat the politics of evasion has been to protect the rights of patients and to hold service providers more accountable. Because various rights are sometimes in conflict with one another, the interplay of these forces explains why change comes so hard. None of them operates in isolation, and they are contradictory and contentious. Understanding the ways in which they complement and counteract one another makes the program of hospital closings more comprehensible.

THE SHIFT TO PRIVATIZATION

Hardly anything could have prepared the residents of Massachusetts who had just experienced the prosperity of the so-called Massachusetts Miracle, for the economic and fiscal disasters that would befall them in the years between 1988 and 1992. As a prosperous economy faltered and then collapsed, the business community began to downsize and lay off employees. The high-tech and defense industries were especially hard hit. By the summer of 1990, the Bay State, like the rest of the nation, was in the midst of a full-blown recession turning into a depression. Banks failed, the savings and loan industry collapsed, investments turned sour, depositors lost their savings, retail sales slumped, housing construction declined, major industries went out of business, and unemployment rose to new heights. Chelsea's city government declared bankruptcy and was placed in receivership. Cries for downsizing were heard in both the public and private sectors.

The telltale signs that people were hurting were evident as early as 1986. State and local debt had doubled since 1980, and expenditures almost doubled in those six years. These events caused a serious decline in public revenues, which in turn led state officials to increase taxes and cut services. This intolerable situation produced enormous pressures to economize. Faced with a fiscal crisis, the executive and legislative branches of state government were compelled to cut back on social services and welfare funding.

As the state's fiscal crisis deepened, the Democratic legislative leaders on Beacon Hill began downsizing state government. Such a course of action ran contrary to the central thrust of their party. Since the days of the New Deal, most Democrats had favored an active, involved role for government, particularly when it came to meeting the needs of low-income families. Nevertheless, the Democrats made good on threats to slash the state budget. They cut $36 million from the DMH budget for fiscal year 1991, reducing it from $497 million to $461 million. They also reduced the authorization for assisted housing for deinstitutionalized patients. The battle over these budget cuts was bitter and acrimonious.

Under the pressure of fiscal deficits, anti-tax pressures, and the rising costs of human services, the lame duck Michael Dukakis administration began making drastic budget cuts, but they were not sufficient to cover the revenue shortfalls. The state constitution requires a governor to submit a balanced budget, but despite two consecutive billion-dollar tax increases, Massachusetts had a $1.8 billion deficit when Dukakis left office. The state's credit was in jeopardy, and its bond rating had sunk to almost that of a junk bond. All these events generated intense public anger, for many tax-payers believed that the politicians themselves were to blame for the state's fiscal problems. Public fury reached a boiling point during the 1990 state elections.

In the primary election, which was only a warm-up for the main event, the two major parties selected gubernatorial candidates who ran as self-styled political outsiders. In the general election, Republican William Weld, a politician of patrician pedigree, was pitted against Democrat John Silber, the outspoken and controversial president of Boston University. (The two were literally outsiders as well, Weld having moved to Massachusetts from New York and Silber from Texas.) It turned out to be a hotly contested and bitterly fought race in which the outcome remained very much in doubt until the end.

A graduate of Harvard Law School and a former U.S. attorney in the Ronald Reagan administration, Weld was pro-choice and pro–gay rights, but he was a hard-liner when it came to crime, spending, and taxes. In addition to his base of mainstream Republicans, he appealed primarily to women, gays, minorities, and disaffected Democrats. The alienated voters had become increasingly distrustful of and cynical about government. As the campaign wore on, Weld railed against big government and extolled the virtues of free enterprise and the workings of the marketplace. His disdain toward bureaucracy was vitriolic. At one point he derisively referred to state employees as "walruses," a comment that did not especially endear him to them. Privatization, reinventing government, and total quality man-agement were the popular buzzwords of the day. Ideologically a freewheeling libertarian, Weld promised the voters no new taxes. This popular rhetoric quickly translated into a politically viable philosophy that was shrewdly attuned to the temper of the times. In the closing days of the campaign, Silber seemed to stumble. Strident and contentious as ever, he bungled a television interview and that cost him dearly. In the end, Weld narrowly defeated Silber, with the women's vote carrying him to victory.

Pressures were strong on the newly elected governor—the head of the first Republican administration in more than sixteen years—to overcome past tradition and cut through the complexities to a prompt resolution of the budget deficit. Given the prevailing skepticism about the fiscal capacity of state government, the impulse to "privatize" was almost irresistible. Vig-orous gubernatorial action would be possible under these circumstances. Fresh from the campaign, Weld called on state administrators to privatize functions wherever they believed such action would save money or improve services. He moved aggressively to gain control of a recalcitrant bureaucracy and to reduce the large deficit he had inherited. Dukakis holdovers, who were plentiful, departed only with the greatest reluctance, compounding the atmosphere of distrust and deception. Persuaded as to the policy utility of privatization, Weld eagerly embraced public-choice economics—that is, favoring the private sector—as a substitute for institutional development. His was a minimalist approach to government. As a deliberate strategy, Weld sought to reduce the size of state government from its current level of 72,000 employees. These were trends thoroughly consistent with the governor's temperament and philosophy.

For more than a decade the state's human service budget had been growing at an alarming rate. Because of its legislators' liberal commitment to the poor and needy, Massachusetts spent more money on human services than any other state except New York. Unfortunately, at the very time when the demand for these services was steadily increasing, the Commonwealth was losing the economic capacity to finance them. A disproportionate share of the mental health budget went toward financing the state's antiquated hospitals. By 1991 the average annual cost of caring for a mental patient in a state hospital was $120,000. To put it another way, 6 percent of DMH consumers were using 47 percent of its resources. Although more than 750 inpatients were ready to be discharged, they could not be placed in the community for lack of assisted housing. As of January 1991, the adult inpatient census at all DMH facilities, which included seven state hospitals and eight community mental health centers, was 2,021.

Even before Weld was inaugurated, the immediate focus of his principal economic advisers was to bring the fiscal crisis under control. They proposed doing so by imposing effective cost containment measures that would harness the so-called budget busters, identified as Medicaid, debt service, pensions, group health insurance, and the Metropolitan Bay Transportation Authority. It was these big-ticket items that caught the public eye. There were no magic solutions to the perplexing issues that Weld chose to tackle. Alarms were sounded from various quarters in the spring of 1990. The gap between public revenues and expenditures had been documented in a report published by the McCormack Institute, which analyzed the state's fiscal crisis and sent warning signals of trouble ahead.[2]

Responding to this crisis, the Republican governor placed a cap on spiraling debt service costs which limited capital spending over the next five years to $4.5 billion. Weld refused to borrow money to cover the deficit. He refinanced the outstanding debt and spread it out over a longer period of time and threatened to veto any tax increases. By adopting such a strategy, the governor had put the legislature in a box. It was a well-executed political squeeze play.

Over and beyond this, the Weld administration discovered how to milk the federal cash cow by way of reimbursements. In 1991 Kathy Betts, an obscure state employee, spotted a loophole in the Medicaid regulations. The provision was originally designed to reimburse hospitals that treat a disproportionate share of poor people, but almost every state discovered its dual use as a means of financing other projects. The result was a $500 million windfall for Massachusetts, an instant remedy for its fiscal crisis. The official clinical rationale for closing the mental hospitals was that patients do better in community settings. But the fiscal rationale was even more compelling. Although Medicaid (a joint federal-state program that helps pay medical costs for low-income people) did not cover mental patients in state institutions, it paid half the costs for patients in community care. The yield was $21 million a year in federal funds.

The overall strategy called for the purchase of service contracts. Packaged under the policy tag "public managed care," the DMH program consisted of five components: (1) closing state hospitals through privatization; (2) moving more resources into the community; (3) developing a comprehensive community support system model; (4) creating an infrastructure for quality and utilization management; and (5) integrating the dual systems of care that existed between the Department of Mental Health and the Division of Medical Assistance (the state's Medicaid agency). These sweeping policy changes, which were introduced by the newly appointed commissioner, Eileen Elias, shifted much of the burden for mental health care from the state to private management. Hindsight was to reveal that the length of public hospital stays was substantially shortened, and the number of institutionalized patients was sharply reduced, from 2,330 to 1,160. Contracting with private agencies to provide services formerly supplied by state government was not exactly a new idea. Since the 1960s, services had been increasingly provided by private, not-for-profit agencies under government supervision. What was new, of course, was shifting the locus of service delivery to private enterprise.

Central to the policies then being fashioned were two recent changes in state law that signaled a move toward privatization. The first, a statute passed in 1987 (Chapter 167), authorized the creation of psychiatric units in private or general hospitals. The second, legislation passed in 1990 (Chapter 150), authorized Medicaid to implement a managed care program for recipients. The economic theory behind managed care was to move people out of high-cost institutional settings. Chapter 167 allowed the state to share the cost of mental health care with third-party payers by transferring Medicaid patients out of ineligible hospitals and into reimbursable acute care facilities. The hospital financing law was due to expire in October 1991 and its renewal was regarded as problematic. Subsequently, new hospital financing legislation reduced regulatory requirements and created opportunities for selective contracting with health care providers. This legislation was particularly helpful in removing barriers to caring for patients with long-term serious mental illness in private or general hospitals.

His alert sense of these trends shaped the strategy of Governor Weld, who described himself as a social liberal and a fiscal conservative. On February 26, 1991, as the pressures of office descended on him, he appointed a seventeen-member special commission to study the problem of state-operated hospitals. This blue-ribbon commission comprised four state legislators—two Democrats and two Republicans—a labor union official, a family member, six experts on health care and housing policy, three agency commissioners, and two cabinet secretaries. It was stacked in the sense that most of its members were favorably disposed toward shifting care for persons with disabilities from large state institutions to private community-based organizations, hospitals, and nursing homes. As secretary of the executive office of Health and Human Services Governor Weld had appointed David Forsberg, head of the regional office of the U.S. Department of Housing and Urban Development. The commission's work began immediately under the direction of Forsberg, who served as chair. His able deputy, Charles Baker, who chaired a working subgroup of state employees, assisted him. As the point men for the Weld administration, Forsberg and Baker worked well together. A politically savvy administrator, Forsberg possessed well-honed political skills, while Baker, who had come over from the Pioneer Institute, a conservative think tank, was a good numbers cruncher and a superb technician.

With a specific focus and genuine political clout among its members, the commission moved at a rapid pace. In whirlwind fashion, the members took their show on the road and inspected most state health facilities. This tour consisted of thirty-one site visits and fifteen hours of public hearings that were held in various parts of the state. After spending numerous hours deliberating and studying background materials, they found, among other things, that the state had a shrinking patient population and an excess capacity of hospital beds. The nature and extent of this problem were clearly outlined in their report:

> The Commonwealth's inpatient facilities system, which was built to accommodate over 35,000 individuals at its peak, today cares for 6,200 clients. Encompassing some 10,500 acres and over 1,000 buildings, stretched over 34 campuses, the inpatient system is grossly oversized for the number of people in its care. Moreover, of those 6,200 individuals receiving care in institutions, at least 2,200 would be more appropriately cared for in community-based settings. Today, the state's inpatient facilities, which do fill an important need for very specific kinds of clients, would be appropriately sized with capacity to care for 4,000 clients.[3]

A spirit of open inquiry prevailed among the commission members. Much of their deliberation focused on the impact of federal aid and what states were able to do with it. The major problem was how to maximize federal reimbursements for mental hospitals. Only those patients twenty-one years of age and under and sixty-five years of age and over were eligible for Medicaid reimbursement. Commission members recognized the national trend of moving mental health care toward a noninstitutional approach. After crisis intervention and acute care had been rendered, the integration of community services was viewed as a better solution than restricted institutional care. In shifting to such an approach, the trick was to separate housing needs from treatment needs. Clients could not obtain Medicaid money for housing except through waivers. Drawing on their experience in the housing field, both chairman David Forsberg and Eleanor White, who served as deputy director of the Massachusetts Housing Finance Agency, played a critical role in reminding their fellow commission members of considerations that they might otherwise have ignored. The recent crash in the real estate market made it easy for clients to obtain assisted housing. For his part, Charles Baker knew how to access housing that was not treatment oriented. In addition, new federal and state laws made it illegal to discriminate against the mentally disabled.[4]

Four months later, on June 19, 1991, the governor's special commission released its report, "Actions for Quality Care." Charged to develop a specific plan, it concluded that a systemwide solution was warranted. Devising what it termed a "right-sizing" hospital reduction strategy, the commission recommended closing nine of thirty-four inpatient facilities over a three-year period, with patients being moved either to the community or to public or private hospitals. Among those facilities recommended for closing were three adult mental hospitals, three public health hospitals, and three schools for the mentally retarded. Describing community-based services as "highly desirable, highly effective, and less expensive than institutional care," the commission also called for the development of two thousand new community residential placements and associated community support programs (seven hundred of these specifically targeted for persons with mental illness). In addition, it recommended that three hundred new general hospital acute care beds and two hundred new long-term-care nursing home beds be created for former state hospital patients.

As a sign that it was operating in good faith, the commission explicitly acknowledged the failures of past efforts to deinstitutionalize clients and therefore promised that no patient would be moved from a state facility slated for closure until an "equal or better" alternative care setting was available.[5] The commission estimated that its recommendations would save the state approximately $60 million in annual operating costs and another

$144 million in capital avoidance; in other words, funds would not have to be spent to bring antiquated facilities up to the standards of the Joint Commission on Accreditation of Healthcare Organizations and the Health Care Finance Administration.

This was not a policy brought forward by overwhelming popular demand. Activists and mental health professionals had talked about it for years, but no political groundswell existed in its behalf. In the fall of 1990, the Massachusetts Association for Mental Health had published a working paper suggesting that three state hospitals—Danvers, Metropolitan State, and Northampton—were prime candidates for closure. According to Bernard Carey, its executive director, the intent of the group was to give this paper to the winner of the gubernatorial election.[6] As it turned out, these were the same three hospitals that the governor's special commission decided to shut down.

Much like the military base closings on the national level, this was a process not without pain and considerable conflict. Before DMH could close any of its hospitals, Governor Weld first had to accept the commission's recommendations. Barriers to policy implementation, such as collective bargaining agreements, stood in the way of executive action. Closing underused hospitals would prove to be very difficult politically. Previous administrations had been either unwilling or unable to take on the legislature and the powerful state employee unions. Stimulated by the work of the governor's commission and given the green light by Weld, DMH quickly moved to close three of its seven remaining adult hospitals and Gaebler, its one children's hospital. All signals remained go.

From a political standpoint, the governor's special commission had the practical effect of shifting the locus of decisionmaking. It thus provided a convenient buffer for Weld. A bipartisan consensus existed among the four state legislators who served on the commission. Democrats Edward Burke and Barbara Gray and Republicans Arthur Chase and Edward Teague voted in favor of the plan. Laura Spenser, a labor union member (AFSCME Council 93), cast the only negative vote. Taking a strong stand against privatization and the laying off of state employees, she filed a minority report.

Among those hospitals placed on the "hit list" of recommended closings was Metropolitan State in Waltham, where a planned phasedown from 400 to 120 patients was already well under way. The two other adult mental hospitals scheduled to be closed were Danvers and Northampton. Selection of these three institutions was based mainly on the grounds of their inefficiency, costly operation, and underutilization. Beyond these criteria, all three were situated in areas where there was a large provider base and private hospitals to handle acute care. Finally, their closure was deemed politically feasible.[7]

The downsizing of Metropolitan State predated Weld's appointment of Eileen Elias as mental health commissioner in June 1991. The governor was eager to appoint women to high-level positions. Elias replaced Henry Tomes, a holdover Dukakis appointee, who had resigned a month earlier. Before coming to Massachusetts, Elias had worked for twenty-five years as a psychiatric rehabilitation counselor in both the private and public sectors. She had recently served as area director on Cape Cod and the offshore islands. Not only was she the first woman commissioner in a state renowned for its entrenched old boy political network, but also she was even more of an outsider in that she came from Philadelphia and New Jersey. Furthermore, she had no formal connections to the prestigious Boston medical institutions which exercised considerable influence in the mental health policy environment.[8]

Feisty and determined, Elias fought hard to achieve her goals. In response to the agenda for change mandated by the Weld administration and her own reform vision, she worked with people from across the state, developing and articulating the vision of change and challenging them to work with her to develop a blueprint for improving the system. Her concept was based on principles of consumer empowerment, community-based organized systems of care, flexible use of resources, protection of the local service system, and accountability. But these principles carried consequences that, unless anticipated and managed, ensured policy disasters.

Dr. Annette Hanson, a psychiatrist from the private sector, was named deputy commissioner for clinical and professional services. (By law, the department's second in command is required to be a board-certified psychiatrist if the commissioner is not.) Both were assisted by general counsel Jennifer Wilcox and by two other deputy commissioners, Valerie Fletcher in charge of program operations and John Ford in charge of budget and finance. This team was responsible for implementing the recommendations of the governor's special commission.

The hospital closings, so painfully generated, aroused intense opposition. Hostility to the plan was concentrated in those areas where the targeted hospitals were located. The battle to keep them open was fought by those most directly threatened and most capable of effective defense and counterattack. They included adversely affected special interest groups such as, the American Federation of State, County, and Municipal Employees and the Massachusetts Alliance for the Mentally ill, a grassroots family advocacy organization whose main purpose is to lobby on behalf of the powerless. In addition, Governor Weld received a petition signed by more than five thousand citizens urging him not to close the facilities.[9]

Undeterred by this opposition, Weld remained firmly committed to his restructuring initiatives. Emboldened by his commission's plan and convinced that it would result in a substantial reduction of public spending, the governor forged ahead. At a press conference he declared, "While the top priority of the special commission is client care, their recommendations will result in tremendous savings to the Commonwealth."[10] Even so, DMH administrators first had to close the hospitals before any savings could be realized. Operating with money from a reserve account, they faced the problem of how to free up existing resources for community services while keeping the hospitals open until they could be emptied. This was a formidable task.

By the end of January 1992, DMH had closed Metropolitan State Hospital, which was then the largest public mental hospital in Massachusetts. With a 412-bed capacity, it served twenty-three communities located within the greater Boston metropolitan region. Five months later, in June 1992, Danvers State Hospital, which served the northeastern region with 155 beds, was closed. As a subsequent recommendation of the governor's commission, the Gaebler Children's Center, which housed fifty-six emotionally disturbed children under the age of fourteen, was closed in September 1992.

But already a reaction was taking place. Northampton was the only state hospital in western Massachusetts. It housed 145 patients and was operating under a court-ordered consent decree. The legislative delegation from this region was strongly opposed to its closing, fearing that the prospect of losing a major facility would have a negative impact on the local economy. The lawmakers therefore gave Commissioner Elias an exceedingly hard time and tried to persuade her to change her mind. Despite their strenuous objections, Northampton was closed on August 26, 1993.

The Weld initiative prevailed because of the perceived benefits of privatization. It had considerable appeal. The fact that the general public was angry with state government fueled support for Weld's program. Public opinion polls indicated as much. A poll conducted by the Becker Institute in 1993 showed that 53 percent of those surveyed approved of privatization, while 39 percent were opposed to it. A similar poll commissioned by the *Boston Globe* showed a favorable rating of 45 percent and an unfavorable rating of 33 percent.[11]

The trade-offs between political ideology and political reality are always tricky, whether played out nationally or at the state and local levels. This restructuring program proved to be no exception. According to the figures released by the governor's special commission, closing the three adult mental hospitals would save the state an estimated $36.94 million annually in net operating expenses and another $40.03 million in capital costs. Considering Metropolitan State Hospital by itself, the commission estimated that its closure would result in operating savings of $12.93 million annually and $16.78 million in capital savings.[12]

These cost-benefit arguments did not sway those who believed that the proposed hospital closings would forever preclude the existence of a safety net for the mentally ill. Skeptics questioned the accuracy of the figures. Despite the differences in numbers, most of the money saved would have to be reallocated to financing a wide array of community services, facilitating patient access, and expanding appropriate care options. Mental health professionals considered residential care more cost-effective and less stigmatizing than institutional care. A similar managed care approach, aimed at reducing Medicaid expenditures, was evident in public welfare. With this goal in mind, the Division of Medical Assistance contracted with Mental Health Management of America, a private vendor, to deliver mental health and substance abuse services to Medicaid recipients. These were fundamental shifts in conventional definitions of mission, in development of resources, financial and human and in the physical siting of mental health services. Case management, however, was not privatized. All in all, the plan represented a major restructuring of the mental health care system in Massachusetts.

Not surprisingly, labor unions strongly opposed the hospital reduction policy, arguing that closures would significantly worsen the intolerable situation of hundreds of state workers already laid off owing to severe budget cuts. Furthermore, they argued that increasing privatization of the mental health system would lead to disparities in the quality of services for the profoundly mentally ill. In late 1991 the Service Employees International Union Local 509 filed suit against the Weld administration, charging it with illegally implementing privatization of the mental health system. The suit accused state officials of illegally laying off more than eight hundred state employees who worked in private agencies. Many of the discharged state workers were then rehired by private providers, but at lower wage and benefit rates. Although the litigation was unsuccessful, the unions continued their efforts to roll back state privatization policies.

The political fallout from the closings made most state legislators unhappy. Weld's restructuring program was anathema to Democrats on Beacon Hill, who, by the end of 1993, had mounted a concerted counterattack. The Senate Committee on Post Audit and Oversight criticized DMH for not ensuring that enough private hospital beds were available before closing Northampton.[13] The House Committee on Post Audit and Oversight, chaired by Democrat William Nagle of Northampton, was even more critical. State senator Marc Pacheco, a Democrat of Taunton, feared that Taunton State Hospital, which was located in his legislative district, would be the next one closed. In December 1993, Pacheco introduced legislation that prohibited a state agency from privatizing services unless it could document a minimum savings of 10 percent of its costs. Governor Weld vetoed

Pacheco's "anti-privatization" bill, but the Democrats mustered the necessary two-thirds vote in each house to override his veto, and it became law. In July 1994 the irate lawmakers overrode another gubernatorial veto of a legislative rider attached to the budget that prohibited the closing of any more state hospitals.

FRAMING THE ISSUE: WHY CLOSE METROPOLITAN STATE?

In what follows I focus on the impact of the consolidation and transfer of services at Metropolitan State Hospital as a point of departure. The episode raised several hard questions that did not yield easy answers. Why such a major change? What would happen to the clients in its custody? Where would they go? Could they be transferred to alternative hospital facilities or community group homes without jeopardizing their health and safety? Could the Department of Mental Health protect the safety of the larger society and the rights of the mentally ill at the same time? What would happen to the clinical treatment staff and other hospital personnel who faced imminent layoffs? Could they find jobs elsewhere in the system?

These questions of public policy and public management and their ramifications have been debated with increasing fervor over the past several decades. They found their origins in the policy option of deinstitutionalization, which resulted in the wholesale discharge of patients that started in the 1960s and continued throughout the 1970s. This controversial reform exposed the cracks in the system, which in turn led to the first round of hospital closings in the mid-1970s. The remaining sections of this chapter summarize the painful history of these efforts and the mistakes that were made along the way. Acknowledging the embarrassing failures of deinstitutionalization, one must ask the obvious questions: Why again? If this strategy failed then, what made the policymakers think that it would succeed a second time? What was the critical difference? As we shall see, these are questions worth examining.

Opened in 1929 on the eve of the Great Depression, Met State, as it was popularly known, had been in operation for sixty-three years. During this extended period it had provided both acute and long-term care for patients suffering from various mental and personality disorders. Over the years, thousands upon thousands of patients had been treated there on their road to recovery or stability. Most referrals originated with families who found themselves unable to cope with the bizarre and erratic behavior of a troubled member. The hospital admitted people from three of DMH's nine catchment areas. These included the Cambridge-Somerville area; the Beaverbrook–Concord–Mystic Valley area; and the Tri-City area, which encompassed the cities of Everett, Malden, and Medford.

As it happened, the quality of care at Met State in the late 1980s left much to be desired. Most of its patients suffered severe mental illnesses ranging from paranoid schizophrenia to bipolar disorder. Some of these illnesses are associated with chemical changes in the brain which cause their victims to lose touch with reality. Theirs was a world haunted by failed treatments and fearful delusions and hallucinations. Those who suffered psychotic relapses returned to the hospital for repeated commitments. The recidivism rate was fairly high. The most costly aspect of mental health is hospitalization: the average cost per patient per year at Met State in 1991 was $98, 500. By marked contrast, a similar stay at a community setting cost, on average, $55,000 per client, which included residential, day, and support services.[14]

In carrying out its responsibilities, Met State was plagued by numerous problems. Client concerns that had been so troubling to so many were legendary, serious care deficiencies and staffing shortages being among the most prevalent.[15] This led to many reports of abuses, for example, individuals being misdiagnosed or overdrugged and neglected in back wards. The factors accounting for these problems were both episodic and long-term. After beginning with high hopes and large budgetary outlays, Met State prospered in its early years. Before long, however, it encountered financial problems and found itself continually underfunded and understaffed. Year after year it experienced successive expansions and contractions of public and political support. This pattern of unstable funding explains in large measure why the hospital declined. Indeed, it was no stranger to cycles of reform and retrenchment, nor was it spared sordid scandal, corruption, and incompetence. For better or worse, it had weathered these storms and withstood the passage of time and change. By 1991 it had become a remnant of an era when bigger and better hospitals were seen as the only viable option for treating the mentally ill.

The decision to close Metropolitan State was based largely on the worn-out condition of its buildings, their replacement value, the costs of maintenance and capital funding, and their physical and functional obsolescence. In short, this sprawling hospital complex was underutilized and too expensive to operate. Another consideration was the excess capacity of private hospitals in the area. Adopting conventional cost-benefit analysis and long-established criteria used in hospital consolidations and mergers, the governor's special commission concluded that Met State lacked an appropriate "physical environment." It politely explained its rationale this way:

The Metropolitan campus was built in two groups of buildings. The buildings are in fair condition but are inappropriately built for today's health care standards. The layouts add to inefficient operating costs for staffing, energy, security, communications, and maintenance. The site utility structures and power plant are original and need significant repairs/rebuilding. Estimates to rebuild the newer portion of the campus for 120 institutional beds and 80 transitional beds approaches $17 million. These funds would be more appropriately invested in community programs and other state facilities.[16]

Clearly, Met State was one of the most inefficient and least cost-effective hospitals in the system. Like a rusty old battleship about to be withdrawn from active service, this imposing hospital facility was ready to be decommissioned and mothballed. From start to finish, the two-stage decommissioning process took fourteen months to complete. The initial phasedown took place during the eight months from November 1990 to June 1991. The second stage began shortly thereafter and concluded when Marylou Sudders, the hospital's chief operating officer, closed its doors on January 31, 1992. In truth, the decision to close Met State had been in the works for some time. It was implicitly made by Dukakis and explicitly affirmed by Weld. Given the downsizing that was already taking place, the hospital was on its way out by the time the latter assumed power.

With Met State's continued existence threatened, its 827 employees were confused and outraged at this turn of events. They were not simply afraid of losing their jobs; their anxiety was deeply rooted in feelings of individual self-worth. Worried employees asked one another, "What will happen to us once the hospital is shut down? Will we lose our jobs and have to go on unemployment? Or can we exercise our bumping rights and get transferred to other state hospitals?" Unwilling to see Met State expire, they engaged in a power struggle for institutional survival. Like their counterparts at Danvers and Northampton, who faced a similar predicament, they fought hard to keep the hospital open. Their resistance to change—especially to change imposed from outside—was extraordinary.

Patients and their families were even more upset. After all, they had the most to lose. The sudden change of conditions meant disrupting the normal routine of patients, breaking up their social networks and the continuity of the clinical treatment that was an integral part of their support system. Closing the hospital caused severe hardship and required adjustments for all parties involved. The whole episode provided a compelling example of organizational change in a volatile environment.

Trying to anticipate the consequences of their actions proved especially important to the administrators. They sensed the probable organizational impact and understood that it would cause much pain and anxiety. Consequently, they devised strategies to help the affected stakeholders cope with their losses, both real and feared. Most important of all, they wanted to maintain the clinical integrity of the process. Related to this, and a matter that sharpened each of the issues they faced, was the complexity of transferring patients to alternative facilities without compromising their health and safety. For many this involved moving from a restrictive setting to a less restrictive one. It was an enormously complicated task that was fraught with risk as well as the uncertainties and complexities inherent in organizational reality. A few months beforehand a class-action lawsuit had been filed by lawyers who sought to protect the basic civil rights of patients. This raised the question whether cooperation among the parties involved in the closure process could flourish or whether the situation was destined to be adversarial.

As principal participants reconstruct the Metropolitan State case, community involvement was extensive. It included consumers, families, employees, trustees, and advocates. After stubborn resistance at the outset, all parties eventually came around in advance of the closing. But the appearance of cooperation on the part of both labor and management did not come easily. To acknowledge sharply divergent views, mutual accommodations and adjustments were the order of the day. The administrators had to invent new ways of allowing the various stakeholders to participate in the planning and decisionmaking processes that affected their lives so deeply. They all showed genuine respect and sympathy for the patients.

Ultimately, it was this sense of shared purpose that made it possible for all parties to work closely together. Labor relations in the past had left much to be desired, both as a process and as an impediment to new policies. The failure of past attempts to create a viable framework for talks was attributable to the lack of trust and credibility on both sides. First, DMH placed a hiring freeze on all job vacancies and promised to give Metropolitan State employees first crack at them. The major negotiations among the nine public employee unions and the senior management team took place at the hospital site in Waltham. Specific grievances were handled at the Office of Employee Relations in Boston. In conjunction with state employee unions, DMH set up an Office of Competitive Bidding to assist employees in bidding on contracted work. What emerged was a policy process that mixed outside and inside participation.

Herbert Kaufman, a prominent political scientist, has identified three internal reasons why organizations resist change. First, the members of an organization almost always make contradictory judgments as to whether the change is necessary. Second, ineffective decisionmaking processes usually obtain. Third, the implementation of new directions is imperfect; slippage between decision and action occurs because the instructions are likely to be ambiguous or impractical or require that members cease doing what they are accustomed to and do something different.[17] Reinforcing Kaufman's explanation of organizational resistance to change is the theory of escalating commitment to the status quo. Institutional officials, employees, and constituency groups become so emotionally, intellectually, financially, and structurally committed to an ongoing pattern of behavior that they inevitably find themselves buried "knee deep in the big muddy."[18] This resistance to change is intensified when an individual or group perceives itself as personally responsible for an action or outcome so that stubbornness compounds formal commitment and informal lethargy. Furthermore, civil service rules and collective bargaining agreements make it extremely difficult to lay off state employees.

All these factors were present in one form or another and to varying degrees in the closing of Met State. Failure to consider them promised a recipe for disaster. The well-organized state employee unions wielded substantial power, as did the medical clinicians, who saw their authority and professional turf at stake. The full range of contending forces made themselves felt. For the most part, the administrators anticipated the resistance and dealt with it as sensibly and expeditiously as possible. They had to manage a new and demanding organizational change. For them, knowledge of how a mix of headquarters-field and site-based organizations works was essential to achieving their goals. They realized early on that if not handled properly, layoffs and employee bumping rights could prove disastrous. The same was true with regard to the legal implications of the transfer of each client. The whole operation could easily have unraveled if it had become tied up in adversarial litigation and time-consuming court delays.

Sifting through the evidence, one comes away generally impressed with the orderly and efficient manner in which Met State was closed. Although not all the participants and observers would agree with this general conclusion, the fact is that the closure was implemented with considerable success. Critics such as Philip Johnston, who served as secretary of human services under Governor Dukakis, charged that the hospital closings were entirely budget-driven and had nothing to do with mental health care. As he saw it, the plan was the direct result of a coalition of strange political bedfellows, including the budget cutters and anti-hospital ideologues.[19] Other critics complained vociferously that many patients were transferred to facilities that did not provide the "equal or better" settings they had been promised.

As far as the media were concerned, the partisan *Boston Globe* directed the most fire at DMH in general and Commissioner Elias in particular. The agency also took a pounding from other media observers. Mark Leccese, the political editor of the *Boston Tab*, leveled what was perhaps the most searing criticism. In a 1994 article titled "Too Much, Too Fast," he wrote, "The Weld administration has spent three years closing state mental hospitals and farming out services to private contractors. It has cut the number of long-term patients in state mental hospitals nearly in half, and the toll on the mentally ill, especially children, has begun to show."[20] Coupled with this barrage of criticism was the accusation that privatization amounted to union busting and that Weld was hostile toward state employees. These arguments had some merit, yet they were not entirely convincing. However much opinions and perceptions varied, few informed observers could quarrel with the key fact that the Met State closing did work. It was a bold stroke well executed.

What follows, then, is a plausible but not definitive reconstruction of the rise and fall of Metropolitan State Hospital, drawn from imperfect documentation and even more imperfect memory. It traces the evolution of the mental health system in Massachusetts in terms of both history and policy. Successive sections characterize the economic and political environment in which the demise of the hospital took place. I treat the clinical, legal, human resources, and labor relations constraints involved, as well as the political and personal agendas that influenced the decision. The last sections of the chapter suggest what lessons we can draw today. But the reader must remember that these conclusions are those of a political scientist, not a mental health professional.

THE POLICY PROCESS AND BUREAUCRATIC SETTING

In elaborating on the key features of the Massachusetts mental health care system, one observes that the bureaucracy is far more a life unto itself than even Max Weber imagined. In policy and organizational terms, it clearly qualifies as a complex system. The state is the sole mental health authority, for there is no local or county mental health control as exists in other states. Over time, the Department of Mental Health has evolved into an agency that sets policy and oversees program development. The central actors in DMH policymaking—politicians, administrators, and medical experts— provide most of the ideas for most of the strategy in the various phases of the process. The drama also features the involvement of the private sector in what is now known as public-private partnership.

Although the DMH bureaucracy has a life of its own, it no longer operates as an autonomous line agency reporting directly to the governor as it once did. Thus, it has limited agency discretion. The mission of DMH is "to improve the quality of life for adults with serious and persistent mental illness and children with serious mental illness or severe emotional disturbance." The department also assumes responsibility for providing emergency services to adults, children, and adolescents who experience a psychiatric crisis and request assistance.

In April 1971, Governor Francis Sargent reorganized the executive branch of Massachusetts state government, creating a new super-agency known as the Executive Office of Human Services. DMH, which was then responsible for both the mentally retarded and the mentally ill, was placed under its jurisdiction and budgetary control. As a result of this reorganization, the commissioner of mental health reports to the governor through the secretary of human services.

To make things more complicated, mental health advocates, who tend to adopt an adversarial position, began using legal means to challenge the way in which DMH administered its facilities. In 1972 Benjamin Ricci, an activist from Amherst, filed a class-action lawsuit against the department on behalf of a group of clients at the state school for the mentally retarded in Belchertown who were subjected to dreadful living conditions. The case of *Ricci v. Greenblatt* triggered other lawsuits that sought to hold DMH accountable for its alleged neglect and mistreatment of clients. Since the civil rights of the patients were involved, this litigation wound up in federal district court, where it was assigned to federal judge Joseph Tauro. Subsuming all these issues under a consent degree, Tauro ordered certain improvements to be made at these institutions. Subsequently, in 1986, DMH was split into two separate agencies. The legislature created a new Department of Mental Retardation, which necessitated a parallel bureaucracy and parallel funding. After retaining jurisdiction of the case for twenty-one years, Tauro finally disengaged on May 25, 1993.

Operating under this structural fluidity, DMH no longer had exclusive command of its own turf. For example, the Department of Public Health is responsible for treating substance abuse, yet DMH treated many substance abusers. A web of intricate relationships—contracts, interagency agreements, intergovernmental grants—binds public and private agencies together in almost every important endeavor. It is under these policies and programs, which are multiagency, multigovernmental, and both public and private in character, that DMH administrators are frequently required to work with intervening elites. Functioning always under powerful political oversight, these women and men perform the critical role of turning simplistic and often contradictory policies into operational programs that the street-level bureaucracy can carry out.

Since its inception in 1938, the Department of Mental Health has functioned as a headquarters-field organization with its central office located at the state capital in Boston. In 1990 its field operations were divided into seven regions and twenty-four area offices, which were scattered across the state. Later that year, Commissioner Henry Tomes decided to reorganize the department with the intention of giving area directors more power and keeping case managers in area offices.[21] This decision was driven by budgetary and political constraints. To trim expenses in hard times, Tomes put a stop to the leasing of expensive area offices.

As state employees, DMH personnel are part of the permanent civil service, working regular hours in regular places. Their behavior is governed by rules, regulations, and directives formulated at headquarters with the expectation of uniform responses in the field. Field actions, which are routinely reviewed at headquarters, can vary all the way from surreptitious evasion and outright obstructionism to enthusiastically embracing the opportunity to initiate reform. Beset by conflicting demands from the field, central office personnel have been known to distance themselves from area directors and hospital administrators, especially when trouble arises or policy initiatives go awry. This difficult terrain is known as the quicksand of bureaucracy, where the footing is slippery and at times treacherous.

Throughout its sixty-three-year history, Metropolitan State Hospital had operated as a site-specific organization where bureaucrats and clients coexisted with one another. Located off Trapelo Road in Waltham, it was run in 1990 by a chief operating officer and a staff of physicians, nurses, hospital attendants, social workers, security guards, and building managers. As one participant recalls, "Met State was a fiefdom in and of itself; it had its own rules and its own code of conduct."[22] Most of its employees worked in rotating shifts around the clock. The hospital was a highly labor-intensive enterprise that typically allocated about 85 percent of its budget to personnel. As Robert Wood, a noted political scientist, explains:

> These organizations have visible physical structures in which "service-providers" and "service-receivers" live together continually or for a substantial portion of the day. There are aspects of communities here—entire cultures with mores and practices that are indigenous and with attitudes never described in manuals. They bear little resemblance to the offices of motor vehicle, employment, transportation, and economic development agencies. Nine to five is not the order of the day. Site-based organizations simply do not work according to the usual rules.[23]

Making the distinction between public and private hospitals is also useful. Perhaps the most notable example of the latter is McLean Hospital in Belmont. Located one mile from Met State, it is a psychiatric teaching hospital that offers high-quality care but serves a very different client population, a more affluent and less troublesome group than was likely to appear at Metropolitan State. Although McLean provides substantial free care, it mainly admits those who are less disturbed and have the ability to pay. This practice is called creaming. By marked contrast, Met State accepted anyone who needed help regardless of an individual's financial circumstances. Its patients were among the most disturbed and the most vulnerable. Lacking medical insurance, they were unable to pay for care.

That there are similarities and differences between public and private hospitals is hardly surprising, but the inequities are striking. They underscore the fact that there was a two-tier mental health system operating in Massachusetts—one for the rich and upper-middle class and one for the poor and dispossessed.[24]

EVOLUTION OF THE MENTAL HEALTH SYSTEM

It is important to examine how the state mental health system evolved. Historically, of course, Massachusetts has been in the vanguard of caring for the mentally ill, a pioneer in building a series of public asylums that became its trademark. From colonial times until the first quarter of the nineteenth century, the insane had been kept in local jails and county almshouses or with family and friends. Founded in 1830, under the leadership of Horace Mann, the first state mental hospital in America was built in Worcester on a site overlooking Lake Quinsigamond. Opening in 1833 and administered by Samuel Woodward, its influential and well-respected superintendent, this hospital became a model for the rest of the nation to emulate. Originally designed to accommodate 120 patients, Worcester served three basic functions: treatment, custody, and social control. By 1850 it had more than 500 patients.[25]

It is well to remember that during the Jacksonian era the states did most of the governing in America. By contrast, the national government played a smaller role. The tradition of local autonomy, which began in colonial times, was strong in New England, and states' rights sentiment reached its zenith in the Civil War. Not since anti-Federalist days had the fervor of grassroots democracy and states' rights burned more brightly. Other states followed the lead of Massachusetts, and by 1844 eleven of the existing twenty-six states had public asylums.

In 1839 the city of Boston established its own asylum for the insane on 214 acres of prime land in Mattapan. This was a time when Irish immigrants were arriving in Boston in large numbers. Strangers in a new land, mired in abject poverty, and devout in their Catholicism, these urban newcomers confronted a hostile environment. Fear of and antipathy toward Irish Catholics had reached new heights in 1834, when an angry mob of nativists set fire to a convent in Charlestown where Ursuline nuns ran a boarding school for children. The intensity of hatred between Catholics and Protestants continued for generations as they fought over their ethnic and religious differences. The unprecedented flood of emigration from Ireland during the late 1840s and early 1850s shocked nativists as ever more Irish fled their famine-stricken homeland to escape the ravages and devastation of the "great hunger." Almost all these people were descended from families who had clung to their faith through centuries of persecution. Starvation and disease, humiliation, and brutal oppression at the hands of the British scarred their lives.[26] In antebellum Boston the abolitionists, who abhorred slavery, were caught up in their own moral self-righteousness and the glory of their cause. The Irish underclass, with few such defenders, was despised and discriminated against as much as, if not more than, the black underclass.

In 1841, Dorothea Dix uncovered widespread neglect and abuse of the mentally ill in Massachusetts. In East Cambridge and elsewhere, she found them chained in jails and almshouses, locked in cellars, and isolated on farms. Appalled by what she saw, Dix spearheaded a personal crusade for their humane treatment. A social reformer with true grit and determination, she worked tirelessly in their behalf and lobbied the state legislature for expanded facilities and proper institutional care.[27] In Dix's time, psychiatrists and lay reformers believed that insanity was as curable as most other ailments. Confinement, they insisted, was not a punishment but a cure. Given the extent of medical knowledge in 1833, there was little else to be done. All these factors gave rise to the cult of curability.

Over the course of the next century, Massachusetts developed an elaborate network of public asylums. At the outset, state and local governments shared responsibility for mental health. According to historical accounts, state funds were used to pay for the buildings and the superintendent's salary, but much of the financial burden remained at the local level. Counties, towns, and villages paid a per capita fee for their indigent patients, but local officials tended to be parsimonious. Most of the state hospitals were constructed during the second half of the nineteenth century, which was the heyday of the "moral treatment" movement. These lunatic asylums, as they were commonly known, came into operation one at a time, each in response to a distinct need. Overcrowding at Worcester led to the creation of new asylums at Taunton in 1854 and Northampton in 1858. Each served a localized area but accepted patients from other parts of the state.

Upper-class Yankees, who were mostly Whigs and abolitionist Republicans, made up the ruling elite. They sited these hospitals in quiet, rural farming towns where land was cheap, purposely separating them from the community. Such a serene and idyllic environment afforded patients plenty of fresh air and a retreat from the pressures of modern society while improving their physical health and vigor. Here the patients were sealed off from the outside world and wrapped in protective custody. Little thought was given to the stigma that such isolation and social exclusion imposed. Pejorative terms such as "lunatics," "nut houses," "loony bins," and "funny farms" were even more stigmatizing. The general public considered insanity a shameful form of deviance.[28] They viewed victims as social misfits.

Individual hospitals were operated independently by a board of lay trustees appointed by the governor. The psychiatrists complained about lay control, but this made them accountable to the public. The trustees hired superintendents to manage the asylums. Hundreds of employees were needed to staff the wards of these large hospitals and to maintain their physical plants. In many ways these asylums became self-contained communities that contributed to the local economy. Most of the hired staff were native-born white Anglo-Saxon Protestants who lived on the hospital grounds in dormitories built for this purpose. They often managed to get their family members put on the payroll, and before long nepotism became rampant. Social and recreational activities were organized to promote staff morale, and interfaith and Catholic chapels for religious worship were eventually built on each campus.

Much of the hospital land was used for farming. Patients were put to work tending crops and large dairy herds. The revenues earned from the sale of agricultural produce went to defray operating costs. Under the superintendency of Pliny Earle, who was in charge from 1864 to 1885, Northampton had the most efficient patient work program in the country. The hospital was virtually self-supporting. As the historian J. Michael Moore observes:

> The patients were to receive humane and dignified treatment under the watchful eye and direct care of the superintendent, the doctor who attended to every medical and administrative detail of the hospital. Combined with regular physical and intellectual activity and a tightly regulated schedule, this system of "moral treatment" would lead the ill back to health. Both the location and the physical design of the buildings were intended to enhance the therapeutic effect of the hospital.[29]

During the late nineteenth century, Massachusetts changed from a largely rural and agricultural to a largely urban and industrial state. Its society was different in the Gilded Age, more diverse in its demographic pluralism and more demanding in the workplace. Up to that time most emigrants had come from the British Isles, France, Germany, and the Scandinavian countries, but now the diversity of immigration began to increase dramatically. By the 1890s, the majority of immigrants were coming from southern and eastern Europe, from Italy, Hungary, Greece, and the Balkan countries, as well as Poland, Lithuania, and Russia. They were recruited as a source of cheap labor to work in the state's textile mills, leather tanneries, and shoe factories. Their assimilation into the larger society was slow and painful. In the meantime, the downtrodden Irish, who often suffered depression, anxiety, and distress, had filled the asylums. The historian David Mechanic describes their plight in language worthy of lengthy quotation:

> The general contempt of Massachusetts society for the Irish immigrants, who constituted a growing proportion of the insane, led to increasing pressures on the mental hospital to take on many new patients. With the growing number of patients—the mass of them held in low esteem by the community as well as by mental hospital personnel—it was impossible to maintain the administrative and environmental attitudes necessary for moral treatment. Moreover, with a growing number of patients and limited resources, it was necessary to develop more efficient custodial attitudes and procedures. The contempt in which the hospital held its clients and the low social value accorded them by the society at large neither stimulated hospital administrators to demand greater resources to care for their patients nor encouraged the community to provide further and more intensive support.[30]

The incidence of mental illness was on the rise in part because, insanity was defined loosely enough to permit egregious abuses. The wording of the law was so vague that it could be applied to persons whose real problems were poverty, homelessness, and physical disability. Under such conditions, unprecedented numbers of people were declared insane and confined to mental hospitals. The sheer magnitude of the problem resulted in overcrowded and understaffed asylums. Madness was increasing at a much faster rate than society's ability to cope with it.

Party politics and patronage also influenced the growth and expansion of asylums. Like other social control institutions, such as prisons and reformatories, public asylums were viewed as lucrative sources of jobs and contracts that party politicians could bestow as a reward on their loyal supporters. Steeped in this political culture, Massachusetts built several hospitals during the post–Civil War era. A palatial asylum designed and built on a grand scale was erected in Danvers on a hill overlooking the countryside. This facility was completed in 1878 at a cost of more than $1.5 million, an expenditure deemed extravagant at the time. Before the end of the century three other asylums appeared—at Westborough in 1886, Foxborough in 1893, and Medfield in 1896. These institutions made new spaces available and gave local officials a good excuse to redefine their senile poor as insane and shift the financial burden to the state.[31]

There were then 219 almshouses in Massachusetts, which were populated by the homeless poor, the disabled, drunkards, vagrants, and common criminals, many of whom were immigrants. As reformers succeeded in closing these institutions, state asylums were forced to absorb increasing

numbers of the aged poor. Almshouses at Bridgewater, Monson, and Tewksbury, established in the early 1850s, were converted into public asylums for
the mentally ill and mentally retarded. Bridgewater became a prison hospital
for the criminally insane. Operated as a maximum-security prison, it now
falls under the jurisdiction of the Department of Corrections.

These public asylums were overseen and inspected at least twice a year
by a state Board of Health, Lunacy, and Charity, which was created in 1879.
This agency was replaced in 1886 by the state Board of Lunacy and Charity,
which in turn was replaced by the state Board of Insanity in 1898. Many
reformers, who favored centralized administration of asylums, argued that
they were vulnerable to patronage. Despite this concern, the asylums jeal-
ously guarded their local autonomy and enlisted important political support
whenever a governor or a state agency threatened to tighten central control.
Whenever a serious threat to their independence arose, local officials could
be expected to voice strong objections. With the Republicans securely in
control of state politics, the asylum system increasingly served as a patronage vehicle for their party.

Expansion of the public asylums took place in close correlation with the
rise of the Progressive movement. Since the medical profession claimed
responsibility for treating insanity, citizen influence was only peripheral to
the closed world of the asylum. To be sure, the doctors exercised absolute
control, and the public came to accept a medical explanation of madness.
Sociologist John Sutton argues that "late nineteenth-century policies toward
the insane and the poor were premised on an ideology that portrayed social
problems as fundamentally individual and moral in origin. Throughout the
Progressive era, the imagery of Protestant moralism that underlay this
ideology gradually gave way to a medical model of deviance, but the basic
discourse of individualism remained intact."[32]

Given the state's expansion mode, another public asylum appeared at
Gardner in 1901. Three years later the state assumed full financial responsibility for care of the insane. As a result of this takeover, Massachusetts
entered into negotiations with the city of Boston and purchased its municipal asylum in 1908 for the sum of $1 million. Seven years later, in 1915, yet
another asylum appeared, this one at Grafton, at a time when the nation
was witnessing the emergence of the mental hygiene movement. Its proponents argued that mental illness could be eradicated through education
in human relationships, but the millennium failed to arrive. In due course,
moral treatment was replaced by a focus on the incurability of psychiatric
disorders and the somatic basis of mental disease.

Research was a luxury that most mental institutions could not afford.
The Boston Psychopathic Hospital was an exception. Established in 1912 as
the research arm of Boston State Hospital, it sought to develop new medical

approaches for combating mental illness. As a result, Boston soon became the mecca for psychiatry in America. While Boston State served the "incurable" of the day, the experimental Boston Psychopathic Hospital attempted to accommodate "incipient, acute, and curable insanity." This teaching and research center was renamed the Massachusetts Mental Health Center in 1956. On a smaller scale, a pathology laboratory was established at Westborough. It operated under the direction of Solomon Carter Fuller, a distinguished black neuropsychiatrist who conducted research on the biological influences of mental health.

Meanwhile, Massachusetts, like the rest of the country, had swung from the conservatism of Grover Cleveland and William McKinley to the progressivism of Theodore Roosevelt and Woodrow Wilson, and then, in the 1920s, back to the conservatism of Calvin Coolidge and Herbert Hoover. At this time Metropolitan State appeared at Waltham, the last asylum to be founded. It was the biggest and most modern hospital in Massachusetts. Collectively, the thirteen state institutions functioned as an extended system that proved beneficial to all of the state's 351 cities and towns.[33]

As the years went on, the state mental hospitals gradually fell into a long decline, victims of circumstances largely beyond their control. They had deteriorated during the Great Depression and World War II. Incremental decisions were being made which, in the long run, would have serious negative consequences. Eventually the system would break down, but long before reaching the point of collapse it found ways to correct itself. Operating on tight budgets, the hospitals struggled with fiscal problems, staff reductions, low morale, and the departure of clinicians. Continual turnover and staff burnout became a perennial problem. Party politics and patronage also contributed to the decline. While the Republicans continued to dominate state politics during the first half of the twentieth century, the construction and maintenance of asylums channeled state and local patronage to loyalists of both major parties. The reporter John A. Farrell paints this picture:

> There were riding stables, cocktail parties and other luxuries for administrators, while the wards were left in filthy disrepair. Services given to patients by the "Mental Disease Department," as it was known, were sapped by graft. In 1938, Commissioner David L. Williams had been assaulted on his own front steps, and his skull fractured, when he declined to steer contracts to a politically well connected food supplier who had been suspended for chiseling the system.[34]

Through the New Deal, the Fair Deal, and the Eisenhower administration, the public asylums became more custodial than therapeutic, mere dumping grounds for those afflicted with alcoholism, epilepsy, or senility and other chronic geriatric illnesses. Admitted and left to be forgotten, these people were consigned to living and dying in these institutions. As was true in other states, the asylums had become human storage bins. Treatment was abusive, uncaring, and unresponsive. In 1946, Mary Jane Ward wrote a graphic personal account of her incarceration in a state hospital. Her best-selling book, *The Snake Pit*, was made into a movie in 1948. That same year, the pioneering psychiatrist Erich Lindemann set up the first community mental health center America, the Human Relations Service, in Wellesley.

The demanding nature of care for the mentally ill has always taken a toll among those who provide it, for their jobs are filled with stress and tension. They are constantly exposed to physical danger and assaults by violent patients. Says one observer:

> The state hospital was a hard place to work. Hospital workers provided care to many of the neediest members of society; people who often could get help nowhere else. They provided this care at a hospital that was constantly under-funded and over-crowded, as part of a system which often thwarted their best intentions. They endured the stigma that haunts the mentally ill in our society. Most of these employees were good and caring people who tried hard to help their patients.[35]

Although reformers persisted in their efforts to achieve more centralized administration and greater control of the state hospitals, inevitably the bureaucracy continued to evolve. In sparse outline, it passed through successive stages of evolution that witnessed the creation of a Commission of Mental Diseases in 1916, a Department of Mental Disease in 1919, and finally a Department of Mental Health in 1938.[36] DMH's initial emphasis was constricted. It stressed the overriding importance of state hospitals and the molding of people to fit the system rather than the search for alternatives. With the outbreak of World War II and the staffing shortages that resulted from emergency wartime mobilization, the major emphasis was placed on occupational rehabilitation. Psychiatrists in America played an important role in screening military recruits and in treating soldiers who broke down mentally under the prolonged stress of combat. After the war, the establishment of the National Institute of Mental Health in 1948 was a watershed event legitimating a new federal role in mental health.

In 1949 Governor Paul Dever and Massachusetts House Speaker Thomas P. O'Neill received a sixty-page report from Commissioner Clifton Perkins, who warned them of a long-simmering crisis at DMH and indicated that it would take $43 million to correct the system's failings. The mental hospitals housed 25 to 40 percent more patients than they were designed to handle, and one in every four jobs in the system was vacant because of poor pay and working conditions. Speaker O'Neill's interest in the state's decaying system of mental hospitals was piqued when a constituent with a Down's syndrome child sought his help in getting the child hospitalized. O'Neill drove the child to the state hospital in Belmont and was turned away; the waiting list already had 3,600 names on it. So he simply walked out—leaving the child in the waiting room—and then called from a telephone down the street to say, "The child is in your hospital. Find a bed."[37]

In response to these conditions, the Democrats pushed through a pay raise for mental health employees and redoubled the state's efforts to fill the vacant positions. Governor Dever asked for $16 million to fund new construction—the highest one-year capital outlay in the state's history—and for a legislative commission to investigate conditions at the hospitals, especially those that served children. A new children's hospital with 1,500 beds was planned for Taunton.[38]

Despite these improvements, the old pressures returned to haunt the 1950s agenda. Staff shortages continued to be a major problem. Because better-paying jobs were offered elsewhere, it became increasingly difficult to recruit and retain a reliable workforce. Replacements, while available, were not always of the highest quality; many were untrained and unqualified. Psychiatrists entered private practice to earn more money and shunned work at state hospitals. Foreign physicians were hired to take their place. New pressures reinforced the old ones. Client admissions were again skyrocketing. Staff shortages meant that patients received mostly custodial care and very little treatment or therapy. The system reached its peak capacity in 1953 with a combined census of 23,560 patients. At this point the hospitals were in danger of being overwhelmed and imperiled by overcrowding. Influential reformers became increasingly disenchanted with the characteristically custodial institutions. In short, the hospitals had become part of the problem rather than part of the solution.

In February 1955, Congress commissioned a study of the human and economic problems that emotionally disabled people faced and agreed to fund demonstration projects that sought to improve services. The Joint Commission on Mental Illness and Health, a nonprofit corporation, conducted this study. Jack Ewalt, then commissioner of mental health in Massachusetts, served as its executive director. The report, *Action for Mental Health*, published in 1961, drew from the experiences at Worcester State Hospital with regard to patient reduction and outpatient and aftercare services. It called for creating community mental health centers and reducing the size of state hospitals to no more than one thousand beds. These new ideas were promoted by President John F. Kennedy, whose legislative initiative was enacted by Congress as the Community Mental Health Centers

Act of 1963. Signing this statute shortly before his assassination. Kennedy declared that the time had come for a bold new approach. Local services locally administered: this was to be the bold new approach. The hope was that the large state hospitals would become a thing of the past. In 1964, Massachusetts produced its own report, "Strategies of Mental Health Change," which reiterated the theme that local care was the wave of the future. That goal was the central thrust of the ensuing law.

THE SYSTEM DISASSEMBLES

In 1966, when Republican John Volpe was governor, the state legislature passed the Comprehensive Mental Health and Retardation Act. This land-mark legislation, Chapter 735, and subsequent programs stemmed from the idea of creating community mental health centers. Venturing into this do-main was a pioneering endeavor, for there were virtually no residential care or psychiatric day treatment programs available in Massachusetts. Central to this legislation was the concept of a service area, a designated geograph-ical locale in which clients would receive coordinated services from various agencies. Chapter 735 divided the state into seven regions and forty area offices, each with its own citizens' advisory board. Citizen participation through a monitoring role was a major breakthrough of this venture, anal-ogous to the Great Society programs that called citizen involvement.

In 1967, Governor Volpe appointed Milton Greenblatt, a man with im-peccable credentials that satisfied demands for both professional achieve-ment and administrative experience, as commissioner of mental health. A graduate of Harvard Medical School, Greenblatt had previously served as assistant director of the Massachusetts Mental Health Center and as super-intendent of Boston State Hospital. The task of implementing the new statute and setting up citizen area boards fell to him. Soon to follow was the "unitization" of all state hospitals, a policy designed to give area direc-tors clinical and administrative control of inpatient units. Unitization as-signed patients to hospital wards by their community of residence. A shaky and unpredictable process, it at least linked inpatient care to a fledgling community-based service system.[39]

Almost simultaneously, the deinstitutionalization movement forced itself on the nation's agenda and captured public attention. This crusade launched a stinging counterattack on the efficacy of state hospitalization, which soon became a rallying cry for mental health champions across the country in the late 1960s and throughout the 1970s. This reform, fueled by federal money, was designed to place patients in community residences and halfway houses as an alternative to warehousing them in large custodial institutions.

For at least a generation or two, the pressure to deinstitutionalize increased in almost all the states in the nation, but the pace was agonizingly slow in some of them.[40] If there was a social laboratory in which to test this reform, it was Massachusetts, for nowhere else was it advanced so vigorously.

In 1969, Lieutenant Governor Francis Sargent was thrust into the governor's office when Volpe left to accept the cabinet post of secretary of transportation in the Nixon administration. After Sargent was elected to a full term as governor in 1970, his attention fell on reorganizing the executive branch, creating "super"-agencies, and controlling the bureaucracy by political appointments that reached far down into the middle ranks of departments and agencies. He named Peter Goldmark as the first secretary of human services. One of Goldmark's objectives, shared by Sargent, was to move as many people as possible out of the large human service institutions and into smaller community facilities. Goldmark's strategy relied on forcing bureaucratic agencies to act by applying pressure from constituency groups at the grassroots level.

While this was going on, the state legislature amended Chapter 123 in 1970 to clarify hospital admissions and commitment policies. The law's provisions were changed to protect the civil liberties of mental patients and to prevent abuses in admissions and undue incarceration. No longer could people be committed for mere vagrancy. Only those who were deemed a danger to themselves and others could be locked up involuntarily.

Whatever its merits, the Goldmark strategy of citizen participation ran directly counter to Greenblatt's philosophy of keeping the physicians on top. Perceived as a doctor's doctor, Greenblatt did not attempt to close any state hospitals. Reluctant to adapt to shifting policies, he wished to maintain the status quo. Not surprisingly, the hospital superintendents, all psychiatrists, loved him, but this affection was not shared universally. Greenblatt came under fire from a citizens' task force on "children out of school" after stonewalling their efforts to monitor the implementation of Chapter 750, a law that called for the delivery of mental health and educational services to emotionally disturbed youngsters unable to function in a traditional public school. The children's task force was led by Hubie Jones, a black social worker and community activist who engaged the task force in public advocacy and confrontational politics.

After a series of disagreements on programs and policies and a steady drumbeat of criticism from citizen area boards and other constituency groups, Greenblatt crossed swords with Jones in a clash that became highly visible.[41] The commissioner was also called to task by the so-called Lolas commission, which had investigated the deaths of four mentally retarded clients at the Belchertown State School. Although an internal probe conducted by DMH absolved Greenblatt of any negligence in the matter, the commission, which was headed by State Representative Alexander Lolas of Monson, found him partially responsible and called for his resignation. These events led to his forced departure in December 1972. In *Managing the State*, Martha Weinberg wrote, "Buffeted by a department that was changing rapidly but in no single clear direction, by new constituency groups with which he had few natural ties, and by a superior who wanted to move the department more quickly and in different directions than he did, Greenblatt left his post."[42]

The search for Greenblatt's successor produced a changed atmosphere. Legislation was passed making the commissioner's appointment coterminous with the governor's incumbency, a move that was intended to ensure greater accountability. To quote Weinberg again, "pressure was also building to have a commissioner whose primary experience and training had been administrative and political rather than medical; and in the spring of 1973, as the search was being conducted, the General Court abolished the requirement that the commissioner be a board-certified psychiatrist."[43]

After a six-month search, Governor Sargent appointed William Goldman, a San Francisco psychiatrist, as commissioner of mental health. Sargent had heard Goldman speak at a governors' conference in Colorado and was impressed by him. Although Goldman had attended medical school in Boston, he had spent most of his career in California, where he had been director of a community mental health center and a leader in the national movement to establish more such facilities. Goldman, realizing that Massachusetts lagged far behind other states in obtaining its share of federal funds, brought with him fellow Californian Edward Sarsfield, who was put in charge of federal relations. The experienced Sarsfield knew which kinds of programs qualified for federal assistance.

Ambitious, energetic, and often abrasive, Goldman was an extraordinary agent for social change and accordingly his actions deeply affected DMH. He set a new tone as well as a new direction for the department by allowing the citizen area boards to participate in the budget process and by refusing to curry favor with the medical establishment, which was viewed as a sacred cow. The direct opposite of Greenblatt, he saw doctors as stubborn resisters of change and impediments to new policies. Goldman infuriated them by refusing to fund psychiatric residencies at many university-affiliated hospitals and clinics; he also prohibited psychiatrists who were on the state payroll from working more than half-time in private practice.[44]

A complex and controversial personality, Goldman knew where he wanted to go and didn't mind running roughshod over people in order to get there. In an interview he candidly revealed his style and strategy as a public person:

What this department needs is unambiguous authority. Nobody knew what the hell they were supposed to be doing. I can't promise that I have the right answers, but at least I could give some leadership to people who didn't know where to turn. I wanted to establish that the citizens were going to have some control over the department and that there was nothing sacrosanct about the medical community. I don't go in for the consensus mentality, which has dominated this department for years. It's fine if you don't intend to do anything, but by pursuing a consensus you lose years. It's better to let everybody know where you stand and to shove yourself and the department out onto the firing line. Everybody here is desperate to have somebody to follow. That's the only way to manage this department—by leading it.[45]

Goldman was the original architect of the plan for closing hospitals, and under his leadership DMH began disassembling the system. Of the eleven state hospitals still in operation, three were closed within a span of three years. In 1973 Grafton was the first to be shut down, in 1974 Gardner was closed, and in 1975 Foxborough followed suit. These were the so-called snake pits, but they were hardly the worst.[46] Most of their clients were transferred to other state hospitals. No money was saved in closing Grafton, but the state did manage to save $5 million in closing Gardner. These savings were immediately put into community programs, which was no small accomplishment. The first round of hospital closings broke new ground and paved the way for subsequent closures.

As a result of these events and initiatives, the Massachusetts inpatient population declined steadily. Between 1960 and 1972, the combined census was dramatically reduced from 23,000 to 9,800 patients. At the end of 1975, 4,876 people were in state mental hospitals. Dependency on these institutions had become the lowest of any eastern state. Hospitals continued to empty their wards throughout the 1970s and early 1980s, the total figure was reduced to 2,950 by 1984, 23 percent of what it had been in 1955. New psychotropic drugs and the infusion of federal Medicare and Medicaid funds spurred this large-scale reduction. For instance, Medicaid picking up the cost, the state made a policy decision in 1990 to launch trials of the new drug clozapine, which DMH wanted to make available to more patients. The advent of clozapine was expected to have a significant impact on the management of serious mental illness, and it was hoped that it would help to reduce the future need for long inpatient stays. Many of those discharged during this period were elderly patients who were placed in nursing and rest homes. Times had changed, and federal intervention was critical. This reform set the stage for the events that followed.

DRAGGING RECALCITRANT INSTITUTIONS INTO COURT

Michael Dukakis was first elected governor in November 1974. After a divisive campaign and an upset victory over incumbent Francis Sargent, he set out to appoint men and women of substance and ideas to his administration. During the campaign Dukakis had attacked Sargent for mishandling the Russell Daniels case. A former patient at Belchertown, Daniels had been convicted and sent to prison for murdering an eighty-three-year-old woman. Advocates argued that his confession had been coerced and signed without legal counsel. In another campaign issue, the Massachusetts Psychiatric Association had endorsed Dukakis on the condition that Commissioner Goldman be let go. This was the context in which the governor entered office and found a sizable fiscal deficit awaiting him. When he appointed Lucy Benson as secretary of human services, she refused to meet with Goldman, a Sargent holdover, who had put together a package of new ideas for her. Soon afterward Goldman was fired, in part for referring publicly to Dukakis's policies as neo-Nazi.

Lee Macht, who had been director of a community mental health center in Cambridge, was brought in to replace Goldman for a brief stint as interim commissioner. Picking up where Goldman had left off, Macht oversaw the closing of Foxborough State hospital, which was accomplished in an orderly and well-structured manner. Robert Kaplan, the regional administrator, was able to reach an agreement with the public employee unions which made jobs available to their members at state institutions within twenty-five miles of Foxborough. This agreement went a long way toward ensuring union cooperation.

In 1975 Massachusetts had the second-highest unemployment rate in the country and the largest state deficit. Confronted with the problems of urban minority populations and challenged by well-organized state employee unions, liberal-minded public officials had responded to their demands at a level that tax revenues could not support. Many people feared that Massachusetts was becoming a welfare magnet. Social demographics were changing rapidly as the newest urban immigrants arrived in the state—blacks, Hispanics, and Asians who had come to the Bay State seeking the same economic opportunities that had attracted the struggling European immigrants two or three generations earlier.

As people of color, they met with racism and bigotry, but their demands for accommodation were more far-reaching and more costly than the European immigrants' had been. Marching under the banner of civil rights and affirmative action, they demanded affordable housing, better jobs, and integrated schools. After nearly a decade of political and legal battles, reflecting more than a century of stored-up fears and antagonisms, desegregation came to the Boston public schools. The tensions brought to the surface by court-ordered busing exploded into the ugliest racial violence in September 1974.

Brought up short by the large deficit and inflation, Dukakis made deep budget cuts and reduced spending on welfare entitlements and social services. He applied a "meat cleaver" to bring the budget under control. State spending for public higher education was greatly reduced. Although economic factors prompted this action, it had political repercussions. To the extent that minorities represented a growing political force, first in urban and then in state politics, they created a countervailing response to Dukakis's effort to reduce spending. Political responsiveness to group pressures remained the norm, but the traditional sources of patronage had not disappeared.

Cross-pressured, the governor incurred the wrath of prominent liberal Democrats and a coalition of human service groups, who were clearly estranged. The chasm between them became wide and deep. For purposes of Dukakis's first term, their political support was critical, but it was strained to the breaking point. State Representative Barney Frank, a liberal Democrat, openly attacked the governor as a "perfect political ingrate." To add to Dukakis's fiscal woes, the energy crisis and the Arab oil embargo set off a new scramble for scarce public resources, while the previously secure world of state administrators was invaded by the third branch of government, the judiciary. The threat to mental health programs across the state was real.

Advocates began to stir up trouble. Seeking to advance the rights of mental patients and to disclose widespread deficiencies, they used the legal system to bring the Department of Mental Health to the bar of justice. A new breed of lawyers, spawned during the civil rights movement and the halcyon days of the Great Society, fashioned complicated remedies intruding on the most detailed practices of state administrators. The filmmaker Frederick Wiseman produced the 1967 documentary *Titicut Follies*, which revealed the horrible conditions at Bridgewater State Hospital and sent shock waves throughout Massachusetts. Initially sealed by the courts, it was subsequently released, but only after advocates began court proceedings to allow it to be shown to the general public. Even so, the state Supreme Judicial Court limited the viewing audience and conditions under which it could be screened.[47]

Activists continued to disclose that the Massachusetts mental health system was fraught with abuses, neglect, filthy and unsafe conditions, and mismanagement on a systemwide scale. Slapped with a class-action lawsuit in 1976, officials at Northampton State Hospital were hauled into court. In the famous case *Brewster v. Dukakis*, the plaintiffs charged that they had a legal right to psychiatric treatment in a less restrictive setting than a state hospital and that the state had an obligation to provide such a treatment setting. A similar fate befell the schools for the mentally retarded at Belchertown, Fernald in Waltham, and Monson, which allowed their clients to live in squalor. These recalcitrant institutions had to be dragged into court before they would do anything to improve the despicable conditions that prevailed. The consent decree was the preferred instrument of judicial intervention. In effect, the courts became the administrators. The world of mental health practice was becoming more complex.

After Foxborough was closed, Lee Macht stepped down as commissioner. Dukakis replaced him with Robert Okin, who was strongly committed to community mental health services. Only thirty-three years old, Okin had served as commissioner in Vermont from 1973 to 1975. Prior to that, he had been a consultant to the Boston regional office of the National Institute of Mental Health. Okin was a dedicated, hardworking, and driven administrator who recognized that the care of psychiatric patients needed to be further brought into the mainstream. Psychiatry was still outside the realm of medicine. Realizing that the system was broken, Okin declared that his goal was to close all the state hospitals and single-mindedly went about creating such change. No one tested the limits of deinstitutionalization more than he did. What Okin understood well but did not acknowledge was that the cities and towns were ill prepared to receive such a massive influx.

A commissioner with a compelling vision, Okin foresaw the day when mental illness would be treated not within state hospitals but at private general hospitals. In this respect he was a true visionary and a forerunner to privatization. For the time being, however, Okin insisted that community services take precedence over everything else. As he told one colleague, "I would rather see mental patients eating out of garbage cans in the streets than to see them endure the miserable conditions on the back wards."[48] Believing that the systemic problems could not be fixed until the hospital functions were located elsewhere in the mental health delivery system, he was adamant that state employees not be allowed to move into community settings or private group homes. The commissioner felt that they were trapped in the same institutional mind-set as the patients.

As a zealous reformer obsessed with his vision, Okin pushed vigorously to advance the cause, putting intense pressure on regional administrators to scale down the hospitals. Caught in the middle, they were viewed as the enemy by both the hospital superintendents and the unions. Here the state missed a rare opportunity. DMH could have reached an agreement with the unions but failed to do so. Union officials were apparently willing to help the state downsize and close its hospitals, provided that their members would be assured jobs in community-based group homes. That proposal was on the table, but the state never acted on it. This intransigence at the bargaining table resulted in an unfortunate standoff.[49]

Metropolitan State Hospital was supposed to be closed in 1978, but that did not happen. The plan was for McLean Hospital to replace Met State in terms of acute and long-term care, but the Public Health Council turned down the plan.[50] Meanwhile, the eight remaining state hospitals continued to decline and decay, becoming little more than holding cages for the acutely and chronically insane. All eight were guilty of flagrant neglect and harm to nearly helpless people. The back wards were filthy and appallingly inhumane. Patients were stripped of their self-esteem and human dignity, the restive and unruly ones forcibly placed in seclusion and mechanical restraints, some forced to take medication against their will. Grim stories about physical and sexual abuse abounded. Hospital attendants often mentally abused patients by threatening to send them to Bridgewater, a state hospital for the criminally insane, if they acted up or otherwise caused trouble. Since the law called for strict security, this kind of intimidation and cruelty was no idle threat.

As Dukakis came to the end of his first term in 1978, he was unable to patch up the differences and bitter feelings that had split the Democratic Party into warring factions. Seizing the opportunity to take advantage of dissension in the ranks of the Democrats, Edward King, a conservative Boston Irish Democrat and former director of the Massachusetts Port Authority, challenged Dukakis in a party primary. By appealing to disaffected party members, King scored a stunning upset victory and went on to win the governorship in the general election.

A few weeks later, in December 1978, the state and the plaintiffs, who had been engaged in the *Brewster* case for two years, entered into what became known as the Northampton consent decree. It mandated that "clients were entitled to live in the least restrictive, most normal residential alternatives and to receive appropriate treatment, training, and support suited to their individual needs."[51] This decree buoyed Okin's prospects. Some colleagues suspected Okin of playing a double-agent role in aiding and abetting this litigation. In truth, he supported the consent decree. Governor King reappointed Okin as commissioner on February 5, 1979.

Measured by federal standards, Northampton was not the worst mental hospital. That dubious distinction belonged to Boston State Hospital, which housed 3,600 patients as late as 1964, when it was considered a disaster. The hospital was slated to be closed in 1975. In fact, in 1976 some 100 geriatric patients were transferred to Lemuel Shattuck Public Health Hospital in Jamaica Plain. But this phase-down proved to be politically sensitive and unacceptable to the community, so Okin was forced to back off. He subsequently accelerated the pace of deinstitutionalization. In March 1981 the average daily census at Boston State had dwindled to 147 patients. After 142 years of operation, Gerard O'Connor, its superintendent, closed this venerable institution.

At this juncture Okin left DMH to accept a job as chief of psychiatry at San Francisco General Hospital. By this time he had become too expensive for the King administration, which was not committed to a vision of community services. Among his many talents, Okin had the ability to get the money he needed from the legislature. Upset by the budgetary implications, King no longer wished to keep such an independent commissioner aboard. Okin had obviously worn out his welcome.

On April 7, 1981, King appointed Mark Mills to fill the vacancy. Mills, who had served as chief executive of the Massachusetts Mental Health Center, took the job as a stepping-stone. Before his last position, he had been chief resident in psychiatry at the Veterans Administration Hospital in Palo Alto. He held a law degree from Harvard and a medical degree from Stanford University, an educational background that well equipped him to handle his new job. But during his two-year tenure, few if any significant ideas were transformed into policy. Some colleagues viewed Mills as being too narcissistic to accomplish much of anything. He defended the practice of DMH clinical personnel working part-time in community clinics, although the state Ethics Commission had ruled that such a practice was in violation of the conflict-of-interest laws.[52]

In December 1979, Okin had appointed a blue-ribbon commission to examine the state's mental health services and to project what lay ahead. After seventeen months of studying the vexing problem, this group released its report, "Mental Health Crossroads," in May 1981, a month after Mills had come aboard. Some of the suggestions in the report read like prophecies. Echoing Okin's sentiments, the commission recommended closing all state hospitals, but nothing came of its report—for good reason.[53]

The Department of Mental Health was then engaged in political battles over funding on Beacon Hill. The beleaguered department came under increasing attack as the largest and most poorly managed state agency. Mills publicly acknowledged in 1981 that no one knew exactly how many employees the department had on its payroll. Management weaknesses were glaring. As a complacent bureaucracy, DMH lacked standards of accountability as well as standards for ensuring quality care. There were few if any incentives for personnel to perform well. The department suffered from poor staff recruitment and training as well as the inability to transform new ideas into workable programs. Along with this complacency came an unwillingness to admit mistakes and take corrective action. All these signs were indicative of a public agency that had lost its sense of mission, confused its priorities, and forgotten the public it was supposed to serve.

Clearly, DMH was an agency in continual disarray and turmoil. Its administrators were taking a beating not only from legislators but also from advocates and unions, which became obstreperous and obstructive. DMH was beset on all sides. Proposition 2½, which limited local taxation, was causing problems in public finance at the municipal level. The politicians on Beacon Hill were taking public money away from state agencies in order to finance local aid. Between 1981 and 1982, DMH lost 1,200 positions. During the remainder of the King administration, the agency behaved in self-serving and self-protective ways. Hunkering down in a siege mentality, it stonewalled not only advocates but also compliance with court-ordered consent decrees.

Amid this turbulence, employees at several state hospitals went out on strike in 1982 to protest their low pay and poor working conditions. Faced with a crisis, Governor King mobilized the National Guard and sent in state troops to run the hospitals. In the fall of 1982, King turned out to be a one term governor as Dukakis defeated him in a much-heralded intraparty rematch and recaptured the governorship.

WHAT WENT WRONG?

Anticipating the consequences of any policy is always difficult at best. New ideas are not easily translated into policy, and policymakers usually land in trouble if they do not identify correctly the attributes of a problem and the options for its resolution. In essence this is what happened in Massachusetts. Moreover, the reformers seriously underestimated the economic and political power needed to close hospitals such as Northampton and Boston State, which were an important source of jobs for the local community.[54]

I will not detail the horrors of what one finds inside the walls of a state hospital, but suffice it to say that it is not a pretty picture. Only those who have endured such experiences or observed what goes on can describe the reality of such an institution. The cruel and sadistic treatment that was typical is vividly portrayed in Ken Kesey's novel *One Flew Over the Cuckoo's Nest* and the movie based on it. Unitization was supposed to have corrected these abuses, but they still persisted. Despite the similarity of all mental hospital experiences in their broadest outlines, each has its own daily agonies and occasional small triumphs.

Displeasure with the mental health system was widespread at the end of the 1970s. The recurring public outcry for better treatment grew louder and more persistent. Administrators such as Rae O'Leary, who had spent most of her career in state hospitals, were thrust into crisis management. O'Leary's experience was typical of many who ended up frustrated and angry. O'Leary expressed her anger when she said, "Conditions were so horrible in these hellholes that they should have been blown up."[55] Barbara Hoffman, who began her career as a hospital attendant at Met State in 1956, was somewhat more philosophical. Interviewed by Okin for the job of regional administrator in 1978, she told him, "I hope to see daisies growing on the hill were Met State stood."[56] By the time she ended her career in 1986, Hoffman had seen eleven commissioners come and go, but Met State remained standing. The average tenure for a state mental health commissioner nationwide was eighteen months.

After years of neglect at Danvers State Hospital, the aging infrastructure was crumbling. Although most of its older buildings had been condemned and were no longer in use, the hospital stood, in the words of one journalist, as "a monument to society's neglect of the mentally ill."[57] Much the same could be said for the other state hospitals. Collectively they symbolized the politics of evasion and the decaying status quo. To record the substantial decline of these institutions is not to suggest that they had outlived their usefulness. As ragged as it was, the existing system was better than nothing. At rock bottom, the state hospitals provided support of last resort for the indigent mentally ill. There was no place else for them to go. This conundrum, which lay at the heart of the policy paradox, explains in large measure why Dukakis was reluctant to close them.

Deinstitutionalization may have been a sound concept, but it was a policy almost bound to backfire, for the consequences of its implementation on community life were not anticipated. Because of poor planning and inadequate funding, the Department of Mental Health lacked the necessary resources to handle a wholesale discharge of patients. It faced the classic dilemma of need versus capability. As a consequence, the policy was implemented untested and irresponsibly. Most patients were simply dumped into the streets, where they roamed aimlessly, hungry and ragged, and slipped through the cracks in the system. Without the necessary community infrastructure, the reform was doomed to failure. Little wonder that the policy resulted in chaos and ambiguity.

Left to fend for themselves, the ex-patients were too disoriented and too confused to make their way through the maze of public bureaucracies to get the help they needed. For the most part they tended to cluster in urban centers, where, in Massachusetts, an estimated 1,500 to 3,600 mentally ill persons—no one knew the exact figure—ended up homeless. Some found temporary lodging in jails, in general hospital emergency rooms, and in rundown tenements and shabby rooming houses. Other slept in store entrances or in homeless shelters such as the Pine Street Inn in Boston. Still others wound up back in the revolving door of the state hospital system. Under these circumstances, the end result was bound to be disappointing. To this day Robert Okin believes that deinstitutionalization did not fail. On the contrary, he contends that it was never given a real chance to succeed. Okin's argument may find favor in academic circles, but not in government.[58]

Some programs survived to prove themselves in the 1980s. The Reagan administration used block grants mainly to combat drug abuse. The federal government continued to provide planning grants to states for community mental health services but virtually abandoned direct funding of services. By 1983 there were only ten community mental health centers operating in all of Massachusetts. Most areas of the state had psychiatric day and residential programs, but these were always filled to capacity with waiting lists for admission. Community opposition was a major obstacle to assisted housing and residential services. Local residents, anxious about their property values, recognized the problems of the mentally impaired but insisted that the solution should lie somewhere else, not in their neighborhoods. These frequently voiced protests became known as the NIMBY—"not in my backyard"—syndrome. By default, DMH left it to the homeless shelters to provide for those who resisted conventional treatment and wandered the streets. Some general hospitals had psychiatric units, but only voluntary patients were admitted.

ONCE MORE UNTO THE BREACH

At the beginning of his second term as governor, Michael Dukakis appointed Manuel Carballo as human services secretary. Severely criticized in his first term for not appointing people who had campaigned for him, Dukakis was not about to repeat that mistake. Carballo, who had unimpeded access to the governor, started searching for a replacement for Mark Mills. Both he and Dukakis wanted a manager. In February 1983, Carballo told the press, "We need someone able to manage an agency that has lost a sense of direction and has been subject to a great deal of criticism."[59] Seven people, not one of whom was a physician, were under consideration for the position. As Miles Shore, a psychiatrist at the Massachusetts Mental Health Center, wryly observed, "The commissioner should have real experience in public administration to rebuild the department. To have someone identified with program development would send the wrong message for these times."[60]

Five months later Dukakis decided that James Callahan met the requirements and appointed him to the post in May 1983. Callahan, the first nonpsychiatrist to hold the position, was a capable and experienced administrator. He had previously managed two public health facilities, Lemuel Shattuck Hospital in Jamaica Plain and the Massachusetts Hospital School in Canton, and served as secretary of elder affairs in the first Dukakis administration. The governor, along with his top aides, distrusted the Department of Mental Health as an inept and clumsy bureaucracy, considering it weak and ineffectual. He suggested that Callahan might want to clean house. On November 10, 1983, in an effort to shake up the agency, Callahan fired three assistant commissioners and seven regional administrators. This famous incident, involving four women and six men, became known as "bloody Thursday." Robert Porter, the chief operating officer, gave the dismissal order, which no one had anticipated, for it was shrouded in utmost secrecy in a department known for its leaks. Callahan could now start with a fresh slate.[61]

Insiders felt that the ten administrators had been unfairly scapegoated. They saw their firings as a ploy to divert public attention from the strains on the system, when in fact, after a decade of huge expenditures, the Dukakis regime was refusing to pour any more money into deinstitutionalization.[62] Ironically, two of those dismissed went on to become mental health commissioners in other states. Danna Mauch, who had served as assistant commissioner from 1981 to 1983, became commissioner in Rhode Island, while Michael Hogan, following a similar route, became commissioner first in Connecticut and subsequently in Ohio.

A few weeks after this incident, the state Supreme Judicial Court ruled in *Rogers v. Okin* that patients committed to mental hospitals have a fundamental right to refuse treatment with mind-altering drugs, or if not mentally competent to speak for themselves, to have a judge make that decision for them. The case had been brought on behalf of Ruby Rogers and six other patients at Boston State Hospital. Originally filed in 1975, it was a landmark battle that had gone all the way from the federal district court in Boston to the First Circuit Court of Appeals and then to the U.S. Supreme Court, where it was remanded for state adjudication.

Justice Ruth Abrams, who wrote the unanimous decision for the state high court, declared, "The doctors who are attempting to treat as well as maintain order in the hospital have interests in conflict with those of their patients who may wish to avoid medication."[63] Psychiatrists attacked the decision as an unwarranted intrusion by the courts into medical decision-making which would render access to treatment more difficult for the most seriously ill. Advocacy groups were delighted with the court ruling because it gave patients a choice.

Meanwhile, a series of tragic events combined to dramatize the housing problem that ex-patients faced in Massachusetts. In June 1981, Cookie Wilson, a mentally ill woman, died as fire engulfed an abandoned town house in Boston where she was spending the night. Two rooming house fires, one in Worcester on April 19, 1983, and the other in Beverly on July 4, 1984, claimed the lives of fourteen others. These tragedies sparked a legislative investigation and focused media attention on the plight of homeless ex-patients.[64] The ensuing publicity raised the level of public awareness.

So the pressure built within the Dukakis administration, with notable public support and debate, to improve the mental health system. In January 1984, Manuel Carballo died of meningitis at the age of forty-two. Governor Dukakis appointed Philip Johnston to replace him as human services secretary. A liberal and compassionate Democrat, Johnson was a former state legislator who had once worked as a hospital attendant at Northampton. He saw the mental health system as "one big hole that needed to be reformed."[65] Dukakis and Johnston each had a personal stake in the issue, since both their families had been touched by mental illness. Both felt that the policy of deinstitutionalization had gone too far. They saw the possibility of midcourse corrections and changes in Dukakis's second term, but before they could take action, they first had to organize politically.

In August 1985, Edward Murphy was brought over from the Department of Youth Services to replace Commissioner Callahan, who returned to his academic duties at Brandeis University. Murphy, who came from a criminal justice background, had a reputation as a strong manager. Before leaving office, Callahan warned against any move toward reestablishing large hospitals to warehouse people. Consensus on the future direction of mental health, however, was hard to achieve. From Johnston's perspective, a war had been waged for the past twenty years over whether to pour more money into hospitals or to put it into community services. Given the incidence of mental illness, Johnston wanted to know exactly how many state hospital beds would be necessary to solve the problem. The number, in his judgment, had to be defensible. Ultimately he arrived at the figure of 2,150 beds.[66]

Not coincidentally, policy control remained securely in the governor's office. Catherine Dunham, the executive director of the Massachusetts Council of Human Services Providers, was brought in to replace Johnston as Dukakis's human services policy adviser. Having started her career as a teacher in a reform school, she was pro-deinstitutionalization and was highly regarded by service providers. Dunham was expected to build bridges with the provider community. Amid this flurry of activity, media observers failed to note the critical centralization of power signified by these personnel assignments.

By 1985, the Dukakis administration was committed to a specific program of mental health reform. It began with an initiative known as the Mental Health Action Project, which brought together a coalition of human service advocacy groups. A covey of medical experts, departmental specialists, and constituency group leaders served on its steering committee. It was an impressive working group whose thirteen members represented a variety of perspectives and posts. Anita Pyatt, who headed the state Alliance for the

Mentally Ill, took a lead position. She persuaded the steering committee to endorse the idea of using vacant state land for establishing therapeutic communities and assisted housing for the mentally ill. This would enable them to live independently and alleviate the burdens on aging parents faced with having to care for them. After much debate on the efficacy of the programs of the 1970s, a consensus emerged in shaping the policy agenda. The technique yielded a written document as a departure point for subsequent discussions with the governor.[67]

Major improvements were to be made at the seven remaining state hospitals. The goal of DMH was to bring them up to the standards of the Joint Commission on Accreditation of Healthcare Organizations for purposes of approval. Metropolitan, Taunton, Worcester, and Westborough were targeted to become regional specialized care facilities that would provide long-term inpatient and quarter-way residential services for clients with a variety of clinical needs. A battery of suggestions emerged from the meetings of the steering committee. Essentially, its work resulted in three major policy proposals: a capital outlay program, a quadrupling of housing units, and a package of community living and treatment options. The committee submitted its recommendations to the governor in late November 1985.[68]

Dukakis was in western Massachusetts on December 19. He flew by helicopter to Met State, where he delivered his special message, a propitious event in terms of both timing and location. The governor called for a five-year plan designed to renovate and refurbish the existing hospitals and to overhaul the outpatient care system. He saw the problem as one that had been deteriorating for decades and was sure to become worse if ignored. Only a massive infusion of money and new construction would suffice. With a soul-searching review of successes and failures, Dukakis declared:

> We are painfully aware the system of care envisioned in 1966 is not yet fully developed. Many areas of the Commonwealth lack emergency screening and crisis services; housing opportunities for chronically mentally ill persons remain extremely limited; and little support is provided for families caring for mentally ill relatives. Hospital care for those needing acute or long-term psychiatric treatment does not in many cases meet even marginally acceptable standards. We are all well aware of the tragic plight of homeless mentally ill.[69]

Dukakis's speech was typically objective, detached, and measured, clearly the result of long reflection. It boosted the morale of those who labored anonymously in the field of mental health by bestowing on them the public recognition and appreciation that were long overdue. George Segal, the medical director at Met State, who had served on the steering committee, was more than pleased. His reaction was noted in the press: "We are overcrowded and operating at two-thirds of the staff we need. This is the first expression that the work we do is of value there has been in years."[70]

Dukakis was then riding the crest of his power and popularity in Massachusetts. In 1986 he was easily reelected to a third term as governor with an overwhelming majority. He had the best of both worlds. With a prosperous state economy, there was plenty of money to go around and no reason to rock the boat. His presidential ambitions may have made him more accessible to group pressures. In any event, a master plan for each state hospital was developed during 1986, and the first phase of improvements actually began. For instance, the boilers and oil pumps at Met State were replaced. Systemwide improvements were to be completed over the next five to seven years.

But financial and political constraints soon prevented Dukakis from delivering on the recommendations. Three factors doomed his revitalization efforts. First, wrangling over the proposed plan of state representative Angelo Scaccia to redevelop Boston State Hospital hurt badly. Chapter 579, which mandated the process for disposition of surplus property, required the participation of local officials and citizens from the communities in which the vacant land was located. In this case, the citizens' advisory committee got bogged down in petty squabbles and could not overcome its disagreements. Second, legislative inertia caused considerable delay and inaction. Stalled for two years in the General Court, the $340 million capital appropriation was not passed until the spring of 1987. Third, and by far the most crippling blow, the state economy suddenly went from boom to bust.

In 1987, when the state economy was still booming, Dukakis decided to run for president largely on the strength of the "Massachusetts Miracle." During the ill-fated 1988 presidential campaign, George Bush's attacks on Dukakis and his record damaged his reputation as an efficient manger. At the same time, the climate changed as the state's inflated economy began to falter. Tax revenues fell well below projections. Hard-pressed for resources, the state raised taxes and cut services. Johnston was forced to make budget cuts totaling $1 billion and to eliminate five thousand human services positions from a base of thirty thousand jobs. Bowing to reality, the governor abandoned the struggle. As Johnston recalled, "We were barely under way when the bottom dropped out of the Massachusetts economy and our project was stopped dead in its tracks."[71]

Despite his public pronouncements, Dukakis was unable to deliver. But the human services coalition did not attack him as it had done during his first term. This was no time for recriminations. Motivated by a desire to cast himself in a favorable light, Dukakis was eager to maintain a liberal image in his quest for higher office. Disagreements and disappointments were papered over in the interests of party politics. Nevertheless, the truth is that neither the governor nor the family members of patients wanted to close any more hospitals.

Although a cadre of distinguished people was actively involved in the Dukakis administration, ideologues came to the fore in policy matters. In May 1988, at the height of the presidential primaries, the Department of Mental Health joined forces with the state Alliance for the Mentally Ill in promoting an anti-stigma campaign. As its central theme this campaign resisted the idea of isolating mental patients from the mainstream community, an issue on which the governor and the anti-stigma ideologues parted company. The latter feared he was trying to rebuild the institutional settings that had led to the problem in the first place. After the failure of the Mental Health Action Project, the promising coalition of citizens, politicians, administrators, and experts broke apart. The steering committee dissolved, and in the end its impact on mental health policy was negligible.

THE HISTORY OF METROPOLITAN STATE HOSPITAL

Now let us turn to a brief history of Metropolitan State Hospital. In 1927, two years before the Great Depression began, state officials purchased 378 acres of farmland in the western suburbs of Boston. This property, then valued at $68,922, intersected the municipal boundary lines of Belmont, Lexington, and Waltham, which at the time were still quiet farming communities set in a rural New England landscape of rolling hills, woods, and streams. Stone walls that once formed boundaries between farms still stand even today. Under construction from 1927 to 1935, the sprawling hospital complex took eight years to build at a cost of $1.8 million. Some of the work in the later stages was done by the federal Works Progress Administration. At the time, it was considered the most modern mental health facility in America.

Many towns and cities openly resisted the siting of housing for the mentally ill, but Waltham, which had repeatedly demonstrated its support for the hospital and its clients, was an exception. Although local town and hospital relations were relatively good, the three surrounding municipalities hardly communicated with one another. The typically narrow perspective of local governments kept them preoccupied with their own problems and conflicts over zoning and land use issues.

Groundbreaking for the administration building took place on December 27, 1927. Two years later, on December 26, 1929, the first thirty-six patients were transferred from Grafton State Hospital to Met State, whose official opening was celebrated on October 29, 1930. Among the dignitaries on hand for this occasion were acting superintendent Clifford Moore, Governor Frank Allen, and former governor Alvan T. Fuller, two stalwart Republicans.

This was a transition year that marked the end of the old political order and the coming of the New Deal in Massachusetts. Democrat Joseph Buell Ely, a lawyer from the western part of the state, was elected governor in 1930. Though the Republicans still dominated the state legislature, Yankee hegemony was beginning to give way to the Irish political ascendancy, as Democrats such as James Michael Curley and Charles Hurley soon followed Ely into the governor's office.

Met State was a hospital within a hospital, treating patients with both mental health and general health problems. The original group of seventeen buildings that made up Met State included the medical-surgical building with its domed rooftop and six patient living areas, which was not completed until 1935; the cafeteria building where food was prepared and served; the continuous treatment group (CTG) building for patients; and two large employee dormitories. The heating plant, originally fueled by coal, was later converted to oil. An elaborate system of underground tunnels, which ran beneath all these buildings, carried the steam lines, enabling employees to travel from one building to another during inclement weather and to transport food the same way. The Furcolo Building, named for the deceased wife of the sitting governor, was added in 1957. There were two admission wards, one for women and the other for men. Chronic patients were sent to the backwards.

The massive CTG building provided eight wings of patient accommodations connected by a continuous circular corridor. Each wing housed three wards, for a total of twenty-four, which were lettered alphabetically. At the center of the complex was a secure courtyard, used for recreation, whose orientation provided significant advantages to the patients and staff, offering controlled access to all parts of the facility. The individual wings afforded each ward a secure open porch area with a southern exposure for maximum sunlight and fresh air.

This new enterprise got off to a good start. The hospital, designed for a capacity of 1,248 beds, admitted some 1,182 patients in 1931. They were to require a minimum of staff supervision and were expected to participate in work programs such as agriculture, laundry, and hospital industries. Some forty-five acres of land were under cultivation as part of the working farms, which continued to operate until the late 1960s.[72] But by 1932, Met State had already exceeded its capacity with 1,315 patients. In the depression-ridden 1930s, the hospital was partially staffed with working patients from other hospitals. Regular employees, who lived off campus, had to get to and from work on their own, since no direct public transportation was available. Hospital administrators tried for years to obtain some kind of bus service, but to no avail.

Several hospitals were located in the immediate vicinity. Nearby were both the Fernald School for the mentally retarded and Middlesex County Hospital, the latter established in 1930 as a tuberculosis sanatorium. McLean Hospital in Belmont was a short distance down the road. Adjacent to the Met State campus was the Gaebler Children's Center, a sixty-bed facility built in 1952. It accepted referrals of emotionally disturbed children from across the state. Although Gaebler was a separate entity, it shared Met State's laundry, pharmacy, groundskeeping crew, and engineering and electrical staff.

On entering the Met State grounds, one could not help but notice the name of William F. McLaughlin inscribed in bold letters above the white portico of the main administration building. Dr. McLaughlin, who served as its dedicated superintendent from 1952 until 1974, was by all accounts a powerful father figure and a highly respected physician whose entire professional life was wrapped up in Met State. A kind, gentle, and dignified man, McLaughlin lived on the grounds and cared deeply for the people in his charge. Conciliatory by nature, he was not a fighter. He accepted his lot and rarely clamored for more funds or complained but did his job with the resources at hand. He left the day-to-day management of the hospital to his administrative assistant Paul O'Leary. Whatever his shortcomings as a superintendent, he inspired people to accomplish what they otherwise might not have done. Beloved by his staff, he was the last of a vanishing breed of superintendents who attended patients and made their rounds on the hospital wards.

While at the helm, McLaughin succeeded in maintaining the hospital's Joint Commission on Accreditation of Healthcare Organizations (JCAHO) accreditation, which ensured a steady flow of federal funds, but state money gradually diminished, much of it reallocated by the central office to other hospitals. With tight budgets, state funds slowed to a trickle, forcing deferment of physical maintenance. This inevitably produced deteriorating conditions, a long-term difficulty. Personnel, with its high rate of turnover, was always a major problem. According to Jack MacDougall, who served as personnel director from 1971 to 1989, staffing levels had fallen from the normal standard of 1.3 staff for each patient to 0.3 staff per patient during the Dukakis years.[73] Staff shortages necessitated the use of prison inmates form nearby Concord, who were transported to and from the hospital on a work release program, for general duty.

The patient population at Met State reached its peak of 2,200 during McLaughlin's tenure. Although he did not officially retire until September 1978, he had stepped down as superintendent four years earlier. He was followed by a succession of ten administrators with various titles, including Arnold Abrams, Ernest Cook, Barbara Hoffman, Melvin Tapper, Frank Karlon, Katherine Olberg, and Phyllis Oram. Audrey DeLoffi, who took over in December 1985 and was given the new title of chief operating officer, was succeeded by Fernando Durand and Marylou Sudders. Nothing better illustrates the managerial turnover problem than this line of succession from 1974 to 1992.

There was a pattern of incompetence and poor management. Met State lost its JCAHO accreditation in 1980, and from then on ran downhill. By this time the physical plant was in bad shape; incrementalism had taken its toll, and patients complained about poor heating, poor ventilation, lack of air conditioning, foul odors, and filthy conditions. Only three of the seventeen original structures still housed patients. The aging buildings were falling apart: crumbling bricks, leaking roofs, and a wasteful heating system characterized their physical deterioration. In August 1983 a fifty-five-year-old water pump broke and caused the water tower to run dry.[74] For two days water had to be trucked in by the National Guard. Since the old steam lines had few operable control valves, much vacant space in the abandoned buildings remained heated, resulting in huge energy losses. It was estimated that the hospital wasted about three-quarters of its annual $1.7 million heating budget. Other mechanical, electrical, and emergency systems were outdated and inefficient. It was the politics of evasion run amok.

Citizens who sat on the Cambridge area board were outraged by such waste, for they took their monitoring role seriously. While observing patients huddled together in dilapidated wards and dingy day rooms, board chairman Bruce Houghton told a group of visiting state legislators in April 1984, "These people are at the end of the line, the last to be deinstitutionalized, the last to get other services. Some are violent. Others have no place else to go. If any were covered by medical insurance, they wouldn't be here. But no one questions whether they are better off here than as victims of the street."[75]

Many other illustrations of Met State's dilapidated condition could be cited, but a few more examples will suffice. The superstructure supporting the wooden roof of the Furcolo Building had rotted to the point where it was deemed structurally unsound; engineers feared that the roof might collapse with a heavy snowstorm; the elevators frequently failed to work, which meant that physically disabled patients had to be carried up and down stairs during fire drills; the electrical wiring and lighting were wholly inadequate; spare parts were hard to obtain; and water faucets had to be removed from one building to repair broken ones in another. Some sixty-six acres of the hospital property adjoined the Beaverbrook reservation, an area that had been designated as a protected wetland. When a fuel oil spill near the boiler building was detected by the Department of Environmental Protection, it cost the state $30,000 to clean up this hazardous waste.

Virtually no aspect of the operation was functioning at acceptable federal standards. In April 1989 the Division of Capital Planning and Operations hired an engineering consulting firm to study the problem. The engineers estimated that restoring Met State to meet these requirements would cost $38.8 million.[76] Even Philip Johnston, the secretary of human services, admitted that the cost was prohibitive.

MET STATE ROCKED BY SCANDAL

What goes on inside a state mental hospital is a mystery to the public and elected officials alike until dramatic events draw attention to it, usually when a dangerous patient escapes or when a scandal breaks out. Such incidents prompt an investigation and sensational media coverage. A major scandal occurred at Met State in February 1990, when four male employees—a security guard, a mental health worker, a nursing supervisor, and a plumber—were charged with having sexually abused five female patients. This sordid affair reached into a fairly high level of management, and the story was widely reported in the local press.[77]

Initially, DMH conducted its own internal probe. Scott Harshbarger, the Middlesex County district attorney, then made a separate investigation. Charges were filed against the accused, administrative hearings were held, the four state employees were found guilty, and all were fired for cause. In addition, thirty-one other hospital employees who knew about the incidents were reprimanded for having failed to report the sexual misconduct as they were required to do by law. Under pressure to clean up the mess, Audrey DeLoffi resigned as chief operating officer. She was replaced by Fernando Duran, who took charge for a brief period, staying long enough to sign the disciplinary actions.

Marylou Sudders, who had been recruited by Assistant Commissioner Katherine Olberg, replaced Duran. Sudders was a social worker and the area director for central Middlesex County. Although she had never worked in a state mental hospital before, Sudders was brought in to close Met State.[78] Her more immediate objective was to improve the patient environment, and she moved vigorously in her first months to meet this goal.

Adept in relating to people, Sudders proved herself an able administrator. She realized that the repercussions of the scandal had seriously damaged staff morale. Most employees believed that they were victims of guilt by association. Working in an atmosphere of suspicion and intimidation, they all felt tainted. As she struggled to take the initiative, Sudders decided to address the problem head-on, her goal being to change the culture. On November 30 she sent the staff an initial memo detailing what she expected of them by way of improving patient care, maintaining patient dignity, and protecting patient rights.[79] Whatever the inspiration, Sudders's statement allayed the fears of some. But the issue would not go away. Many employees still believed that their thirty-one co-workers had been given a bad rap.

THE TRANSITON TEAM DEVELOPS A PLAN

When the fiscal crisis broke in October 1990, Henry Tomes, who has succeeded Edward Murphy as mental health commissioner, realized that his organization faced a specific problem which he had to solve. Because of sharp reductions in state funding, he discovered a $10 million deficit in the Met State operating budget. Tomes decided that the only way to recoup this revenue shortfall was to downsize the hospital. He therefore asked Rae O'Leary, the Metro West area director, to devise a plan to compensate for the deficit, expecting her answer within an hour. O'Leary mapped out a plan later that evening at home.[80]

The major responsibility for this downsizing initiative rested with the Metro West area. In September 1990 a total of 827 employees worked at Met State, approximately 475 of whom were direct care staff (415 nursing personnel and 60 clinicians). Of the total full-time equivalents, 53 percent were minorities, mostly Haitians, who worked in food service and housekeeping. As the newest wave of urban immigrants, they were willing to accept low-paying menial jobs, but they experienced various cultural barriers. Since the Haitians were assigned entry-level positions, they ranked low in seniority and civil service status, and their bumping rights were affected accordingly.

A veteran of the Foxborough State Hospital closing in 1975, Rae O'Leary was a career psychiatric nurse who had risen through the ranks in the Department of Mental Health. A tough bureaucratic infighter, she not only knew the territory but also believed that anything could be done if managed correctly. In her view, the client always came first. O'Leary detailed the specifics of her plan in a public document and identified a set of key functional areas that needed to be addressed. These included the clinical process, human resources, labor relations, legal issues, communications, physical plant and property, and administrative operations. O'Leary believed that a specific work plan had to be developed for each area before any client transfers could be made. In budget and management terms, she analyzed the problem as follows:

> The budget reduction which would occur January 1, 1991, resulted in the ability to fund only 439 staff, a reduction of 288 [full-time employees]. This, in turn, defined the number of clients who could be cared for at the facility. With an overall staff to patient ratio of 2 to 1, a marginally acceptable level, 220 clients could be cared for by a staff of 439. Therefore, the census would need to de-

crease from 400 to 220, a reduction of 180, during the nine-month period between October 1990 and June 1991.[81]

For O'Leary the next step was putting together a transition team. Anticipating opposition that might emanate from DMH headquarters, she sought ways of effectively neutralizing this threat by putting central office staff in place as liaisons to the key functional areas of the transition team. Acting as chair of the team, she persuaded Dan Nakamoto, assistant commissioner for community programs, to serve as liaison to her. She then picked the rest of the personnel and gave them their assignments. They included Marylou Sudders, clinical concerns and placements; Connie Doto, patient transfers; Maryellen LaSala and Jeff McCue, labor relations/human resources; Doris "Chip" Carreiro and Richard Ames, legal affairs; Brian Devin, administrative operations; Lauren Flewelling and Mary McGeown, internal and external communications; and Peter Callagy, physical plant and property. Their participation proved critical in the development and execution of the plan.

O'Leary assembled everyone in a room and explained her ideas about downsizing the hospital. She told them bluntly that they could either accept the challenge or leave. She also let them know that she would be as committed to them as they were to her. Her forthright leadership inspired the team members. No one left the room. As Doris Carreiro recalled, "Rae's brilliance was in her capacity to recognize the people who could get things done."[82] Above all, O'Leary wanted to manage and was ready to move. Throughout the phasedown, no one mentioned the possibility of closing Met State Hospital.

With O'Leary in charge the transition team became the symbolic hub of the wheel that moved the operation forward. The goal was to articulate a set of principles to guide the members in their decisionmaking and other activities. The team defined these principles as follows: (1) the process must be client focused, sensitive, and clinically appropriate; (2) no client will move to a treatment setting clinically less appropriate or in poorer physical space, and most will move to improved care in improved space; (3) the process must be open to allow input and assistance from affected individuals, including clients, involved citizens, families, staff, and providers, and the communication system must be ongoing and impeccable; and (4) the process must be sensitive and supportive to staff whose positions have been defunded but who are responsible for client care during the phasedown. Layoffs would occur only as a last resort.[83]

For O'Leary, making up the $10 million deficit was the defining problem. Brian Devin, the operations manager for the Metro West area, soon discovered that this figure was $1 million short. At first glance, O'Leary feared that this discrepancy might have been a miscalculation on her part. She quickly realized, however, that it was due to the cost of maintaining the Cambridge-Somerville unit, where most of the patients were hospitalized. The Metro Boston area office wanted to keep this unit open. Since the funds followed the consumers, any cost overruns were ultimately rectified by the central office.[84]

It should be noted that the DMH reorganization in 1990 had strengthened O'Leary's hand. In her capacity as Metro West area director, she had been in charge of two hospitals, Westborough and Met State. This situation worked to her advantage, because most Met State patients were eventually transferred to Westborough.

Marylou Sudders was a key actor in the transition; she was a quick study with the capacity to listen and to bring people on board. She managed the daily activities at Met State while O'Leary supervised the interfacility and interagency details. Both were strong-willed women whose managerial styles differed and whose personalities clashed at times, but both were heavily invested in the hospital closing. O'Leary sought greater control and more rigid lines of responsibility and authority, whereas Sudders seemed more flexible and ready to meet unforeseen contingencies. Sudders saw the issue as being larger than Metro West. She believed that someone from the Cambridge-Somerville area office should have been put on the transition team and felt that other area directors should have been involved. She also felt that the time lines were too tight and too abbreviated. O'Leary's managerial approach was more a case of "my way or the highway."

IMPLEMENTING THE PHASEDOWN

No sooner had the plan been announced than trouble arose. The hospital trustees opposed the downsizing, which was hardly surprising. Of the fifteen trustees who served on the board, eight were either mental health clients or family members. In a written statement distributed to employees on November 27, the trustees declared: "As a citizen board, we recognize that the current fiscal crisis in our state requires that some difficult decisions be made, and we also acknowledge that there are some logical components to this plan. However, as advocates of the patients at Met State, we strongly believe that the timetable for implementation is extremely unrealistic and unacceptable."[85] In disseminating this statement, the trustees had set the tone of resistance for the entire organization.

Internal squabbles among staff members surfaced. Most employees considered the transition team a "hit squad" that was following orders from the central office. Others believed that Met State was being closed as punishment for the sex scandal. Surreptitious obstructionism appeared in the form of an underground newspaper that opposed the phasedown. Its editors, who were identified as clinicians at Cambridge Hospital, viciously attacked Sudders, derisively referring to her as "Queen Boney." Some of this criticism amounted to personal hostility and bitterness. Sudders snuffed out further publication of this house organ by threatening to report its editors to the medical licensing board.

Anonymous and alarming rumors began circulating. Emotional statements were made to the effect that the transfer of long-term chronic patients would result in their deaths. A review of the literature was launched immediately by O'Leary to determine the validity of such charges, but there was little evidence to support them. These obstructionist tactics were described by Alan Greene, a member of the Alliance for the Mentally Ill, as "a rearguard action designed to stop the closing."[86]

Much confusion and consternation prevailed. In the midst of all the turmoil, a dangerous patient escaped from the hospital but, fortunately, was taken into custody by local police within forty-five minutes and returned to the hospital. (It was DMH policy to search for a patient on hospital grounds and to notify state and local police to look for the patient outside the campus boundaries.) Once the immediate uproar subsided, Sudders contacted Dr. Mona Bennett at the central office and had the patient transferred to Medfield, a more secure facility.

The initial phasedown began on November 5, when the central Middlesex area closed its admissions. This decision allowed for the shutdown of a receiving ward on December 17, but the administrators soon realized that it would be necessary to maintain admissions to serve patients from the Cambridge-Somerville area. The Tri-City area made alternate plans to divert acute admissions to Danvers, which enabled them to close their admissions by January 1. The census at Met State on November 30, 1990, was 382 patients.

O'Leary sensed from the start that the trustees might be a problem. She therefore asked Henry Tomes to meet with them in order to address their concerns and to request their assistance. He did so on November 28 and explained to them that it was his decision to downsize. On January 29, Tomes met with interested family members and told them essentially the same thing. By so doing, the commissioner took responsibility for the decision and provided a buffer for O'Leary.

At these meetings Tomes specifically addressed the clinical issues along with hardship and access issues. He spoke about plans to install special telephone lines at Westborough and Worcester and to provide a shuttle bus service between the two hospitals. An independent psychiatrist was selected to review individual hardship cases, and a contact person was identified at each hospital for family questions and concerns. Family support meetings were scheduled at Met State. A patient transfer packet was developed and distributed to unit directors and department heads. Arrangements were made for patients to have their funds and medical records transferred, to have their pictures taken prior to transfer, and to have luggage purchased for them. These steps were taken at the end of the third Dukakis administration, at a time when the economy and social structure of the state were undergoing wrenching changes.

Meanwhile, when Fernando Durand was still in charge of Met State, Cambridge and Somerville Legal Services had filed a class-action lawsuit on behalf of Joann Dottin and seven other patients who were in custody there. These patients were ready to be discharged, but DMH had been unable to place them. The suit charged state officials with failure to release them and to provide appropriate community services. Their lawyers—including Steven Schwartz, who had argued the Northampton case—contended that their clients were being held illegally. Realizing that this litigation (*Dottin v. Dukakis*) could bring the phasedown to an abrupt halt, Richard Ames, who was general counsel for DMH, set up a meeting with the plaintiffs' lawyers. At this meeting Doris Carreiro, Rae O'Leary, and Marylou Sudders presented the transition plan. During these prelitigation negotiations, Ames and Carreiro were able to persuade counsel for the plaintiffs to hold the case in abeyance. Their clients agreed to cooperate if they could exercise some kind of veto power in the community placement process. This agreement allowed the phasedown to go forward without further delay.

Both Marylou Sudders and Katherine Olberg provided testimony by way of an affidavit on behalf of the plaintiffs, whereas Rae O'Leary testified on behalf of the department, which was in her view the right thing to do. As it turned out, the legal issue was never contested on the merits because DMH found community placements for all but one of the eight patients. The eighth, it was determined, required continued hospital care, so she was transferred to Medfield.

Once this major hurdle had been cleared, the phasedown proceeded on schedule. All patient records were carefully reviewed for legal status, guardianship status, and the need for court decree modifications. Judge Kevin Doyle of the Waltham District Court agreed to hold special court sessions for cases needing review or modification prior to transfer. Transfers were made pursuant to law (Chapter 123, section 3). Few if any patients contested the transfers.

Met State staff attempted, where possible, to elicit patient input in the process of planning for new community programs and services. Patients' ideas concerning transfer options were also elicited. In addition, patients assisting in planning their discharge into the community retained the right to refuse specific placements during the planning process. Once patients were discharged, they were systematically tracked by DMH for ninety days.

TRANSFER OF PATIENTS AND REDUCTION IN FORCE

The medical director of Westborough met with Met State clinical staff to review clients identified for transfer on December 7. A reciprocal meeting was held at Westborough the following week. On January 2, 1991, two weeks before Governor William Weld was sworn into office, the initial twenty-five patients were transferred to existing vacancies at Westborough, where a new ward was established later that month to accommodate an additional twenty-five to thirty clients.

Simultaneously, a request for proposal (RFP) was issued for forty-two residential beds in the Metro West area and eight residential beds in the Cambridge-Somerville area. Another sixteen-bed RFP was issued by the Metro North area. Area staff were involved in site searches with local realtors and Community Development Corporation housing partnerships. In addition, a twenty-bed housing program was set up on the Met State campus, consisting of three homes that were scheduled for occupancy in January and February 1991.

Once the phasedown began, the hard work and commitment of hospital employees allowed for the supportive and orderly transfer of patients. The first few months were the most difficult, mainly because the institution was still reeling from the sex scandal. Local telephone lines for towns surrounding Met State were installed at Westbrough and Worcester hospitals, thus facilitating family-to-client and client-to-client communication at no increased expense. A twice-a-week van service was established. Family support meetings run by Worcester and Westborough staff were begun at Met State and transferred to the receiving facilities.

In terms of media strategy, Sudders did not talk with the press until she had first cleared it with the central office in Boston. She was very protective of the hospital and relied on the clinical leadership to hold the ranks together. Obviously, there was considerable disruption in the treatment of patients, but they continued to receive their medications and psychotherapy.

The transfer process was difficult, even heart-wrenching. Mistakes were made, plans were changed or modified, and unexpected events arose. According to Sudders, the toughest decisions involved which patients to send to other hospitals and which to send to community settings. Dr. Kenneth Minkhoff was brought in as a consulting psychiatrist to review difficult placement cases when the staff could not reach consensus. He was assisted by Marilyn Berner, a clinical social worker and lawyer. They evaluated individual situations and made their recommendations accordingly. The purpose of this independent review was to obtain another opinion to help reach consensus rather than to override an unpopular decision.

Those patients who were ready for community placement were accommodated in new residential and day programs in their area of origin. Since they originated from Metro Boston, Metro West, and the North Shore, these three areas were where the new residential expansion took place. Some 311 new residential beds were developed between fiscal years 1991 and 1992. Three other state facilities—Danvers, Medfield, and Westborough—received patients who needed continued inpatient care. These institutions developed new community programs and quarter-way houses to accommodate their patients awaiting discharge, which allowed for the creation of sufficient inpatient bed space for Met State transfers.

The transfer to Danvers presented a special problem. Careful consideration was given to the fact that patients were being moved from one closing state hospital to another that was scheduled to close six months later. Since the newly built psychiatric unit at Tewksbury Public Health Hospital was not ready for occupancy, these patients would have to be moved twice. This troublesome issue was thoroughly discussed with family members and the affected patients, for only with their concurrence would this move take place. Rae O'Leary strenuously objected to these transfers. Given the overcrowding and understaffing at Danvers, she felt that the double move violated the principle of providing an "equal or better" setting.

Hospital employees who received a reduction in force, or layoff, notice were understandably upset at the prospect of losing their jobs, their main fear being loss of job security. In the early stages, DMH provided fourteen days' notice to employees opting for a voluntary layoff and those who received no reassignment or bumping options. At the outset, the employees encountered a cold, impersonal bureaucracy they found maddening. In their eyes, DMH exhibited what seemed to them a callous disregard of their worth as individuals and their many years of loyal service. In short, they felt devalued. Some blamed the government or Michael Dukakis for their predicament. Others believed that privatization would never happen or that they could wait out the Weld administration. They were counting on the legislature to oppose the closing and to protect the unions. Many seemed to be saying, "We won't believe it until they put a padlock on the door." A lot of people were stuck in denial, buried knee-deep in the big muddy.

While sensitive client care and the clinical integrity of the process remained the top priorities for administrators, appropriate planning for staff ran a close second. During the phasedown and closing processes, significant efforts were made to avoid the necessity of staff layoffs. To begin with, Rae O'Leary persuaded Henry Tomes to install a hiring freeze throughout the system and to give first consideration to Met State employees for transfer. On November 26, Deputy Commissioner Stephen Day issued a memo to all area directors, which read in part:

> Consistent with the movement of patients from Metropolitan State Hospital to clinically appropriate settings, there is a resulting need to lower staffing levels within this facility. The coordination of these staffing reductions with the lowering of the hospital census poses unique obstacles which can best be addressed by the transfer of affected employees. While it may not be possible to avoid layoffs totally at Metropolitan State Hospital, it is the position of the agency that every avenue will be exhausted for accomplishing these reductions before proceeding to layoff activities.
>
> Utilizing the transfer language which already exists with union collective bargaining agreements, all DMH areas will be required to provide priority consideration to Metropolitan State Hospital transfer requests. Accordingly, no positions are to be filled without full and fair consideration of appropriate Metropolitan State Hospital transfer requests.[87]

This memo set in motion a series of events arranged mostly by Jeff McCue and Maryellen LaSala. Their main objective was to develop a plan for laying off as few employees as possible. They discussed their plan with labor union officials and solicited their feedback regarding staff bidding for jobs.[88]

Several staff meetings were held for the purpose of answering employees' questions. An informational booth was set up to advertise employment opportunities and to assist with résumé writing. The career counseling center in the Division of Employment Training held employee seminars on site. Hospital job fairs were also scheduled. As of December 11, 1990, there were fifty-seven requests for transfer on file, and forty-eight informational postings had been received. Somewhat later, a daylong seminar on retirement was presented by William Farmer of the state retirement board.

Meanwhile, Marylou Sudders appeared on the wards almost daily, her presence an important factor in calming tensions. She made it a point to visit all rotating work shifts at least twice each month to talk with staff and to answer their questions. Informal conversations and observations were as important as the formal ones. Sudders was ready to provide information, squelch rumors, listen to complaints, give moral support, soothe chafed egos, and deal with people who were angry and upset. The staff needed to know what was happening in the community as well as the hospital. Even partial information, if it was true, was better than none. Bulletin boards provided the latest information on the opening of community programs, movement of clients, current census data, and so on. Printed updates were occasionally distributed with the payroll.

A combination of fiscal incentives and market forces was employed to implement the reduction in force. Negotiations regarding a bonus incentive program and an early retirement option were under way. Employees who elected voluntary layoff received a lump sum cash payment of $2,268, based on their health insurance costs, an option that proved attractive to many workers. They were also eligible for unemployment compensation. In the interest of clinical continuity and stability, DMH granted an extended notice period for voluntary layoffs. The early retirement program was soon in place. The bonus incentive program, however, was not approved. It was turned down by Peter Nessen, the secretary of administration and fianance, who did not see it as being cost-effective.

On November 14, 1991, Rae O'Leary sent Commissioner Eileen Elias a status report, saying: "Our initial commitment to staff to avoid layoffs during the phasedown did not appear to be realistic when the hospital closure was being confronted. Now, however, our optimism is again increasing. We intend to make every effort to provide employment options to Met State employees who are interested in such options."[89] In the end, most opted for them. The following data summarize employee attrition from the phasedown through the closing:

Transfers within DMH	365
Transfers to other state agencies	22
Mothball crew	27
Voluntary layoff	240
Retirements	40
Resignations	38
Laid off (no bumping option awarded)	17
Functional eliminations	27
Discharges	12

Of the 365 transfers, 153 staff were transferred laterally with the patients, and 68 were bumped into other facilities as a result of the functional eliminations. Of the 240 voluntary layoffs, 183 were processed after December 13, 1991, and 166 employees met the eligibility criteria for the insurance incentive. All vacation and incentive cash-outs were completed on February 20, 1992. Only 17 employees were involuntarily laid off. Only one grievance was filed, and that was an affirmative action complaint. When the early retirement plan was put into effect in July 1992, 40 employees took advantage of it.

FROM PHASEDOWN TO CLOSURE

As of June 19, 1991, the same day that Governor Weld's special commission released its report, the census at Met State was down to 207 clients. For all practical purposes, this concluded the phasedown. The next day Commissioner Elias, who had just been appointed, visited the hospital to announce to families and staff that it would be closed, a traumatic moment. Since no one had told them about the closing, this unenviable task fell to Elias, who broke the news as best she could. She spoke about the death of an institution and the grieving process that has to accompany it. Her visit was more like a wake.

Movement of patients continued throughout the summer and fall of 1991. As of November 19, the census was down to 180 patients. By this time 324 employees had left, and the remainder of patients and workers would leave within the next two months. The other significant development was the opening of a DMH replacement unit at Cambridge Hospital. A contract was signed on December 16 to provide seventeen acute care beds to accommodate Cambridge and Somerville patients.

As Metropolitan State headed for closure, there was an increase in petty theft as some wards were closed. This was stopped by moving all furnishings and equipment from the unit and sealing off the closed area immediately after the last patient had left. The final displacement of the 382 patients was achieved as follows:

DMH inpatient transfer	163
DMH community placements	156
Admissions diversion	37
DMR community placements	14
Long-term-care placements	5
Other	7

On January 25, 1992, the last group of patients and staff was moved out and relocated. Six days later, with the hospital wards completely empty, Marylou Sudders invited the trustees and a few special guests to lunch. Afterward she bade them farewell, packed her personal belongings, and locked the hospital doors. The previous day she had sent a letter to all employees, paying tribute to them for their professionalism and their care in a job well done. Commissioner Elias later met with a group of mental health professionals. At the end of the meeting, Catherine Dunham, who had served under Dukakis, shook hands with Elias and congratulated her by saying, "You have achieved what we tried for so many years to accomplish, but we were unable to do."[90] It was a gracious gesture.

On that poignant note, the history of Metropolitan State came to an end. The skeleton crew then put the facility in mothballs. Vacant and boarded up, the hospital currently resembles a ghost town. Former patients occasionally return, seeking to gain entry. The three adjoining municipalities, the state Division of Capital Planning and Operations, and the Metropolitan District Commission have reached a consensus with regard to the disposition of the 346 acres of abandoned property. There is something in the reuse proposal for each town: conservation land for Belmont, a nine-hole municipal golf course for Waltham, and affordable housing for the elderly in Lexington. The golf course is designed to have the least impact on the natural environment, preserving wetlands and providing for minimum deforestation of Mackerel Hill.

EVALUATING POLICY IMPLEMENTATION

As may be seen from this historical review of mental health care in Massachusetts, different eras are defined by different problems. From the founding of the first state hospital in Worcester in the early 1830s until the Civil War, the problem was seen as one of social control and institutional care. From the Civil War until the New Deal, the problem was associated with the expansion of public asylums. From the New Deal until the New Frontier, the problem was one of skyrocketing admissions and warehousing of patients. From the New Frontier until recently, the problem was one of deinstitutionalization and community programs. The defining issues of today's era are privatization and public managed care.

Once a state assumes responsibility for a public function, it cannot easily discard it. The policy conundrum of providing institutions of last resort makes disengagement that much more difficult. The obsession with state hospitals blinded participants to the fact that they were protecting their own interests and distorted their understanding of the new realities that had emerged in recent years. Other states—for example, Michigan and New Jersey—have attempted to close their mental hospitals, but they have experienced much difficulty.

In the effort to restructure mental health in Massachusetts, ideology did prevail, and the working of the system in a managerial sense improved. Most important, the consequences of its implementation on community life were anticipated and dealt with responsibly. What had gone wrong with deinstitutionalization did not go wrong this time. The major policy achievements closely followed the classic implementation scenario. Policy goals were stated in precise terms such as "Four mental hospitals to be closed by 1993." Policymakers and implementers—the governor, the health and human services secretary, DMH, some of the mental health lobby—shared these goals, and the public generally supported them. Power to control the implementation process was centralized hierarchically. The implementers were granted the technical authority and possessed the technical competence to carry out the policy goals.

Crisis alone can empower. An early reckoning of the impact of budget reductions and simplified management showed that the Elias strategy was working. The extremely tight time constraints permitted those in charge to decide on and implement the closure policy without prolonged debate. Attaining policy goals required bold leadership and the political will to stay the course. Previous administrations had faltered for lack of such will. In a major restructuring of this kind, the commissioner is definitely in the hot seat. Eileen Elias took most of the heat. As she says, "Managing change in a public bureaucracy necessitates determination, tenacity, vision, strategic and systemic planning, and implementation."[91]

In both reducing spending and consolidating hospitals, the Weld administration achieved substantial success. In the first three years, the total savings were $62 million. It cost $34 million to expand community-based services and $26.7 million to develop replacement units. In addition, the Commonwealth avoided an expenditure of $43.7 million in capital resources that would have been needed to bring the closed mental hospitals into compliance with federal certification and accreditation standards. The Department of Mental Health generated $17.9 million in new revenues as a result of its initiatives and saved $11 million in state employee health insurance costs for a net savings to the state of $69 million. Unlike what occurred in previous efforts to deinstitutionalize, this time the resources followed the consumer.

Completing tracking studies of patients who had been discharged helped to ensure that they would not slip through the cracks. According to DMH tracking data, from July 1991 to the end of 1992, a total of 963 patients were discharged to DMH-funded community residences; 274 were placed with their families, with non–family members, or in independent living settings; 255 were transferred to another state facility; and 114 were moved to other treatment facilities. Only two patients were discharged to the street to become homeless persons. Replacement units for acute care were set up through contracts with general hospitals, which resulted in a significant drop in the length of stay. State hospitals reported longer stays, while general hospitals reported much shorter ones. Fewer than 6 percent of the state employees who worked in the system were laid off. Most of the others were absorbed elsewhere in the system or hired by private providers.

Much of the program duplication and overlap that existed within the system was substantially reduced so that the fiscal and management goals were largely realized. As mental health professionals Barbara Leadholm and Joan Kerzner point out, however:

> The restructuring of the system has not come without a price. Along with the successes, there were some unavoidable disruptions in services. Hospital closures, consolidations, and privatization resulted in the dislocation of some staff as a result of layoffs and bumping, and particularly affected vendor-operated community clinics to which DMH clinical staff had historically been assigned. This practice was discontinued in June 1991 when the department cashed out the state positions. The clinics (and subsequently, a number of clinical staff) were offered contract funds instead. Not unexpectedly, clients of these clinics and their family members resented the disruptions and the uncertainties regarding continuity of care.[92]

The apparent success of the Met State closure is instructive. It provides a textbook solution to the problem. The entire operation worked almost to perfection. From an insider's point of view, Doris Carreiro felt that the plan was executed superbly from start to finish. Scholars have usually applied three criteria to evaluate policy implementation: efficiency, effectiveness, and equity. Using these criteria, I would give the implementers generally high marks for their performance. The transition team led by Rae O'Leary and Marylou Sudders deserves much of the credit for planning and implementation. They elicited trust and performed well.

The efficiency criteria attempt to evaluate quality of performance in relation to cost. Here the statistics generated by the Met State closure between fiscal years 1990 and 1994 reveal the following: state funding savings, $28.9 million; inpatient replacement cost, $2.3 million; community expansion cost, $7.1 million; revenue enhancement savings, $0.9 million; group insurance savings, $5 million; and capital cost savings, $16.7 million. These produced a total saving of $42.1 million.

The effectiveness criteria also attempt to measure consumer and constituency satisfaction. After Met State and Danvers had been closed, the Division of Capital and Planning Operations, the state agency that oversaw the consolidation process, contracted with the University of Massachusetts to interview clients and families of these two hospitals. The purpose of the study was to determine whether the state's promise that clients would have "equal or better" care in their new settings had been fulfilled. A total of eighty-six clients were interviewed—fifty-nine former Met State and twenty-four former Danvers patients. While most Met State patients had been placed in community group homes or apartments, most Danvers patients had been transferred to Tewksbury.

No client interviewed rated his or her current placement as worse than the prior hospital placement. In the case of the fifty-nine former Met State clients in community settings, 69 percent rated their overall post-hospital experience as better, while 31 percent rated it as equal to their hospital care. In addition, a majority reported that they felt involved in and satisfied with the transfer process. The twenty-seven Danvers patients had less positive responses, with only 30 percent rating their new inpatient setting as better, while 67 percent rated it as equal. Most reported little or no involvement in, and lack of satisfaction with, the process of moving from one facility to another.[93]

Most family members indicated that the client's new placement was better than the state hospital in a variety of areas, including living space, cleanliness, opportunity for social activities, and privacy. Only a few family members indicated feeling that the closing of the state hospital where their relative had received care had had a predominantly negative impact on their family member. Many reported not having been informed that the facility was closing or that the client would be moved. Many also felt excluded from discharge planning for the hospitalized relative.[94]

The equity criteria deal with fairness in delivery of public services. Here the policy mandate in dispute worked better than most critics were willing to admit. For one thing, patients now spend less time in a restrictive setting. Formerly they could spend anywhere from five months to five years at Met State in a deplorable environment. Closing hospitals was only part of the story. Changes in approaches to care were another important factor, involving looking at mental health from a broader perspective. The problem lay in seeing clients solely in terms of their acute status and not from the point of view of recovery and rehabilitation. DMH needed to capture that model. Elias was a commissioner who understood recovery and rehabilitation. During her tenure she won praise from constituency groups for encouraging treatment in the least restrictive settings and for getting patients more involved in their own care. On the fairness issue, the restructuring went a long way toward eliminating the inequities of the two-tier system that had prevailed for so many years. No longer were patients discriminated against because they were poor or disadvantaged. The practice of "creaming" was eliminated.

The policy jury is still out on the quality and consequences of privatization. Time will tell whether the quality of services has been enhanced. The most severe critique was offered by Robert Dorwart and Sherrie Epstein, who see privatization of mental health care as a fragile balance:

This tension between whether human services should be supplied because of a public obligation or mission to serve community interests or because of a desire to sell a service in order to generate a profit is one that we believe to be at the heart of many current policy debates in mental health. Pressures toward increased competition and cost containment are likely to exacerbate the stress already building as protagonists wrestle with various options for financing and organizing mental health care.[95]

This stress became evident in June 1995, when a DMH internal report of patient deaths and suicides was released on an information request. The data revealed that deaths in the mental health system had risen by 79 percent during the restructuring period from 1990 to 1994. When this information reached the public, it was used by some advocates and the media as evidence to support their position that the public managed care initiative was detrimental to the seriously mentally ill.[96]

Commissioner Elias, called on to explain the statistics before the House Post Audit and Oversight Committee, a legislative watchdog group, explained that in 1992 the criteria for reporting client deaths were expanded to include a broader range of people having contact with DMH.[97] Neither the advocates nor the media accepted this explanation. Instead, they continued to use these data as proof that the restructuring initiative was linked to increased patient deaths and demanded the resignation of Commissioner Elias.[98]

To deal with the problem and to satisfy the Post Audit Committee's desire to get the facts from an unbiased source, DMH commissioned an independent team of researchers to investigate the matter further. More specifically, the researchers were asked to examine the reported increase in patient mortality and determine whether it was related to the restructuring and public managed care initiative. The team's report revealed an actual decline in the rate of consumer deaths from 1991 to 1993.[99]

One can argue about the desirability and feasibility of these policies, but they were not just rhetoric or ideology; they were in the mainstream of mental health policy and program development. The choice between privatization and state hospitals will continue to require a search for an appropriate balance among competing values where no final resolution is possible. With the amelioration of one problem, new difficulties will emerge, compelling public attention. The restructuring at least permits a cost-benefit analysis to be debated in light of the Pacheco law requiring evidence of substantial savings before a state facility can be closed. The important question is whether the taxpayers are willing to invest sufficient resources to provide for a broad range of services. Only if the reply is in the affirmative will a comprehensive community support system become a viable entity.

Whatever the possibilities for a new range of services, a few lingering questions remain. In closing its hospitals, is the state government shirking its responsibilities? Is it evading necessary duties? Is it relinquishing its oversight function? These are sobering thoughts for policymakers to ponder. In the final analysis, the managed care concept can be made to work, but its success depends largely on keeping people out of the hospital.

EPILOGUE

After the closure of Met State, Marylou Sudders left to become head of the New Hampshire mental health system. Meanwhile, the pressures on Eileen Elias continued to mount. Displaying a penchant for oversimplifying events, the media coverage had sparked a public controversy that would not subside. Several high-profile patient suicides added fuel to the fire. As a result, the Massachusetts Alliance for the Mentally ill continued to demand Elias's removal. Under intense scrutiny, she continued to defend her much-maligned agency. But the drumbeat continued nonstop. On January 9, 1996, Elias announced that she would soon be leaving her post. Three days later, as fate would have it, Marylou Sudders was brought back to replace her.

Several key developments occurred once Sudders took over the helm. In July 1996, DMH signed an interagency agreement with DMA (the state's Medicaid agency) whereby DMA agreed to expand eligibility for its behavioral health care "carve out" (mental health and substance abuse services) to uninsured adult DMH clients, and to ensure access to such services for children. Under this agreement, most acute care and emergency services are managed by DMA's behavioral health care vendor. DMH continues to provide continuing care inpatient and community services.

In October 1997, Commissioner Sudders launched a mental illness awareness campaign. A task force, aided by a statewide survey of public attitudes, developed a two-pronged strategy for educating the public about mental illness. This public relations effort, known as "Changing Minds," was designed to remove the stigma of mental illness and to deal with the problem of avoidance of treatment. Tipper Gore, wife of Vice President Al Gore, agreed to appear in a public service announcement about mental illness. Shortly thereafter, CBS newsman Mike Wallace was recruited to speak about his own depression and successful treatment. In all, the campaign proved worthwhile.[100]

There have also been several significant legislative accomplishments. In 1997 the "Five Fundamental Rights Bill" was passed, which assures patients in private psychiatric hospitals and community programs five of the same basic human rights afforded to patients in DMH hospitals: the right to make and receive phone calls, see visitors of their choosing, read and receive uncensored mail, have a humane physical environment, and have access to legal advocacy services. In August 2000 the civil commitment law was revised, aligning Massachusetts with most other states regarding the length of involuntary hospitalization prior to judicial review. This statute (Chapter 249) shortens the time in which a patient can file a petition for release from ten days to four business days. It also reduces the time in which a court must hear such a case from fourteen days to four business days.

Another area where Massachusetts lagged behind other states was in mandating equal coverage of health and mental health problems under private insurance. Although widely supported by mental health advocates, providers, and DMH, parity legislation had been staunchly resisted by insurance companies and employers who wanted to avoid the costs. Under pressure from advocacy groups, the legislature enacted a parity law in May 2000 requiring insurers to end discrimination in coverage of mental illness. This legislation (Chapter 80) became effective in January 2001.

In June 2000 a series of newspaper reports documented the problem of emotionally disturbed children and adolescents, who were confined in locked psychiatric wards for weeks and months for lack of a place to go. The system was backed up. These were called "stuck kids" because they lacked suitable community placements.[101] In response to this crisis, the legislature appropriated $10 million to expand residential programs and to provide home-based services for children. Despite this infusion of state money, services for mentally ill children remain so overburdened that many of them needing hospitalization have been turned away because all the available beds are full.[102]

DMH is no longer the sole agency dealing with mentally ill children. It shares responsibility for this population with the Department of Social Services, the Department of Youth Services, DMA, the school system, and the court system. DMH now runs the juvenile court clinics and acts as a bridge between the courts and the health care system. This endeavor is still a work in progress.

Of the estimated nine thousand homeless adults living in Massachusetts, approximately two thousand have severe and persistent mental illnesses. According to DMH, these numbers continue to rise, and the shelter system is being strained beyond its capacity. This is a priority problem for DMH, and substantial new state resources have been directed into this program area in recent years. The annual budget for the homeless mentally ill is over $21 million. This money is being used for expanding housing, residential services, and rental assistance.

One final comment. The verdict is now in on the treatment revolution, and it seems to be that the mental health care system in Massachusetts had made substantial gains. Clearly the community rather than the old asylum is the best place for patients to get better. "This is nothing short of a transformation," says Danna Mauch. "Most are clearly better off; there are few who dispute that."[103] Responding to her statement, Larry Tye wrote in the *Boston Globe*:

> That is not the tale advocates typically tell of mental health in Massachusetts or the nation, as they hammer the system's manifest shortcomings. Thousands are waiting for group homes and other residential services, which generate backups everywhere from psychiatric hospitals to homeless shelters. And too many former mental patients still wander the streets from the South End to Springfield, convinced they are Christ or Madame Curie.
>
> But such shortfalls notwithstanding, the progress made in treating mental illness has been revolutionary. More than 75 interviews by the Globe in recent weeks—with health professionals and patients, in hospitals, at group homes and on the street—suggest that the mental health system finally has found a series of solutions, even if it lacks the cash to fully implement them.[104]

That was where things stood in April 2001. The lives of these vulnerable people haunt the ending of the system reform story.

4

THE SEARCH FOR
A CHANCELLOR
OF HIGHER
EDUCATION

Money is what makes the world of higher education go round. We all rely on it. We all—public and independent institutions alike—look to the state, as well as to the federal government, for help in getting it. And we all have an abiding interest in finding ways to convince public policymakers that we need and deserve more of it to do our job with the kind of effectiveness we aim for.

Clifton R. Wharton Jr., Askwith Lecture, 1986

AUTONOMY AND POLITICS IN HIGHER EDUCATION

Among the concerns about the quality of American education that seem to abound in our age are the challenges to the public university. Retaining the ability to make fair and autonomous decisions is of critical importance to its operation. Inappropriate political interference in the governance of higher education threatens that independence. The threat is a grave one because it goes to the heart of the academic enterprise. In delivering the Askwith Lecture at Harvard in 1986, Clifton Wharton Jr., then chancellor of the state higher education system in New York, explained the crux of the problem: "Public colleges and universities are identical to their counterparts in the independent sector in having no margin of tolerance for political quid pro quo. That which compromises the integrity of their administration and governance also compromises the integrity of their teaching, research, and service. It is a short step to making faculty appointments or awarding tenure on the basis of political persuasion and ideological preference."[1] Educators therefore tend to take a very dim view of political intrusion into

Chronology, 1985–86

December 10	Chancellor Duff resigns; search committee appointed.
January 8	Search committee meets with governor and obtains commitment from him to press for early legislation to increase the chancellor's salary.
February 11	Board of Regents adopts procedural resolution to abide by search committee's recommendations.
March 15	Application deadline; 107 candidates apply.
March 27	Pay raise bill (H-5474) filed.
April 3	Screening subcommittee recommends thirty-two candidates.
April 16	Public hearing on pay raise bill (H-5474).
April 17	Search committee narrows field to twelve candidates.
May 2–3	First round of candidate interviews.
May 6	Pay raise bill in new form (H-5639) reported favorably by the Public Service Committee.
May 14	Ylvisaker alerts Board of Regents that search committee will not be able to report final selection of candidates on June 9 as originally planned.
May 22	Search committee makes penultimate cut and reduces field to six candidates.
June 9	Board of Regents attempts to abandon search but instead authorizes a maximum of six finalists.
June 12–18	Second round of candidate interviews. Speaker Keverian refuses to advance pay raise bill unless Collins appears among the finalists.
June 19	Search committee selects four finalists; Collins eliminated.
July 1	Board of Regents ignores four finalists and elects Collins as new chancellor; Ylvisaker resigns in protest.
July 2	Governor intervenes in dispute, replaces Regents chairman Beaubien with Lashman, and announces his intention to overturn the Board of Regents' decision. House of Representatives unanimously endorses Collins as chancellor.
July 3	Governor contacts Collins and warns him not to resign from legislature or to proceed on present course.
July 6	*Boston Globe* breaks story that Collins asked Duff to sell tickets to Speaker's campaign fundraiser.
July 7	Eisner resigns from Board of Regents in protest of Collins's appointment.
July 8	Collins rejects ninety-day contract offer by Lashman.
July 10	Collins appears on television to argue his case.
July 18	Six Regents call for special meeting of board to act on stalled contract negotiations.
July 24	Seven Regents ask attorney general to rule on legality of Collins appointment.
July 25	Attorney general rules Collins legally elected but serves at pleasure of Board of Regents.
July 31	Governor appoints three new Regents and gains control of the board.
August 5	Board of Regents reopens search and denies Collins one-year performance contract.
August 18	Newell drops out of race, claiming atmosphere too politicized.
September 9	Board of Regents fires Collins and elects Jenifer as new chancellor.

the academic community, where it is seen as an infringement on the cherished principles of academic freedom and institutional autonomy.

In legal terms, public colleges and universities are creatures of the state. As such, they operate in a political environment that makes them accountable to the public and at the same time exposes them to steady external pressures. One can argue that such influence over a publicly funded institution is appropriate in ensuring democratic responsibility. Similarly, the argument can be made that a university, like a hospital or a motor vehicle office, ought to be autonomous. In reality, however, no university, whether public or private, enjoys complete autonomy. Both are subject to the constraints imposed by government funding and to the decisions handed down by state and federal courts. In the public domain, the boundaries between democratic accountability and academic autonomy are not always clearly defined. Most controversies in state higher education involve the clash of these competing demands.[2]

For higher education as a whole, the issue of autonomy arises when a new chief executive officer is hired. Here the differences between the public and private sectors are revealing. Hiring a president at a private university is typically a process shrouded in secrecy. New England institutions such as Brown and Dartmouth, for example, neither reveal the names of their candidates nor keep the outside world informed of the progress of the search. Furthermore, formal offers are not made to qualified prospects unless their acceptance is assured. By sharp contrast, public institutions operate virtually in a glass house when performing the same function. The recruitment of campus executives in the public sector is at best a delicate and arduous task, as various groups and individuals, each with their own agenda, seek to become active if not predominant in the selection process. Such searches must be done in compliance with affirmative action rules and with the requirements of "open meeting" laws, which are designed to ensure accountability. Studies indicate that in states such as Florida, these laws (sometimes referred to as "sunshine legislation") may be more of a hindrance than a help in attracting the most qualified people.[3] Preserving confidentiality, as the private sector well knows, is often the key to a successful search. Candidates for the job do not want their names bandied about for fear of jeopardizing their current positions. And if they are not accepted for the post, such disclosure may impair their future opportunities elsewhere. The courts generally recognize certain privacy rights of the individual placed in such circumstances. Balancing these rights against the obligations of sunshine laws is indeed a difficult and perplexing exercise.

Procedures are normally adopted to protect the confidentiality of the candidates and to guard against the impact of publicity and the cruder forms of direct interference. Even the most elaborate procedures, however, do not necessarily guarantee such protection. Leaks to the press and other premature disclosures are almost bound to occur.[4] Public awareness of the candidates is unavoidable after a certain point. Since the selection process involves dynamic tensions among the competing interests, it may well become politicized. Once this happens, the politics of the search run a course similar to the politics of any other controversial dispute in a democratic society. Some people want something from government and build a coalition of influence to get it, while other people want something different and build a countervailing coalition to block or modify the design of the first group. Compelled to conduct its educational business in a highly charged political atmosphere, a search committee may stray from its proper course despite its best efforts and intentions.

Perhaps there is no better illustration of this phenomenon than the search for a chancellor of higher education that took place in Massachusetts in 1986. During the first six months of that year, the state Board of Regents conducted a national search for a new chancellor to head its public higher education system. Before long, the search developed into a fierce power struggle both inside and outside the board. The media seized on it. Powerful forces—some obvious, some subtle—exerted tremendous pressures in their attempts to influence the outcome. Much of the politics and press attention focused on James Collins, a state representative from Amherst and an erstwhile supporter of public higher education, who became a central figure in the struggle. Bypassing the four finalists their search had produced, the Regents appointed Collins as chancellor and thereby invoked a storm of protest. The fact that they had picked a state legislator rather than a professional educator did not sit well with Governor Michael Dukakis and his supporters. Claiming that the selection process had been seriously flawed, the governor intervened in the dispute and proceeded to pack the sixteen-member board with a new chairman and three new members who were favorably disposed to his own position. By so doing, he was able to get the Board of Regents to reconsider the appointment and to remove Collins from office. Meanwhile, Speaker of the House George Keverian criticized the governor's intervention and vigorously defended Collins. Subsequently, the realigned board chose Franklyn Jenifer, a black educator from New Jersey and a previous finalist. Values and vested interests were at stake as well as personal pride and ambition.

The chancellor search controversy must be understood in the context of a very complex political system involving history, culture, personalities, institutional arrangements, special interests, and ethnic group participation. To be sure, the political culture of Massachusetts colors all aspects of its institutional life, including the most rarefied and lofty level of higher education, highlighting perhaps more than simply a division between academic and political interests. Over time, politicians in the Bay State have adopted a proprietary attitude toward its public colleges and universities. They regard them as their prized possessions, if not their own creations. In the parlance of Beacon Hill legislators, they "own" them. Some of these institutions had become legislators' fiefdoms. In addition, the higher education system was a patronage haven for several ex-legislators. Unless one understands these dynamics, one cannot fully comprehend or appreciate the particulars of this specific case.

In many respects, the battle over the search for a chancellor reflected what had been going on in Massachusetts higher education for twenty years: a struggle between the traditional politics of the Boston Irish and the new politics of insurgent reformers. It also set in motion the bifactionalism within the state Democratic Party that pitted conservative Ed King Democrats against liberal Michael Dukakis Democrats and the legislative and executive branches of state government against each other. Urban-rural rivalries and other old antagonisms were rekindled between those who favored centralization of the system in Boston and those who favored decentralization. Among the latter were those who sought to restore the University of Massachusetts at Amherst to its once preeminent position. The controversy was further aggravated by the enduring tension between public and private institutions of higher learning. Indeed, the state's elite private institutions, especially those of world-class caliber, have always enjoyed center stage, much to the chagrin and intense jealousy of the public sector. Before the battle ended, it was transformed into a public-versus-private skirmish with the trappings of an Irish-versus-Harvard, town-and-gown confrontation.

To add to the political drama, Regent James Howell was accused of a conflict of interest by the state Ethics Commission in arguing against the approval of a graduate nursing program at the University of Massachusetts in Boston. The new program would be competing with a financially troubled one at Boston University, a private institution where Howell served as a trustee. Although he actually abstained from voting on the issue, he was nonetheless charged with a conflict. As a consequence, legislation was passed that clarified the relationship between the law establishing the Board of Regents and the law establishing the Ethics Commission. The matter did not end there, however. The legislation was promptly vetoed by Governor Dukakis, and the governor's veto, which evoked additional public criticism from Speaker Keverian, was later overridden by the General Court. But the furor over this effort to censure and then to exonerate Howell took a back seat to the controversy sparked by the effort to remove Collins.

All of this activity occurred in 1986 at a time when the newly created Board of Regents was still struggling to organize itself and define its role. For the most part the public was baffled by the intricate political game being played at the State House. Public opinion on the governor's handling of the chancellor search controversy was strongly divided. Some people looked on the whole affair as smart politics, especially for an incumbent governor who was then seeking reelection and planning to run for the U.S.

presidency in 1988. Others viewed it as a manipulative exercise of power that was as blatant as it was transparent, and of doubtful legality as well. Still others were too confused by the Board of Regents' overturning of its original decision to know quite what to make of it. Before the political smoke settled, the participants themselves felt that something had gone wrong. My own recollections are those of an interested faculty member who viewed the dispute from a discreet distance. The account that follows is based primarily on the public record and on personal interviews obtained from the principal participants.[5]

On the assumption that a look backward may illuminate the way ahead, I examine the central issue of process and analyze why things went awry. Inevitably mistakes were made, and these were mostly procedural. Some of the troubles were systemic and thus unavoidable. Others were not, although they could perhaps have been predicted by considering the difficulty the Regents had encountered in their search for a chancellor in 1981. (That botched effort will be discussed shortly.) Anyone looking at the events that took place in 1986 cannot adequately explain why they occurred without raising a set of deeper questions: What was the nature of the decision process itself? What preconceptions did the participants bring with them? How did their perceptions play against one another? Under what sorts of pressures were they operating? In what specific ways was the process flawed? What midcourse corrective measures were at their disposal? Did the Regents act in such a way as to reduce their own autonomy? If the Collins forces were able to control the Regents, why could they not also shape a search committee to serve their interests? How did it come about that the anti-Collins faction depended on the search committee to achieve its ends while the pro-Collins group relied on the Regents to do so, when the former was a creature of the latter?

Answering these kinds of questions should shed light on what happened. The questions, of course, answer themselves much more clearly after the fact than before. My list is far from complete. Many other questions may need to be asked and answered. Even so, this approach at least takes into account the different ways in which key actors saw the episode and their roles in it.

THE STRUGGLE FOR AUTONOMY

American public higher education began in Massachusetts in the late 1830s, when Horace Mann left the General Court to become the state's first secretary of education. An educator of great vision, Mann presided over numerous reforms, including the establishment of several normal schools to train teachers. These were the prototype public colleges. In 1862 the U.S.

Congress passed the Morrill Act, which gave land grants to each state for establishing colleges to train students in agriculture and mechanics. The Massachusetts Institute of Technology accepted the mechanical training mandate of this federal program. To address the other mandate, a state college of agriculture was created in Amherst in 1863.

Before the Civil War, Massachusetts was largely rural, Yankee Protestant, and agricultural. By the turn of the century, it had become largely urban and industrial and increasingly Catholic. The public colleges met these new social realities as best they could, but they were competing with an illustrious array of private institutions that benefited greatly from capitalist philanthropy. Bridging the gap between them was costly, and the public colleges suffered as a result. Subjected to benign neglect, they were starved financially and abused politically.

The hegemony of the independent sector explains in large measure why Massachusetts was so slow to provide more generous support for public higher education. Under these circumstances, the state college of agriculture at Amherst remained small in size and stature. It did not achieve university status until 1947, when its enrollment still hovered between two and three thousand students. At that time it paled by comparison to the large land grant schools in the midwestern and western states. "Mass Aggie," however, yearned to play catch-up and to emulate states such as California, Ohio, Michigan, and Indiana, which had a healthy mixture of strong private institutions and eminent public universities. But change came slowly. During the 1950s, Governor Foster Furcolo championed the establishment of a network of community colleges. Despite its success, Massachusetts sent a smaller proportion of its high school students on to college than any other state except Maine and Mississippi. Lacking the prestige and financial clout of their distinguished private counterparts, the public institutions suffered from an inferiority complex, considering themselves second best. This attitude, which was rooted in financial deprivation persists to some extent today.

By the early 1960s, conditions began to change sharply. The era of the Great Society, which witnessed increased federal involvement in and funding of higher education, marked a decisive turning point in the evolution of public of higher education in the Bay State. During that decade, enrollment at UMass/Amherst soared to 23,000 students, and more than seventy new buildings were constructed to accommodate them. Capital outlay funds at the state university rose from $1.6 million to $89.8 million. New campuses were created at Boston in 1964 and at Worcester in 1968. The state built a medical school in Worcester with federal assistance, and the new teaching hospital overlooking Lake Quinsigamond was soon providing better care than had previously been available in the area. Mergers of small technical colleges led to the establishment of Southeastern Massachusetts University in 1969 and the University of Lowell in 1973. At the same time, the community college system was expanded, and the old normal schools were converted into modern liberal arts colleges. New community colleges appeared in cities such as Brockton and Lynn in the east and Pittsfield and Springfield in the west.

Spearheading this expansion drive were leading Irish Democratic politicians including Maurice Donahue, Kevin Harrington, Robert Quinn, and George Kenneally, who were all close to the party's blue-collar base. Solving the problem of changing conditions with such dramatic expansion required the combined efforts of both the executive and legislative branches. What had happened? Apparently the demand had always been there. Why was the legislature now willing to meet that demand? Or, to put it somewhat differently, why did it take the Boston Irish so long to commit public funds to the education of their children? No single explanation is satisfactory. Part of the answer lies in the fact that the Republicans controlled the governorship and both houses of the legislature, with few exceptions, from the Civil War to almost the middle of the twentieth century. The Democrats did not gain control of the House of Representatives until 1948. They did not capture the Senate until 1958. Another part of the answer had to do with the dramatic transformation of Catholic institutions such as Boston College and Holy Cross, which began to recruit faculty and students nationwide. Such private colleges became too expensive for middle-income and working-class families. Even more prohibitive were the skyrocketing tuition costs at the private medical schools. Consequently, Senate president Donahue and Speaker Quinn made increased funding a top legislative priority. In fact, it was mostly Boston College alumni on Beacon Hill who pushed for the creation of UMass/Boston. They saw it as a way to pick up the slack in the private system and to serve their blue-collar constituents. UMass/Boston, dedicated to the pursuit of the liberal arts, was envisioned by its founding faculty as a "Harvard for the working class."

With the passage of the landmark Willis-Harrington Act in 1965, the public sector won considerable fiscal and institutional autonomy. As former UMass president Robert Wood observes:

All through the sixties, higher education in Massachusetts was on a roll. Enrollments swelled as post-war baby boomers came of age. Federal support for research and development, the student aid programs of the Great Society, liberal state appropriations for public institutions, and the first sizable endowment drives for many private ones provided sufficient and occasionally ample resources. Civil-rights legislation released the pent-up college demands for minorities. Capital outlays for new campuses, classrooms, and laboratories were often authorized even before architects completed plans. The times were golden.[6]

Values and social demographics were changing. The new informational age spawned by computers was dawning. With the abundance of state and federal funding, the entire system prospered. Nothing since has matched that period of accomplishment.

CREATION OF THE BOARD OF REGENTS

Those years of euphoria placated all but the most ardent proponents of expanded growth. Regulating such growth and the way in which the public system was governed presented a formidable challenge. Under the Willis-Harrington legislation, the system was loosely organized into five "segments," with governance delegated to separate boards of lay trustees. Their efforts were coordinated by a central Board of Higher Education, whose primary functions were to develop a master plan and to review budgetary requests. But the Board of Higher Education never obtained from the legislature a budget or staff that was sufficient to carry out these responsibilities. Opposition to the Board of Higher Education came mostly from UMass/Amherst, which did not want any state agency interfering with its flagship status or with its plans to catch up with the more prestigious Big Ten state universities. Much of this resistance was engineered by Winthrop Dakin, an astute Yankee attorney from Amherst, who had opposed the creation of the Board of Higher Education. Ironically, Dakin wound up as its chairman. In this capacity he implemented the Amherst game plan, which was to keep the Board of Higher Education weak. The private sector, which also wished to protect its independence from the Board of Higher Education, aided and abetted that plan.[7]

A succession of chancellors (Richard Millard, Patrick McCarthy, Leroy Keith, Edward McGuire, and Laura Clausen), whose selection was embroiled in controversy, managed the Board of Higher Education. Keith, who later became president of Morehouse College in Atlanta, was the first black to head the Commonwealth's system. In addition to its being underfunded and understaffed, the Board of Higher Education was further compromised in 1971 with the awkward presence of a secretary of educational affairs, a position that had been established as part of an extensive reorganization of state government. This institutional arrangement resulted in substantial overlap of statutory authority and responsibilities.

By the mid-1970s, with the Arab oil embargo, soaring inflation, general economic uncertainty, and the first Dukakis administration imposing across-the-board funding cuts for public higher education, this cumbersome bureaucracy proved unsatisfactory. The hegemony of the segmented boards not only resulted in a disparate set of academic programs and duplication of effort but also replicated budget hearings that were prone to internecine battles in the competition for what were now scarce state funds. As John Millett observes, "What had been demonstrated in Massachusetts was the inability of a state coordinating board and a secretary of education to bring about substantial change."[8]

As a result, Kevin Harrington of Salem, who had succeeded Maurice Donahue as Senate president, was anxious to replace the Board of Higher Education with a better institutional arrangement. A special legislative commission headed by state senator Walter Boverini of Lynn was established in 1977 to study the problem, but its work was interrupted by a gubernatorial election in 1978 that saw conservative Edward King defeat the liberal incumbent Michael Dukakis in a bitterly contested Democratic primary. Buoyed by his startling upset, King went on to win the governorship. Like his two predecessors in the corner office, King advocated the creation of a strong central governing board, but he could not break through the stalemate of forces surrounding the reorganization of public higher education. The main obstacle was James Collins. Strongly influenced by Winthrop Dakin, the young state representative from Amherst, who chaired the House Education Committee, remained vehemently opposed to the idea of a central board. He saw it as a major threat to the autonomy of UMass/Amherst. Although no Irish symbolism attaches to the rural town of Amherst, the flagship campus was nevertheless located in his base of political power. From the mid-1970s on, Collins succeeded in blocking a series of reorganization proposals.[9]

In the meantime, it took three governors (Francis Sargent, Dukakis, and King) to restructure public higher education and to streamline its bureaucracy. In May 1980 the Boverini commission submitted its report, but its recommendations were torpedoed. Exasperated by such obstruction, the Irish Democratic troika of Governor King, Speaker Thomas McGee, and Senate president William Bulger (by this time Bulger had succeeded Harrington in the top Senate post) broke the stalemate and agreed to enact major reform. The deal was supposedly struck while the three men were on a trip together to Ireland. In what amounted to an end run around Collins, they achieved the reform measure by use of an "outside section" that was appended to the appropriations bill for the 1981 fiscal year. (For an explanation of "outside sections," see chapter 7.) Since the issue was resolved by a conference committee, it did not require either a public hearing or a floor debate. Hence, Collins could not kill the measure. Both state representative John Finnegan and state senator Chester Atkins, who chaired their respective Ways and Means committees, were responsible for engineering this feat. What became known as the Higher Education Reorganization Act of 1980 was thereby enacted.

The new law abolished the Board of Higher Education, the community college and state college boards, and the position of secretary of educational affairs. These entities were replaced by a powerful Board of Regents which was given both coordinating and governing functions. Under this legislation, the Board of Regents was made responsible for long-range planning, personnel policies, collective bargaining, and review and approval of academic programs. In addition, it was given oversight responsibility for independent degree-granting institutions in the private sector. All in all, the Board of Regents was assigned the broad powers necessary for achieving unity and cohesion in what was then a highly fragmented and unwieldy system.[10] What this meant in blunter language was that the authority of the central board would be increased at the inevitable expense of the local boards.

By statutory language, the Board of Regents was granted a seven-month transition period before it became operational. During this orderly transition, which extended from August 1980 to March 1981, Secretary of State Paul Guzzi, a former state representative from Newton, served as its temporary chancellor. While he presided in an interim capacity, the Board of Regents conducted a search for his permanent replacement. Guzzi himself did not become a candidate. Worth momentary note is the fact that the search committee in 1980–81 was composed exclusively of regents. There were no outsiders. The chancellor's salary was fixed by statute at $54,500, which proved to be a significant drawback to attracting the best applicants. According to Regent George Ellison, everyone entered the search expecting that the salary would be raised to $95,000. Four highly qualified educators from out of state were selected as finalists. Albert Bowker, the chancellor at the University of California at Berkeley, was the leading contender. But the Regents were unable to persuade the General Court to increase the chancellor's salary, and none of the finalists would accept the job because of the low salary. Consequently, the first phase ended in stalemate. Seven months of searching amounted to an exercise in futility. The search had to be reopened.[11]

In the second phase, three contenders emerged. They were David Bartley, Kermit Morrissey, and Franklin Patterson. All three came from within Massachusetts. Morrissey was the former president of Boston State College, and Patterson was the former president of Hampshire College. The frontrunner, Bartley, was no stranger to state politics. He was the former Speaker of the House and the sitting president of Holyoke Community College. The Regents rejected him because he came across in his interview more as a politician than as an academic leader. They also failed to agree on either Morrissey or Paterson.[12] In a surprise move, they drafted a transplanted New Jersey educator, John Duff, president of the University of Lowell. Duff was also the founder and head of the Public Council of College and University Presidents and as such was serving as academic adviser to the search committee. Although he apparently did not seek the job, some people resented the fact that he was an insider choice.

Duff was promised a $10,500 salary increase, but he never got it. This feisty Irishman proved to be controversial. Scorned by skeptics and journalists, Duff nevertheless provided strong leadership, especially in dealing with systemic problems, but his direct and decisive managerial style eventually landed him in trouble.

Among Duff's more notable accomplishments was the successful merger of Boston State College with UMass/Boston in 1983. More than anything else, this merger demonstrated to a tax-conscious public the willingness and determination of the Board of Regents to terminate programs that were no longer cost-effective. Their decision was unpopular locally. Boston State College, which had been founded in 1852, had powerful allies on Beacon Hill. A hue and cry went up, but the Board of Regents stuck to its decision. In implementing the merger plan, the Regents acted as a buffer by taking the political heat off the Boston legislative delegation for the demise of its state teachers' college.

By 1986 the public system had grown huge and complex. Taken together, it encompassed three state universities, nine state teachers' colleges, and fifteen community colleges, with a total enrollment of 180,000 students and a workforce of 14,000 employees. The Board of Regents chancellor administered a budget in excess of $700 million, which included a $58 million scholarship program and a capital outlay plan. In addition, he supervised a staff of seventy-two people and an office budget of $3 million. As the primary advocate for higher education, he was its most visible leader, both symbolically and operationally. His continued effectiveness depended in large measure on his personal style and his professional competence.

Members and Terms of Office Massachusetts Board of Regents of Higher Education, 1986

Appointees of Governor Edward King	Appointees of Governor Michael Dukakis
*David J Beaubien (1980–88)	Mary Lou Anderson (1984–89)
*Nicholas Boraski (1982–92)	Paul S. Doherty (1986–91)
Gerard F. Doherty (1982–87)	Ellen C. Guiney (1986–91)
Janet Eisner (1980–86)	Kathleen Harrington (1984–88)
**George Ellison (1980–82; 1984–88)	Joseph M. Henson (1986–91)
*J. John Fox (1981–89)	L. Edward Lashman (1986–90)
James Howell (1982–86)	Paul Marks (1984–90)
David Paresky (1980–86)	Norma Markey, student member (1986–87)
**Elizabeth B. Rawlins (1980–82; 1984–88)	Hassan Minor (1984–89)
Edward T. Sullivan (1982–87)	Paul N. Ylvisaker (1984–86)

*Initially appointed by King and reappointed by Dukakis
**Initially appointed by King and then appointed by Dukakis

A NEW SEARCH COMMITTEE

On December 10, 1985, John Duff suddenly resigned as chancellor under the cloud of allegations of improper political fundraising. He had sent a letter to the Regents soliciting them to buy tickets to a $100-a-plate dinner given for the benefit of Speaker George Keverian. Subsequently, the print media revealed that it was James Collins who had asked Duff to sell the tickets. This solicitation, many State House observers believed, was part of a larger scheme by Regent John Fox to rehabilitate Collins politically.

After Duff's departure, the picture was further clouded by the revelation of a sex scandal that eventually led to the indictment of the president of Westfield State College and the payment of $10,000 as a legal settlement to the student involved. The fallout from this sordid affair was widespread. To add to the administrative chaos and disarray, a $2 million discrepancy was discovered in the Board of Regents' computer account.

Gerard Indelicato, the governor's educational adviser, was involved in a bitter feud with Duff that stemmed from Indelicato's actions with regard to the Teaching and Learning Center. Duff distrusted Indelicato, whom he had found to be duplicitous in dealing with the legislature. Both men disliked each other intensely. Indelicato saw the fundraising incident as the perfect excuse to oust Duff. This, as we shall see, was the precipitating event that set off a political chain reaction. Before leaving office, however, Duff warned Governor Dukakis about Indelicato. Later, the governor's inner circle of Frank Keefe, John Sasso, and Steve Rosenfeld voiced their displeasure with Indelicato and urged that he be replaced.

Against this background, Board of Regents chairman David Beaubien moved quickly to fill the leadership vacuum created by Duff's departure. Beaubien had served on the board since its inception in 1980. He was a senior vice president for a high-technology firm (EG&G), where he was responsible for new business ventures. A UMass/Amherst graduate in engineering, Beaubien lived in Montague in western Massachusetts. His residence was located within state senator John Olver's district and near James Collins's district in Hampshire County.

As its December 10 meeting, which Regent Gerard F. Doherty missed, the Board of Regents named Joseph Finnegan as the acting interim chancellor. Finnegan, whose brother had helped create the Board of Regents, came from a well-known political family in Dorchester. He was not an academic. (Doherty, who soon became a major player in the search, was a former state legislator and former chairman of the state Democratic Party. He had helped deliver Bunker Hill Community College, along with an MDC hockey rink, to his predominantly Irish working-class constituency in Charlestown.) At the same meeting, the board approved Beaubien's appointment of an eleven-member search committee. Unlike the original search committee, this one was composed of six Regents and five non-Regents. Since 1980 the Board of Regents had adopted a new policy governing searches which followed a national model and called for adding outside people to meet the demands from the various constituencies within public higher education. The new policy also specified that once the Regents delegated the screening function to a committee, they could not resort to an alternative means for picking candidates.

Six of the Regents volunteered to serve on the search committee. Three of those were chosen and three other Regents were drafted. Of the volunteers, Doherty, Howell, Harrington, and Sullivan turned out to be Collins supporters; Rawlins and Minor were the other two volunteers. The additional Regent representation on the search committee consisted of Mary Lou Anderson, Janet Eisner, James Howell, Hassan Minor, Edward Sullivan, and Paul Ylvisaker. The non-Regents were Joyce King, a trustee of Roxbury Community College; David Knapp, president of UMass; Robert Lee, a faculty member at Fitchburg State College; Laura Clausen, former Board of Higher Education chancellor who now served on the Board of Regents staff; and Eileen Parise, a student trustee at Southeastern Massachusetts University. Obviously, Duff's departure was anticipated, and Beaubien received help in producing these names. He had consulted with Duff and with vice chancellors Joseph Finnegan, Peter Mitchell, Roger Schinness, and Clare Van Ummersen. Staff member Jan Robinson had recommended Eileen Parise.[13]

There was no shortage of expertise among those responsible for screening candidates. Nor did they lack gender and racial balance. There were six men and five women. Nine of the eleven brought substantial experience in higher education, though from different vantage points, and the other two were a student and a member of organized labor. There were two blacks and one Asian.

Paul Ylvisaker was asked to chair the search committee. He did not volunteer for the assignment. As the former dean of the Harvard Graduate School of Education, he brought with him both academic and political experience. In the mid-1960s he had served as the first commissioner of community affairs in New Jersey. Before accepting his new assignment, Ylvisaker made his conditions known. If he was going to put his professional reputation on the line, he insisted on conducting a fair and open search.[14] Hassan Minor, a black academic who had taught courses in organizational behavior at MIT, was chosen as vice chairman. Janet Eisner, president of Emmanuel College, was the only person who had served on the original search committee in 1980–81.

PROBING ASSUMPTIONS

The participants approached their task with concerns and objectives colored by assumptions based on past experience. Even before the search had gotten under way, rumors began circulating that James Collins had sufficient votes on the Board of Regents to win the chancellorship. These rumors, which were not entirely without substance, created the impression that the outcome was predetermined. Meanwhile, Collins, who wanted to redeem his political stature, was busy lining up potential support. He discussed his candidacy at separate luncheon engagements with Mary Lou Anderson and David Knapp. Anderson, who lived in Worcester, belonged to several professional women's group and chaired the Regents' subcommittee on affirmative action. Such early maneuvering raised questions about whether there was to be a genuine search or merely the ratification of a decision that had already been made.

Not unexpectedly, the participants soon divided into pro-and anti-Collins camps. The Collins backers saw the chancellor's job primarily in terms of generating legislative support for public higher education and obtaining the funds necessary to finance it. In 1984, while lobbying for a salary increase for the chancellor, Regent Edward Sullivan discovered that John Duff had become persona non grata on Beacon Hill.[15] Duff's credibility problem stemmed in part from what was widely perceived as his expensive lifestyle. His deteriorating relations with the General Court had impaired his continued effectiveness.

As a result, the holdover King appointees on the Board of Regents, three of whom were on the search committee, now wanted to find someone whom the legislators liked and respected. In their eyes, James Collins was the ideal person. Endowed with abundant Irish charm and wit and popular among his peers, he was a seasoned Democratic politician with fourteen years of legislative experience. Thus, he could serve their interests well in the competition for state funding. As the former chairman of the joint Education Committee, the thirty-nine-year-old Collins had won his reputation in leading the fight for elementary and secondary school reform. The son of a taxi driver, the Hampshire County Democrat had graduated from UMass/Amherst in 1968 and from Suffolk Law School in 1984. He was also the protégé of Regent John Fox, who had close ties with former Speaker David Bartley.

Regent John Fox saw the chancellorship as a way of rehabilitating Collins, who had been stripped of his committee chair in a House leadership fight in 1984. Collins had backed incumbent Speaker Thomas McGee in that fight, but McGee lost to George Keverian, who had promised rules reform in the lower house. No one played the inside political game better than Judge Fox. He had served as chief secretary to former governor Paul A. Dever from 1949 to 1952. In 1972 he co-sponsored the Bartley-Fox bill, which served as a national model for handgun control legislation. As a former trustee of UMass, Fox was closely identified with its Boston campus.

It became clear that a combination of ethnic, class, and Democratic Party loyalties was the main factor that shaped the thinking of the King appointees on the Board of Regents. The fact that Collins was an alumnus of UMass/ Amherst made him all the more attractive to them. With the availability of a homegrown product of the public system, they gave some thought to putting Collins in office without going through the formality of a search, but they decided against such a move.[16]

The anti-Collins camp, which was composed of Dukakis appointees led by Ylvisaker and Minor, operated with fundamentally divergent attitudes. They wished to find either the best educator in the nation or someone who knew how to manage a complex public organization. If that person happened to be a minority or female, so much the better. Affirmative action and the advancement of women's rights were values that they prized. Clearly they did not want to have another Irishman or a Beacon Hill crony in the post. Although they wanted a chancellor who could develop a good rapport with the legislature, they did not see this as an absolute prerequisite for the job. If they had to accept a legislator, they much preferred state senator John Olver, who had a doctorate in chemistry from MIT and had taught for several years at UMass/Amherst. Above all, they were looking for a tough-minded administrator who had experience in shaping academic policy and was familiar with the way bureaucracy works. In other words, they wanted a "change agent" who could shake things up and turn the Board of Regents around in much the same way that banker Ira Jackson had done at the state Department of Revenue. Whether they could find such a person remained to be seen, but they were determined to cast as wide a net as possible.[17]

At a courtesy meeting held on January 8, 1986, Governor Dukakis revealed his assumptions to the search group. He indicated that he wanted a "cracker-jack" appointment but was hopeful that they might find a qualified person within the state since, in the past, there had been a large turnover of people who had been recruited from out of state. He also wanted someone with political savvy who knew local politics and could hit the ground running. Hassan Minor recalled the governor's saying, "I'm not the least bit interested in academic deans who can't find their way through the State House." Dukakis expressed his dismay that no candidate from Massachusetts had surfaced in the recent search for a new commissioner for the state Board of Education, which oversaw elementary and secondary schools. At one point in the meeting Ylvisaker attempted to flush out the truth by asking the governor a loaded question. "We have heard stories to the effect that somebody already has been picked for the chancellorship. How do you respond?" Dukakis said that he had heard similar "rumors coming over the transom," but as far as he was concerned there was no inside candidate for the job. He ended the meeting by telling the committee that he wanted "to keep politics out of the search" as much as possible.[18]

Reaction to the meeting varied. The pro-Collins forces interpreted the governor's remarks as a "backhanded endorsement" of their man. The anti-Collins camp felt encouraged by his disclaimer about an inside candidate. Obviously the governor had given them mixed signals. Had he defined more clearly the objective he had in mind, subsequent events might have been different. They might even have produced a happier result from his standpoint. Privately he confided to Beaubien that he could live with a candidate who was not an academic. In fact, the governor seriously considered his close friend and political adviser Edward Lashman as a possible candidate. But Lashman, who had come out of the labor movement, lacked even a bachelor's degree. After discussing the matter with David Bartley, Lashman concluded that his candidacy not only would be an affront to the academic community but also would damage the governor politically, and he declined to be considered.[19]

Dukakis did agree to the need for a more competitive chancellor's salary, and he promised to press for early legislative action. He did not keep his promise, however, and that in itself became an issue. As James Howell lamented, "The pay raise issue was the albatross that hung above our ship."[20]

Even more revealing was the exchange that took place between the governor and *Boston Globe* reporter Steve Curwood. In an exclusive personal interview for publication, Curwood asked Dukakis about his priority and about charges that his administration was not fully supportive of UMass/Amherst as the flagship institution. Dukakis answered, "We aren't California, we're not Texas, and we're not Michigan. We're a different state. We do happen to have some of the finest [private] academic institutions in the world. And I don't think it makes sense for us to try to duplicate that."[21] Such words inflamed smoldering tensions. The interview infuriated the constituencies who identified themselves with public higher education. Many of them feared that the governor lacked sympathy for their cause and was not genuinely committed to providing educational leaders of superior quality. Besides leaving himself vulnerable to charges of favoritism, the governor inadvertently undercut the search. His comments went a long way toward explaining his failure to play a more aggressive leadership role, particularly in the early stages of the search.

A short time later several Regents, including Beaubien, Fox, Minor, and

Ylvisaker, paid courtesy calls to both Speaker Keverian and Senate president Bulger. Among other things, they discussed the salary issue as a major problem facing them in the recruitment of a new chancellor. Keverian promised that he would not interfere with their seeking corrective legislative action. While Bulger indicated that he did not favor a salary increase, he told them that he would not block their efforts.

The drafting of the necessary legislation soon bogged down in an intramural spat between James Samels, the attorney for the Board of Regents, and Stephen Rosenfeld, the governor's legal counsel. Consequently, the pay raise bill (H-5474) was not filed until March 27. The governor's bill was designed to eliminate the practice of setting the chancellor's salary by statute. It delegated this prerogative to the Regents, subject to the approval of the commissioner of administration and finance, at that time Frank Keefe. A public hearing on the bill was held by the public Service Committee on April 16. Since Ylvisaker was out of town that day, Beaubien and Minor testified at the hearing.

On May 6 the pay raise bill was reported favorably out of the Public Service Committee, but it now appeared in much different form. The new draft (H-5639) allowed the Regents to set the salary, but the first increase had to be approved by the Ways and Means committees of both houses. The legislative intent was to retain the power of the purse as a means of exerting leverage on the Board of Regents. H-5639 was then referred to the House Ways and Means Committee, where it languished and never resurfaced. The bill, which became an instrument of control for Speaker Keverian, succumbed to a slow and painful death.[22]

THE SELECTION PROCESS

The selection process was essentially a two-stage affair. The first stage, which extended from January 8 to June 19, involved establishing procedures, organizing the search, and screening the applicants. The latter two functions were performed by the search committee. Procedures were set by the Board of Regents itself. The second stage was shorter but more intensive. It covered the twelve days between June 20 and July 1, when the Regents interviewed the four finalists and then finally picked the chancellor.

During the first stage, the search committee held fifteen meetings. These were all duly announced as required by the state open meeting law. Minutes were recorded and made publicly available. Janet Eisner hosted most of the meetings at her Emmanuel College campus in Boston. Those involving candidate interviews were held at MIT's Endicott House in Dedham and at the Park Plaza Hotel in Boston. Ylvisaker, who was designated as the sole spokesman for the search committee, reported about its progress at each meeting of the Board of Regents. He delegated the staff work to Hassan Minor, who was director of a nonprofit community organization head-quartered on Commonwealth Avenue in Boston. Candidate files were kept sequestered there during the first stage. The committee originally contracted with the Association of Governing Boards (AGB) of American Colleges and Universities to conduct reference checks on semifinalist candidates. Because of a scheduling conflict, the AGB was later replaced by the firm Peter Levine Associates, which performed the same service.[23]

Given the divergences between the rival factions, it could have been predicted that they would have difficulty working with each other. Ylvisaker may have foreseen that prospect; at least he came to recognize it right away. He showed a meticulous concern for maintaining a delicate balance between politics and education, although to the King appointees, Ylvisaker seemed more interested in process than in outcome. He was afraid that unless he developed a fail-safe mechanism for protecting the process, it would be rigged or otherwise subverted. Ylvisaker's concern was heightened by the rumors of a "political fix." He soon found a way around the dilemma.

The Board of Regents meeting of February 11 was held at Roxbury Community College. Because of a winter snowstorm, six Regents were absent, including James Howell and Kathleen Harrington. At this meeting Ylvisaker introduced a resolution that committed the Regents to make their appointment from a list of three to five candidates recommended by the search committee. If none of them proved acceptable, Ylvisaker's resolution further stipulated that the process was to be remanded back to the search committee, which would then provide additional recommendations. This provision was designed to guard against the repetition of the stalemate that had occurred in 1981. It was a masterstroke that was deceptively simple. Since the resolution passed by a vote of 8 to 1, the Collins forces either were caught off guard or were slow on the uptake. Only Gerard Doherty opposed it.[24]

More lay behind this maneuver than met the eye. The subtle message it conveyed to the Collins people was that they were not operating in good faith and therefore could not be trusted. More significant was the reality that it moved power away from the Board of Regents and put it in the hands of outsiders. Gerard Doherty, who had missed the December 10 meeting when the Regents had approved the composition of the search committee, strongly objected to Ylvisaker's resolution on the grounds that it transferred his authority as a Regent to five non-Regents, who did not share his statutory responsibility or political accountability. In his view, the Ylvisaker maneuver was reminiscent of the "politics of exclusion" that had banned certain people from the 1968 Democratic national convention.[25]

In that issue lay the misunderstanding. Ylvisaker, who privately referred to his scheme as "shark repellent," got his way in the adoption of the binding resolution but stored up trouble for himself in its execution, thereby setting the stage for gubernatorial intervention. For the time being, calm prevailed.

The search committee had established a set of procedural guidelines that were appended to Ylvisaker's resolution. The committee members also rewrote the chancellor's job description, but not without some difficulty. Given the wide gaps in perspective, they found it hard to agree on the kind of person whom they wanted to fill the position. After extensive deliberation, they finally reached a consensus. Much emphasis was placed on the leadership and managerial skills required to run a comprehensive system with twenty-nine campuses. Another criterion called for "sensitivity to the educational needs of a changing population, and a record of commitment to affirmative action."[26] Although the job description mentioned that an "earned doctorate" was desired, the wording was ambiguous enough to allow for a candidate who lacked such a degree. In fact, the guidelines specifically allowed for "exceptional talent or accomplishment" as a qualification equivalency. They intentionally steered clear of making a Ph.D. the litmus test. It was preferred but not required.

The Massachusetts chancellor vacancy was advertised in the *Chronicle of Higher Education, Black Issues in Higher Education*, and Boston and national newspapers, with March 15, 1986, set as the deadline for applications and nominations. In an effort to attract women and minorities, letters were sent to women's organizations and traditional black colleges encouraging applications. With these tasks completed, a wide net had been cast.

The next step was the screening of candidates. By the March 15 cutoff date, the committee had received 107 nominations, constituting a rich pool of both national and local candidates. A subcommittee composed of Ylvisaker, Knapp, and Minor did the initial screening. The first cuts were relatively easy. Some thirty-nine either withdrew or failed to complete their applications. Another thirty-six were eliminated for various reasons. By March 31 the pool had been reduced from 107 to thirty-two. Of the remaining candidates, six were people of color, sixteen were white, and race was indeterminable for the remainder. There were six women and twenty-six men.[27]

SURVIVING THE NEXT TWO CUTS

On April 3 the search committee unanimously approved the work of its screening subcommittee. The members spent the next two weeks examining candidate files. On April 17, Bruce Rose, the Regents' affirmative action officer, gave the list of thirty-two names his official stamp of approval. He found its racial and gender composition to fall within the prescribed guide-lines.[28] On the same day, the committee winnowed the field from thirty-two to twelve. Those who survived this cut were Alice Chandler, James Collins, Robert Corrigan, Elbert Fretwell, Leon Ginsberg, Franklyn Jenifer, William Monat, Barbara Newell, John Olver, Lawrence Pettit, Donald Stewart, and Blenda Wilson. This first short list consisted of three women and nine men; three were black.

The first indication of trouble was the leaking of these names to the press. On learning of the leak, Ylvisaker became visibly angered by the breach in confidentiality. The main casualty was Blenda Wilson, a black female educator who headed Colorado's Commission on Higher Education. She immediately dropped out of the competition to protect her quest for the presidency of Spelman College in Georgia. This post was being vacated by Donald Stewart, whom she did not want to offend. Up to that point, Wilson, along with Barbara Newell, were Ylvisaker's favorite contenders. Wilson had previously worked for him as an assistant dean at Harvard. It was generally conceded that someone in the Collins camp was responsible for the news leak.

To no one's surprise, two state legislators survived this cut. Most participants felt that Collins and Olver were being paired to offset each other. The Ylvisaker group clung to a stereotype of Collins as a "hack politician" who was only marginally qualified. His critics considered him an opportunist. They deplored the fact that he lacked a doctorate and that he did not come from a traditional academic background. His detractors grudgingly admitted that Collins had been passionate about elementary and secondary education but argued that he was a "Johnny-come-lately" when it came to higher education. Another complaint was that Collins had never managed a large-scale public organization. The only job that the legislator had held prior to entering politics was assistant director of an Upward Bound program at UMass/Amherst. For that matter, state senator John Olver suffered from the same deficiency. He had not managed a large public organization either. Perhaps that flaw was inevitable. It speaks to the legislative careers and the overlapping interests that the two prominent men shared: both chaired legislative committees, both were politically qualified, and both came from Amherst.

The Collins advocates rebutted their opponents by arguing that through his legislative accomplishments, their candidate more than met the qualification equivalency as specified in the procedural guidelines. They were quick to point out that even the president of Harvard University had only a law degree, not an earned doctorate. They saw an attack on Collins as an attack on legislators in general. Senate president William Bulger stayed out of the chancellor search controversy largely in deference to state senator

John Olver. Although Bulger liked Collins personally, he did not want to embarrass his colleague Olver by opposing him publicly. It was a form of senatorial courtesy on Bulger's part.

While this furor continued within the Board of Regents, House Speaker Keverian threatened to block the chancellor's pay raise unless Collins was among the finalists. That pressure grew in intensity as the "ownership mentality" of the General Court asserted itself. In legislative circles, Keverian's support of Collins was seen as a symbolic act intended to show that the Speaker was not vindictive toward his previous opponents in the 1984 House fight so long as they accepted his leadership.

Further complications arose when selection of the chancellor was attempted across sex lines. Gender and race were affirmative action criteria that had to be taken into account. The same was true of other factors such as social class, age, and ethnicity. Any combination of these variables made the search committee's choices that much more complicated. Inherited memories of the past gave certain options added weight and at the same time tended to exclude others.

In early May, as the emerging controversy surfaced publicly, the search committee began its first round of interviews. Professor Robert Lee from Fitchburg State College prepared a list of questions that solicited pertinent information about each candidate's record and about his or her commitment to salient issues in public higher education. Owing to scheduling problems, these interviews progressed slowly. Ylvisaker notified the Board of Regents that the search committee would not be able to present its final slate of candidates by the board's June 9 meeting as originally planned. He also expressed his concern that the search was becoming politicized. The Collins entourage was especially active in May. Judge Fox lobbied hard to line up the necessary votes for his protégé. The tactics of the Collins forces appeared heavy-handed to those who were not impressed by him.

Beaubien, who readily admitted that his business interests were interfering with his job as chairman of the Board of Regents, was content to play a passive role. He studiously refrained from taking sides. In comparison with the forceful leadership exercised by James R. Martin, the board's first chairman, Beaubien seemed weak and inept. He did not have the organizational skills to prevent the drift that the agency was experiencing. Without a firm hand at the helm, coupled with the custodial chancellorship of Joseph Finnegan, the Board of Regents was left operating with a loose rudder.

On May 22 the penultimate cut from twelve candidates to six was made. By this time, three of the contenders had dropped out. In addition to Blenda Wilson, they included Alice Chandler of the State University of New York at New Paltz, and William Monat, chancellor of the Illinois Board of Regents, who accepted a job elsewhere. That left nine remaining. Of these,

Robert Corrigan of UMass/Boston, Leon Ginsberg of West Virginia, and Lawrence Pettit of the University System of South Texas were eliminated. Corrigan was seen by the Collins backers as a threat to both Boston University and the resurgence of UMass/Amherst, and they thought it inappropriate for him to move ahead of his boss, David Knapp. At the conclusion of the meeting to narrow the field, the committee sensed a move afoot by Ylvisaker and Minor to limit the number of finalists to four.[29]

THE FINAL FOUR

As the search entered its final stages in June, the Collins phalanx became alarmed, and with good reason. Since their native son candidate had barely edged out Leon Ginsberg for the sixth spot, they feared that he might be eliminated in the final cut. To avoid such a possibility, they now attempted what they had flirted with doing back in December. At the Board of Regents meeting of June 9, which met in executive session, the Collins camp moved to dispense with the search and thereby clear the way to put their man in office. Ylvisaker firmly resisted this move and warned that if the search were disrupted, he would be forced to go public. His counterthreat worked. The Collins faction backed off and withdrew their motion. As a compromise, the Board of Regents took the easy way out and authorized the submission of six names as finalists. And indeed, for a time it appeared that the search committee would take this way out.[30]

For a meeting that was called for the purpose of reducing internal strife, it did not succeed. Strong differences of opinion split the Board of Regents. At one point Janet Eisner walked out of the meeting in complete disgust, but Elizabeth Rawlins talked her into coming back. Eisner deplored the fact that the board had spent five hours discussing the search, compared with one hour discussing the crisis at Westfield State College. Only fragmentary accounts of the confidential discussions leaked out, some of them a year later. The discordant factions now went their separate ways as the dispute headed for its first major showdown.

Three days later, on June 12, Eisner notified her fellow Regents that since she would be leaving the country for the next few weeks, she would not be participating in their upcoming decisions. This announcement came as a blow to the Collins camp, which had been counting heavily on her vote. Some thought that she "took a walk" to avoid trustee pressure on her campus. Emmanuel is a Catholic women's college that was founded by local Irish Catholics in 1919. As might be expected, many of its alumnae favored Collins. How much pressure they actually applied to their trustees and president cannot be ascertained. Eisner herself denied such allegations, claiming that she had scheduled her trip months in advance. For her, the

Collins candidacy presented a quality issue. She definitely preferred E. K. Fretwell, who she felt would bring stature to the Commonwealth.[31]

Maneuvers on both sides heightened the impression of a political fix. Distracting bombshells, including the Westfield State scandal and the conflict-of-interest charges leveled against Regent James Howell, exploded in their midst. The mudslinging continued unabated. Collins was severely criticized for his opposition to the creation of the Board of Regents and his subsequent attempts to repeal the enabling legislation. It seemed ludicrous to his detractors that he would now be chosen to head the agency that he had previously tried to dismantle. In a similar vein, John Olver was taken to task for his stance in favor of abolishing the president's office at UMass. The pro-Collins Regents complained bitterly that the non-Regents were usurping their prerogative to select the chancellor. Failure by chairman Beaubien to clarify this confusion in roles not only exacerbated the process issue but also led to a serious concern about accountability.

On June 12 and 18, the six semifinalists were invited back for a second interview with Regents in attendance who were not members of the search committee. Complete reference checks were made on each candidate. At the beginning of the search, Collins had asked several well-known educators to nominate and endorse him. Gregory Anrig, the president of Educational Testing Service and former state secretary for education, nominated him for the chancellorship. Collins also obtained recommendations from the renowned historian Henry Steele Commager and from Peter Pouncey, the president of Amherst College. In addition, he received endorsements from a legislative delegation composed of UMass alumni and from the Massachusetts Black Legislative Caucus.[32] The latter endorsement was considered to be a real coup for affirmative action. But the outside consulting firm downplayed the impact of these endorsements. The consultants indicated that such letters of recommendation were unreliable because their authors could be sued if they wrote comments that might be construed as damaging.

What particularly irked the Collins camp is that the Regents not on the committee were not allowed to see these letters or to attend the meetings. As staff director, Hassan Minor kept the letters under tight security in his private office. This procedure distorted the process by giving the anti-Collins group an unfair advantage. As James Howell put it, "He who controls the mail has the power."[33] The Collins faction was peeved at Minor for other reasons. They felt that he had his own agenda, which was to get Franklyn Jenifer elected chancellor. Minor's close friendship with Steve Curwood of the *Boston Globe* also disturbed them. In their view it was no accident that Curwood's articles were highly critical of Collins and his supporters. Both sides were guilty of leaking information to the press. But not all of the sources were detectable—at least not immediately. A year later, in 1987, the

Boston Globe revealed that it was John Sasso, the governor's top aide, who had leaked damaging information about Collins's academic record in law school.[34]

Amid the swirl of conflicting information, UMass president David Knapp played a crucial role in promoting Collins. He was largely responsible for getting him into the semifinal round. Knapp warned his cohorts that there would be a major uproar if they excluded Collins.[35] Some saw Knapp as acting in his own self-interest in not wanting a strong chancellor who might overshadow him. Others believed that if Collins became chancellor, he would have to depend on Knapp for advice and counsel. Still others felt that Knapp was under heavy pressure from both the UMass Alumni Association and the public college presidents' group to fall in line behind Collins. Knapp's motives may have been mixed but surely were more complex than his critics would acknowledge.

During the second round of interviews, Donald Stewart, the president of Spelman College in Georgia, impressed everyone, but he suffered from the same drawback as Olver and Collins in not having managed a large public organization. Barbara Newell came across as an upper-middle-class professional woman who knew Massachusetts from her earlier days as president of Wellesley College. Since then she had been chancellor of the Board of Regents in Florida, where she ran into difficulty with the state legislature. In 1986 she was a visiting scholar at Harvard. Over the years she had been friendly with Ylvisaker. The Collins faction found Newell not only aloof but also unsympathetic to their concerns. Franklyn Jenifer, who felt that a few questions in his first interview had been "flagrantly racist," fared somewhat better in his second interview.[36] He was able to use his central office experience in New Jersey to advantage. The chancellor position was a career advancement for him, since he would be moving up from a deputy position to the top spot. E. K. Fretwell, who had done his graduate work at Harvard, came right out of central casting. He was an orthodox candidate of the sort typically revered in the halls of academe. In this sense, he had a superb résumé. At sixty-two years of age, the chancellor of the University of North Carolina at Charlotte had spent a lifetime in education and had gained a stellar reputation nationally. Although Fretwell was seen as nearing retirement, the age factor did not seem to harm his chances. He was on everybody's short list.[37]

Salary remained the big stumbling block. Paradoxically, Massachusetts had one of the largest systems but one of the lowest salaries. Speaker Keverian was now holding the pay raise bill hostage as a means of promoting Collins. Of the six semifinalists, only Olver and Collins were willing to accept the job at the current salary of $65,000, plus a housing allowance of $18,000. This combined figure paled by comparison with the $178,000 that

California paid the head of its system. The other four candidates felt that the total compensation package was too low, though Newell and Jenifer were willing to negotiate. Fretwell and Stewart were not. Stewart, in fact, was astounded to learn that the Massachusetts chancellor earned less than some of the public college presidents within the same system. Frustrated in their attempts to change the law, the Regents were powerless to rectify the situation. Keverian's tactics had stymied the search committee. Ylvisaker found himself with little room to maneuver.

The final meeting of the search committee was held at the Park Plaza Hotel in Boston on June 19. Before commencing, the committee waited over an hour for the arrival of the student member, Eileen Parise, who was stuck in a traffic jam on the Southeast Expressway. Both sides insisted on waiting. As a result of the absence of Janet Eisner, Parise's vote had become more crucial. Still young and inexperienced, Parise was pliable.

Intent on circumventing the Regents' June 9 directive, Hassan Minor proposed a three-step process. One was to reject the Regents' directive that authorized six candidates. A second was to submit only four names. The third was to select the four people and submit them in unranked order. All three steps were discussed at length and approved. The results of the tally on the third option put Fretwell on top with the maximum ten votes, followed by Olver with nine, Jenifer with eight, and Newell with six. Eliminated from the short list were Collins with four votes and Stewart with three.[38]

The Collins group was shocked by the outcome. They were particularly disappointed in Eileen Parise. Hers was the one vote they had miscalculated. Mary Lou Anderson, who was promoting Barbara Newell, believed that the Collins backers had exhibited sexist behavior in their questioning of Newell. They in turn accused Anderson of exerting undue influence on Parise in persuading her not to vote for Collins. Both Anderson and Parise denied that any sort of arm-twisting had taken place.[39] But the Collins backers claimed to have overheard conversations to the contrary. In any case, they were furious. Suspecting that Ylvisaker had engineered the outcome, they accused him of having rigged the process to prevent Collins from making the list of four finalists. There was an element of truth in their accusations when one considers that Ylvisaker's own binding resolution allowed for a maximum of five candidates. Whatever the grievance, Edward Sullivan stormed out of the meeting taking a binder of confidential material that was supposed to remain sequestered. Sullivan's hostility toward Ylvisaker and Minor had become caustic.

Shortly afterward, Collins had an unexpected meeting with former state representative Mel King. Collins told the black leader that he was disappointed in King's wife, Joyce, who had not voted for him. She favored

Jenifer and Stewart, whom she saw as risk takers. In her view, Collins did not meet the quality standard. Because of her involvement in her husband's Boston mayoral campaign, which witnessed the emergence of the "rainbow coalition," the Roxbury Community College trustee had missed several search committee meetings.[40]

COLLINS APPOINTED AND YLVISAKER RESIGNS

Through the remainder of June, the political pressures and maneuvering intensified. The sense of urgency in the Collins camp bordered on frenzy. Panic seized the members as they realized that the terms of three Regents (Eisner, Howell, and David Paresky) were about to expire.

Afraid of losing their numerical advantage on the board, they pressed for a final decision by July 1. As David Knapp had warned, a major uproar now erupted. Still smarting from their defeat on June 19, the Collins faction not only got mad but, in the Irish vernacular, they also got even.

While this fighting was going on, Ylvisaker convinced Dukakis that he was getting battered by his adversaries, who were belaboring the point that his committee had come up with only one viable candidate, John Olver, who would accept the job at the prescribed salary. The governor was reluctant to intervene. He did not want to pull a power play. In the words of one critic, "Dukakis does not thrive in such circumstances, because he is above all a consensus politician uncomfortable with open conflict."[41] The governor admitted that he did not have the votes to prevent Collins from being elected chancellor. He therefore asked Ylvisaker to play the "heavy" until he could appoint new members to the Board of Regents. By that time, however, Ylvisaker was perceived by the opposition as a "tool of the Duke." This perception was based in part on a personal affinity that had evolved between the two men beginning in the early 1950s, when Dukakis was a student of Ylvisaker's at Swarthmore College in Pennsylvania, and continuing when their paths crossed again at Harvard in the late 1970s.

At the board's special meeting of July 1, in which the full panoply of tensions erupted, chairman Beaubien had one purpose in mind: to elect a chancellor. After Ylvisaker gave a brief summary of the search, the first ballot was taken. Jenifer received five votes, Olver one, and Fretwell one. Strangely, Newell received none. At the time, both Newell and Fretwell were traveling as part of an exchange program in China, and most of the Regents read their absence as a signal that they were no longer interested in the position. The Collins faction showed its strategy by registering eight abstentions. Then came the second ballot. There were six votes for Jenifer, three for Olver, and six abstentions. The third ballot produced the identical result. Thus, the stalemate that Ylvisaker had anticipated did in fact occur.

At this juncture the process should have reverted to the search committee, but it did not, and that was the fatal flaw. In a series of parliamentary maneuvers designed to scuttle the search, George Ellison moved to discharge the search committee, to rescind the resolution of February 11, and to take nominations from the floor. All three motions passed and thereby cleared the way for Collins to reenter the picture. This pressure caused Beaubien to cave in. Then came the final ballot.

When the votes were counted, Collins received eight, Jenifer three, and Olver three. David Paresky of Weston abstained. As a fellow UMass/Amherst alumnus, Beaubien cast the decisive vote for Collins. It was shades of Winthrop Dakin. Norma Markey, the student Regent, who attended North Shore Community College, also voted for Collins.[42]

Ylvisaker was outraged. The implications for the Commonwealth seemed alarming to him. He believed that the integrity of the process had been grossly violated. He resigned that same day, charging that the selection of Collins had been "politically wired" and that it amounted to "politics as usual."[43] Soon after, Eisner, who had returned from abroad, tendered her resignation. She wrote a letter to the governor that reinforced Ylvisaker's argument.[44] As a matter of principle, Ylvisaker rejected the governor's offer to place him back on the Board of Regents.

GUBERNATORIAL INTERVENTION

As much as any politician in the country, Michael Dukakis, who had regained the governorship with an exciting comeback victory in 1982, understood the essence of the political game. His battle in 1983 to remove a "midnight" appointee of outgoing governor King as director of the Massachusetts Port Authority was a perfect illustration. Some people saw a close parallel in the chancellor case. Initially Dukakis took a cautious wait-and-see attitude. He was not particularly worried about Collins because he believed that Ylvisaker would come up with a host of first-rate candidates who would eclipse him. He saw Collins as a political candidate rather than a substantive one.

On another front, the governor never delivered on his promise to obtain legislation boosting the chancellor's salary. Publicly he favored the pay increase, but privately he complained to Beaubien that he as governor did not earn the kind of money they had in mind. Dukakis, who carried the liabilities as well as the assets of a long political career, was unable to deliver because of his rift with Keverian. This broken promise hurt him with his own Regent appointees.

But the political intrigue was more complicated. Gerald Indelicato, the governor's special assistant on education, did not keep his boss apprised of what was happening. Nor did he inform the Regents how Dukakis might react if Collins were elected. This failure of communication caused surprise on both sides. Indelicato, who aspired to become president of Bridgewater State College, was apparently operating in his own self-interest when he told the Collins forces that the governor had no problem with their candidate. Therefore, Kathleen Harrington of Fall River, a Dukakis appointee, felt free to support Collins. By all accounts, Indelicato took advantage of the political bargaining that was going on and parlayed it into the Bridgewater presidency. His actions wreaked havoc and caused major misunderstandings among all parties. According to Edward Lashman, Indelicato did a double disservice to the governor, not only by withholding information from him but also by not protecting his relationship with Speaker Keverian.[45]

When Harrington talked with the governor's aides on June 30, she learned that Dukakis still did not have a favored candidate, though she was told that if the choice boiled down to Olver and Jenifer, he would go with Olver.[46] Actually, the governor would have accepted Olver, but the state senator was not his first choice. He leaned more toward Fretwell. Dukakis had talked with former governor James Martin of North Carolina, who spoke highly of Fretwell.[47]

No one can know for sure what might have resulted had Dukakis gone for Olver. In hindsight, however, almost everyone in his administration believed his final acceptance of Jenifer to have been wiser and more fruitful. The political significance of that acceptance transcended the immediate issue. Like most politicians who move into the front ranks, the governor realized that the political system within which he had to operate was not only shaping his decisions but also formulating his options. Standing for reelection in the fall, he could ill afford to do nothing, especially given the persistent embarrassment caused by the Westfield State sex scandal. Some thought that this episode was the catalyst that spurred him to action. Facing criticism for his indecision, Dukakis decided that the political imperative of defeating Collins outweighed the moral one of cleaning up the mess at Westfield. As his top aide, John Sasso, put it, "This is about winning."[48]

Echoing similar sentiments was David Nyhan of the *Boston Globe*, who declared, "Governors running for reelection, and maybe for president, cannot afford to get their tail so publicly kicked on something as visible as Collins and his legislative backers made this."[49] The *Globe*, which had begun as a neutral observer, now found itself an active participant attempting to influence the outcome with its blistering editorials and its investigative journalism. Except for the public television station WGBH, the weekly newspaper the *Boston Phoenix*, and the communications media in western Massachusetts, which sided with Collins, press coverage tended to be biased in favor of Dukakis. This was especially true to the *Globe*, whose editorial writers and political cartoonists gleefully attacked the Collins forces. The *Globe*, Boston's newspaper of record, did not want to detract from Dukakis's presidential aspirations.

The key to leadership is seizing the initiative. With this in mind, the governor intervened in the dispute on July 2. Angered by the unfolding events, he chastised the Board of Regents, replaced it chairman, David Beaubien, with Edward Lashman, and announced his intention to have its election of Collins overturned. His anger was due in part to the violation of process and in part to his having been taken by surprise. He wanted to challenge the election of Collins in court, but Lashman, feeling that it was clear from the statute that Collins had been elected legally, talked him out of doing so. Whenever Dukakis spoke of the matter, he emphasized his personal commitment to restoring public confidence in a badly shaken system. Wrapped up in those claims were implicit values of competence, integrity, and good government.[50]

It was vintage Dukakis. In his second term he had received a great deal more from the legislature than he did during his first term. Few governors had done better. But he had to pay a heavy price for his intervention. It put him on a collision course with the legislature in general and with the Speaker in particular. After all, Keverian had helped him produce many striking public policy changes in his second term. Their relationship was now seriously ruptured, if not irreparably harmed. The Speaker had been deeply hurt by being tarred in the media as a "shabby" Massachusetts politician. The charges of improper fundraising that were leveled against Duff, followed by an investigation ordered by the governor, were the precipitating events that now made it difficult for Dukakis and Keverian to work out an accommodation. John Sasso was furious at Indelicato for failing to protect the relationship between the governor and the Speaker. Furthermore, Keverian was hurt by the disparaging comments about presumed "patronage."

Stung by the rejection of one of their own, legislators in both political parties rallied behind Collins. They bitterly resented his being labeled a political "hack." Many of them, including the new House education chairman, Nicholas Paleologos, took the insult personally. They felt it demeaned the entire legislature. To show their support, the Democrat-controlled House unanimously passed a resolution endorsing Collins as chancellor. There were no dissenting voices. Even the Republicans joined in the heavenly chorus.

What surprised most political pundits is that Collins had been a longtime supporter of Dukakis. He had remained loyal to him even after Dukakis had lost his primary battle against Edward King in 1978, when most mainstream Irish Democratic politicians threw their support behind King. The same was true in the much-publicized rematch of 1982. Two years later, Dukakis had a serious falling-out with Collins over education reform efforts. In 1984, Collins insisted on pushing a costly bill mandating large increases in teacher salaries, despite the governor's concern that the bill would necessitate a tax increase. This put the governor in the awkward position of failing to support a House leadership bill that had the strong backing of the Massachusetts Teachers Association.

Convinced that his party leader was "hoodwinking" the public, Collins broke with the governor over this issue. His criticism of the Dukakis administration was shrill and persistent. Such strident rhetoric planted the seeds of discord. From then on, the governor no longer considered Collins to be a "team player."[51] Reporter Scot Lehigh, writing for the *Boston Phoenix*, correctly attributed their current difficulties to this break in relations: "Clearly, from the viewpoint of a governor with no real higher-education goals, agenda, or philosophy—outside of a desire not to be embarrassed— Collins's tendency to be blunt, uncompromising, and outspoken made him an uncomfortable choice for chancellor."[52]

On July 3, Dukakis telephoned Collins to see if they could resolve their differences. The chief executive advised Collins not to resign his House seat and to stop holding press conferences. He also warned Collins not to go down the path on which he was headed because he was the only person who would get hurt. Spurning this advice, Collins decided to stay the course and promptly resigned from the legislature. Forewarned, he figured, was forearmed. But the crisis had not been resolved—only postponed.

Three days later, on July 6, reporter Bruce Mohl of the *Boston Globe* broke the story that identified Collins as the person who had asked former chancellor Duff to peddle the tickets for Keverian's fundraiser. Collins frankly acknowledged the truth of the story but claimed that the tickets were intended for Duff's personal use. Contacted by the same reporter, Duff, who had taken a job as a commissioner of the Chicago Public Library, denied such intent.[53]

On July 10, Collins went public with his fight by making a brief appearance on television. Citing relevant statistics, he deplored the fact that one out of four public school students in Massachusetts dropped out. He pointed out that only 18 percent of the graduates of Chelsea High School advanced to college, while over 85 percent of those in Amherst did. By skillfully publicizing the issue, Collins hoped to overcome his perceived liabilities and win grassroots support as Horace Mann had done in the late 1830s. Wrapping himself in the mantle of the legendary Mann, who had faced a similar crisis, the ex-legislator made his case. In so doing, he continued to stress elementary and secondary education, thereby lending credence to those who attacked him for not having a grasp of the issues facing higher education. The television broadcast, which was paid for by the UMass Alumni Association, did not generate the groundswell of favorable public opinion that he had anticipated.[54] Even worse, it infuriated the governor, who felt that Collins had gone too far. The conflict was now reduced to hardball politics.

As the governor's handpicked troubleshooter, Edward Lashman played his role to perfection. The new Board of Regents chairman was superb at delay. In a flurry of hastily arranged meetings held at the Harvard Club in Boston, he negotiated with Collins and offered him a short-term contract, no longer than ninety days. This offer was promptly rejected. Collins insisted on a one-year performance contract, but he did not get it. His requests to continue negotiations were refused. At this point, Michael West, an attorney for Collins, threatened to file an unfair labor practice suit against Lashman, who, he contended, was not bargaining in good faith. Pressure was also put on him to the effect that if he did not cooperate, Dukakis's presidential plans would be sabotaged. Undaunted, Lashman remained steadfast. He let West know that he was going to Maine on vacation for the last two weeks of July. By leaving the state, Lashman bought the governor the time he needed to reshape the Board of Regents with his new appointees.

Frustrated by Lashman's delay tactics, the Collins group on July 18 attempted to call a special meeting of the board to award their man a long-term contract. Lashman denied their request. An embittered Edward Sullivan broke with his cohorts on this issue. He wanted to hold the meeting without Lashman and let Lashman take them to court. But cooler heads prevailed. The Collins backers did not choose to go the litigation route because it was doubtful that they could have obtained injunctive relief. To do so they would have had to prevail on the merits and prove imminent damage. To save face, they tried to send Harrington as an emissary to John Sasso to see if they could reach a compromise. She never heard back from him. It would be hardball to the end.[55]

Frantic to stave off the removal of Collins, on July 24 seven of his supporters asked Attorney General Francis X. Bellotti to rule on the legality of the matter. Responding the next day, Bellotti gave them good news and bad news. The good news was that Collins had been legally elected chancellor on July 1. The bad news was that the chancellor serves at the pleasure of the Board of Regents and is "subject to removal by the board with no legal entitlement to serve out any contractually specified term."[56] On this prophetic note, Collins's fate was for all practical purposes sealed. Although his days were numbered, the outcome was by no means a foregone conclusion.

Almost simultaneously, television station WBZ in Boston announced the results of a public opinion poll that it had commissioned. When asked if Collins should receive a contract, 27 percent of those polled responded affirmatively; when asked if the search should be reopened, 39 percent agreed and 33 percent said they didn't know. When asked whether Dukakis's actions were politically motivated or whether he was acting to preserve the legitimacy of the search process, 33 percent responded affirmatively to the first question; 27 percent agreed with the second; and 39 percent fell into the "don't know" category.[57]

COLLINS REMOVED AND JENIFER APPOINTED

Through July and August the pressure did not subside. Collins, who had dug in his heels, visited the Westfield State campus in an effort to stabilize the unrest there. He also asked the state Ethics Commission if it would be proper for him to hire his former legislative aide, who was a nephew of Regent John Fox. To top it off, Collins announced plans for the establishment of a public-private partnership for the purpose of helping disadvantaged youth go on to college. These moves were more symbolic than substantive. Most knowledgeable observers interpreted his actions as a concerted public relations effort to rescue an embattled chancellorship.

On July 31, Dukakis appointed three new Regents. He chose Ellen Guiney, director of Boston's citywide educational coalition; Paul Doherty, a Springfield attorney; and Joseph Henson, president of Prime Computer. These appointments made political sense, but the academic community was not impressed. While the governor did not exact a pledge from his appointees to vote against Collins, he did ask them for a commitment to vote on procedural matters and to reopen the search. Speaker Keverian accused the governor of "packing the board" to ensure that Collins would be removed. With the three new members aboard, Lashman now granted the Collins faction its request for a special meeting. It was held on August 5. By identical votes of 9 to 7, the Board of Regents reinstituted the search and denied Collins the one-year performance contract that he was seeking.[58] The balance of power had clearly shifted in the governor's favor.

Because they already had a list of candidates, the Regents agreed informally not to expand the reopened search. Instead of starting from scratch, they merely picked up where they had left off in late June. This time, however, only the Regents participated, thus restoring their lost autonomy. Lashman had a difficult task in persuading the former finalists to return to the race. He did not try to convince Barbara Newell, who dropped out of contention on August 18 because she felt that the environment had become too politicized. To avoid the potential embarrassment of a candidate's refusing to accept the position because of the low salary, Lashman insisted that all the candidates give him a commitment in writing that they would accept the job if offered it. Since Collins was still legally the chancellor, he presented a special problem. Nevertheless, Lashman insisted that he declare his intentions in writing if he wished to be considered. Collins grudgingly complied with the request.

At about the same time, the press announced that Donald Stewart had been hired as president of the College Board in New York City. This prompted the *Boston Globe* to criticize the Dukakis administration for allowing Stewart to slip through its hands.[59] Ironically, Gregory Anrig, who had nominated Collins, was the head of the parent organization that hired Stewart. Anrig was effusive in his praise of Stewart.

During the month of August, the Regents interviewed the four candidates once again. It was clear to them that if either Collins or Olver were chosen, the system would become a captive of the legislature. If Fretwell were picked, they would be getting a custodial chancellor who was approaching the end of his career. Fretwell's performance in this interview was disappointing. By contrast, Jenifer was most impressive. He offered something different both in style and in substance. The former high school dropout and Rutgers biology professor made it clear that his loyalty would be primarily to the people of the Commonwealth rather than to the General Court. He came across as a mover and shaker, a policymaker who intended to stir things up and to plan on a systemwide basis.

But the fight was not over yet. A campaign was now undertaken to discredit Jenifer in order to scare him off. A number of New Jersey Democrats, including members of the state legislature, advised Jenifer to drop out of the race. He was also warned that he would never get a pay raise if he accepted the Massachusetts post. Even worse, rumors were spread that Jenifer was involved in a sexual harassment case in New Jersey. On learning of this, Lashman launched an immediate investigation by the Massachusetts State Police. Playing it safe, he also had Jenifer checked out independently by a private detective agency. The results of both investigations cleared Jenifer completely of the charges. The attempted character assassination had failed.[60]

In the meantime, the governor met with both Fretwell and Jenifer at Lashman's home. After talking with them, Dukakis still entertained a preference for Fretwell. In the governor's mind, Fretwell was the safer candidate because he was better known and he fit all the criteria. Dukakis remained unconvinced about Jenifer's suitability. Quite apart from the smear campaign that was rearing its ugly head, the governor had some reservations about him. As September approached, support for Jenifer coalesced. Henson flew to New Jersey to check him out, while Regent Nicholas Boraski spoke with his contacts there at General Electric. In the end, Jenifer became Lashman's candidate.

The stage was set for yet another showdown. Appointment and removal were the two items on the agenda at the Regents' September 9 meeting. Knowing that the Collins cause was futile, Sullivan did not even bother to show up for this meeting. Without much fanfare, the Board of Regents elected Franklyn Jenifer as its new chancellor. He won nine votes to Collins's six. Strange as it may seem, Collins insisted on being fired. He wanted to force the Regents to dismiss him face-to-face. Complying with his wishes, the Regents terminated him as chancellor effective September 12. This ended the protracted and hard-fought battle that left its weary combatants either traumatized or elated.[61]

LESSONS LEARNED

Looking back over these events and analyzing their implications, one has to ask why this episode is important. In more ways than one, the search for a Massachusetts chancellor illuminates the course not to take. There can be little doubt that the initial outcome had been the result of faulty decisions or decisionmaking processes. Putting aside the clash of personalities, which cannot be minimized, the major difficulties were systemic as well as procedural. More to the point, the political domain has an ownership stake in the Board of Regents, and that in itself flaws the process. Appointments to the Board of Regents are made primarily from the private sector. This is a structural problem that has since been rectified to some extent with the clarification in the state ethics law. Private college officials should not be in the business of regulating their public sector counterparts. In addition to the glaring conflict of interest involved, such regulation also contravenes the Board of Regents' oversight function with regard to private institutions.

By allowing five outsiders to participate in their search, the Regents unwittingly gave up a certain degree of autonomy at the outset. Ostensibly this action was taken to make the process more democratic, but it resulted in leaving the Board of Regents susceptible to political manipulation that it could not withstand in its bureaucratic infancy. Autonomy is especially fragile during this nurturing stage. To compound the difficulty, the Ylvisaker resolution gave away more of this perishable commodity. In the future, the Regents will have to proceed more cautiously before dispensing with any of their autonomy.

This issue naturally leads to the question of predetermination. To what extent was the candidacy of James Collins doomed from the beginning, given the widespread perception that the "fix was in"? Answers to this question remain uncertain and partisan. Nonetheless, given the climate that existed in Massachusetts in 1986, the Collins candidacy seemed almost destined to fail. Public opinion polls reflected the strains of the dispute. Collins probably suffered more from being stereotyped as a "hack" than he did from not having the right academic credentials. Embedded in that shopworn stereotype lay a virulent antilegislative bias. The General Court was not held in high esteem by the citizenry. But this provides only a partial explanation. The Hampshire County Democrat personified at once the Irish establishment, the public-versus-private factor, the rebirth of UMass/Amherst, and the cultural values of rural, small-town western Massachusetts, where he was perceived as a popular folk hero who was standing up to the pressure of the powerful elites in Boston. The urban-rural rivalries, in their subtle variations, worked to Collins's detriment.[62]

It is also revealing to note that the triumvirate of Ylvisaker, Lashman, and Dukakis all emerged from Harvard, an institution steeped in tradition and seen as the bastion of elitism. In terms of the new politics, they represented a throwback to the old Yankees who had excluded the Irish in an earlier era. Both Doherty and Keverian were also graduates of Harvard, but they had come from working-class origins. To be sure, their close bonds of friendship were cemented in the snobbery and class distinctions they had experienced during their undergraduate days, when they had gotten to know each other at Dudley House, the center at Harvard for commuting students. The student "brown baggers" who rode the MTA trolley cars to Cambridge were not accepted socially on the same terms as those privileged to live in Harvard Yard. These ethnic and class relationships, as well as those of gender and race, were manifested throughout the chancellor struggle.

Nevertheless, the role of the Irish as depicted in the media was overblown. It should be noted that neither Keverian nor Fox was Irish. Ethnic loyalty was not as much a binding factor as legislative loyalty. In the words of Maurice Donahue, "The only time the Irish stand together is at Sunday Mass during the reading of the Gospel."[63] Personally, Collins felt that he had been the victim of elitism and academic snobbery. Like Dukakis, who had been jolted by his humiliating defeat in the gubernatorial primary in 1978, Collins had learned the lessons of adversity and humility. But the taxi driver's son suffered from more than hurt pride and a bruised ego. He also suffered to some degree from an anti-Irish bias. Negative ethnic stereotypes definitely played a role. As Martin Nolan of the *Boston Globe* told Collins afterward, "You didn't have the right stickers on your back."[64] To the Collins camp, Ylvisaker epitomized Harvard elitism with his insistence on a doctoral degree. The fact that Harvard's own president lacked such a degree merely added fuel to the fire. Much of the internal acrimony and resentment on the Board of Regents was caused by Ylvisaker's promoting his own friends in academia for the job. Cronyism as an issue cut both ways.

Obviously the Collins faction misread the signs and overestimated their political strength. Their numerical superiority may have lulled them into a false sense of security. Essentially they played a political insider's game, but they came up against a governor who refused to back down. Much to his credit, Collins declined to accept a "golden handshake" in the form of a job offer at his alma mater.

A case can be made that if there was a conspiracy to foist Collins into the chancellorship, there was likewise a counter-conspiracy to deny it to him. The anti-Collins forces contended that the opposition used tactics that were political in the pejorative sense. Although they differed on objectives, Ylvisaker and Minor resorted to much the same kind of devious tactics in their efforts to control the process. Ingenious people, working hard, can always think up ways of circumventing constraints on authority. This was likewise true of the governor, who in the view of several members of the search committee had conveyed the impression that he wanted anybody but Collins. That the chief executive aroused heated opposition is not surprising, for he took on the established order and offended mainstream Irish Democrats. If the Collins phalanx wired the process for their man, the governor certainly rewired it for his choice. He allowed the change precisely because he now accepted what he had earlier rejected. Ambition for higher office induces politicians to support options that will enhance their electoral appeal and strengthen their political alliances.

By opting for Jenifer, or at least by concurring with the Board of Regents' decision, Dukakis made a critical choice and adjusted his gubernatorial campaign strategy to conform with Massachusetts's changing electorate. His nimble skills as a consensus politician were severely tested. But smart politics is not the same as wise politics. The real bone of contention between the Dukakis reformers and the Irish regulars was political control.

Seen in this light, the Irish regulars took a bad rap because the governor and his followers played the identical political game. They too were not above reproach in their discrediting Collins and bashing Keverian. The latter amounted to sheer political folly. Moreover, no one on the governor's side was managing the crisis at the Board of Regents until Lashman took over the reins. The supporting evidence indicates that Indelicato's deceit was compounded by lackluster performances from a weak chairman and a stand-in chancellor. Even so, the buck stops with the chief executive. After all, John Sasso and Frank Keefe, along with John Duff, had warned Dukakis about Indelicato. Beyond that, his latest appointments to the Board of Regents also lacked luster.

This brings us, finally, to the question whether the struggle was worth the price. On the positive side, it forced the governor to address the problems of public higher education; it dramatized the issue of the chancellor's salary; and it prevented the General Court from capturing the Board of Regents. On the negative side, the relationship of the Board of Regents to the other institutions within the system was damaged and its struggle for autonomy lost. The agency's credibility was weakened and the legitimacy of its governance was undermined. Given the fragile bonds that hold the public academic enterprise together, the viability of the Board of Regents itself was called into question.[65] At the moment of truth, Beaubien, a political innocent, cast the decisive vote for Collins. With his capitulation at such a critical point, autonomy went down the drain. But even Ylvisaker lost in the end. Both he and Beaubien were defeated on the autonomy issue.

On balance, one can reasonably argue that a politicized search is far too high a price to pay for the good of the Commonwealth. The world of public higher education is simply too fragile and too skittish to accept this sort of rift. The whole is bound to suffer from the unintended consequences. This episode provides ample evidence to support such an argument. As John Millett concludes, "To avoid open political warfare, higher education boards have to find some way in which to engage in political dialogue with state government officials."[66] Otherwise the warring factions are certain to inflict mutual damage. The answer lies in properly managing the dichotomy of tensions between legitimate political objectives and legitimate academic objectives. To ask for prudence is perhaps asking too much, but to expect that we can keep politics out of education is to perpetuate a myth that invites disappointment.

In the aftermath of the controversy, the Regents were finally given the power to set the salary of the chancellor. Surprisingly, it was Speaker Keverian who sponsored the corrective legislation in 1987. He did so not only to extend a peace offering to Franklyn Jenifer but also, perhaps more important, to restore his own image and to prove his critics wrong. This was no small accomplishment. It added to the positive consequences and made Keverian an unlikely hero. The struggle, in all its rich and poignant detail, had swung full cycle.

All of this seems clear in retrospect, but because of the political smoke screens, it may not have been so clear during the heat of battle. Yet the search for a new chancellor was exceedingly difficult and divisive in 1981, as had been the search for the chancellor of the former Board of Higher Education in 1967. From these events, along with the details already noted, it should not have been hard to infer that trouble loomed on the horizon in 1986. Every search had been harmed by a welter of recurring tensions. But these tensions, as we have seen, have their historical roots. They will not go away. Whether or not the actors can free themselves from their affinities for the remembered past and permit a fair and open search remains to be seen. One thing is certain. Massachusetts will still have to grapple with the problem of providing democratic accountability that does not threaten academic independence. Achieving this goal will enable the public institutions of higher learning to operate in a complex political system in which they can meet difficult challenges without bowing to inappropriate pressures. In the last analysis, the future of the public university ultimately depends on the confidence of its citizens.

EPILOGUE

Much has happened in the field of public higher education in Massachusetts since my analysis of these events was first published in 1988. Chancellor Jennifer left his position in April 1990 to assume the presidency of Howard University. Since then there has been a series of chancellors—Randolph Bromery (1990), Paul Marks (1991–92), Peter Mitchell (1992–93), and Stanley Koplic (1993–2000). Koplic died in office in January 2000 and was replaced by his deputy, Judith Gill.

The quest for effective governance of public higher education in Massachusetts has been a difficult one. In truth, the problem has never been adequately resolved. Over the years, politics, personalities, and instability have characterized the governance structures. The Commonwealth has passed through the successive stages of a Board of Higher Education (1965), a Board of Regents (1981–91), a Higher Education Coordinating Council (1991–96), and back full cycle to a Board of Higher Education (1996), all within the span of forty years. It has been an uncertain and unsteady course with its ups and downs and its cycles of centralization and decentralization. Suffice it to say that stability and accountability in governance are as much needed as stability in funding. For the long haul, the system needs a real reform in governance that de-politicizes the management of higher education and provides independent leadership that is knowledgeable about academic quality and devoted to its advocacy.

5

THE HARRINGTONS OF SALEM

It is never easy to explain to a later generation the
achievements of an earlier one in shattering an unacceptable status quo, because these achievements in turn
have become a status quo beyond which it wishes to
advance.

Frank Freidel, *New York Times*, January 18, 1971

ETHNICITY AND RELIGION IN SALEM POLITICS

The city of Salem, on the North Shore about twenty miles from Boston, is
steeped in American social and political history. Settled by the morally rigid
Puritans in 1626, it was the place where, in the 1690s, men fearing the sor-
cery of witches hanged many women and some men, too. Later its courageous sea captains sailed to the Far East in search of trade and returned with
their ships laden with silk, ivory, and other precious cargo. These prosperous
captains built their stately mansions on Federal and Chestnut streets in
Salem. Designed by the noted architect Samuel McIntire, these venerable
homes were adorned with the traditional "widow's walk" on the rooftops.
The small city was also where Nathaniel Hawthorne worked as a customs
inspector and wrote his famous novel *The House of the Seven Gables*. Joseph
Smith, the Mormon prophet whose writings inspired the founding of the
Church of Jesus Christ of Latter-Day Saints, once predicted that gold would
be found in Salem. In 1836, Smith returned to Salem to explore the possibility of establishing a Mormon religious colony there.[1]

Until 1836 the town of Salem was governed by a board of selectmen.
When the municipality became a city and adopted a mayor-council form
of government, Leverett Saltonstall was elected its first mayor and served
from 1836 to 1837. The Saltonstall ancestry traces back to the fourteenth
century in England. The original Saltonstall, Sir Richard, came to Massa-

chusetts in 1630. Throughout the remainder of the nineteenth century, all the Salem mayors were Protestants of native stock. These old-line Yankees were mostly Whigs and Republicans by party affiliation. Abolitionists, temperance men, anti-Catholic nativists, and moral reformers were often the same men.

Protestant hatred of Catholics and fear of papal authority played a large part in American nativism. As the historian John Higham observed, "Anti-Catholic nativism, aiming at stiff naturalization laws and exclusion of Catholics and foreigners from public office, completely overshadowed every other nativist tradition."[2] For nativists, Romanism inevitably conflicted with free inquiry and liberty of conscience. Playing on fears of popery was a chief means of both fundraising and reducing internal strife among Protestants. Ethnicity, religion, temperance, and the controversy over slavery all shaped party loyalties. These Yankee politicians embodied an ideal of public service with their sense of noblesse oblige and social consciousness. The Bay State, like the rest of the nation, was traumatized by the Civil War and transformed by industrialization. Massive immigration and expansive urban growth produced an increasingly diverse population; it also produced fierce rivalries among ethnic communities.

Irish Catholics first arrived in Salem around 1833. Many worked in the leather industry, the woolen mills, and on the railroads. Their assimilation into society was slow and painful as they encountered a hostile environment of religious intolerance and systematic bigotry. With their strange brogue, peculiar clothes, and wrong religion, as well as their willingness to work for low wages and other distinctive but unloved traits, the Irish suffered discrimination and prejudice. They felt isolated in Salem and moved preponderantly to the northern side of town, where a new ward was created encompassing most of "Corktown." There the Irish built St. Mary's Catholic Church. When that chapel proved too small to accommodate the increasing number of Catholic immigrants, in 1857 ground was broken for the Immaculate Conception Church. On its completion, the entire congregation of St. Mary's was relocated to the new edifice.

As a despised minority, the Irish already had reason enough to resent middle- and upper-class Protestants who possessed wealth and status and seemed disposed to social snobbery. Relations between the two groups were abrasive. Even when exploitative economic relationships and class differences did not exacerbate tensions and resentments, religion and the clash of cultures would cause hostility. The Irish politicians came to City Hall as outcasts, and, as people scorned, they had no great respect for the scorners or their vaunted principles of government. Scarred emotionally by their experience of cruel oppression at the hands of the British, they brought with them clannishness, a talent for extralegal politics, and a tradition of personal loyalty to leaders. Somewhat in the manner of ex-colonials who have grown used to bribery and other means of cheating the prevailing powers, the Irish immigrant bosses set some unsavory records for public plundering. But they were no more unethical than the mill owners and business moguls who oppressed and exploited their people.

Over the years the issues that divided the Yankees and Irish were rooted in two political cultures competing for dominance. As political scientist Paul Peterson points out:

> On the one side, the Catholic immigrant, whose culture emphasized family, neighborhood, and friendship ties, treated politics as another marketplace in which particularistic self-interests could be pursued. On the other side, the middle-class Protestant, reared in a milieu that delineated man's individuality, separateness, and equality before God, understood politics to be the pursuit of "justice," the ground upon which one created a "city on the hill" that would radiate its worth to the surrounding countryside.[3]

There is much to be said for this analysis. Many conflicts in Salem and other Bay State cities divided sharply along these lines. Patronage and corruption lubricated the friction between the world of equality and the world of privilege.

In cities like Salem, successive waves of new immigrants came to the fore and elected mayors. Over the years the office gradually passed from Yankee to Irish, Jewish, French, Italian, and Lithuanian ethnics, in that order.[4] The turning point for the Irish came in 1900, when John F. Hurley was elected the city's first Catholic mayor. Ordinary working people had discovered their power. Religion and ethnic politics obviously blended well.[5]

THE ASCENT OF THE HARRINGTONS

It was against this background that the Harringtons plunged heartily into ethnic politics in Salem, where they built their political base and gradually attained considerable power. As political aspirants, they used city office-holding and Democratic Party politics as a stepping-stone. They were part of the Irish political ascendancy that witnessed generations of bitter and unyielding conflict between Yankee Protestants and Irish Catholics. As ardent Democrats, they maintained their power mainly through the use of patronage, attention to the demands of competing ethnic groups, and the provision of public services through partisan channels. In an era when class hatred, religious antagonism, and ethnic resentment were rampant, it was important to take care of one's own. North Salem was a neighborhood of the lower working class, most of whom were "shanty" Irish. The "lace curtain" Irish lived in the upscale Broad Street section of the city. Over the years, these voter-rich precincts provided the Harringtons with a reliable base of Democratic support.

The Harringtons came from humble origins in Ireland. Cornelius Harrington, the family patriarch, was born in Skibbereen in 1833. At the age of fourteen, he left his famine-stricken homeland to escape the devastation of the great hunger. Skibbereen, which lay in the western part of County Cork, was one of the worst-afflicted towns. Cornelius and his parents belonged to the masses of landless or evicted peasantry who wandered into cities and took whatever job they could find. He emigrated as a young man to London, where he eventually found work as an English bobby. Like most ethnic policemen, he was assigned to patrol the dreadful Irish slums in the Limehouse section of the city. His son, Cornelius F. Harrington, was born in London in 1864 on a street called Petticut Lane. When he was five years of age, his immigrant parents brought him from London to Beverly, Massachusetts. They lived at 12 Rantoul Street in an area called Goat Hill. Young Cornelius grew up in Beverly and became familiar with its class and ethnic tensions. An Irish immigrant with neither family support nor education, he worked in the shoe and boot trade until he gained enough experience to become a union activist. He was arrested for organizing shoe workers in the mill cities of Haverhill, Massachusetts, and Manchester, New Hampshire. Before long, Cornelius married Ellen T. Griffin, who worked in the Pequot mills in Salem. Her mother, Ann Conroy, an Irish girl who worked in the woolen mills, had come to Lowell with a rich English Protestant. The head of the family had been hired to manage the mills.[6]

City directories indicate that the Harringtons moved from Beverly to Salem in 1893. They lived briefly at 1 Ferry Street and then at 2 Essex Street, before they acquired their own home at 57 Osgood Street. This modest house was located off Bridge Street on a dead end that backed up to Collins Cove. Cornelius F. Harrington (1864–1943) was listed in the city directory as an "edge setter" by trade. He outlived his son Cornelius J. Harrington (1890–1935), whose occupation was that of a plumber. Both men became active in Salem politics and were part of the Hurley political machine, which was well organized.

Reform of the Salem police force required a supportive marshal. Mayor Henry P. Benson appointed Cornelius F. Harrington as city marshal in 1916. This plum patronage appointment was the equivalent of city police chief. Benson, one of Salem's wealthiest men, managed the Naumkeag Steam Cotton Company, which had been established in 1847. Later known as the Pequot Mills, this company was the largest employer in the city. Presumably, Benson appointed Harrington in order to curry favor with the Irish, but most Protestants resented the Irish courtship. Recalling what life was like at her grandparents' home at 57 Osgood Street, Carol Harrington Mulholland writes:

> For my part, I found the Harringtons quite fascinating. On Sundays my father [Leo F. Harrington] would take my brother and me to his family home, a very short walk from our house, first because he adored his mother and wanted to visit with her, and second because he wanted to give my mother a few hours respite. Those were great times for me. The Harrington household was very "casual." The kitchen table covered with an oil cloth, was never unset. Someone was always eating. The beds were never made, someone was always sleeping. There were in the family six sons and three daughters. Grandfather Harrington, and the male members of the family sat around the kitchen table or out on the porch and discussed politics and unions. Grandmother Harrington, a tall, long-necked woman, straight as a ram rod, with a sharp tongue and a keen sense of humor waited on the men, all the while making sarcastic remarks about her husband's fondness for poetry and conversation and his complete lack of fondness for physical labor. (If she were alive today she would be the president of "NOW"). Meanwhile, hordes of grandchildren ran unrestrained through the house, whooping and screaming and being totally destructive. Generally, I preferred sitting with the grown-ups listening to their talk and would remain there as long as I was permitted to do so.[7]

The Harrington household was typical of many Irish Americans.

At the time, the French Canadians outnumbered the Irish in Salem. During the second half of the nineteenth century, the owners of the Pequot Mills had imported Canadian laborers to work at substandard wages. As recently as 1980, 43 percent of Salem's population, which hovered around 40,000, was French Canadian. Constant rivalries sprang up between the French, Irish, and Polish populations. The French and Irish hated each other. But the Irish were more efficient at organizing their community. They also had the advantage of speaking English and being familiar with county government as a result of their experience in Ireland. Since the French Canadians frequently quarreled among themselves, they had difficulty in putting together a winning coalition, though they could defeat a candidate for mayor if they disliked him enough.[8] Given their lack of cohesiveness, they had to wait until 1973 before Jean A. Levesque became the first French mayor of Salem. He filled the unexpired term of Samuel E. Zoll, the first Jewish mayor, who served from 1970 to 1973 before departing the mayor's office in order to accept a state judgeship. Levesque then served a total of five terms, from 1973 to 1983. The first Italian mayor, Anthony V. Salvo, served three terms from 1984 to 1989.

With the appointment of Cornelius F. Harrington as city marshal in 1916, the family had gained a political foothold, and soon thereafter they were on their way. They advanced politically and learned how to survive in the hurly-burly of Massachusetts politics. For better or worse, they experienced the perils and travails that went with public life, and these experiences shaped the way they looked at the world, at the public, at duty, at religion, at responsibility, at democracy, and at the cruel caprices of life. For some Harringtons, political life was like a bumpy roller-coaster ride of electoral victories and defeats. Most of all, they were doers, who seemed more interested in getting things done than in perpetuating themselves in office. Public service was their calling, and they served the public well.

Over the years, the Harringtons provided leadership that inspired loyalty and cooperation among their supporters. In all, one served as city marshal and two as mayor of Salem; two served in the state Senate; two in the Massachusetts House of Representatives; and one was sent to Congress. Four of them served at one time or another on the Salem City Council. They saw politics as an honorable profession as well as an exciting adventure. For a period of eighty-one years they were a force to be reckoned with in the Democratic Party. In their differing ways, each made his presence felt in the political arena.

A DEMOCRATIC PARTY WHEELHORSE

A formidable adversary, Joseph B. Harrington, who was born in Salem on November 22, 1908, enjoyed a long public career in the Democratic Party. He was the son of the city marshal and the second family member to seek elective office. His older brother Cornelius had run for a city council seat and lost. Possessed of charm, wit, and intelligence, Joe Harrington was a magnetic character who described himself as a self-made man well tutored by life experience. Educated at St. Mary's Commercial School in Salem, he went to work at the age of fifteen. While holding down a state job as a clerk-stenographer he completed his schooling at the Salem Evening High School, where he graduated as valedictorian. He was a voracious reader and a self-educated man. Although his family could not afford to send him to college, he was sufficiently motivated to earn a law degree, attending Suffolk Law School at night.[9] To pay his way through law school, he trained trolley car operators, whose jobs were being eliminated, to become bus drivers.

In those days a prospective lawyer did not need a college degree in order to take the bar exam. Following his admission to the bar in 1932, Joseph Harrington married Elizabeth C. Kenneally, who worked as a secretary for Salem mayor Edward A. Coffey. A smooth talker, Harrington soon became a leading attorney in his hometown. He joined the Knights of Columbus and entered politics. A slightly built man who stood six feet tall, he had charisma as well as a social conscience. His identification with lower-income groups was important to him. He was popular with party regulars, many of whom were working-class people. These personal qualities, along with a playful sense of humor, became his trademark. He liked nothing better than to make lighthearted mischief.

In the 1930s, Harrington ran several times for city council before he was finally elected in 1937. Like his contemporary James Michael Curley, he was a brilliant and instinctive politician endowed with that gift for symbolic gesture so beloved by the Irish community. His was a political world in which geniality, compassion, and opportunism were all given equal play. The Great Depression of the 1930s instilled in Harrington a genuine compassion for the unemployed, who were hungry and desperate. Of such endearing instincts lasting friendships were made. What he learned then shaped his subsequent thinking. He was intent on doing good and helping the less fortunate, especially alcoholics who were down-and-out. Unlike the Protestant elite, he did not show disdain for the drunkard. Quite the contrary, he founded the North Shore Council on Alcoholism, which set up a network of services for taking care of alcoholics and making sure they were not treated like common criminals.

In the late 1930s, Joe Harrington's embrace of isolationism put him at odds with his party's leadership, for he was an Al Smith Democrat, not an FDR loyalist. The national prominence of New York governor Alfred E. Smith stirred his Irish pride. When Smith ran for the presidency in 1928, Harrington supported him enthusiastically. Smith in turn unleashed a powerful force for the Democratic Party. "One of their own kind, Irish, Catholic, big city son of immigrants," as Jerome Mileur observes of Smith, his "candidacy galvanized the 'newer races' of working class Democrats in Massachusetts, who marched to the polls in unprecedented numbers to make him the first Democrat in the state's history to win a majority of the popular vote for President."[10]

There are great waves or cycles to the rhythm of politics, and the 1928 presidential election marked a significant turning point in Massachusetts, when one wave was ebbing and another was ready to advance. Since the Civil War, the Bay State had been safely Republican. But the 1928 election would be the last time the Republicans would monopolize state politics. During the three decades from 1930 to 1960, the Democrats won six of eight presidential elections, divided the two U.S. Senate seats evenly with the Republicans, won the governorship in nine of sixteen elections, split those for attorney general and secretary of state, and dominated elections for treasurer and auditor.[11]

Active in Democratic politics in Essex County, Joe Harrington was blessed with a magnificent baritone voice, and he was much in demand as an after-dinner speaker. His ability to beguile the urban masses attracted the attention of party bosses. Joe Harrington was a man on a mission, trying to win elections but also trying to build a party. The milieu made possible the emergence of the man. In 1940 he ran for the state Senate against Raymond H. Trefry of Marblehead, whose Yankee Protestant credentials were impeccable. A lawyer by profession, Trefry was no run-of-the-mill politician. A well-known Republican and Marblehead town counsel, he was a two-term incumbent seeking a third term and was the heavy favorite. At the time, the second Essex senatorial district, encompassing Salem, Beverly, Danvers, and Marblehead, was considered an impregnable Republican stronghold. The local Republican committees had agreed, however, that the seat should be rotated among the party faithful in these four communities. Trefry was supposed to have vacated his seat at the end of his second term to make it available for some other deserving Republican. Intoxicated with the elixir of power, he decided to run again and was therefore in trouble with the base of his own party.

Trefry's predicament, coupled with election year presidential politics and the gravitational pull of FDR's candidacy, contributed to Harrington's stunning upset victory. He collected 22,675 votes, compared to 22,252 for Trefry—a narrow margin of 423 votes. The Salem Democrat carried his hometown by 7,877 votes. Commenting on the outcome, the *Salem Evening News* proudly boasted, "In the most stunning upset in local political history of recent record at least, Councillor Joseph B. Harrington of Salem, veteran of many political storms despite his youth, staged a knockout over his Republican opponent, Raymond H. Trefry of Marblehead, in the hotly contested battle for state senator in the Second Essex district. It was an amazing victory and came as a stunning blow to Republicans who have always carried this district before without any trouble."[12]

Nor would Joe Harrington's hunger for office subside there. Up or out became his credo. Counting on his continuing popularity, party leaders asked him to run for Congress in 1941. Since this was a special off-year election, he could run for higher office without giving up his state Senate incumbency. That is what is known in politics as being in the catbird seat. He had everything to gain and nothing to lose. But things did not turn out the way he expected, as we shall see in the next section.

By the time Joe Harrington retired from politics, the politician had become a legend and the man had become a myth. Governor Foster Furcolo honored him by appointing him a state judge. Judge Harrington often had lunch at the Hawthorne Hotel in Salem, where a special table was held for him in the dining area known as the "main brace." There he discussed politics with his political cronies. For relaxation he bought a used thirty-six-foot cabin cruiser, which he named the *Wanderer*. During the summer months, when court sessions were light and the judiciary normally adjourned by noon, he would invite friends to cruise with him in the waters off Salem. Sometimes the judge traveled to Gloucester by boat to preside over trials there. All his life he took pleasure in his daily work, in using his power and celebrity to help others less fortunate than he.

THE SPECIAL ELECTION OF 1941

To appreciate the events of the 1941 special election, it is necessary to reconstruct American history as Joseph Harrington and his generation understood it. This was an extraordinary time of domestic social change, international struggle, and political extremism. Perhaps the best place to start is October 19, 1941. On that day, Congressman Lawrence J. Connery died in office. A lifelong Democrat and native of Lynn, he had succeeded his brother William P. Connery, who likewise had died in office in September 1937. The latter had long been recognized as a staunch advocate of labor in Massachusetts. He had co-sponsored the Wagner-Connery Labor Act of 1935, which created the National Labor Relations Board.[13] This key piece of New Deal legislation reasserted the right of workers to form unions without being harassed by their employers. It also empowered the NLRB to determine "unfair labor practices" against which wage earners could complain without fear of reprisal from their employers.

Congressman Lawrence Connery's death created a vacancy in the Seventh Congressional District, to be filled by a special election. The date of the primary was set for December 16, 1941, while the special election itself was to be held two weeks later on December 30. This meant that the candidates vying for the vacant seat had only two months to campaign.

A total of nine Democrats and two Republicans took out nomination papers. In addition to Harrington, the other Democrats included Thomas J. Lane, a state senator from Lawrence; Charles Hogan, a state senator from Lynn; Fred Manning, a twelve-year mayor of Lynn; Edward D. Connery of Chelsea (obviously trying to trade on the similarity of names with the deceased congressman); Frederick J. Myers of Boston; Arthur M. McCarthy of Winthrop; George J. O'Shea, a state representative from Lynn; and V. Frederick Sano of Lynn. Since the Seventh Congressional District was overwhelmingly Democratic, the Republicans provided only token opposition. They recruited John H. Gavin of Lawrence and C. F. Nelson Pratt, a former state representative from Saugus. Pratt and Harrington were mortal political enemies. Not all of these candidates, including Harrington, lived in the district—because of Republican gerrymandering, only

Ward 4 in Salem was part of the district—but there was no residency requirement.

With a population of one hundred thousand, Lynn was the largest city in the congressional district and the fifth largest in the state. It was a major center of shoe manufacturing. The district also contained two of the biggest industries in the Commonwealth: the General Electric plant in Lynn, which employed over twenty thousand workers, and the American Woolen Company in Lawrence, the world's largest woolen mill. At the time, Lawrence was the nation's leading producer of worsted goods. Its mills provided jobs for more than thirty thousand workers.

Unless either Harrington or Hogan dropped out of the race, the pundits were saying, Tom Lane would be the next congressman. Harrington and Hogan were competing for the same bloc of votes, and it was expected that they would knock each other off, to Lane's benefit. So Hogan decided to drop out. This cleared the way for Harrington, at least in southern Essex. It was still a crowded field, in which Lane, Manning, and Harrington soon emerged as the early front-runners.

During his first year in the state Senate, Joe Harrington had acquired a reputation for being a silver-tongued orator who could rally followers to a cause with the power of his deep, rich voice. But there was a cutting edge to his florid oratory. He often laced his speeches with a touch of wit and sarcasm. Whenever he took the floor in the Senate, the word quickly spread throughout the State House and people rushed to the gallery to hear him speak. Cornelius Dalton, a veteran reporter for the *Boston Traveler*, wrote, "There were a few men who had his eloquence and a few men who were as effective in debate, but no legislator in modern times had both these gifts in such abundant measure."[14] Harrington was also a press favorite, always good for a photograph and a ready quote. Sometimes he was too outspoken for his own good. Seldom did he pull his punches.

In 1941, Harrington had gained considerable recognition at the impeachment trial of seventy-six-year-old Daniel H. Coakley, an attorney from Brighton and a member of the Governor's Council for the previous nine years. By all accounts Coakley was a despicable character who specialized in blackmail and operated a sexual entrapment racket or "badger game." His accomplices in these sexual shakedowns were Nathan Tufts and Joseph Pelletier, the chief law enforcement officers of Massachusetts's two most populous counties. "A prostitute hired by the trio would lure a rich elderly gentleman to a hotel room," Jack Beatty explains. "When they were in flagrante delicto, an irate 'husband' or 'father' of the woman would burst in, or the police would enter and charge the man with fornication or contributing to the delinquency of a minor. The man would be told that an alienation of affection suit could be avoided only by hiring attorney Coakley, who by a miracle of legal art would persuade either District Attorney Tufts or District Attorney Pelletier, depending on the location of the tryst, to 'noi pros' the suit" [nolle prosecui: a decision not to take a case to court].[15] In 1922 all three lawyers were disbarred, and the two district attorneys were removed from office by the Supreme Judicial Court.

Fourteen charges of fraud and misconduct in office were leveled against Coakley by the lower house of the Massachusetts legislature. The charges involved pardons granted to Raymond L. S. Patriarca, later to become notorious as an organized crime boss, and Frank W. Potter and Maurice Limon between 1935 and 1938. Coakley was defended by Senator Harrington and a prominent black lawyer, William H. Lewis, a former assistant United States attorney. The impeachment trial was conducted by the Republican-controlled Senate, and Harrington and Lewis were under pressure not to yield to the Republicans. At midnight on October 3, 1941, the verdict was returned. The Republican senators found Coakley guilty and voted to remove him from office and to disqualify him from ever holding public office again.[16]

Of course, Harrington came to the Senate with this problem already on his agenda. He could see the partisan storm coming, seeking in the timing of the impeachment some clue to Republican motives. Those motives soon became evident. At stake was control of the eight-member Governor's Council, a vestige of colonial times that served as a political check on the governor. The councilors not only approved pardons and parole but also confirmed judicial appointments. By ousting Coakley, the Republicans were able to gain majority control of the council. Politics was a blood sport. Republican governor Leverett Saltonstall was no doubt pleased with the ultimate outcome. No longer did he have to worry about the Democratic councilors blocking his contemplated courses of action.

Harrington had entered politics in the face of the impending European war. With the rise of Adolf Hitler in Germany during the 1930s, a series of international events had long dominated foreign news. Everyone who read the newspapers knew that Japan had seized Manchuria from China in 1932, and that Italy had invaded and conquered Ethiopia in 1935. Then the Rhineland crisis broke in 1936, when Hitler suddenly marched troops into that presumably demilitarized zone. This was followed by the Czech crisis of 1938, when Britain, France, and Italy bought temporary peace at the Munich Conference by giving Hitler crucial portions of Czechoslovakia. These disturbing events contributed to cautiousness abroad and at home. Paralyzed by the fear of war and by the Great Depression, Britain and France at first acquiesced to German expansion, but after Munich they concluded that Hitler could not be appeased. The British signed a defense pact with Poland,

and when Hitler invaded Poland on September 1, 1939, Britain and France declared war on Germany. Ignoring these warning signs, many Americans of all political persuasions latched onto isolationism as their security blanket. Nowhere was this phenomenon more prevalent than in Massachusetts. The state was a hotbed of antiwar sentiment, especially among the Irish. Indeed, it grew ever stronger.

In May 1940, as the Nazis overran Norway and marched west, Neville Chamberlain, the British prime minister associated with Munich, won a vote of confidence from the House of Commons but with forty abstentions on his own side. That vote so compromised Chamberlain's standing in the conservative Tory Party, the press, and the country that he felt compelled to step down as prime minister. Winston Churchill, who succeeded Chamberlain as prime minister, never forgot either the event or the lesson. He was widely regarded as having been right about the dangers of appeasement.

The presidential election of 1940 raised the question whether America would intervene or stay out of the war that was raging in Europe. President Roosevelt's exchange with England of aging destroyers in return for naval bases alienated most Irish Americans. In Massachusetts, the Irish praised Ambassador Joseph P. Kennedy for his reluctance to aid the British. U.S. senator David I. Walsh, who was a strong isolationist, was reported to be in "a towering rage" when he learned about the sale of navy ships and munitions. He threatened to force legislation prohibiting such sales.[17]

In Wendell Wilkie the Republicans had a far more energetic nominee than Alf Landon had been in 1936. Unlike Landon, who had stayed out of Massachusetts, Wilkie twice visited Boston, where he spoke to a large crowd of 35,000 people at Braves Field and received a cordial audience with Cardinal William O'Connell. He promised to restore prosperity and to keep "our boys out of Europe." If Roosevelt were reelected, Wilkie predicted that American "boys" would be fighting within six months.

Alarmed by Wilkie's attack, local Democrats patched up some of their differences and rallied behind the president. Boston mayor Maurice J. Tobin and Congressman John W. McCormack vigorously campaigned for him. Even a reluctant James Michael Curley, who played on the hatreds, fears, and insecurities of the Irish, reminded voters that he had been the first politician in America to endorse Roosevelt eight years earlier. In addition, the state Federation of Labor, with all its political muscle, came through with a ringing endorsement of FDR.

The Democrats pulled out all the stops. Outside speakers were summoned to the rescue. New York mayor Fiorello La Guardia wooed Italians on Roosevelt's behalf. The long-dominant Irish leadership of the Democratic Party was being challenged more and more by emerging Italian leaders. Many Italian Americans, however, voted the Republican ticket. From their perspective, Roosevelt had stabbed dictator Benito Mussolini in the back on the eve of the United States' entry into World War II. Without their defection, the dominance of the Republican Party in Massachusetts would probably have deteriorated much sooner.

Meanwhile, the Detroit radio priest Father Charles Coughlin continued his savage attacks against Roosevelt and his New Deal programs. He also spewed forth the venom of anti-Semitism. His Jew-baiting Christian Front endorsed Wilkie, and the priest's followers combed Irish neighborhoods in search of Republican votes. Italians in Boston's North End demonstrated in support of Mussolini and his armed aggression. Like the Italian community, the Irish too were stirred by events abroad. They despised the English for their cruel, oppressive rule in Ireland and did not want America to bail them out. Hence, they strongly objected to FDR's destroyer exchange. Their rabid Anglophobia was as blatant as it was transparent.

In January 1941, President Roosevelt pushed the isolationist nation closer to war when he persuaded Congress to pass the Lend-Lease bill, which empowered him to transfer war materiel to any country deemed vital to American interests, deferring payments for those ships and arms. Almost simultaneously, John McCormack, who personified the Boston Irish, was the first Catholic to be named majority leader of the House of Representatives. McCormack served under Speaker Sam Rayburn of Texas. Their political relationship soon developed into what eventually became known as "the Austin to Boston connection." As a dyed-in-the-wool New Dealer, McCormack remained loyal to Roosevelt and steadfastly supported his foreign and domestic policies. Social security had been enacted in 1935, and by 1941 the problem of massive unemployment had been substantially reduced. The depression was almost over, although some of its effects still lingered.

After spending three years abroad (during which time he met with various Nazi leaders), Colonel Charles Lindbergh, the famed aviator, returned home in 1941 to speak against American involvement in the European war. A celebrated international hero, Lindbergh had flown nonstop from New York to Paris in the *Spirit of Saint Louis* in 1927. He became the leading spokesman for the isolationist group known as Defend America First, a broad coalition that included such diverse personalities as Burton K. Wheeler, Democratic U.S. senator from Montana; Kathleen Norris, a popular novelist; Kingman Brewster, president of Yale University; and socialist Norman Thomas. Lindbergh's father had been a Minnesota congressman and a staunch pacifist. As midwesterners, they were diehard isolationists. The popular aviator was by far the biggest draw for the America First movement. He made thirteen public appearances as its featured speaker in practically every region of the country, but he could not conceal his thinly veiled anti-Semitism.[18] His speech in Des Moines, Iowa, revealed his negative feelings toward the Jews. Walter Winchell, the nation's most powerful columnist and a popular radio commentator, hounded him with charges of anti-Semitism. These events set the stage for what followed in Massachusetts.

As the darling of the Irish, Joe Harrington read these signs accordingly and tapped into what he perceived as a rich vein of isolationism. To that end he deliberately distanced himself from Roosevelt. An outspoken America Firster, he adopted the campaign slogan, "American defense at any expense, but no foreign war." The Salem Democrat insisted that his congressional campaign should be devoted entirely to a debate over foreign policy. The *Salem Evening News* observed, "Harrington, a leader in the America First Committee, is running on an out-and-out isolationist platform."[19] He was stridently noninterventionist. Such a stance won him the solid support of the Irish. President Roosevelt's recall of Joseph Kennedy from his ambassadorship at the Court of St. James's outraged many of Harrington's constituents. Most Republicans were opposed to American involvement in the war because they hated Roosevelt and all that he stood for. The New Deal, with its social welfare programs, was anathema to them. More significantly, FDR's internationalist views were in direct opposition to the powerful isolationist wing of the Republican Party. At the end of World War I, U.S. senator Henry Cabot Lodge Sr., had led the charge in torpedoing America's entry into the League of Nations.

Whatever its merits, the Harrington strategy ran directly counter to the philosophy of Tom Lane and Fred Manning, who were his two main Democratic opponents. They both supported FDR. Lane declared unequivocally that he was "casting my lot with the kind of Americanism typified by President Roosevelt. I pledge my full support to his foreign and domestic policy." In addition to being pro-labor and an Irish Catholic Democrat, Lane was also a military veteran who had fought in the trenches during World War I. He gained the support of the American Legion and other veterans' groups. Straddling the political fence, Manning equivocated by saying that he would "never vote for war," but he would support Lend-Lease and other interventionist measures.[20] He was trying to have it both ways. But Manning was going nowhere at this stage of the campaign.

In marked contrast, Harrington stood before the public as opposing the use of American military power. Whenever he spoke, he emphasized his personal commitment to a policy of nonintervention. Speaking more bluntly, he boldly asserted that he was "100 per cent opposed to President Roosevelt's foreign policy and 100 per cent in support of the Wheeler-Nye faction in Congress."[21] This statement drew the ire of important labor leaders, who read an ominous portent into his words. The Massachusetts

CIO, which was riding high, launched a concerted drive to defeat him. They insinuated that Harrington was flirting with Nazism. Joseph A. Salerno, president of the state CIO, along with other labor leaders, endorsed Lane. Their endorsement was revealing in terms of both substance and tone. As Salerno put it, "We must unite on one candidate if labor is to defeat the appeasers and the candidates of the American Fascist party, known as the America First Committee."[22] Salerno was also the head of the Clothing Workers Union, many of whose members were Jewish. They were not about to support an isolationist.

Although Harrington came from a staunch union family, he did not win the support of organized labor. "Massachusetts unions [were] for the most part led by men rather like the state and local leaders of the Democratic party," wrote two observers, "men whose orientation toward social problems [was] 'meat and potatoes,' immediate short-run economic benefits rather than broad social programs."[23] Since the Roosevelt administration had initiated progressive labor legislation like the Wagner-Connery Act, labor felt obliged to support FDR and those Democrats who identified with him. So Lane was the direct beneficiary. In fact, Lane was under tremendous pressure from organized labor to fall in line with FDR. Much of this pressure came from the mill town of Lawrence, which had been the scene of the famous "Bread and Roses" strike in 1912.

To add to his momentum, Lane was endorsed by the Connery Associates. This political action committee, which bore the name of the two former congressmen, was headquartered in Lynn. Ironically, their sister Mary A. Connery was married to James Harrington, who was Joseph's older brother. No doubt this awkward situation created family discord.

To offset labor's opposition, Harrington sought the blessings of the America First Committee. Several of its national leaders came to Massachusetts to campaign for him. Among them were U.S. senator Gerald P. Nye of North Dakota and John T. Flynn, who was a columnist for the *New Republic* and leader of the liberal flank of the America First movement. They appeared together on the same platform with Harrington at antiwar rallies. In addition, Charles Lindbergh endorsed him, a major coup for Harrington, or so it seemed.

These endorsements turned out to be a mixed blessing, however, because they did not sit well with liberals or with the Jewish community. Liberals, of course, equated pacifism with appeasement. Boston Jewry had rallied against Hitlerism and raised money for those who were fleeing Nazi Germany, although at this point the facts of the Jewish genocide were not well known. The America First movement offended most Jews, who could only have felt antipathy. They did not support Harrington or contribute financially to his campaign. Because he was a pacifist, Harrington was tagged as anti-Semitic. This charge was unfair. Lindbergh's biographer Scott Berg writes:

> While many of the other antiwar organizations had distinctly reactionary—often anti-Semitic—taints to them, America First seemed to attract men and women of all ages, political persuasions, and religions—including a number of influential Jews. These included Sidney Hertzberg, their publicity director, and Lessing Rosenwald, one of the Sears-Roebuck heirs. Furthermore, noted an FBI report on the organization, there was "a tremendous Jewish group" subsidizing the movement, using the Guggenheim Foundation as its front.[24]

From Harrington's perspective, American intervention in a European war was too high a price to pay. In words that would resonate in the political life of his son Michael twenty-eight years later, he felt that Americans should not have to fight someone else's war. Despite organized labor's support of Lane, Harrington held a commanding lead. Public opinion polls showed him well ahead of his primary rivals. Boston mayor Maurice Tobin considered Harrington a shoo-in.[25]

Timing, of course, was absolutely critical as far as Harrington's prospects were concerned. He remained the favorite right up until December 7, 1941. On that fateful Sunday morning, the Japanese bombed Pearl Harbor in a surprise attack. The next day, President Roosevelt appeared before a joint session of Congress and declared war against Germany and Japan. Now the congressional race took an electrifying turn.

Fate had delivered an unexpected jolt. Almost overnight the steam went out of the America First movement. The public quickly rallied behind its president in a time of national crisis. As a result, Harrington's prospects evaporated. Isolationism quickly became his Achilles' heel. With only a week to go before the election, the avalanche of war buried him.

When the voters went to the polls December 16, they cast their ballots in the spirit of national unity. Lane benefited most from this show of patriotism. In the Democratic primary, Lane received 17,275 votes, Manning 8,994, and Harrington finished a humiliating third with 4,498.[26] It was a crushing defeat and one that was hard for the Salem Democrat to swallow. He had been literally bombed out of the election. Who could have foreseen the shocking surprise at Pearl Harbor? Who could have predicted that the election would turn on the political accident of international events? Given Harrington's plight, his supporters felt some sympathy for him as a politician. In the Republican primary, Nelson Pratt picked up 5,268 votes, compared to 1,533 for John Garvin. Two weeks later, on December 30, Lane drubbed Pratt by 7,616 votes in the special election.[27]

THE INTERVENING YEARS

A basic rule of American politics holds that timing is everything. Paradoxically, Joe Harrington had gotten where he was because of good timing and lost because of bad timing. It was difficult for him to erase the memory of his defeat. Years later, upon leaving Dini's Restaurant in Boston, he remarked to some friends, "Remember Pearl Harbor? Will I ever forget it!"[28] Yet he saw his career after 1941 in exactly the same terms as before. Now he returned to the state Senate, where he finished the remainder of his unexpired term.

Harrington did not seek reelection in 1942 and for good reason. The Republicans were determined to regain the seat that Raymond Trefry had lost in 1940. To counteract Harrington's popularity among the Irish, they ran J. Frank Hughes of Danvers, who won back the seat for them. Hughes was a popular Irish politician who had agreed to rotate the senatorial seat. In 1944, Republican J. Elmer Callahan succeeded Hughes. Callahan lived in the "lace curtain" Broad Street section of Salem. Both Hughes and Callahan had been purposely recruited to split the Irish vote.

Seeing the writing on the wall, Harrington decided to run instead for district attorney of Essex County. His Republican opponent in 1942 was Hugh A. Cregg, a well-known attorney from Methuen. At the outset of the campaign, William Enwright, the editor of the *Lynn Telegram News*, who loathed Harrington, launched a vicious smear campaign against him. Their personal feud stemmed from an earlier libel suit that Harrington had won against the editor in court. Enwright now sought revenge and accused Harrington of being "a fascist and pro-Nazi." It was a completely bogus issue designed to deflect and destroy, but the strategy worked perfectly. Under wartime conditions, Enwright's poison pen editorials proved damaging. Harrington lost Lynn by 4,116 votes. The city was a blue-collar community that normally went Democratic. In the end, Cregg defeated Harrington by a margin of 8,569 votes.[29] The year 1942 was a banner year for Republicans in Massachusetts. Leverett Saltonstall won the governorship and Henry Cabot Lodge Jr. was elected to the U.S. Senate.

Two years later, in 1944, Harrington ran for state representative and won. He defeated John M. Gray by polling 4,643 votes to 3,443 for Gray.[30] Because of redistricting in 1945, Harrington did not seek reelection, but he did not lose his taste for public service. In 1947 he ran for mayor of Salem and defeated the Republican incumbent, Edward Coffey, who had held the office since 1938. Although municipal elections were by now nonpartisan, this was the first time a Democrat had won the office in over twenty-four years.

As things turned out, Joe Harrington was destined to serve only a single term. While serving as mayor, he suffered a severe heart attack. During the weeks of recovery and recuperation, he conducted city affairs from his home. Upon seeking reelection in 1949, he inadvertently alienated the city's French Canadians. The popularized story, still believed in Salem's political community, was that the insult was intentional, but that version is not quite accurate. He was too smart to make such an incredible blunder. What really happened was that a motorcycle policeman by the name of Wilfred Dansreau was apparently seeking a promotion in rank. He went to see Monsignor Arthur Mercier, the pastor of St. Joseph's Catholic Church, whose congregation was predominantly French. Dansreau, who was notorious for nabbing speeding motorists, asked the monsignor if he would intercede with the mayor in his behalf. Mercier gladly obliged. Persuaded finally that under civil service rules this promotion was not possible, Harrington turned down the request. Speaking from the pulpit at Sunday Mass, Monsignor Mercier told his congregation, "Obviously, the mayor must feel that he doesn't need the French vote." This comment, however, was mistakenly attributed to Harrington. Nevertheless, no insult was more keenly felt than to be considered irrelevant or unneeded.

Consequently, Franco-Americans voted overwhelmingly for Harrington's opponent, Francis X. Collins, who had previously served on the local school committee. His political strength lay in the "Gallows Hill" section of the city. There was no primary election in those days. In a closely contested race, Collins defeated Harrington by 9,194 to 8,971 votes. As the returns showing his narrow defeat came in, Harrington challenged the vote, but it was upheld after an official recount.

Capitalizing on good public relations, Collins remained in the mayor's office for the next twenty years. As an undergraduate at Harvard, Collins had majored in mathematics. He was considered "a genius with figures" and was able to keep the property tax rate down. That was the secret to his success. But he benefited greatly from the legacy of his predecessor. Mayor Joseph Harrington had persuaded the New England Power Company to build an $80 million electricity generating plant in Salem in 1949. During the 1950s, this private utility paid nearly 50 percent of the city's total taxes.

Collins kept city spending to a minimum but allowed Salem's run-down public schools to deteriorate even further. Because a majority of the school-children in Salem attended parochial schools, local taxpayers had been reluctant to improve their public schools.[31] Fourteen years later, in 1963, Michael J. Harrington, who was Joseph's son, would challenge Collins for the mayoralty, declaring unequivocally that he would raise taxes to pay for better public schools. Such a posture, while courageous on his part, no doubt cost him the election. But he believed in telling the truth, no matter the consequences.[32]

After his mayoral defeat in 1949, Joe Harrington did not seek public office again. His whole life had been wrapped up in politics, but his time had come and gone. In 1948, Governor Paul Dever had asked him to run for attorney general, but he declined. In 1957, Governor Foster Furcolo appointed him a state judge. Harrington was assigned to the First District court in Salem, where he presided for the next seven years. He seemed the very essence of a judge, for he was charming, articulate, and intelligent. An icon of the local establishment, he impressed both sides with his fairness and good sense. More than one associate characterized him as compassionate, especially in dealing with youthful offenders and alcoholics. Because of his leniency, some people referred to him as "Let Him Go Joe."

In 1960, Judge Harrington suffered a second heart attack, but this one was milder than the first. In 1962, although he had retired from politics, he backed Endicott (Chub) Peabody for governor and could not resist taking a swipe at both Edward M. Kennedy and George Cabot Lodge, labeling them "wealthy interlopers" who were not deserving of being elected to the U.S. Senate. Harrington's heart problems continued to plague him. He flew to Texas, where he had open-heart surgery at Houston Methodist Hospital. This surgery was performed by Michael DeBakey, then considered the leading surgeon in the country for this type of operation. A few years later, on February 3, 1964, while shaving in the morning before going to work, Harrington suffered a heart attack and died at age fifty-six. The *Salem Evening News* paid him this tribute:

> Joe Harrington liked the little people because he was one of them and mingled among them in his exciting life. The judge had known fame and frustration in his more than half-century on earth and he was far and away the most colorful figure in this city's politics in this generation. His spell-binding oratory, his extemporaneous brilliance in a living room, or on a political rostrum or on the bench, will not soon be duplicated. His humor was matchless. Judge Harrington was a loyal friend to some and worthy foe to others, but most of all, he was human. He made politics a noble and attractive calling and was quick to defend those in the profession. He was the patriarch of a family clan dedicated as few have been to the public service and a community stricken with grief is quick to send condolences to his gracious widow and four sons.[33]

THE RISE AND FALL OF KEVIN HARRINGTON

Thomas Lane served in Congress for twenty years, from 1942 to 1962. Since Lane came from a relatively safe Democratic district, he had no trouble holding on to his congressional seat. But Lane was hardly an asset to the party. He had been convicted of tax evasion and sent to federal prison. Shortly after his release from prison, he was reelected to Congress in 1956.

A protégé of his uncle Joe, Kevin B. Harrington, who served on the Salem City Council, was encouraged to run for the state Senate in 1958. It was the same year that Maine's governor Edmund Muskie, the son of a Polish-born tailor, won a special election as U.S. senator. For a Catholic to be elected in such a rock-ribbed Republican state as Maine meant that the political dynamics in New England were changing. Sensing this change, Kevin Harrington ran successfully for the state Senate.[34] The Democrats won twenty-four of the forty Senate seats in 1958, the year they first took control of the upper chamber.

The General Court was redistricted in 1959 on the basis of the 1955 state census. Under this plan the city of Salem was made a "double district" with regard to the House, and would now elect two representatives. Moreover, the town of Marblehead was dropped from the second Essex senatorial district and the city of Peabody was added to it. This plan was challenged in the courts, but the Supreme Judicial Court upheld it. Michael Harrington, Joe's son, was first elected as a state representative from Salem in 1964, about the time that the United States was becoming more involved militarily in Vietnam.

When it came to the U.S. Congress, Massachusetts had not been redistricted since 1940. But the 1960 federal census figures showed that states such as Florida and California were growing faster than Massachusetts. This meant that the Bay State would lose two House seats, thereby reducing its congressional delegation from fourteen to twelve members. As fate would have it, Kevin Harrington chaired a special legislative committee on redistricting in 1962. Under a plan that he devised, nine of the twelve new districts would be Democratic. It was shades of Elbridge Gerry, who had invented the practice of gerrymandering back in 1812. Republican governor John Volpe threatened to veto any redistricting plan that was unfair to Republicans. He insisted that the two major parties split the loss of the two congressional seats.

Four members of the Massachusetts congressional delegation met with Governor Volpe to discuss the problem. They included Democrats Thomas P. ("Tip") O'Neill and Edward P. Boland and Republicans Silvio Conte and William H. Bates. Given the fact that the negotiating group was bipartisan, their performance was extraordinary. They reached common ground with remarkable dispatch. Seeking to protect their own districts, they devised a bipartisan plan that differed significantly from Kevin Harrington's. The Republicans sacrificed the seat that was held by Laurence Curtis of Boston's Back Bay, allowing it to be eliminated. The Democrats had an easier decision. Embarrassed by the scandal of Thomas Lane languishing in jail for income tax evasion, they were willing to jettison him. He was placed in the same district with Republican F. Bradford Morse of Lowell. Although the new district was Democratic, Morse was a strong favorite because of his popularity and he defeated Lane in the 1962 election.[35]

A small irony arose when Democrat George J. O'Shea Jr. sought the Sixth District congressional seat in 1962. Like his father, who had run unsuccessfully in the special election of 1941, he was a state representative from Lynn. The younger O'Shea lost to the Republican incumbent William H. Bates, who had been in Congress since 1950, despite the fact that the heavily Democratic cities of Lynn and Peabody had been added to the new district. A former football star at Salem High School, Bates was a very popular Irish Catholic Republican. He was reelected in 1964, 1966, and again in 1968.

The political career of Kevin Harrington is worth examining in greater detail. Born in Salem on January 9, 1929, he was the son of Cornelius, a plumber. His mother was the former Mary G. Whalen, whose father had been an Irish stonemason. Kevin's parents lived at 7 Barton Street, where they raised six children—three boys and three girls. Cornelius died of a heart attack in June 1935 in the depths of the Great Depression. The three boys retained for life the questing intensity of children too early deprived of a father.

Typical of the Irish, Kevin entered politics. Another of the brothers became a diocesan priest. The Reverend Cornelius J. Harrington (commonly known as Father Neil) taught at St. Sebastian's Country Day School in Newton beginning in 1947 and later became pastor of Sacred Heart parish in Manchester. The eldest brother, Joseph B. Harrington, worked as an engineer for the New England Telephone Company. He was a political operative in his spare time. In 1962 he had coordinated the successful gubernatorial campaign of Chub Peabody in Essex County. As a reward for his efforts, Governor Peabody appointed him to the Alcoholic Beverages Control Commission. Tall, ruggedly handsome, and a hulk of a man physically, he was nicknamed "Joe the Monster." Unfortunately, he died prematurely in December 1967 at age forty-five, leaving behind a wife and five children.[36]

Standing six feet nine inches tall, Kevin Harrington cut a large figure and towered above most other people. In his youth he had played basketball, first at St. Mary's Boys' High in Lynn and then at St. Louis University, where he received an athletic scholarship and was educated by German Jesuits. There he met and fell in love with the attractive Kathleen Carney. After graduation, Kevin obtained a job teaching at the newly created Merrimack College in North Andover. He taught courses in modern European history and American government and also coached the basketball team. While teaching, he entered local politics and was elected to the Salem City Council, where he served from 1957 to 1959. From there he advanced to the state Senate.

In relatively short order, Kevin showed a unique ability to connect with people across racial, religious, and class lines. He also demonstrated the ability to negotiate and compromise that is necessary for success in politics. His temperament disposed him toward achieving compromise. He accepted the inherent messiness of the real world and displayed a tolerance for chaos and ambiguity. At the same time, he could efficiently sort out, accommodate, and integrate conflicting views. An astute and flexible politician, Harrington was receptive to new ideas and always tried to keep his options open. Seldom did he allow himself to become rigidly boxed in without finding some avenue of retreat.

Early in his career, Kevin became a key player on Beacon Hill, where he earned a reputation as a cautious realist. He was more concerned with delivering for his constituents than in undertaking the risky political ventures on which his liberal colleagues constantly wanted to send him. No one was more adept at listening to people, at understanding the nuances of an issue, and at finding new ways to move forward. It was the kind of wisdom that can come only from hard-won political experience. He had been a freshman Democratic state senator when the Democrats first took control of that body in 1959.

For as long as he was in office, Kevin Harrington, whom no one would mistake for a liberal, made the most of his political opportunity. He soon became a mover and shaker in the state Democratic Party. With his background in college teaching, he served on the joint Committee on Education. In 1962, Harrington led the battle over fiscal autonomy for the public university. That same year he chaired a blue-ribbon commission that made a comprehensive study of public education in Massachusetts. Benjamin C. Willis, the superintendent of schools in Chicago, served as staff director of the commission. Its 624-page report laid the groundwork for a sweeping reorganization of the Commonwealth's educational system. The landmark Willis-Harrington Act of 1965 established a new Department of Education and an independent Board of Higher Education. The passage of this important piece of legislation won Harrington statewide recognition.[37] Some party leaders began to see him as a potential gubernatorial candidate.

In similar fashion, Kevin Harrington used his power as a senator to make sure that Salem State College received its share of state funding. He obtained passage of legislation to restore its physical plant and to add several new buildings that were desperately needed. In 1964 he fought to obtain fiscal autonomy for the nine state colleges. This afforded them the same protection that had been granted to the University of Massachusetts in 1962. In taking such action, he helped to put Salem State College on the map. He also worked for the passage of bills to permit industrial and business expansion along Route 128 in Peabody, Danvers, and Beverly. These were important trophies for a legislator to take home to his constituents.

Over a period of twenty years (1958–78), Kevin Harrington became a lawmaker of considerable skill and experience. His other main concern was to gain power within the Senate. When John Powers stepped down as Senate president, Maurice Donahue of Holyoke was chosen to succeed him in April 1964. At the outset of the next legislative session, in January 1965, Harrington was promoted to majority floor leader. He later succeeded Donahue as Senate president and served in that position from January 1971 to July 1978. It was a chamber crowded with commanding egos and strident voices.

Both friend and foe alike acknowledged that Harrington was a powerful Senate president. He sometimes single-handedly moved or blocked legislation. He held the office longer than all but two of his eighty-two predecessors. No other man had so much influence in the General Court for so long a period—an influence derived mainly from his strong personality and the patronage he controlled. Mockingly referred to as "King Kevin" by his colleagues, he ruled the Senate with an iron hand and was adept at playing political hardball. Mike Barnicle, in a column for the *Boston Globe*, described him in masterly fashion:

> In an age when politics is being played mostly by colorless clerks, Kevin Harrington has always been Babe Ruth in a 48 extra-long. He is a tall Tip O'Neill, after eight months at Weight Watchers; Lyndon Johnson without the cowboy boots; a back room guy; a consensus builder. He is a pol to the teeth. . . . He has led the Senate sometimes with brute force, sometimes by juggling the different egos, playing off the different cast of characters against one another, always knowing just how far he could push, twist, shove, or coerce to convince the others.[38]

Even allowing for Barnicle's expansiveness, this is a remarkable portrait of the Salem Democrat as a versatile and accomplished politician. Barnicle knew Harrington well, and often spoke to men who knew him better. For his part, Harrington worked hard at achieving consensus. Capable of working with partisans of a different persuasion for the common good, he got along well with Republican governor Francis Sargent.

At this stage of his political career, the Salem Democrat fully understood the intricacies of the legislative process and the ethics of the Senate. As its presiding officer, he knew how to advise without being patronizing, how to bargain without promising more than he could deliver, and how to appeal to personal honor or party unity without seeming overly solicitous. Moreover, he knew where each of his colleagues in both parties stood, or wavered, and what each wanted or feared. He concealed his own position until it was absolutely necessary to divulge it. Few people knew what he really wanted other than to come out on the winning side.

Harrington, however, disagreed with Sargent when it came to the governor's handling of the prison riots that erupted in 1971–72. These uprisings plunged the runaway state prison system into chaos and endangered public safety. The riots, including acts of brutality and murder, resulted in a strike by the prison guards, culminating in the firing of Corrections Commissioner John O. Boone. Despite his disagreement with Governor Sargent, Harrington blocked attempts to kill the prison furlough program.

During the mid-1970s, agitation for reinstatement of the death penalty was gathering steam in the legislature. Public opinion strongly favored the death penalty, but many people saw it as unfair and unethical. The latter viewed capital punishment as state-sanctioned murder. The Commonwealth had last executed a prisoner in 1947. Almost three decades later, in 1976, the U.S. Supreme Court allowed the states to reinstate death penalty laws. The high court ruled that the death penalty was constitutional in the sense that it did not violate the Eighth Amendment's prohibition against "cruel and unusual punishment." Since then, thirty-eight states have reinstated the death penalty. In October 2001, the Georgia Supreme Court outlawed the electric chair, leaving Alabama and Nebraska as the only state using it as the sole method of execution. The issue as debated in Massachusetts focused on the morality of the state's taking a life in the pursuit of justice. Beset with conflicting demands on both sides of this highly charged issue, Kevin Harrington blocked the death penalty legislation in the Senate and thereby prevented its passage, much to the delight of liberals. The Boston Catholic Archdiocese was also pleased with the outcome.

To his credit, Harrington took more principled positions on legislation than most of his predecessors. In 1975 he showed exemplary leadership during a fiscal crisis and crafted a plan that enabled the state government to remain solvent and avoid bankruptcy. This was no small accomplishment. At one point he fast-gaveled a budget through without taking a roll-call vote. Republican senators were furious at him, but such a move carried the day. Harrington also worked closely with Robert C. Wood, president of the University of Massachusetts, in helping to restore the draconian budget cuts that Governor Michael Dukakis had imposed on the public higher education system.

Oddly enough, Harrington got along better with Republican governor Sargent than he did with Democratic governor Dukakis. Upon taking office, Dukakis stood firm on his "leadpipe guarantee" of no new taxes, though he conceded that the fiscal situation was much worse than he had anticipated. Harrington offered to help him by getting a tax bill passed to finance the deficit, but Dukakis spurned his offer. The two men seemed constantly at odds with each other. During his first term as governor, Dukakis was arrogant and did not reach out and listen to people. Consequently, he alienated many local Democrats, especially those who had backed him. His budget cuts in the field of human services angered them, and they made trouble for him as a result. His party position was weak at the end of his first term, when he appeared to be losing political strength.

In 1978 political insiders viewed Harrington as the Democrat most likely to oust Dukakis from the governorship. Looking back, reporters Charles Kenney and Robert Turner summed up the situation:

> The one most talked about, Harrington, was a smart, intimidatingly tall politi-cian who smoked huge cigars and took pleasure in wielding the considerable power of his office. The Senate was his private reserve; to give it up would be difficult. Yet Dukakis's perceived vulnerability among insiders convinced Har-rington that he could become governor. He intended to declare his candidacy formally at the end of January, and in the months preceding, he signed on people to raise money, take polls, and create advertising.[39]

Harrington's strategy of bringing together all the disaffected voters was risky. It would have involved his pushing aside the titular party leader and unseating a sitting governor within his own party. Yet there was precedent for doing so. In 1964, Lieutenant Governor Frank Bellotti had narrowly beaten the incumbent governor, Endicott Peabody, in a Democratic pri-mary. Bellotti then lost to Republican John Volpe in the general election.

In any event, the anticipated showdown between Harrington and Dukakis never materialized. Unfortunately for Harrington, his career ended abruptly when it was revealed that a $2,000 check made out to him had been cashed at his Salem bank. This check was issued by the New York consulting firm of McKee, Berger, and Mansueto, which had overseen the construction of the Boston campus of the University of Massachusetts at Columbia Point. Corporate campaign contributions had been illegal in Massachusetts since 1946. This disclosure came on the heels of a major scandal. On February 25, 1977, Joseph J. C. DiCarlo, Democratic floor leader of the Senate, and Ronald C. MacKenzie, the Republican whip, were convicted of extortion, conspiracy, and related federal crimes. The charges against them involved the payment of $40,000 in bribes by the same firm. After losing an appeal, they were both sentenced to one year in federal prison and fined $5,000 each.

Asked by reporters about the check, Harrington admitted that the en-dorsement on the back appeared to be his, but insisted that he did not remember either endorsing or cashing it. But the damage had been done so far as his position was concerned. What internal battling had not done to destroy his power, the scandal charge did. So fragile can political power be. Under the circumstances, Kevin Harrington did his best to appear philosophical and statesmanlike, saying, "Napoleon said history is an agreed-upon myth. Well, this myth has been agreed upon, and I don't think it will change regardless of what happens. The myth is set, and has jelled."[40] The controversy abruptly terminated Harrington's gubernatorial plans and hastened his political demise. Whatever the facts of the case, he resigned from the Senate on July 31, 1978. He lamented the next day to the *Salem Evening News*, "Doesn't 20 years count for anything?"

Kevin Harrington was relegated to the sidelines, where he would remain for the rest of his life. Although he was only forty-nine, he would never hold elected public office again. The ultimate irony is that two months before leaving office, he pushed through legislation that created an independent state Ethics Commission and a financial disclosure law. But if his career seems to have ended on a note of despair, the impression one has of him is not of failure but of highly effective leadership.

ALL IN THE FAMILY

In the meantime, Michael Harrington, who was Kevin's first cousin, had been elected to Congress. He used his power on Capitol Hill in Washington to see that Salem received federal funds to finance a revitalized downtown and waterfront. He was the driving force behind the creation of the "Salem partnership," which was both public and private in character. In masterminding this initiative, he brought together all the major players who could help shape the future of the small city. Once the partnership was launched, however, he quickly went off and pursued other matters. He was a man in a hurry and not especially given to patience. Because of his cerebral approach to politics and his penchant for independence, opponents saw him as a different kind of Democrat. He was a complicated man, not easily deciphered. No politician was more inscrutable or difficult to fathom. Ultimately, he was a man stubbornly determined to do what he thought right regardless of the consequences.

Throughout the 1960s and most of the 1970s, the dynamic duo of Kevin and Michael Harrington wielded substantial political clout. To be sure, there was a certain potency to the Harrington name. Perceived power often translates into real power. A reputation for strength, however, is dependent on more than just personal qualities. Possession of the means to punish or reward is also important. The Salem businessman William Follett once remarked, "If the Harringtons can't do it, it can't be done." Such was their reputation for power.

Nancy Harrington, who was a first cousin to Kevin and Michael, made her mark as a professional academic administrator. She became president of Salem State College in 1990, having finished as runner-up in a previous presidential search. Her predecessor had lasted only a short time and resigned as the result of a scandal. She earned the position on her own merits and not through political patronage, as some suspected. A smart and talented woman, she was the first graduate of the college to assume its top executive post. She had previously been its dean of graduate and continuing education. She performed admirably at the helm despite her critics, like most successful administrators surrounding herself with a highly competent staff.[41]

Her older sister, Carol Mulholland, was considered by her two siblings to be the brightest of the three children. She graduated from Radcliffe College in 1944 with a major in sociology. Her late brother, Lee F. Harrington, served as president of the Massachusetts Maritime Academy in Buzzards Bay from 1972 to 1980. He had been educated at St. John's Prep in Danvers, where he graduated in 1941 as valedictorian and was considered the best athlete in his class. After finishing Holy Cross College in 1944, Lee joined the navy during World War II and saw combat in the South Pacific aboard the heavy cruiser U.S.S. *Pittsburgh*, achieving the rank of lieutenant commander. Donald Flynn, a former student of Harrington's at Massachusetts Maritime Academy, recalled him as a fine math teacher and an excellent baseball coach.[42] He was very popular with his students. Sad to relate, he died prematurely of cancer in July 1980 at age fifty-five.

A fifth generation of Harringtons appeared on the Salem political scene in the early 1980s. Given his grandfather's name out of family pride, Cornelius J. Harrington was the son of Kevin Harrington and Kathleen Carney. He was educated at St. John's Prep and at St. Louis University. Known by his nickname, Neil, he was elected to the local city council and then served as mayor of Salem from 1990 to 1997. He was a well-intentioned and conscientious mayor who took his job seriously, but he was always in his father's shadow and had trouble finding his political footing. During these years he experienced some painful disagreements with his second cousin. There was a fraying of the friendship, or what everyone had been led to believe was a friendship, between Michael and Neil. Whatever the grievance between the two men, Michael Harrington felt compelled to say publicly that "Neil doesn't have the stomach to be mayor." They eventually broke with each other politically. In 1982, Neil failed to win a five-way race for the state Senate seat previously held by his father. After serving four terms in the mayor's office, he ultimately found his rhythm, but by then it was too late. He lost his bid for reelection to a fifth term, and then lost another bid to become sheriff of Essex County.

A REBEL WITH A CAUSE

Michael J. Harrington was the son of Joseph and Elizabeth Harrington. His date of birth, September 2, 1936, made him a "depression baby." Like his father he was born and raised in Salem. The family lived at 35 Winter Island Road, which was at the far end of a long promontory jutting out into the ocean with a commanding view of the sea. Their house was in the "Salem Willows" section of the city. At the time, this was a close-knit neighborhood, where the city's "poor farm" and the U.S. Coast Guard station were located. Originally developed in the 1880s as an amusement park for the urban masses, the Willows was the site of the world's largest outdoor saltwater swimming pool, which was built during the depression by the federal Works Progress Administration.[43] The so-called Smith pool was a New Deal pump-priming project of FDR's.

A quarter-century later Michael Harrington followed in his father's footsteps and pursued a similar career path, though he had taken a different route in obtaining his education. From the parochial schools of Salem he went on to St. John's Prep, where he played baseball and excelled in his studies. As a youngster Harrington often accompanied his father in making the political rounds of the local fire stations. He was a "golden boy," who graduated as class valedictorian from St. John's in 1954. From there he went on to Harvard University (class of 1958) and Harvard Law School (class of 1961). Before beginning the private practice of law in Salem in 1962, he earned a master's degree in public administration at Harvard's Littauer School, which was later renamed the Kennedy School of Government. These ivy covered institutions of higher learning were still Yankee Brahmin preserves. The family had come a long way since the early days of St. Mary's Commercial School. While at law school, Michael married Dorothy M. Leahy, who lived on North Street in Salem. She was a bright woman who was considered a prize catch.

Some politicians are born to opportunity, others create opportunity, and still others have opportunity thrust upon them. In the case of Michael Harrington it was a combination of all three. Drawing on the political connections that his father had established, he was elected to the Salem City Council at the age of twenty-three. Inspired by the idealism of President John F. Kennedy, he served on the council from 1960 to 1963. He then ran for mayor of Salem but lost to the popular incumbent Francis X. Collins, who had held the office since 1950.

An Irish Catholic Democrat and a Harvard alumnus, Collins had unseated Joe Harrington as mayor in 1949. He thus defeated both father and son. Collins, who served an unprecedented ten terms as mayor from 1950 to 1969, disliked the Harringtons for any number of reasons, including their mayoral battles. There was bad blood between them. Years later, Mayor Neil Harrington would name the Middle School in Salem after Collins. This magnanimous gesture was an exercise in political reconciliation, but Neil also felt that it was the right thing to do. Collins in turn appreciated the gesture. Asked near the end of his life to estimate the value of the mayor's office, Joe Harrington concluded that it was a political dead end. This was a fair assessment, considering the fact that both he and his grandnephew Neil ended their political careers as mayor.

Intelligent, energetic, and ambitious, Michael Harrington followed his father's pragmatic ethic of moving "up or out" when it came to politics. The opportunities for political advancement were limited even for the most ambitious of local politicians. Adept at turning adversity to his advantage, Michael quickly rebounded from his mayoral defeat in 1963 and got himself elected to the Massachusetts House of Representative, where he served for three consecutive terms from 1964 to 1969. He was considered a rising political star from his earliest days in the legislature. His intelligence won him grudging acceptance from many of his fellow legislators. He then ran successfully for Congress in 1969 when the antiwar movement was gaining a head of steam. It was a natural progression for a public figure who had long defied the establishment.

The country in Michael's day was vastly different from the America of his father's generation. This was a period that witnessed the emergence of a counterculture and social forces that produced great tensions and fissures throughout society. Families were divided over issues of war, drugs, sex, race, music, fashion, hairstyles, and the prevalent use of profanity in everyday speech. Richard Nixon was president of the United States and Leonid Brezhnev was chairman of the Soviet Communist Party. The cold war had reached its apogee.

Sensing that the present was alive with change, Michael Harrington ran for Congress in opposition to the war in Vietnam. This audacious venture was fraught with risk, for he was up against entrenched establishment power. In taking such a courageous stance, Harrington threw caution to the wind. He defied not only the Nixon administration but his own party's leadership as well. Under the Lyndon Johnson administration, Secretary of Defense Robert McNamara had felt that some way had to be found of neither abandoning Vietnam nor stepping up American involvement. No stranger to controversy, Harrington made the increasingly unpopular war in Southeast Asia the centerpiece of his congressional campaign. He became the antiestablishment candidate.

THE 1969 SPECIAL ELECTION

Only fifty-two years of age, Congressman William H. Bates died of stomach cancer at Bethesda Naval Hospital on June 22, 1969. A lifelong Republican, he had succeeded his father, Congressman George J. Bates, who was killed in an airplane crash at National Airport in Washington in November 1949. The senior Bates had served as mayor of Salem from 1924 to 1937, and his son pretty much followed in his father's footsteps. After graduating from Brown University and the Harvard Business School, Bill Bates had served as a naval officer during World War II. While in Congress, he championed a nuclear navy and the development of peaceful uses of atomic energy. During the Eisenhower administration, he was a frequent golfing companion of Vice President Nixon. His untimely death set off a mad scramble for the open seat. The date of the primary election was set for August 26, to be followed by the special election on September 30, 1969.

Four Democrats threw their hats into the ring. They included Daniel Burke, a colorful Essex County commissioner from Lynnfield; Thaddeus Buczko, the state auditor from Salem; Irving Kane, the mayor of Lynn; and Michael Harrington, a state representative who had since moved from Salem to Beverly, where his great-grandparents had originally settled. The Republicans recruited William L. Saltonstall, a state senator from Manchester, and Francis W. Hatch Jr., a state representative from Beverly Farms, two affluent North Shore suburbs located on what is referred to as the "Gold Coast."

Affectionately known by the nickname "Salty," William Saltonstall was a social conservative and a dedicated environmentalist as well as a strong advocate of land use planning and environmental reforms. He later sponsored legislation to assist the state's fishing industry and to improve bicycling safety. But his greatest single asset was his family name. An archetypal Yankee blueblood, he was the son of Leverett Saltonstall, a Republican powerhouse who served four terms as Speaker of the Massachusetts House, three terms as governor, and twenty-two years in the U.S. Senate. His great-grandfather was a former mayor of Salem. Given his family's illustrious legacy, name recognition and visibility were not a problem for him.

To be sure, the road to the state Senate had been more than adequately prepared for William Saltonstall. Upon his moving to Manchester in 1967, the Republicans persuaded Phillip Graham, the incumbent state senator, to vacate his seat. For accommodating his party in this regard, Graham was amply rewarded with a plum patronage job at the Massachusetts Turnpike Authority. At the time, the employees were not covered by the state pension system. Before departing from office, Graham hastily pushed through legislation that provided such coverage. The political trade-offs were abundantly clear.

Once again, it was a crowded primary field. The Sixth Congressional District had been a traditional Republican stronghold. In fact Republicans had held the seat almost continuously since the end of the Civil War. There was only one interruption: in 1874, Charles P. Thompson, a Democrat from Gloucester, had won the seat in what proved to be an aberration. The dismal failures of Reconstruction, an economic depression, and the corruption scandals within the Grant administration all made 1874 a disastrous year for the Republican Party nationally. Thompson served a single term from 1875 to 1877. Otherwise, the Republicans owned the congressional seat.

This was still pretty much the same congressional district that Governor Elbridge Gerry had carved out in 1812, with only slight alterations here and there. It is a hard district for a candidate to work politically because of its peculiar peninsular shape and geography. Bounded on the northeast by the Atlantic Ocean, the district runs mostly in a southern and westerly direction. Two-thirds of its vote comes out of the highly urban and industrial southern portion of the district. The northern part consists mostly of small rural towns and suburbs, which over the years have been a wellspring of Republicanism. With such a crowded primary field, the Democrats risked fracturing their rich base of support in the cities of Haverhill, Lynn, Peabody, and Salem. Consequently, Thaddeus Buczko, after taking out papers to run, decided to withdraw from the race as the result of pressure from local Democratic leaders, who feared that he would split the ethnic vote and leave the party vulnerable in the special election.

A complex and controversial personality, Michael Harrington ran not as a conservative Irish politician but more as a liberal Irish Catholic with Harvard credentials. He had risen in his party because of four perceptions among his colleagues and constituents, all of which he fostered. First, as a state legislator, he had earned the reputation of being a maverick liberal who was nonconformist in his political behavior. As one observer put it, "There were rules for Michael Harrington and then there were rules for everybody else." Even within the Democratic Party he stood against the wind. Second, he liked to shake things up on Beacon Hill and didn't mind stepping on toes, even if the toes happened to be those of former governor Foster Furcolo, who had appointed Harrington's father a state judge. Third, he displayed a penchant for leftist politics and supported Eugene McCarthy for president in 1968. That year he joined disaffected Democrats who sought to "Dump the Hump," a move to deny Vice President Hubert Humphrey the party's presidential nomination. Fourth, he had several political assets, including family name, financial resources, proven vote-getting ability, and influential allies.[44]

To be sure, Michael Harrington was a complex person who was never easy about revealing himself to others. To some people who knew him he came across not as a warmhearted liberal but as tough-minded and very self-centered. In terms of public perception, he projected multiple images, not all of which were favorable. Some critics saw him as a political opportunist who seemed overly ambitious and greedy for power. Others perceived him as a "knee-jerk lefty" and a "complete flake," whose ideas were simply unrealistic. Still others felt that he was an arrogant politician who played by his own rules. Those who knew him best admired him the most. Few people remained neutral. He was loved and hated with equal passion.

Yet Harrington was shrewdly attuned to the temper of the times. Questioning authority and rebelling against it were very much in vogue among the younger generation. Once freed of the cant of nationalism, the myths and shibboleths of yesterday were not merely disbelieved by the young but became positively abhorrent. Many of the older generation, unable to see the difference between their own noble causes—World War II, Korea—and the attempt to "defend freedom" in Southeast Asia, were outraged by what they perceived as the rejection of patriotism. This generational conflict only worsened.

The rap against Harrington as a state legislator was that he had one of the worst attendance records in the General Court, and that when present he sat in a back row and pouted. Many of these complaints were no doubt justified, in politics criticism usually goes with the territory. In many ways, Harrington was an enigmatic figure who defied simplistic stereotyping. He was a curious blend of idealist and rebel, but he was filled with contradictions and ambiguities. In reality he walked a fine line between overbearing arrogance and supreme self-confidence. He lacked patience, and did not suffer fools gladly. His public persona did not differ much from his private one.

Politics for Harrington was a game of risk. Secure in his convictions about how the world operated, he was willing to take certain positions that offended the establishment. Ultimately he decided to go for broke and make his opposition to the war in Vietnam the central issue of his campaign. Everything else, including local issues such as the closing of shoe factories and the consequent loss of jobs, became secondary. He also benefited from the fact that his father had been a legendary figure in the Democratic Party of Essex County. Unlike his father, however, he won the support of the Jewish community, which was a key Democratic constituency. Many more Jews had moved to the North Shore since the end of World War II. They not only supported Michael Harrington with their votes but also contributed heavily to his campaign coffers. Jewish activists such as Jake Segal of Marblehead, Gertrude Weiss of Swampscott, Adele Ash of Haverhill, and

William Wasserman of Ipswich all played a vital role in his campaign. Wasserman, who owned and published the *North Shore Sunday* newspaper, later became Harrington's administrative assistant in Congress.

Once they decided between themselves which one would vie for the party's nomination, Michael named his cousin Kevin Harrington as his campaign manager. This proved a wise choice on his part, considering what he ultimately set out to achieve. As majority floor leader in the state Senate, Kevin was a respected and knowledgeable player on Beacon Hill. In dealing with fellow politicians, he avoided the tactless errors of his cousin Michael. Kevin had access to influential people and knew reasonably well just about everybody who would matter to Michael's success as a candidate. He understood the dynamics of the race and gave Michael's candidacy a certain degree of political legitimacy. Upon learning of Kevin's role, Thomas McGee, a local Democratic leader in Lynn, felt confident that the campaign would be in good hands with "the big guy" in charge. An ex-Marine, McGee was a rough-hewn, conservative Irish politician, who had seen combat in World War II. He was not particularly fond of Michael's brand of liberalism. As things turned out, Kevin Harrington proved to be an effective campaign manager. Inevitably mistakes were made, but these were mostly scheduling problems and staffing decisions. They were not serious blunders.

Michael Harrington's advertising man, Robert Baker of Marblehead, devised a clever theme for the election campaign. In trying to capture the public's imagination, Baker came up with two campaign slogans: "Congress will never be the same" and "He has the guts to do what's right."[45] Harrington used the latter slogan over and over again. It was plastered on advertising billboards and printed in campaign brochures, accompanied by a picture of Harrington with his sport jacket slung over his shoulder to convey the impression of an activist politician hard at work. When the idea was originally proposed, Kevin Harrington was nervous about it. He felt that the slogans sounded arrogant and somewhat flippant, but Michael overruled any objections. He told his campaign staff, "If my conservative cousin is nervous, then we should do it."[46] Initially, the billboards were field-tested in the northern part of the district, and when they seemed to connect with the public, they were then put in place in the more populous southern tier.

The Democratic primary was a three-man fight. The major issues focused on the ABM (antiballistic missile) system, the proposed federal interstate highway I-95, and the Vietnam War. Sounding the right words and the right tone, Harrington spoke out against the policy in Vietnam. "We are talking out of both sides of our mouths," he said. "The policy is bankrupt."[47] He expressed his dissatisfaction with both Democrats and Republicans alike, and promised that if elected to Congress, he would shake up the system on

Capitol Hill. Irving Kane, by contrast, expressed support for President Nixon's Vietnam troop withdrawal policy and stated that he would have voted for the Hart-Cooper amendment calling for more research on the ABM system before its deployment.

On August 6, Harrington got a big boost when Nicholas Mavroules, the mayor of Peabody, endorsed him.[48] This move helped to offset Kane's expected strength in Lynn, where he was mayor. A week later, on August 18, David Harrison, who was chairman of the state Democratic Party, also endorsed him. Both Daniel Burke and Kane were furious at Harrison. They felt that the party chairman should have remained neutral during the primary. Rumors spread that Harrison's endorsement had the tacit approval of Senator Edward Kennedy.[49]

On the Republican side, Frank Hatch was a decided underdog. Not nearly as well known or as well financed as William Saltonstall, he faced an uphill battle. At a debate in Gloucester, which was sponsored by Cape Ann Concerned Citizens, Hatch attacked Saltonstall by arguing that having a famous political name was not sufficient reason for him to win the Republican nomination. Hatch reminded his audience that he had nearly won his party's nomination for lieutenant governor in 1966, but he lost by a whisker to Frank Sargent. In taking stock of his own legislative achievements, Hatch pointed with pride to the pioneer work that he had done in the area of environmental policy, especially with the passage of the so-called Hatch Act, which provided for wetlands protection. He also cited his fight to obtain better commuter rail service for the North Shore, and his struggle to get overhead electrical power lines buried underground. But Hatch equivocated on Vietnam. Skipping the Gloucester debate, Saltonstall conducted his informal "Walking with Salty" campaign.

In the August 26 primary Harrington topped the Democratic slate with 16,985 votes. Kane came in second with 9,130 votes, while Burke, who had missed several of the debates, ran a distant third with 6,227 votes. In the Republican primary Hatch gave Saltonstall all the competition he could handle. He outdistanced him in Beverly, Danvers, Hamilton, Topsfield, and Wenham for a much closer finish than most political insiders had predicted. Only 2,487 votes separated them. Saltonstall received 14,934 ballots compared to 12,347 for Hatch.[50] After the primary election Saltonstall remarked that he "would try to get out from under the name-brand umbrella and would carry on his campaign as an individual with his own views and his own style of politics."[51] By his own admission, he needed to find his voice, his message, and his campaign style.

Now Harrington would go one-on-one with Saltonstall. It was a classic match-up pitting a staid, conservative Protestant out of Harvard against an upstart, liberal Catholic out of Harvard. The former was the scion of a sterling Yankee blueblood family, while the latter was the grandson of an Irish immigrant. The old ethnic and class tensions had been reactivated. These values were played out as the campaign unfolded. Not surprisingly, Saltonstall, because of his illustrious family name and background, showed an early lead in public opinion polls. It was Harrington's turn to play the role of underdog.

The news media showed an intense interest in the race, mainly because of the defining Vietnam War issue. It became a major news story. News commentators depicted the campaign as a battle between the "hawks" and the "doves." It was not always easy to tell them apart simply by party affiliation. We do well to remember that some Eisenhower Republicans were early "doves," while some Kennedy Democrats were persistent "hawks." In his 1968 book *The Emerging Republican Majority*, Kevin Phillips propounded the theory that Nixon had won the White House with a southern strategy that sent a signal to both parties. No longer could Democrats rely on the South as a dependable redoubt of support. Nor could they take urban ethnic voters in the North for granted. This special election was the first test of Phillips's theory. Moreover, it was imperative for President Nixon to keep the Sixth District a Republican seat. Therefore, the Republican National Committee sent Charles Colson, one of its best political operatives, to help out. Colson, a seasoned back room guy who had a reputation for masterminding winning elections, was subsequently convicted and sent to prison for his role in the Watergate scandal.

The Vietnam War had aroused debate in the United States long before it became Lyndon Johnson's war. In 1965, President Johnson gradually Americanized the war. He decided first to bomb North Vietnam and then to send American ground forces into combat in South Vietnam. The escalating war, which drained the nation's resources for funding LBJ's Great Society programs and fighting the war against poverty at home, was generating a contentious atmosphere. Antiwar radicals had violently demonstrated at the Democratic national convention in Chicago in 1968. Student protests and campus riots, which soon became endemic, disrupted university life. Dissenting groups marched in the streets, took over public buildings, and shut down universities in order to protest what they believed to be an unjust war abroad and inequalities at home.

Against this background, the Americanization of the Vietnam War became the overriding campaign issue. Harrington's strategy was to depict Saltonstall as supporting the war and remaining loyal to Nixon, who was struggling to find an honorable way out, but without much success. The Beverly Democrat was careful to let voters know that he was opposed to *Nixon's* policies as distinct from *Republican* policies, a subtle difference that was not lost on independent voters.[52] As expected, Saltonstall came out in favor of Nixon's policy on the war and on deployment of the ABM system. In March 1969, Nixon agreed to a compromise that altered the purpose of the ABM system to protecting American missile-launching sites against a Soviet first strike. That scaled down its size, reduced its cost, and removed the system to the least populated states such as Montana and North Dakota. The program got through Congress by a single vote in August, and two missile sites were eventually built.

To distinguish himself from his Republican opponent, Harrington called for a speedier withdrawal of American troops from Southeast Asia and opposed the ABM system as costing too much and escalating the arms race. By adopting such positions, he veered to the left and thereby energized his liberal antiwar base, the locus of Democratic restiveness. Both candidates conducted themselves in an exemplary manner. They were dignified, polite, and occasionally eloquent. Although the debates were heated, they never grew personal. Neither candidate resorted to harsh words or negative campaigning. Harrington's support built steadily while Saltonstall's faltered. The Beverly Democrat had a lot going for him that a successful campaign requires: energy, experience, allies, urgency, a break on the issues, and the absence of a charismatic rival.

Near the end of the campaign, both candidates sought outside help by way of surrogates. Michael Dukakis, a liberal Democrat from Brookline who served with Harrington as a state legislator, campaigned for him in the Greek community of Haverhill. Five days before the election, Senator Edmund Muskie of Maine flew in from Washington to campaign for Harrington in Lynn. Former vice president Hubert Humphrey gave him an enthusiastic endorsement as well. Congressman Allard K. Lowenstein of New York, an outspoken opponent of the war in Vietnam, also campaigned on his behalf. For his part, Saltonstall countered with Senator Edward Brooke and Governor Frank Sargent, who campaigned for him in the cities of Lynn and Salem.

The Harrington camp had flirted with the idea of bringing in Edward Kennedy to campaign, but they had second thoughts and decided against it. The Chappaquiddick tragedy, in which Mary Jo Kopechne drowned, had recently taken place on July 18, 1969. This tragedy, which ruined Kennedy's chances for the presidency, was too fresh in the public mind. His moral failings at Chappaquiddick appeared to disqualify him. In any case, it was sufficient reason to keep Kennedy under wraps. A personal appearance by the controversial senator was at best a risky proposition, so the idea was scrubbed. But Kennedy did record a favorable radio message. Harrington had peaked with perfect timing. The final showdown was at hand.

On September 30 the voters went to the polls in a record turnout. After the polls closed that evening, the returns came in slowly from the small rural towns because they did not have voting machines and still counted their ballots by hand. A clue as to how the vote might turn out came early when the town of Swampscott reported its returns. Saltonstall carried this rock-ribbed Republican community by only 37 votes. That was a good omen for the Harrington forces. In the end, Harrington received 72,030 votes to 65,454 for Saltonstall.[53] The Beverly Democrat had not only vanquished his Yankee rival but also vindicated his father's defeat in 1941.

A jubilant victory party was held election night at the King's Grant Inn in Danvers. Harrington and his army of campaign workers were exultant. It was cause for great celebration. Not since 1874 had a Democrat won the Sixth Congressional District. Among those offering their congratulations was the socialist Michael Harrington, who in 1962 had written the popular best-seller *The Other America*. He was often described as "the man who discovered poverty." The social critic appropriately signed his congratulatory telegram "The Other Mike Harrington."

Two weeks later, on October 15, a massive rally was held on the Boston Common to observe the nationwide Vietnam Moratorium. A huge crowd estimated at 100,000 people demonstrated their opposition to the war and shouted cries of "Peace Now!" They heard Senator George McGovern of South Dakota declare, "We seek not to break the President, but to lift the terrible burden of the war from his shoulders and from the American people."[54]

MICHAEL HARRINGTON'S UNFULFILLED PROMISE

There is much to admire in the career of Michael Harrington, who had the courage to speak his convictions. His was a voice of conscience. Fresh from his congressional campaign, he went to Washington in 1969 with what appeared to be a bright political future ahead of him. Much was expected of him as he stepped into the national limelight. He had potential greatness written all over him. Those expectations, however, were largely dashed. He spent the next nine years in Congress, where he had a decent but undistinguished career. The issues he chose to tackle were complicated: national security, arms control, intelligence operations. His record of performance in Congress was at best spotty. No major legislation bears his name. The stunning gap between promise and unrealized potential was reflected in his lackluster and somewhat erratic performance.

From start to finish, Harrington had trouble adjusting to the customs and legislative procedures of Capitol Hill. Although the rule of deference was still very powerful, the late 1960s witnessed major procedural reforms in Congress and a revolt against the seniority system and the power of committee chairmen. As Michael Schudson explains in his magisterial book

The Good Citizen: "Subcommittees proliferated, decentralizing authority and providing multiple new points of access for various constituencies, including minority groups. The members of Congress became more co-equal, each member grew more dependent on his or her own entrepreneurial endeavors and less dependent on currying favor with senior colleagues, and increasingly even freshmen legislators could make speeches on the floor and propose significant policy initiatives."[55]

The Democratic Party in Massachusetts was undergoing significant change. To quote Jerome Mileur again:

> There were reformers in the ranks of the Democrats, organizations like the Americans for Democratic Action, but they remained on the margins of the party until the 1960s when the anti-war movement brought new forces and a new generation into the party. The children of JFK, these activists for peace, environment, women, and minorities, transformed the Democrats in the 1970s and 1980s into a party of social liberalism, marginalizing the older economic pragmatism and cultural conservatism.[56]

It is in this context that Harrington's subsequent political behavior is best understood. As a freshman congressman, he joined the revolt that was already under way. For someone who played by his own rules, he chafed under the seniority system and wanted to do away with it. He felt frustrated by what he perceived as archaic rules and folkways in a Congress that was dominated by a club of elders, especially barons of the Old South. He wanted to act right away and felt impatient with those who blocked action. His impetuous behavior (a telling criticism), coupled with his penchant for stirring things up, eventually landed him in trouble. He was something of a loner and not a particularly collegial member of the House, and a poor attendance record in Congress did not help matters.

Initially Harrington was assigned to the Banking and Currency Committee and the Armed Services Committee, but he quickly became disenchanted with what he considered mundane assignments. Seeking help from fellow Massachusetts Democrat and House majority leader Tip O'Neill, he got himself reassigned to the more prestigious Foreign Affairs Committee and the Government Operations Committee. It was on these two committees where his work had the most impact. He remained a steadfast opponent of U.S. involvement in Vietnam.

The winding down of the war in Vietnam resulted in an examination of the role of intelligence agencies in shaping foreign and defense policy. Moreover, the Watergate investigations of 1974 had revealed the extent to which presidential administrations had attempted to cover up politically embarrassing activities under the guise of national security. Investigative journalists uncovered evidence that intelligence agencies such as the CIA and the FBI were involved in questionable covert operations overseas as well as in domestic surveillance of antiwar protesters and other opponents of government policies at home. It was further revealed that these practices were widespread throughout the late 1960s and early 1970s.

As a result, House Speaker Carl Albert appointed a Select Intelligence Committee in 1975 to investigate these matters. Lucien Nedzi, a conservative Democrat from Michigan, was named as chair. He turned out to be a controversial choice. Shortly after his appointment it was revealed that Nedzi had received secret briefings in 1974 about illegal CIA operations, but he had failed to inform the committee. This situation troubled his fellow Democrats, especially Harrington. They pressed for Nedzi's removal.

In a highly unusual move, Harrington once again threw caution to the wind. He released to the public secret testimony that had been given by CIA director William Colby related to the agency's covert role in the overthrow of Salvador Allende's leftist government in Chile on September 11, 1973. Adam Clymer, the Washington correspondent for the *New York Times,* put it this way: "The [Nixon] administration had poured millions of dollars into efforts to defeat Allende in 1970 and tried to stimulate a coup then. After Allende took power, it sought to squeeze Chile through international financial institutions. There is no evidence of U.S. government involvement in the 1973 coup, but the administration quickly recognized the new government despite the murders of Allende and thousands of others."[57]

Harrington's release of the secret testimony shook Capitol Hill. The fight promised to be a lonely one. The danger of such a game lay in the possibility of retribution and punishment. It prompted Republican congressman Robin L. Beard of Tennessee to file a complaint against Harrington for his apparent violation of House rules. Beard was seeking to have him either reprimanded or censured. The House Ethics Committee voted to investigate the complaint and to hold a hearing.

Harrington, of course, saw the controversy in a much different light and felt that he was being attacked unfairly. Convinced of the rectitude of his cause, he declared: "What is really at issue here is the failure of the Congress to discharge its responsibilities as an overseer of intelligence security. The issue is not Michael Harrington, but the use of the CIA and government secrecy in general to short-circuit the democratic process and cover up illegal activity. I remain convinced that what I did . . . was responsible and proper under the circumstances."[58] He had said all that he intended to say on the subject, but he sent a signal to the Nixon administration. Whether or not the effort to censure him contributed to his disillusionment with politics, it took courage to blow the whistle and expose what the federal government had been doing.

During this stage of the cold war, liberals like Harrington, on the one hand, often warned the nation about the danger of eroding civil liberties. Conservatives, on the other hand, supported virtually every expansion of power by federal authorities (such as domestic surveillance or wiretapping of suspected subversives) as an indispensable weapon in the war against communism.

Given his predicament, Harrington once again sought help from Tip O'Neill, who intervened on his behalf and saved him from a formal vote of censure. Tip warned Harrington, however, that he had used up his political capital and should not expect any further help from him. In this highly politicized atmosphere, the select committee was reconstituted with the same mandate but with a different chair. Both Nedzi and Harrington were disciplined and were removed from the committee.[59]

The energy crisis and the Arab oil embargo had set off a scramble for scarce energy resources. In 1976, Harrington proposed creating a Massachusetts Power Authority. The idea was for the state to build and operate electric generating plants and sell power to local electric companies for distribution to their customers. The private electric companies doing business in Massachusetts were strongly opposed to Harrington's push for state-run electricity. The question was placed on the ballot as a public referendum, but it was soundly defeated by the electorate.[60]

Harrington's impatience persisted, but his patently unfulfilled ambition lent credence to the perception that he was a man possessed. A former aide put it even more crisply: "Look at him. He's gone through seven administrative assistants in seven years for Christ's sake." In a 1977 interview Harrington candidly acknowledged his own conflicting emotions, saying, "I am impatient with myself, with other people and with life." Reporter Charles Kenney wrote in *The Free Paper*, "Harrington's impatience has caused some to question his political maturity and his commitment to his job in Congress. He hasn't mastered the fine art of waiting. Horny dogs do a better job of masking their ambitions."[61]

It was widely expected that Harrington would challenge Republican incumbent Edward Brooke for the U.S. Senate in 1978. Brooke appeared vulnerable because of a scandal over apparently falsifying his personal finances in a divorce proceeding. Harrington was nevertheless concerned that his liberal supporters would view such a challenge as untenable, since it would have pitted a liberal Democrat against the lone liberal black in the Senate. Besides, Harrington also happened to be a close friend of Ed Brooke. They had vacationed near each other on the island of St. Martin. Rather than trying to move up, Harrington decided to move out. His best chance for the U.S. Senate had come and gone. Congressman Paul Tsongas of Lowell, who did not share Harrington's qualms, challenged and defeated

Brooke in 1978. Coincidentally, this was the same year that Kevin Harrington resigned as state Senate president.

Faced with the prospect of strong competition within his own party, from Peabody mayor Nicholas Mavroules and State Representative James Smith from Lynn, Michael Harrington left Congress in 1978 at age forty-two. No longer did politics or the U.S. Senate hold the attraction it once did. Harrington cited personal finances as the main reason why he was leaving. No longer could he support his growing family on the salary of a congressman. Many of his constituents were sorely disappointed by his decision. Compared to his colleagues Tip O'Neill, Edward Boland, and Joseph Moakley, he did not have the same patience or staying power. They did better and lasted longer, underscoring the tragic shortfall of his achievement.

At this juncture Michael Harrington returned to his private law practice in Salem. He became a real estate developer and part owner of the prestigious Hawthorne Hotel, managed by Michael Garvin. Harrington also served for a brief period as a director of the Federal Reserve Bank in Boston. In 1990 he made an abortive run for state treasurer, but after taking out a $20,000 personal loan to finance his campaign, he suddenly withdrew from the race. He was restless still, but seemed to be driven more by business than political ambition.

In due course Harrington's business activities landed him in trouble. In early January 2000 the U.S. attorney's office in Boston charged him with misrepresenting his finances in order to obtain bank loans to buy the Hawthorne Hotel, Museum Place Mall, and other properties in Salem, and to finance his futile bid for state treasurer.[62] He was indicted on Saint Valentine's Day. Under a plea agreement that spared him a jail term, he pled guilty to a misdemeanor and was fined $100,000 by federal judge Edward Harrington.[63]

NEIL HARRINGTON'S POLITICAL DEAD END

In 1997, Neil Harrington, who had already served four terms as mayor of Salem, failed to win his bid for reelection. He was defeated by insurgent city councilor Stanley J. Usovicz Jr. At the time, public opinion polls indicated that Harrington had a high negative rating. Sensing that the incumbent mayor was vulnerable, Usovicz conducted a low-key door-to-door campaign. His emphasis on improving public schools resonated with Salem voters, especially the upwardly mobile business and professional people. Usovicz, whose parents were of Lithuanian and Irish extraction, was perceived by many voters as "a local boy made good." He won overwhelmingly. In fact, Neil Harrington lost every precinct in the city. He had seriously alienated the schoolteachers by his comments that there were not enough votes for increased public school funding. As a result of this political gaffe, the teachers were adamantly opposed to his reelection. The education vote was a big vote in the city. Spearheaded by Jane Dwyer, who organized the anti-Harrington forces, the teachers worked hard to defeat him.

Most big city mayors tend to have a limited "shelf life," especially if they try to accomplish a great deal while in office. This was certainly true in Neil Harrington's case. He could claim a host of accomplishments. Salem, much like Lynn, was an old industrial city that was badly in need of economic revitalization. Harrington was largely responsible for turning the city around and making it more viable economically. He attracted more federal money than any previous mayor. Among numerous other accomplishments, he established the Federal Street School, a unique two-way bilingual school for both English- and Spanish-speaking students. The Saltonstall School was converted to a K-5 grammar school. The mayor initiated the reconstruction of Riley Plaza, thereby eliminating a hazardous rotary and dramatically improving the safety and aesthetics of Salem's main downtown thoroughfare. Significantly, he broke decisively with his cousin Michael Harrington, firmly resisting the latter's attempts to obtain tax concessions from the city for the Hawthorne Hotel. This dispute was his profile in courage.

While Neil Harrington had his strengths, he also had his weaknesses. Outwardly stiff and seemingly humorless, he struck most people as being cold, reserved, distant, and aloof. More telling, he was unable to schmooze with reporters and voters. That personal rigidity lessened his effectiveness. Critics were extremely harsh on him. Some claimed that he was arrogant, pompous, rude, and immature. Others described him as rigid and uptight, secretive and controlling. He had brought into his administration David Shea, a manipulative political operative whom many constituents disliked and distrusted. This only earned the contempt of friends and enemies, all of which worked to the advantage of Usovicz and contributed to Harrington's downfall. He had planned to run for lieutenant governor in 1998, but those plans went awry. Trapped in his own rigidity, he then ran for sheriff of Essex County and lost. The magic had gone out of the enterprise, and the glory days were over. Unable to emerge from the shadow of his father, Neil symbolized the family's political downfall.

All this seems clear in retrospect. Neil Harrington's defeat dashed any serious notion of the Harringtons as a continuing political dynasty. The changing order saw his exit and Usovicz's arrival. It was the last hurrah for the Harringtons.

6

FROM MBM SCANDAL TO STATE ETHICS REFORM

No responsibility of government is more fundamental than the responsibility of maintaining the highest standards of ethical behavior by those who conduct the public business. There can be no dissent from the principle that all officials must act with unwavering integrity, absolute impartiality, and complete devotion to the public interest. This principle must be followed not only in reality but in appearance. The basis of effective government is public confidence, and that confidence is endangered when ethical standards falter or appear to falter.

President John F. Kennedy, 1961
Message to Congress on Ethics in Government

MORALITY AND PUBLIC INTEGRITY

The Massachusetts legislature is under a cloud after decades of intermittent scandals and endless embarrassments. Evidence of occasional bribery, influence peddling, late night "toga" parties, vacations paid for by lobbyists, gratuities in the form of golf games and dinners, favoritism, and shoddy legislative procedures have tarnished its reputation.[1] Certainly newspaper reporters have had a field day. This bad press results mainly from the political corruption that has long plagued state government, including the criminal conviction of top legislative leaders, both Democrats and Republicans alike.

News reporters, often at odds with legislators, tend to overemphasize their negative traits and fail to acknowledge their more positive attributes.

There is a natural antagonism that exists between them. This stems in large part from the kind of investigative journalism that emerged in America in the post-Watergate era. As Senate president Thomas Birmingham put it in July 2000, "Legislators and reporters are like sheepherders and cattlemen, or natural rivals with different world views."[2] The popular image of the modern politician is that of the shady ward heeler, the sleazy state representative, and the pompous senator on the take. The media play a role in shaping these negative perceptions in part for their own purposes. Sweeping moral criticisms of existing institutions and their leaders often take the place of rigorous evaluations of actual performance. This kind of sensationalism sells newspapers and boosts television ratings, but it also contributes to voter alienation.

Civil servants receive similar disparaging treatment by the media. Conventional stereotypes portray them mired in red tape, as venality and stupidity abound. These persistent characterizations lead many people to mistrust them as a class and to lump them together under the derogatory label "bureaucrat." Their role is scorned as so routinized that the particular individuals serving in particular posts are judged irrelevant. "Thus individuals become interchangeable in bureaucracies," writes Robert Wood, "disposable like plastic cups. They are cogs in a wheel, and bureaucratic behavior is uniform, predictable, molded by massive, impersonal pressures and processes."[3]

Despite the media's tendency to oversimplify events, some unscrupulous politicians and civil servants do in fact cheat and defraud the general public. Such disreputable behavior is often referred to as "the fleecing of America." This does not mean that all public employees are dishonest. It does mean that actions tainted with conflicts of interest and corruption do occur. Yet most state workers are honest, dedicated, and hardworking civil servants who stay well within the boundaries of legal and ethical standards. It is well to remember, however, that the odor of the barrel originates with the rotten apples, not the honest ones.

Fighting and preventing fraud is not something new in Massachusetts. As early as 1795, the legislature prohibited extortion by public employees. In 1862 it prohibited state and municipal purchasing agents from accepting gifts and gratuities from vendors. This restriction was extended in 1872 to cover all elected and appointed city officials; in 1875 to include state legislators, members of the Governor's Council, and members of state commissions; and in 1893 to encompass county officials. Recounting the state's political history, Robert Wood noted in 1994:

Not all of our public history is in fact exemplary. Since persecuting the Salem witches, our authorities have occasionally erred grievously. Governor Gerry invented gerrymandering in the early days of the Republic. Scandals in public franchises and contracts were almost endemic throughout the eighteen hundreds. In this century, the public arena became the battleground for successive waves of ethnic struggle—Yankee vs. Irish vs. Italian most prominently. They produced the cynical politics of spoils and plunder, bosses and machines that stuffed the ranks of the civil service with office-holders chosen on the basis of family or patronage. The modus operandi then was "who you knew, not what you knew." By the mid-twentieth century, public service had fallen into disrepute. Fed by media accounts of crime and corruption, the citizenry increasingly has come to view public service as a refuge for scoundrels, or at the very least for the untrained, the unmotivated or the uncaring.[4]

In the modern era, three special legislative commissions have investigated crime and political corruption in Massachusetts. The first commission was created in 1953 and reconstituted in 1955. Headed by Charles C. Cabot, it focused on organized crime. The second commission was set up in 1962 and was chaired by Alfred Gardner. It concentrated its investigation on corrupt practices in state and local government. The same was true of the third commission, which was established in 1978. It was directed by John William Ward, the president of Amherst College. Collectively, the work of these three commissions pretty much tells the story of the past half-century.

Massachusetts was rife with political corruption throughout the 1960s and most of the 1970s. In 1962 the state legislature passed the first conflict of interest law (Chapter 268A), modeled on legislation then pending in Congress. Under this statute, bribery offenses were punishable by a $5,000 fine or three years' imprisonment. Since its original passage, the conflict law has been amended over forty times, most notably in 1978, 1982, and 1986. The 1978 amendments produced a financial disclosure law (Chapter 268B) that was prompted by the public contracting scandals of the early 1970s and by an initiative petition sponsored by Common Cause, a reform-oriented public interest watchdog group.

House Speaker John F. Thompson, a Democrat, and former Speaker Charles Gibbons, a Republican, were indicted on May 8, 1964, by a Suffolk County grand jury on bribery and conspiracy charges following a crime commission investigation of lobbying activities by small loan companies. Both denied the charges brought against them and proclaimed their innocence. A clever and charming rogue, Thompson, who was dubbed the "Iron Duke," died of acute alcoholism before he went to trial, and the charges against Gibbons were dismissed for lack of prosecution.

Unethical behavior was not confined to the legislative branch. The judiciary was likewise tarnished by unethical conduct. Disciplinary action taken by the General Court during this period led to the removal of both Jerome

P. Troy as a district court judge in 1973, and Robert M. Bonin as chief justice of the Superior Court in 1978. Troy was the first judge removed from office since 1882, and Bonin was the first chief justice to be removed in the history of the Commonwealth. Nor was that all. Several other judges who were involved in scandals resigned while legislative proceedings were either pending or threatened.

The Massachusetts story was a striking illustration of a universal problem. During the early 1970s, political corruption was prevalent in other states as well. In New Jersey, for example, three successive secretaries of state were indicted for bribery between 1971 and 1974; two were convicted, and the third was not tried because the statute of limitations had expired. Moreover, the governors of Maryland and West Virginia were convicted in the early 1970s for engaging in bribery and tax evasion schemes. Spiro Agnew, former governor of Maryland, was indicted for tax evasion and forced to resign as vice president of the United States in October 1973. Several other states were befouled by the problem of corruption.

CORRUPTION IN THE WATERGATE ERA

Nothing did more to undermine public confidence in American government than the unsavory mess that was uncovered in Washington, D.C., during the early 1970s. In June 1972, during the presidential campaign, five men were arrested for burglarizing the Democratic Party headquarters at the Watergate apartments. It turned out that they were working for the Republican Committee to Re-elect the President. When he heard about the arrest, Nixon authorized a cover-up. But the crime could not be concealed. Before long, it was revealed that Nixon's inner circle had planned the Watergate burglary and, when it fizzled, had tried, with the president's help, to keep their involvement a secret.

All sorts of other revelations began surfacing in 1973 and 1974. These included the use of campaign contributions to win government favors, the illegal use of such funds on behalf of the Watergate defendants, a campaign of political "dirty tricks" to ensure Nixon's electoral victory in 1972, and plans to use government agencies to intimidate Nixon's political enemies. In the end, twenty men who had been acting on the president's behalf were convicted of various crimes relating to Watergate. And despite Nixon's repeated protestations of innocence, it became abundantly clear that the president had been involved in the cover-up and obstruction of justice from the beginning.

The Watergate scandal symbolized a new low in political morality and ultimately revealed much more than the misdeeds of its conspirators. Corruption had penetrated the highest levels of the federal government and, indeed, reached the presidency itself. Rather than face the imminent prospect of impeachment, President Nixon resigned from office in disgrace.

In the shocking aftermath of Watergate, the inevitable happened. It stimulated a national movement to prevent such corruption and abuses of power. Reform groups that sought to ensure honesty and integrity in government sprang up across the country. These efforts were spearheaded mainly by local chapters of Common Cause and by public interest research groups founded by the consumer advocate Ralph Nader. In Massachusetts the latter group was known by its acronym "Mass PIRG." These zealous reformers sought to uncover corruption and to ferret out dishonest public employees who acted unethically.

In 1976 both houses of Congress passed codes of ethics with financial disclosure requirements. Forty states, including Connecticut and Maine, adopted similar ethical codes. In most states these reforms were enacted as a consequence of the Watergate scandal. Thirty-two states went the route of establishing an independent ethics commission. After a protracted battle in 1978, Massachusetts did likewise. But before that happened, the state Senate attempted to adopt its own code of ethics. So did the House of Representatives. These actions could be largely attributed to the reform spirit abroad in the land.

IMPACT OF THE MBM SCANDAL

On February 25, 1977, a political bombshell exploded in Massachusetts. On that day, state senators Joseph J. C. DiCarlo of Revere and Ronald C. MacKenzie of Burlington were convicted in federal district court of extortion, conspiracy, and related federal offenses. They had been prosecuted under the Hobbs Act, which makes it a federal crime for public officials to induce payment of money in return for exercising their influence.

At the time the scandal broke, DiCarlo was the Democratic floor leader in the Senate, and MacKenzie was the Republican whip. They had voluntarily given up their leadership posts after their indictment on August 13, 1976, but they retained their Senate seats. The charges against them, denied by both senators, involved the payment of $40,000 in bribes by the New York consultant firm of McKee, Berger, and Mansueto. The bribe money was used to obtain a favorable report from a special legislative committee which in 1971 had investigated construction costs for the new campus at the University of Massachusetts in Boston. MBM had received $6 million, or more than double its original contract, for supervising the work. The contract had been described in the press as a "sweetheart deal" and was criticized by the state auditor.

DiCarlo was chairman of the investigating committee. Although Mac-Kenzie was not a member of the committee, he had been the conduit for payment of the $40,000. The indictment charged that they had threatened officers of the consulting firm, telling them that unless they were paid, the committee's report would be injurious to the business of MBM. The report, when issued in January 1972, cleared MBM of any impropriety.

Senator James A. Kelly Jr. of Oxford, chairman of the Senate Ways and Means committee, was named an unindicted co-conspirator. The trial judge, however, ruled that the prosecution had failed to link Kelly to the conspiracy and ordered that all references to him be deleted from the indictment.

On March 23, 1977, DiCarlo and MacKenzie were sentenced to one year in federal prison and fined $5,000 each. Their sentences were stayed pending appeal. The MBM scandal rocked the establishment and sent shock waves throughout the Commonwealth. It had been uncovered by Wendell Woodman, a freelance journalist, who had published a series of articles titled "Let Me Call You Sweetheart," in which he revealed the suspicious nature of the MBM contract and concluded that it was the result of a "possible conspiracy."[5] Woodman's suspicions proved accurate. The conviction of DiCarlo and MacKenzie evoked an expected public outcry for corrective action to guard against such abuses in the future. As the scandal fed a media frenzy, the state Senate found itself under mounting pressures to put its own house in order.

In response to this growing pressure, the Senate acted. On February 28, 1977, three days after the conviction of DiCarlo and MacKenzie, the upper house created a new standing committee on ethics and assigned it the responsibility for drafting a code of conduct. On March 1, Senate president Kevin Harrington, in consultation with Senate minority leader John Parker, appointed a five-member bipartisan committee consisting of Senators Chester Atkins of Harvard, John Aylmer of Centerville, Robert McCarthy of East Bridgewater, John Olver of Amherst, and William Saltonstall of Manchester. Three were Democrats and two Republicans. Atkins, a liberal Democrat, was named chairman of the committee. James Vorenberg, a professor at the Harvard Law School and a former Watergate prosecutor, served as legal counsel.

Shortly after their appointment, the members of the Senate Ethics Committee investigated the conduct of Senators DiCarlo and MacKenzie. Meanwhile, the besmirched Senate had become paralyzed. No one wanted to take any substantial action for fear of tainting the outcome. On April 1, the Senate Ethics Committee (SEC) recommended the expulsion of Senator DiCarlo.[6] By resigning the day before, MacKenzie had spared himself a similar fate. Displaying an arrogance that some found incredible, DiCarlo refused to resign, but he was expelled by a vote of 28 to 8, four more than the two-thirds required by the Senate rules. He was the first senator in the history of that institution to suffer such an ignominious punishment.

Jeremiah Murphy, a seasoned *Boston Globe* reporter, surmised that the convictions of DiCarlo and MacKenzie had merely revealed "the tip of the corruption iceberg in Massachusetts."[7] He was right. Before entering federal prison, Joseph DiCarlo blew the whistle on other politicians. If he was going down, he was going to take them with him. It was later revealed that MBM had made payments of $66,000 to politicians, although political contributions from corporations had been illegal in Massachusetts since 1946.

Among the politicians damaged in the mushrooming MBM scandal were top legislative leaders, including Senate president Kevin Harrington, whose political career was effectively ended. In October 1970, Harrington, who was then Senate majority leader, and Boston mayor Kevin White had allegedly received $2,000 each from MBM. Speaker David M. Bartley allegedly had received $1,000 in April 1971 through former governor Endicott Peabody, who was MBM's attorney. Senator James A. Kelly, chairman of the powerful Senate Ways and Means Committee, allegedly had received $1,000 in January 1972. All of them denied receiving any money from MBM, though Peabody did acknowledge using MBM funds to buy tickets to a Bartley fund-raiser.

Albert ("Toots") Manzi, a top fund-raiser for Governor Francis W. Sargent, allegedly had received $20,000 in cash payments from MBM in 1971 and 1972. Manzi, along with Worcester businessman William V. Masiello, were indicted by a Suffolk County grand jury for extorting $10,000 from MBM in 1972. Manzi was charged with trying to extort thousands from MBM as part of a plot to buy the 1972 Republican vice presidential nomination for John Volpe, the former governor.[8] Both men were acquitted, but Masiello, under a grant of immunity, later told the Ward commission that he and Manzi had committed perjury at their trial.

Scandals of a different nature came to light in the executive branch, especially in the Department of Corporations and Taxation. Investigative reporting done by the *Boston Globe*'s Spotlight team revealed that several million dollars in revenue had been lost through the failure to collect delinquent taxes. Governor Michael Dukakis took swift action to reorganize that department and to put a stop to such practices. Questions were also raised about the award of a contract to Sci-Tek Associates, which took place without the required competitive bidding.

Meanwhile, a pending scandal was about to break in the Department of Education over the award of consultant contracts with regard to its vocational education programs. Ultimately, the state's "voke-ed" scandal resulted in the conviction of nineteen people. So the executive branch of state government did not escape unscathed either. Many citizens were already angry and alienated. These revelations only exacerbated public distrust. As the odor of corruption intensified, so did the demand for reform.

THE SENATE ETHICS CODE

Feeling the heat, the Senate Ethics Committee set about its task of drafting a code of ethics. Almost simultaneously, the House of Representatives undertook a similar task. In order to find out what the general public was thinking, the SEC held a series of public hearings. Meanwhile, the committee staff (Harry Greenwald, Daniel Esty, and attorney Natalea Skvir) researched conflict of interest laws and statutes regulating lobbying. They consulted with lawyers in the attorney general's office and with the secretary of state and also examined how the judiciary and the local bar associations had gone about drafting their codes of conduct.

At public hearings held during April 1977, civic groups voiced their outrage about the misconduct and wrongdoing on Beacon Hill. Cries of distrust in state government were repeatedly heard at these hearings. Reform groups such as Common Cause, Americans for Democratic Action, Citizens for Participation in Political Action, the League of Women Voters, and Mass PIRG testified in favor of the need for a strict code of ethics. Of these groups, Common Cause led the charge and was a major force in pressing for corrective action. Since 1972 this public interest watchdog group had been pushing for an ethics code and a financial disclosure law, but without success. Spokespersons for these various interest groups agreed with the philosophy expressed by former U.S. Supreme Court Justice Louis D. Brandeis, who once remarked that "sunshine is said to be the best of disinfectants."[9]

The 1970s were tumultuous times. The counterculture engendered a distrust of government and a diminished respect for authority. After a decade of revelations such as the Pentagon Papers, domestic spying by intelligence agencies, closed committee hearings, and the withholding of tapes by President Richard Nixon under the shield of executive privilege, the general public had become cynical about secrecy in government. As might be expected, the convictions of DiCarlo and MacKenzie simply added fuel to the fire. Clearly, the mood of the times called for more openness in government. This mood was reflected in the public demand for open meeting laws, freedom of information acts, declassification of government documents, access to public school records, sunshine statutes, and a myriad of other regulations designed to force government officials to operate under public inspection. Only the judiciary was spared such open-book scrutiny.

Public opinion polls, radio talk show hosts, and other observers and commentators all confirmed that public distrust was widespread. A Clark University opinion survey found that 84 percent of the citizens of Massachusetts believed that their state government was either "very corrupt" or "somewhat corrupt."[10] Thaddeus Buczko, the state auditor, put it more bluntly: "Public confidence in state government is at an all-time low."[11] From the outpouring of public testimony and the voluminous mail received by the SEC, it was clear that the citizenry expected the highest standards of conduct from their state legislators. Most of this mail arrived while the SEC was considering the fate of Senators DiCarlo and MacKenzie. After DiCarlo had been expelled, however, the volume of mail slowed to a trickle.[12]

Such a frenzied atmosphere of scandal and paralysis allowed the media to apply a special kind of pressure on the General Court. Both houses were now under intense pressure to produce a code of conduct for their members. The *Boston Globe* took the lead in applying such pressure and came out editorially in support of a strong code of ethics. Echoing similar sentiments were other major newspapers, along with radio and television stations throughout Massachusetts.

The legislature proved susceptible to this kind of intense pressure. The *Boston Globe*'s Spotlight team published a series of articles that focused on serious ethical issues such as nepotism, "no-show" positions, and preferential treatment in government hiring. These stories also flushed out two Senate staff employees who were engaged in private business activities while supposedly working for the state. This type of investigative reporting produced results. Caught in the glare of such negative publicity, the two employees were immediately suspended from their jobs without pay. In similar fashion, the "I-Team" at Boston's WBZ-TV got into the act by targeting several lawyer-legislators who had been representing their clients before state agencies in an apparent conflict of interest. In this way the media played an important role in keeping the pressure on externally. Some senators chafed under this negative publicity and resented the fact that the media were able to call the shots. Others, who were more reform-oriented, were delighted with the press coverage, which they saw as a powerful catalyst for change.

SENATE RULE 10-B

At this juncture, the SEC found itself caught on the horns of a dilemma. On the one hand, the members took the position that they were only going to report out a code of ethics that stood a reasonable chance of passing on the floor of the Senate. Yet on the other hand, they realized that whatever they reported, such a code would ultimately have to win public approval. Confronted by this dilemma, the SEC walked a political tightrope. As chairman Chester Atkins put it, "We knew that the Senate was going to vote for anything that we recommended. Our problem was to keep reasonable reins on what we were proposing."[13]

The SEC soon reached what it considered a reasonable solution. There were basically two options at its disposal. One way of drafting a code was to draw up a long list of restrictions indicating specifically what a legislator could and could not do. The alternative was to require disclosure of potential conflicts of interest and then allow the voters to decide whether or not such a conflict existed. After examining how other states had fared with codes that contained lengthy lists of restrictions, the SEC decided in favor of placing the judgment with the voters. By so doing, it avoided the problem of forcing the legislative institution to police itself. Once this matter was resolved, the SEC made financial disclosure the crux of its recommendations.

Deciding what exactly should be disclosed was more complicated. The SEC agreed that business associations should be disclosed in order for voters to exercise intelligent judgment. But how were business associations to be defined? Common Cause wanted to define the term to include all customers and clients doing substantial business with the reporting person. Some states, such as North Carolina, relied on numerical formulas, for example, owning 5 percent or more of outstanding stock in a company. The SEC briefly considered this approach but finally rejected it, feeling that it was not a meaningful distinction. Far more important were questions such as whether a reporting person was a partner in a business and therefore shared directly in the profits, and whether he or she was in a policymaking position such as director or trustee. Moreover, the SEC realized that a potential for conflict existed if such a person had a job to which he or she would return on leaving the Senate, or if there was an agreement for deferred compensation.

The SEC saw no point in requiring disclosure of economic interests that were insignificant in size and amount. In its view, anything under $1,000 was not worth considering. At first the SEC proposed a distinction between earned and unearned income, but on second thought realized that such a distinction discriminated against senators who supplemented their salaries with earned income. On the basis of equity, the SEC decided to treat earned and unearned income alike.

In drafting another requirement, the SEC declared that the "value of income" in situations presenting a potential for conflict should be disclosed. After talking with senators who were involved in competitive businesses, the members realized that disclosure of the exact income from such business would put the proprietor-senator in an untenable position, since his or her competitors would be able to extract critical information from such revelations. Those senators engaged in competitive businesses indicated that they could live with disclosure of such income by "category of value"— $5,000, $10,000, $25,000 and so on. The particular categories selected were designed to provide reasonable indicators of a range of values without leaving so much to the voter's imagination as to give an exaggerated impression of a senator's wealth. By requiring disclosure by categories of value rather than exact amounts, the SEC followed a procedure that was currently being used in many other states.

This still left the SEC with the problem of how to distinguish between income that should be disclosed only by source and income that should be disclosed by category of value. Here it opted for simplicity and went with a commonsense distinction, namely, if the source is "regulated" by the Commonwealth or "does business" with the Commonwealth. But this left unanswered the question of what constitutes a regulated business. Once again a simple definition was adopted, to wit, that a regulated business is a business "subject to the discretionary authority" of an agency, authority, board or commission of the Commonwealth. It should be noted that all the proposed disclosure requirements excluded income from a life insurance policy on a spouse, child, or parent, since the SEC viewed such income as being strictly a personal matter that presented no apparent conflict of interest.

Another important concern was whether or not statements of financial disclosure should be sealed or made a matter of public record. Connecticut, for example, merely required its legislators to disclose to its ethics committee, which in turn kept the reports confidential. Since sealed statements left nothing for the voters to decide, the SEC dropped the idea as being incompatible with the intent of the rule. In reality, its members were afraid that if they opted in favor of sealed statements, such a move would provide Common Cause with a perfect excuse to mobilize public support for its initiative petition calling for the establishment of an independent ethics commission. "Cutting back on disclosure," as was acknowledged in a staff memorandum, "is just what Common Cause needs to recruit a few thousand college students to collect signatures for them. It would become the symbol of the legislature's inability to police itself."

With regard to the disclosure of investments, securities, and real property, the SEC wanted a simple requirement that distinguished potential conflict situations. Thus, only real property located in Massachusetts needed to be reported. Likewise, the requirement applied to securities and investments only if they were in a business that was regulated by the state or doing business with the state. In other words, out-of-state holdings did not have to be disclosed. Two exemptions to this requirement were granted, namely, personal residences and balances in bank accounts. Because interest rates were controlled by the Federal Reserve Board, the SEC saw nothing to be gained from their disclosure.

In its endeavor to eliminate loopholes that could thwart the purpose of disclosure, the SEC decided to place limits on gifts that senators received from lobbyists. Few states required disclosure of reimbursements from lobbyists and other groups with a direct interest in legislation. Under these circumstances, a legislator invited to address a professional association out of state could pay his or her way there, then be reimbursed and never report it. This would result in a free trip, but it would be neither a gift nor income in the usual sense. To cover such situations, but to avoid a rule that would prohibit a legislator from making legitimate travel in connection with his or her public duties, the SEC required that reimbursements for expense in excess of $100 must be reported.

As a practical matter, the SEC determined that some debt disclosure was necessary. Because senators, as ordinary citizens, incur debts that have nothing to do with potential conflicts, the members exempted debts arising from consumer credit transactions, medical or dental expenses, home mortgages, and educational loans. Debts of less than $5,000 or less than ninety days' duration were considered too insignificant to be relevant, and these were likewise exempted. Small business owners faced a particular problem with respect to debts. If a business is incorporated, the business debts are not considered personal. But if a senator runs an unincorporated business, then all the "accounts payable" of that business are personal debts. To avoid an invidious distinction between senators with incorporated and unincorporated businesses, the SEC exempted debts incurred in the ordinary course of business.

With these considerations foremost in mind, the SEC then drafted Senate Rule 10-B, which required senators and employees to disclose the following information:

1. Business associations, including proprietorships, partnerships, directorships, trusteeships, agreements for deferred compensation, and leaves of absence.
2. All sources of income from a single sources in excess of $1,000 and the category of value of such income if the source is regulated by the Commonwealth or does business with the Commonwealth.
3. The identity of all securities, investments (except bank account balances), and real property (except personal residences) valued in excess of $1,000. In addition, the category of value must be reported for property located in the Commonwealth, or investments or securities held in a company that is regulated by the Commonwealth or does business with the Commonwealth. If the holdings are in a trust, the contents of the trust must

be disclosed, with a category of value given only if the reporting person is the sole beneficiary of the trust.

4. The source and amount of any reimbursements in excess of $100 from any person or organization having a direct interest in legislation or matters before an agency of the Commonwealth.

5. The name, address, and type of security given to each creditor to whom more than $5,000 is owed. Exempted from the debt disclosure are mortgages on personal residences, debt from consumer credit transactions, medical debts, education loans, alimony and support obligations, debts of less than ninety days' duration (if not rolled over), and debts incurred in the ordinary course of business.[14]

If adopted, these new rules were to apply not only to the senators themselves but also to Senate aides and employees who earned more than $19,600 a year. The SEC believed that such disclosure was necessary to assure the public of the integrity of Senate staff. Moreover, a senator was required to disclose the economic interests of a working spouse and dependent children. For this purpose a single-family statement could be filed in place of individual disclosure forms for each family member. As drafted, Senate Rule 10-B was to go into effect on January 1, 1979. This date was purposely selected in order to give those senators who chose not to run again and those employees who chose to leave the Senate time to make other arrangements. All other rules in the code were to take effect on their adoption. As it turned out, the proposed code placed a maximum emphasis on disclosure and a minimum emphasis on restrictions.

REFORM AND RESISTANCE

The SEC submitted its report to the full Senate on August 16, 1977. Although many of the difficulties encountered in drafting the code had been worked out beforehand, the set of recommendations was not well received.[15] Not surprisingly, the sudden modification of normal conditions presented a threat to the security of individual senators. This was especially true of those who had been in office for a long time. Recently elected senators tended to be more receptive to the idea of disclosure. They found it easier to adjust to the new rules change, in part at least because they had not developed a regimen of political life from which they would now have to deviate under pressure.

At this point Common Cause sought to apply even greater pressure on a recalcitrant legislature. On August 3, 1977, it filed an initiative petition (House Bill 5151) which called for the creation of an independent state ethics commission.[16] This commission was to be given broad powers of investigation and the authority to impose civil penalties for violations of the ethics laws. The petition provided for extensive reporting of outside sources of income by members of the legislature and by state and county employees who earned more than $20,000 annually. Common Cause had conducted a massive signature drive in which 95,506 qualified voters signed its petition. The intent here was to force the hand of the General Court.

Before pursuing this strategy, the leaders of Common Cause had tried for seven years to have a meaningful dialogue with the legislature, but they had been consistently rebuffed. Jay Hedlund, the executive director of Common Cause, indicated that the legislature had taken no action on their proposals during this time. As a result of such stonewalling, they felt that the recalcitrant General Court was not operating in good faith. More to the point, they believed that the legislature was incapable of policing itself. Therefore, Hedlund continued to press for an independent state ethics commission. Hardened lines showed no signs of softening. The Common Cause petition, however, raised some serious constitutional questions about whether the legislature was free to make its own rules and whether it could act as the final judge of the qualifications of its members.

Meanwhile, some senators privately expressed their opposition to Rule 10-B. This was especially true of social conservatives. It was clear that such resistance would crumble publicly. There was nevertheless a good deal of posturing going on. Some senators genuinely believed that their personal and family finances were strictly a private matter, and as such, they should not have to be revealed. From a libertarian point of view, they considered the new rule to be an unjustified invasion of privacy. Their major concern was with trust funds. If a senator was the sole beneficiary of a trust, there was not much of a problem. But if any of his or her relatives were part of that trust, the concern was that their privacy would be violated. There was also a discriminatory aspect of the problem. Since only the wealthy tend to have trusts, the question arose that if trusts were exempted, didn't that exemption discriminate in favor of the rich. This issue subsequently became part of a much broader question that if wealthy people were forced to disclose, would they choose not to run for public office. Family pressure might conceivably force some senators to get out of politics altogether, especially with regard to the trust fund implications. Senator William Saltonstall of Manchester expressed reservations along these lines. Discrimination by social class cut both ways, however. A senator with little or no money and without any significant real property holdings might conceivably be embarrassed if such information were divulged.

Indirectly, there was also a question of possible gender discrimination. Some male senators were concerned about the implications of Rule 10-B with regard to the equal rights amendments. In this context, they worried that the rights of their wives might be infringed. One senator asked what right the public had to know his wife's income, especially if it were separately earned and separately held. Female senators worried about their husbands' privacy as well. This objection was met by fashioning a compromise that stipulated that income for a working spouse would not be identified in dollar amounts.

Perhaps the most important question raised by Rule 10-B was the appropriate role of the legislator and the issue of part-time versus full-time lawmakers. Some senators felt that the rule would drive good people out of politics and do serious harm to the Jeffersonian concept of citizen-legislators, which was deeply embedded in the American political tradition. Republican senator David Locke of Wellesley was among those who objected to the rule on these grounds. He argued that there was much to be gained from having part-time legislators who knew what it meant to own and run a private business. Since the Common Cause initiative petition made financial disclosure much more extensive than Rule 10-B, it therefore raised the question in the minds of some senators whether or not any legislator could have an outside business. At one point the SEC had considered inserting a time disclosure requirement, but after much deliberation the idea was scrapped. The feeling was that any requirement of this type amounted to a pejorative assumption about part-time legislators. Many senators believed that this was going too far.

Despite the misgivings of Republicans senators such as Locke and Saltonstall, other senators insisted that something had to be done if public confidence in state government were to be restored. The latter tended to be the younger and more progressive senators who had been elected within the previous six years. In their view, post-Watergate morality demanded as much, especially if the Senate were to rehabilitate its tarnished public image. Persuaded that it was the right thing to do, Republican senator John Aylmer of Centerville went on record that there would be a code of ethics with a financial disclosure requirement as an integral part of it.

There were other political considerations that all senators had to take into account. To come out against the adoption of Rule 10-B was fraught with risks. The most obvious stemmed from the fact that the so-called House cut was to go into effect the following year. Under this plan the size of the Massachusetts House of Representatives was to be reduced in 1978 from 240 to 160 members. The House cut had been initiated and pushed for by the League of Women Voters. For all practical purposes, this meant that 80 legislators were slated to lose their district seats. It was more than likely that these dispossessed state representatives would be waiting in the wings to challenge a senatorial incumbent whom they considered vulnerable. A vote against Rule 10-B not only would contribute to that vulnerability but also would allow a potential opponent to run a single-issue campaign. In a state where the notion of moving up or moving out was a basic rule of politics, this was not idle speculation.

CREATION OF THE STATE ETHICS COMMISSION

The Senate finally adopted its code of ethics, including Rule 10-B, on October 17, 1977. But the ethics controversy did not stop there. Realizing that the reform movement had gained a full head of steam, Common Cause wanted to go one step further. Having collected 95,506 signatures on its initiative petition, this group continued to press for more sweeping legislation designed to create an independent state ethics commission. If the recalcitrant legislature did not act, the Common Cause proposal was scheduled to appear on the ballot in November 1978 as a binding referendum. So the die was cast. As things turned out, this strategy worked to perfection. By keeping the legislators' feet to the fire, Common Cause got most of what it wanted.

Faced with this predicament, many members of the House expressed fear that failure to approve the Common Cause proposal would be tantamount to political suicide.[17] The Committee on State Administration voted 16 to 5 to report the Common Cause bill to the House without waiting to clarify its ambiguities. On May 1, 1978, the House quickly approved the measure, but the Senate rejected it and passed its own bill. A fierce battle then ensued over which bill would become law. The SEC had staged a legislative confrontation. It offered a new bill that its members felt was more reasonable than the Common Cause proposal. Critics claimed that the Common Cause bill was being stampeded through a "panicky legislature."[18]

As a rejoinder to this criticism, Jay Hedlund accused the SEC of diversionary tactics: "They are seeing what they can do to water down significant conflict-of-interest legislation. The Senate version is weighted to protecting the privacy of the individual, ours is weighted on the side of the public's right to know."[19]

Not surprisingly, the Common Cause bill and the SEC bill both required annual financial disclosures by elected and appointed officials, and both set up an independent ethics commission to enforce the ethics laws. Both sides traded barbs, and each disparaged the other's motivations. Harry Greenwald, the SEC staff director, remarked, "The Common Cause bill is not tailored to specific public purposes. It is a shotgun blast at government."[20] Expressing similar sentiments, SEC staff attorney Natalea Skvir pushed the argument even further: "We want to focus on the purpose of why we want the information and try to gear the information gathered to that purpose rather than have officials give a whole mass of information and have people cull through it and look for what's germane. It borders on voyeurism to want to know names of people who have no relation to government."[21] Barely restraining his anger, Hedlund responded by accusing Senator Atkins and his staff of misrepresenting the Common Cause bill. For his part, Atkins believed that the Common Cause proposal was too flawed for the Senate to act on it responsibly. Thus, on March 23, 1978, he requested an advisory opinion from the Supreme Judicial Court to resolve the disputed questions.[22]

A month later, on April 27, the SJC issued an advisory opinion upholding the constitutionality of the ethics commission, and declared that it did not conflict with the constitutional right of the Senate and the House to determine their own rules. The court pointed out that nothing in the state constitution prescribes the manner in which the General Court must exercise its rulemaking power. It also said that "the scope of the power of the people to enact laws directly is as extensive as that of the General Court," and it noted that "the matter of regulating legislative proceedings is not excluded from the initiative process." The justices declared, however, that the legislature retained the right to amend or repeal initiative laws adopted by the people.[23] Furthermore, the SJC determined that the broad requirements of the Common Cause proposal did not violate an individual's right to privacy, nor did they infringe on the right to seek public office without unnecessary harassment.[24]

With the SJC advisory opinion in hand, a conference committee worked out a compromise agreement that satisfied all the major players involved, including Common Cause. These delicate negotiations between the two houses were handled by Senators Chester Atkins of Concord and William Owens of Mattapan, and State Representatives John E. Murphy of Peabody and Charles J. Buffone of Worcester. In an unprecedented move, the conference committee allowed Jay Hedlund, director of Common Cause, and Michael Faden, the governor's legislative counsel, to participate as observers. Faden was instrumental in resolving an impasse that had developed over which state employees were to be covered by the legislation. The compromise required financial disclosure by any state employee holding a major policymaking position. The Common Cause salary level of $20,000 was scrapped, but the new ethics commission was given the discretionary power to require disclosure of other state workers.

As a result of these developments, Common Cause withdrew its initiative petition and thereby removed the prospect of a binding referendum. Resolution of this contentious issue defused the situation and cleared the way for final legislative action. During the floor debate in the House, Republican minority leader Francis W. Hatch Jr. of Beverly Farms, who was about to become a gubernatorial candidate, commented, "This is the end of a very,

very long road. The problem has been, in this chamber, that it has been very difficult, if not impossible, to police ourselves."[25]

The language in the final version of the bill called for the creation of an independent five-member ethics commission to which all state and county elected officials and many appointed officials had to make annual detailed personal financial disclosures. It was estimated that five thousand public employees would be covered by the statute. They would be required to:

1. report the source and the amount, within a broad category, of all annual income over $1,000;
2. identify all securities and investments that provide more than $1,000 annual income;
3. report the names and addresses of all creditors holding debts larger than $1,000, except for business debts, educational loans, alimony obligations, medical and dental bills, and mortgages on residences;
4. report all gifts worth more than $100 from anyone other than family members;
5. list all reimbursements for travel or speechmaking of more than $100.

In addition, lobbyists were prohibited from giving public employees or members of their families gifts worth more than a total of $100 per year.

At this point Common Cause publicly acknowledged that it was satisfied with the compromise version of the bill and that it would withdraw its public referendum. Action followed quickly. On June 1, 1978, the House approved the bill by a roll-call vote of 215 to 12. The Senate quickly followed suit and gave the measure routine final enactment.

On June 5, 1978, Governor Michael Dukakis signed the ethics bill into law at a ceremony in his office.[26] A reform-minded chief executive, he took great pride in signing the measure. "This was a case of people working together," he said, "and letting their agreements overwhelm and triumph over their disagreements."[27] On hand for the governor's signing ceremony was Richmond Mayo-Smith, chairman of the board of Common Cause. Delighted with the outcome, he remarked, "The signing of the bill was a landmark victory for the people of Massachusetts who clearly want more stringent controls on conflicts of interest by public officials."[28]

POLITICAL AFTERSHOCKS

The fallout from the new ethics law made some legislators uneasy about their political future. The statute stipulated that public officials who ended their duties before February 1, 1979, would not have to disclose. On July 31, 1978, less than two months after the bill was signed into law, Kevin Harrington resigned as president of the Senate. His successor, William Bulger, sought to restore a sense of integrity to the Senate. Nick King, an experienced reporter for the *Boston Globe*, described the political atmosphere that prevailed on Beacon Hill: "Sullied by scandal, leery of new ethics laws, crippled by the House-cut, fed up with state politics, or opting for higher office and private business, dozens of incumbents have already decided not to seek reelection to the Massachusetts legislature this year."[29]

Among those who indicated that they would not be running for office in the upcoming fall elections were State Representatives Brian Donnelly, Bernard Flynn, Philip Filosa, Peter Harrington, James Segel, James Smith, and Karen Swanson. Smith, a Democrat from Lynn, was planning to run for Congress in a party primary against five-term incumbent Michael Harrington. Others leaving primarily because of the House-cut situation were State Representatives Michael J. DeVito of Everett and John G. King of Danvers, both of whom were planning to run for the state Senate—DeVito for the seat previously held by Joseph DiCarlo, who was now in prison for extortion, and King for the seat being vacated by Senate president Kevin Harrington.[30]

Retiring state senator William Saltonstall, whose decision not to seek a seventh term was based largely on his reluctance to expose the interlocked finances of his entire family, warned that the public disclosure law might make wealthy public officials more vulnerable to robbers and kidnappers.[31] Senator David Locke, who had spent seventeen years in the legislature, did not conceal his dissatisfaction with what was happening to those who had dedicated their careers to public service. He remarked, "It's getting to be a job nobody wants. There's the absolute hazard of public exposure. People assume that if you are in the legislature, you are on the take. Being a legislator should be an honor but instead it's become a stigma."[32]

Expressing similar sentiments was House majority whip George Keverian of Everett, who had been given the unenviable task of drawing up a redistricting plan based on the anticipated House cut.[33] "We are certainly wary of an anti-incumbent sentiment," he said, "and there are those who simply feel that the House is not a very pleasant place to be."[34]

In the executive branch, feelings were not very different. John R. Buckley, secretary of administration and finance, would not have to file a disclosure form because he was leaving state government before February 1, 1979. Nonetheless, he told the press, "The law is having a demoralizing effect on affected state employees and should be changed so the reports are held confidentially unless there is a charge and investigation of wrongdoing."[35] Rebutting this criticism, Common Cause replied that such resistance was part of a painful phase of adjustment that other states had passed through without too much trouble. "This is now an accepted part of government service," said Hedlund. "It will be accepted in Massachusetts. The people have a right to know these things about the people who spend their tax money."[36]

Shortly after the new ethics law was adopted, Chester Atkins resigned as chairman of the SEC. He did not want to continue to play the role of Senate "cop," an assignment he found to be most unpleasant. He recommended that the post be rotated among the forty members of the upper chamber. "If you are perceived by your colleagues as a cop," he said, "it begins to interfere with all your relationships. It's an untenable job as a permanent assignment."[37] In his letter of resignation, which he sent to Senate president Kevin Harrington, Atkins said that it was a logical time to quit the post since the new ethics commission would soon be formed. Subsequently, the incoming Senate president, William Bulger, appointed Atkins chair of the powerful Ways and Means Committee.

COMPOSITION OF THE ETHICS COMMISSION

The law set up a bipartisan ethics commission, with three members appointed by the governor and one each by the attorney general and the secretary of state. Of the five appointees, only three could be from the same political party. Members were appointed for five-year staggered terms, which were nonrenewable. By statute, the governor appointed the chairman. While the law permitted three members to be from the same political party, not all three of the governor's appointees could be. That constraint was designed to prevent the appearance that the commission favored the party of the administration currently in power. Later on, failure to observe this requirement would become an embarrassment for Governor Paul Cellucci.

With these statutory requirements in mind, Governor Dukakis appointed James Vorenberg of the Harvard Law School as the first chairman of the ethics commission. Vorenberg served in this capacity for a five-year term from 1978 to 1983. Prior to this assignment he had earned a national reputation for his role as a Watergate prosecutor. His groundbreaking work in Washington reinforced the principle that no person is above the law, including the president of the United States. His appointment was considered a superb choice.

The governor's two other appointees were Jessie Doyle Deely, an attorney from Lee, and Linda Kistler, a professor of accounting at the University of Lowell. Attorney General Frank Bellotti appointed David Brickman, a newspaper publisher; and Secretary of State Paul Guzzi named Marver Bernstein, a well-known political scientists and president of Brandeis University.

In the early going, Vorenberg had foreseen the difficulties that would beset the commission, and although he was disappointed in its unpromising start, he did not lose hope. Its work, like most reform, would be slow and painstaking, with success often built on failure.

THE WARD COMMISSION VERSUS ENTRENCHED POWER

Reacting to the torrent of public outrage in 1978, Representative Philip W. Johnston, a Democrat, and Republican Andrew Card co-sponsored legislation creating the Ward commission (formally designated as the Special Commission Concerning State and County Buildings). They won for it the power to issue subpoenas and to offer grants of immunity in return for testimony. This commission spent two and a half years investigating the awarding of architectural and building contracts in Massachusetts over the previous two decades.

Governor Dukakis named John William Ward, president of Amherst College, to head the commission. A native of Brighton educated at Harvard, he was an ex-Marine who was widely regarded as a man of enormous energy and unquestioned integrity. Shortly after his appointment, Ward resigned his college presidency so that he could devote his effort full-time to the work of the commission. His favorite expression as an academic administrator was "You know, there must be something better than this."[38] The sentiment held him in good stead in his new assignment. Recalling the electrifying impact of the Ward commission, *Boston Globe* reporter Scot Leigh writes: "Certainly it pulled back the curtain and focused public attention on an unseemly side of politics. With months of dramatic hearings and an exhaustive final report, the commission chronicled rampant bribery, kickbacks, and quid pro quo contributions in the awarding of public design contracts. Back then, the commission's sweeping and scathing criticism of the way business was done in the public sector made headlines across Massachusetts."[39]

The commission's seven members soon realized that to succeed in pressuring the legislature to embrace the sweeping changes they envisioned, they would have to stoke the fire of public outrage. So they did—with carefully culled and corroborated stories of corruption. "That was the way we would get the message out and create pressure on the legislature," says Nick Littlefield, staff director and chief counsel for the commission. "So that became our rule: A bribe a day before lunch."[40]

Upon completing its investigation, the Ward commission submitted its final report on December 31, 1980. It chronicled a litany of bribes paid for contracts stretching back to the early 1960s. Among its major findings were that (1) corruption was a way of life in Massachusetts; (2) political influence, not professional performance, was the prime criterion in doing business with the state; (3) shoddy work and debased standards were the norm; and (4) the "system" of administration was inchoate and substandard.

Between 1962 and 1974, the administrations of Governors Endicott Peabody, John Volpe, and Francis Sargent routinely awarded design contracts worth millions of dollars in return for political contributions. To quote from the Ward commission report: "More than any other single factor, the present method of financing political campaigns in the state creates a climate that breeds corruption and contributes to the deterioration of our system of representative government. Among those who had money and the influence to strike the bargain, the state was for sale." The tough-minded Ward had a superb grasp of the situation. He summed up the commission's findings in these words:

> For at least a decade, across Republican and Democratic administrations alike, the way to get architectural contracts was to buy them. It is not a matter of a few crooks, some bad apples which spoiled the lot. The pattern is too broad and pervasive for that easy excuse. There are, to be sure, honest and hard-working administrators in state agencies, underpaid at best, struggling to do their work well. There are earnest and diligent legislators laboring against the inertia of disbelief that politics can be an honorable calling. In numerical terms, such people are the majority in public life. But at those crucial points where money and power come together, the system has been rotten.[41]

Of the $17.1 billion the public sector had spent on construction projects since 1968, the Ward commission concluded that $7.73 billion had gone for projects with severe defects; another $48.7 million had been wasted on projects that were designed but never built. There were leaking roofs and defective walls at Cape Cod Community College; the library at Salem State College could not support the weight of the books it was built to house; a third of the seats in the auditorium at Boston State College had no view of the stage; and the Worcester County Jail had a malfunctioning locking system. Almost from the day it opened in January 1974, the new campus at the University of Massachusetts in Boston had major problems, from malfunctioning heating and ventilation systems to bricks that fell from the library façade. The report estimated that it would require more than $2 billion to repair all these defects.

Governor Dukakis is widely credited with having cleaned up the shameful mess of state contracting. Looking back, Chester Atkins says, "The practices they [the Ward commission] were after had clearly changed. Dukakis had ended them and the culture died with DiCarlo and MacKenzie."[42] But corruption remained pervasive at the county and city level, and the state system was still producing shoddy buildings. Ironically, Dukakis failed to regain his party's nomination for governor in 1978, when Edward King, a conservative Democrat, defeated him in a party primary.

The Ward commission drove a stake through the heart of the old ways of doing public business in the Bay State. In assessing its unprecedented impact, Nick Littlefield credits the commission's work with effecting a wholesale change in the political culture of Massachusetts. By exposing just how rancid things were, the commission created a constituency for clean government. The reforms it achieved dramatically increased the quality of architects and builders who applied for state work. "Now the best architects in the world," Littlefield says, "are applying for jobs in Massachusetts, whereas before they would not apply because they had not a chance of winning because they weren't willing to pay a bribe."[43]

Those who knew John Ward best say that he entertained gubernatorial ambitions. He believed that the crusading work of his commission, coupled with the notoriety that he received in the media, could conceivably catapult him into political stardom. As an American historian, he was presumably familiar with how Woodrow Wilson, the president of Princeton University, became governor of New Jersey in 1910. This turned out to be wishful thinking on Ward's part. With the loss of architectural and building contracts, the business community turned against him. Indeed, business leaders saw him as the chief whistle-blower and the powerful symbol of reform. His political aspirations quickly faded. Sadly, Ward, who had been despondent over marital troubles, took his own life in 1985.

CREATION OF THE OFFICE OF INSPECTOR GENERAL

The Ward commission filed a package of legislation, which, propelled by public outrage, was eventually passed. These proposals included consolidating construction management in what was then the Division of Capital Planning and Operations (now the Division of Capital Asset Management), and creating an inspector general's office to scrutinize the state's procurement system and to uncover fraud, waste, and corruption. Another law completely reorganized public construction by introducing a rigorous planning, design, review, and oversight process, replete with fiscal controls and safeguards.

By statute authority (Chapter 9B), the inspector general is appointed for a term of five years by a majority vote of the governor, the attorney general, and the state auditor. Joseph R. Barresi of Cohasset was chosen as the first inspector general. He had the support of Attorney General Frank Bellotti and state auditor John Finnegan, but not the backing of Governor Edward King.[44] King apparently had someone else in mind for the post. Barresi had been the director of the Boston Municipal Research Bureau from 1953 to 1975, and subsequently served as vice president of Scudder, Stevens, and Clark, an investment firm, where he worked from 1976 to 1981. Statutorily, the inspector general was limited to two consecutive terms or ten years. Barresi served for two five-year terms from 1981 to 1991.

By all accounts, Barresi took his job seriously and performed well. He was, as many could attest, a man of unusual ability and forcefulness. He had an analytical mind. He was honest, and everyone knew it; emphatically independent by nature, hardworking, frugal—all traits in the New England tradition that made him an ideal inspector general. He was a person of great integrity and above reproach. Most of all, he was professionally competent.

The same cannot be said about his successor, Robert Cerasoli, a former state legislator from Quincy. Although he had served as chair of the House Post Audit and Oversight Committee, he was perceived as a political hack and a Beacon Hill insider. Hearing of his appointment, former governor Michael Dukakis asked "Robert Cerasoli? Couldn't we do better than that?"[45] To be sure, Cerasoli was a dubious choice for the sensitive post. But he had the support of Governor William Weld, Attorney General Scott Harshbarger, and State Auditor Joseph DeNucci. Unsurprisingly, Cerasoli's record of performance was less than inspiring. As veteran newspaper reporter Scot Lehigh wrote, "Too often, too much of what the inspector general has done has been overblown headline hunting."[46]

Echoing similar comments was Boston lawyer Thomas E. Dwyer Jr., who served as deputy chief counsel to the Ward commission. He contended that the inspector general's office has played headline-grabbing games. "It was never contemplated," Dwyer said, "that people would be leaking information out of the inspector general's office and that there would often times be behind-the-scenes press briefings."[47]

In March 2000, Cerasoli became the target of an "I-Team" investigative report on television station WBZ. The report criticized him for doing very little in overseeing the huge cost overruns of the massive highway project known as the Big Dig, whose price tag had skyrocketed from $2.5 billion to $14.5 billion. Nor did Cerasoli do much to detect a $16 million theft from the state treasurer's office. Not only that, but the television exposé caught him on camera doing chores at home during regular working hours and leaving his state job early in the afternoon, well before quitting time. Such lax work habits were not exactly exemplary for a sitting inspector general.

On January 22, 2001, Governor Cellucci threatened to abolish the inspector general's office, but he never made good his threat. [48] Three days later, Cerasoli released a report criticizing Massachusetts Turnpike officials for wasting more than $83 million in public funds on the Big Dig by not holding designers responsible for mistakes.[49]

In the national search that was conducted to find Cerasoli's replacement in the spring of 2001, four finalists emerged. Three of them were homegrown products: State Representatives Maryanne Lewis of Dedham and Joseph C. Sullivan of Braintree, along with Michael J. Sullivan, director of the state campaign finance office. They were all part of the "old boy" network on Beacon Hill. The only outsider, and the only candidate with governmental investigative experience, was Donald Mullinax. He was the inspector general for the Los Angeles school system, and he had previously worked in Washington as chief investigator for the Senate Subcommittee on Investigations. He was by far the most qualified candidate.

Democrat Maryanne Lewis, the House assistant majority leader, was reported to be Speaker Thomas Finneran's choice for the job. Although Finneran had no formal role in this appointment, he apparently lobbied hard on behalf of Lewis. Described in the press as a fierce Finneran loyalist, she was rumored to have the inside track to win the job. In other words, the political fix was in.

Upon learning of this situation, Donald Mullinax concluded that Massachusetts was not interested in filling the post with an independent inspector general and promptly withdrew from the search. "I am concerned," he said, "about what I've seen in their process, putting a politician in an inspector general process. They're supposed to be watchdogs, not housepets."[50] whereupon the *Boston Globe* on May 31, 2001, chimed in with a blistering editorial that demanded "a watchdog, not a lapdog."

The withdrawal of Mullinax prompted Attorney General Thomas Reilly to call for restarting the search and finding someone without ties to the political establishment. "Either we are going to have independent oversight," he said, "or it is going to be business as usual. There is a lot at stake here. State government is a $24 billion enterprise and we need oversight that is free from political pressure."[51]

Joseph DeNucci disagreed with Reilly. "We have three fine candidates who are still in the process," the state auditor said. "If neither of them gets two votes, then, and not until then, should we have a new process. I don't see any reason why we should reopen the process."[52] Three days later, amid growing criticism that the job had been wired for a political insider, acting governor Jane Swift agreed to reopen the search and to hire a firm to recruit and screen candidates. Swift was "concerned with getting an IG who has the public confidence," a spokesperson said.[53]

Meanwhile, it was disclosed that Maryanne Lewis had used her leadership position to promote her husband's career as a policeman and threatened to punish those who stood in the way. Such ethical lapses did not augur well for her. What was at stake was nothing less than the integrity of the office itself. As of this writing, the national search remained incomplete, but Gregory W. Sullivan was named acting inspector general.

CYCLES OF REFORM

In 1982, Michael Dukakis regained the governorship by ousting sitting governor Edward King in a Democratic party primary and defeating Republican Frank Hatch in the general election. Dukakis appointed Colin Diver, dean of Boston University Law School, to succeed James Vorenberg as chair of the state ethics commission. Diver served in that capacity from 1983 to 1989. He was succeeded by Edward F. Hennessy, former chief justice of the Supreme Judicial Court, who served as chair from 1989 to 1994.

During these eleven years, a chrysalis of lethargy had wrapped itself around the prevailing status quo. Clearly, passions had abated, and the uproar over ethics had faded. That is, until May 1993. At that time the *Boston Globe's* Spotlight team dropped a political bombshell. It published a five-part investigative series titled "Beacon Hill's Money Game."[54] Complete with photographs, the Spotlight report exposed state legislators vacationing at tropical resorts and socializing with known lobbyists. It documented several other alleged violations of the conflict law.

First, it identified an elite group of twenty legislators—members of the House and Senate leadership and committee chairmen—who received more than 85 percent of their campaign funds from lobbyists and special interests. Frequently, in the case of committee chairmen, the special interests were involved with legislation that came before their committees. Second, it exposed a four-day lobbyist-financed beach party at a luxurious resort in Puerto Rico attended by House Speaker Charles F. Flaherty and seven other legislators. Third, it described how a nonprofit foundation (funded by tax-deductible contributors from forty corporations and trade associations) had financed vacation trips for Senate president William Bulger. Fourth, it uncovered an apparently illegal payment of $130,000 from the Armed Forces YMCA to two politically wired lobbyists for their role in pushing an appropriation of $12.2 million through the legislature. Finally, it detailed how several legislators, including Speaker Flaherty and former senator William Q. MacLean of Fairhaven, had used campaign funds to defend themselves against corruption charges.[55]

As the shock waves from the Spotlight series spread, the drumbeat for reform was heard once again in Massachusetts. The *Boston Globe* weighed in with a scorching editorial that called on the electorate to take appropriate action: "Ultimately the success of a reform movement at the State House depends on the state's voters. If they are angered by the climate of corruption, they have the power to demand that reforms be made. If they are untroubled by junkets and favors—for most of which they end up paying the bill—then the State House will continue to reek of corruption."[56]

In the wake of the Spotlight series, eighteen legislators were ordered to pay civil penalties. Distracted by personal issues, Speaker Flaherty became the target of a federal investigation. He resigned after pleading guilty to tax evasion and paying a $26,000 fine to the ethics commission. Nine donors of illegal gratuities paid civil penalties ranging from $2,000 to $110,000, the fine paid by John Hancock Life Insurance Company, which at the same time also paid a $900,000 fine to the federal government under the mail fraud statute. As a result of these revelations, Senator Michael Barrett of Cambridge took up the cudgel of reform. He proposed the creation of a special commission to draft tougher ethics legislation.

In 1994 a campaign finance reform law passed by the state legislature created a special commission to study the effectiveness of the existing ethics laws and to recommend changes. This blue ribbon panel consisted of thirteen members (six appointed by the legislative leadership, four by the governor, and three by the attorney general). John T. Montgomery, a prominent Boston lawyer, chaired the panel. Beginning its work in September 1994, the special commission held a series of public hearings, heard testimony from a broad spectrum of experts, and held numerous public meetings.

The Montgomery commission concluded that, although Chapters 268A and 268B of the existing ethics had been reasonably effective, important amendments to the original statutes were necessary to accomplish certain objectives. These were to (1) eliminate ambiguities in the statute and create brighter lines between permissible and prohibited conduct; (2) exempt from the statute certain trivial and inconsequential conduct, especially in the area of gifts and gratuities and multiple officeholding at the municipal level; (3) introduce greater procedural fairness in the administrative processes of the state ethics commission; (4) create mechanisms to enhance involvement in the enforcement of the statutes by the five private citizens who serve on the commission; and (5) strengthen the tools available to prosecutors and regulators to enable them to detect and sanction instances of egregious misconduct more effectively.[57]

The special commission, which took a carrot-and-stick approach to the problem, issued its report on June 12, 1995. It drafted a bill containing its recommended changes in the state ethics statutes. For example, because of certain questions raised by the Supreme Judicial Court, the bill gave the ethics commission subpoena power and established an explicit statute of limitations for ethics violations. Although the recommendations of the

Montgomery commission were largely ignored by the General Court, its final report stands as a coherent and thoughtful set of potential reforms.

THE SAWYER AND SCACCIA CASES

Meanwhile, other cases of ethical misconduct were being litigated. The most egregious involved F. William Sawyer, a lobbyist for the John Hancock Insurance Company, who in 1995 was convicted of criminal violations for treating legislators to trips, meals, and rounds of golf. In addition, State Representative Francis Woodward, chairman of the insurance committee, was convicted of accepting illegal gratuities.[58] These two cases were prosecuted by the federal government.

Almost simultaneously, Angelo M. Scaccia, a veteran Readville legislator, was charged with accepting gratuities from insurance and tobacco industry lobbyists. His case came before the state ethics commission while Judge Edward Hennessy was still chair. When Hennessy stepped down from the post, Scaccia then appeared before the new chairman, George D. Brown, a Boston College law professor. Brown became the hearing officer in the Scaccia case. After the hearing, the ethics commission fined Scaccia $3,000. Rather than pay the fine, as some friends advised him, Scaccia decided to fight the charges in court. He was defended by Morris Goldings, a hard-nosed criminal defense lawyer.

At the same time, the Life Insurance Association of Massachusetts (LIAM), a lobbying organization for ten Massachusetts insurance companies, was ordered to pay a fine of $13,500. Scaccia challenged the commission's findings in state superior court and argued that there was no quid pro quo in exchange for the gratuities, which included two golfing events and one dinner. LIAM also appealed. After losing at the superior court level, both appealed to the Supreme Judicial Court. This litigation was widely seen as a test case of crackdowns on the cozy relationships between Beacon Hill legislators and lobbyists.

On May 5, 2000, the Supreme Judicial Court ruled that Scaccia had not violated the state's gratuity law by accepting $600 in free meals and golf games from lobbyists. But the SJC also ruled that these were gifts and that by accepting them, Scaccia had violated the state's gifts statute, which forbids legislators and their families to accept gifts from a lobbyist totaling more than $100 in a calendar year. It likewise found that Scaccia had violated the state's financial disclosure law by not reporting the gifts. And by creating the appearance of a conflict of interest, he had violated the code of conduct statute. Scaccia was ordered to pay fines, to be set by a lower court.[59] The LIAM case was remanded to superior court for further findings.

Former prosecutors, who eagerly awaited the SJC decision, were disappointed in the outcome. Brian O'Connor, former head of the U.S. attorney's office of public corruption, said that the SJC ruling would make it more difficult for prosecutors to pursue legitimate cases of corruption. "By requiring them to establish a direct link between a gift and a specific act," O'Connor said, "the court has made it clear that the distance between a bribery violation and a gratuity violation is not as great as some prosecutors have believed over the last several years."[60]

In Scaccia's case, the SJC acknowledged the difficulty of obtaining that proof, but it also said that the ethics commission had fallen far short of that standard. "Indeed, the administrative record shows that Scaccia took a position contrary to that advocated by the insurance industry," wrote Justice Roderick L. Ireland, who authored the unanimous decision. "In short, there are no findings, and no evidence in the record, that the gratuities influenced any specified official act by Scaccia."[61] In effect, the SJC ruled that there was no quid pro quo.

Some legislators believe that the state's ethics laws are confusing and contradictory. For example, elected officials are required to disclose publicly those gifts offered that, if accepted, would amount to a violation of the gift law. Given this confusion and ambiguity, Thomas Dwyer, who now heads the Boston Bar Association, named a committee of attorneys to review the laws and to recommend changes to the legislature.

JANE SWIFT ENSNARED IN ETHICAL LAPSES

In the spring of 2000, Lieutenant Governor Jane M. Swift found herself ensnared in charges of ethical lapses and alleged violations of the conflict of interest law. These included her improper use of a state police helicopter to airlift her to her home in the Berkshires for Thanksgiving in 1999; her obtaining a rental apartment at a discount that was below market rates; and use of her staff to move her into a new home, perform baby-sitting duties, and conduct other personal chores.

To top it off, the media revealed that Swift had accepted a part-time teaching job at Suffolk University's Sawyer School of Management. This job apparently had been arranged through Paul Barrett, a partner in a Beacon Hill lobbying firm, after Michael K. Crossen, Swift's campaign chairman, asked Barrett to intercede with Suffolk officials on her behalf. Swift's $25,000 salary far exceeded what most adjunct professors were paid for comparable work. What is more, she was given a light teaching load that involved a six-week course in which only three students were enrolled. Normally, Suffolk cancelled courses that enrolled fewer than six students.

The Suffolk controversy not only damaged Swift's public image but also caused the Cellucci administration considerable grief. In an attempt to douse the political firestorm, Swift resigned under pressure from her teaching position on May 12, 2000. Meanwhile, investigation of the other charges against her proceeded. It should be noted that the state ethics commission is required by law to conduct its business in secret and with the utmost confidentially. As a result, the commission neither confirms nor denies the existence of any complaint or investigation until such investigation is complete and the commission has reasonable grounds to believe that the law was violated.

No sooner had Swift resigned from her teaching post than the composition of the ethics commission was called into question. On May 17, the *Boston Globe* revealed that Governor Cellucci had appointed too many Republicans.[62] In fact, all three of Cellucci's appointees were registered Republicans, namely, Boston lawyers J. Owen Todd and Stephen E. Moore, and chairman Augustus F. Wagner Jr., a Cape Cod lawyer.

With several sensitive cases on the docket, including the probe of Jane Swift, this predicament raised speculation as to whether the ethics panel, already short one member owing to the death of Paul J. Liacos in May 1999, could legally take action on any matters pending before it. Liacos had been the appointee of Secretary of State William Galvin. Subsequently, Galvin appointed Michael Cassidy, a Boston College law professor and former prosecutor, to take Liacos's place.

Former state ethics commission chairman George Brown contended that because its members police the behavior of elected officials and operate in secret, it is crucial that their own ethics be above reproach: "The commission not only has tremendous power but also does virtually everything in executive session. That's not wrong, but it emphasizes the importance of public confidence in the commission."[63] Colin Diver, another former ethics commission chairman, took a slightly different point of view: "If I were a defendant in an action taken by the commission, or a lawyer with a defendant, I would make the argument that the commission is not legally constituted and that the action of the commission is not legal for that reason."[64]

The day after the *Boston Globe* broke the story about the decisions declaring the ethics panel vulnerable to legal challenge, corrective action was taken by Cellucci. Embarrassed by this political gaffe, the governor acknowledged that his staff had not checked the party affiliation of J. Owen Todd, his most recent appointee. Todd, a former superior court judge, resigned by the end of the workday.[65]

Cellucci told the media that his staff had assumed Todd was a Democrat because Governor Michael Dukakis had appointed him to the superior court. "I don't think anyone thought he was a Republican but they should have checked," Cellucci said. "It's a mistake and we've got to straighten it out."[66] A spokesman for the governor said, "Judge Todd has offered to solve the dilemma and we're going to reluctantly accept, because the statute is pretty clear that we cannot have a third Republican as one of our appointees to the commission."[67] Cellucci promised quick action in appointing Todd's successor, but months later the position still remained vacant.

On August 23, 2000, the state ethics commission, after five hours of closed-door deliberations, dismissed most of the allegations that Swift had improperly relied on staff for personal chores and misused a state helicopter. It did, however, find "reasonable cause" to believe that she had violated a section of the law by using her staff as baby-sitters. In so doing, the four commissioners rejected the report of its enforcement division that found probable cause for the other charges. Shortly afterward, Swift offered a public apology. "There's no doubt," she said, "I've made mistakes and the public has lost confidence in my ability to provide leadership on matters they care about."[68]

Two weeks later, on September 19, the ethics commission, rejecting a $750 fine that had been negotiated between its staff and Swift's lawyer, fined her $1,250 for her misconduct. The maximum penalty allowed by law is $2,000.[69] Sadder but wiser, Swift had learned that she needs to behave more ethically. As one commentator put it in early 2001, "Though she's taken her lumps over the past two years, they seem only to have toughened her up. There have been reports of Swift making the rounds of newsrooms and editorial boards delivering a contrite mea culpa for her past sins."[70]

In a capsule assessment of the state ethics commission, one can say that it has maintained high standards of professionalism and nonpartisanship. Most of all it has helped to restore public confidence in state government. No longer is Massachusetts perceived as a "state for sale." Governor Michael Dukakis put a stop to that. There has been a definite change in the political culture. Public employees must now ask themselves, "What's my conduct going to look like if it appears in the media tomorrow." In recent years the ethics commission has been quietly and deliberately moving toward the reforms envisioned by the Montgomery commission. But there is still a long way to go.

7

THE USES
AND ABUSES
OF OUTSIDE
SECTIONS

This is no way to run a railroad.

Stephen Crosby,
Massachusetts Secretary for Administration and Finance,
press conference, August 26, 2000

THE ROLE OF REPRESENTATIVE INSTITUTIONS

Typical of the threats to the viability of democratic institutions that seem to abound in our age is the challenge to the Massachusetts legislature. The threat is a grave one, for the legislature is an indispensable device for representing the diversity of opinion and reflecting the multiplicity of interests that exist in a huge and complex society. In short, the legislature is the only adequate means yet devised for providing representation and compromise in making law; it is a vitally important tool for making responsible and yet authoritative decisions about the basic allocation of public funds.

Because the bicameral legislature reflects many interests, and because it is a practical political institution, I value highly its function of resolving the pressing public issues of the day. Not even the staunchest partisan of the legislature would claim that it does all these things completely satisfactorily, but no one has yet suggested any substitute for the representative legislature as a forum for lawmaking. Neither the executive, the courts, nor the bureaucracy possesses the unique requisites for broad rulemaking fulfilled by the legislature.

Bombarded constantly by evidence of the corrupting influence of soft money in politics and by the concomitant demand for clean elections and campaign finance reform, one can easily lose sight of the crucial role that representative institutions play in the functioning of modern democracy. By definition, democracy rests squarely on the principle of majority rule. The idea of government by the people initially took root in America's small towns and rural villages, where democracy in its purest form was possible. The new England town meeting survives today as a legacy of direct participatory democracy. But democracy could not have been extended to the larger society without the invention of representative government and party politics. Indeed, our representative institutions remain our best hope for keeping government responsive to the people. The delegation of authority to elected representatives and the role that political parties play in conducting a dialogue between political leaders and the body politic are the essential elements of democracy.

EASY RIDERS

Few people understand the intricacles of the state budgetary process, and fewer still understand how much Massachusetts policymakers rely on outside sections of the budget as a vehicle of choice for lawmaking.[1] Outside sections, also known as budget riders, are pieces of legislation attached to appropriation acts. They are called *outside* because these sections are separate from those that specify actual appropriations in hundreds of line items and the amount of local aid each municipality is to receive. These riders become law when the state budget is approved. By attaching these measures to the state budget, their legislative sponsors bypass the regular channels that they would have to go through as separate bills.

Specifically, outside sections avoid committee review, public hearings, and repeated preliminary votes (readings) in both the House and the Senate that regular bills are subject to. What little debate they receive takes place under the constraints of the budget debate, which covers wide ground under the time pressure of an expiring fiscal year. And this deliberation may take place in only one branch of the legislature: an outside section incorporated into, say, the House version of the budget may be "accepted" by Senate delegates in conference committee, so that the measure becomes law without the full Senate's ever having to approve it.

This truncated method allows major legal and policy shifts to be approved with little scrutiny from the legislative membership, the media, advocacy groups, and the citizenry at large. Careful committee consideration of bills and informed debate simply go out the window. These democratic procedures are sacrificed on the altar of political expediency. Some legislators are unaware of the impact of many outside sections until after they have been passed. Nothing could be more undemocratic or more deceptive. It is lawmaking by trickery or sleight of hand.

In many ways, this technique has become a legislative crutch that props up a lame and dysfunctional legislature. Since 1995, well over half the legislation enacted in the Bay State has been approved as outside sections. Lawmaking by outside section is a way to get legislation passed in a complex and contentious public policy environment where stalemate is common. It relieves the legislative leadership of the burden of having to achieve genuine consensus and produce majority votes. As one former legislator, who prefers to remain anonymous, says of outside sections, "They're intoxicating because they're so easy, and if you like policy issues you can make bold changes quickly and with very few amendments." That is precisely why they are so seductive.

If the so-called Fab Four approve, the legislation piggybacked on the outside sections will sail through without so much as a whimper. The Fab Four include the Speaker of the House, the Senate president, and the chairs of both the House and Senate Ways and Means committees. As one frustrated legislator remarked, "Why the hell are we wasting money and time on public hearings and research when it doesn't make any difference what we do? The four of them take care of everything."[2]

Each house passes its own version of the budget with its outside sections attached. Neither house has an opportunity to vote on the other's outside sections. Moreover, a conference committee can take up only those matters that are in dispute between the two houses. Once the appropriations bill is approved by conference committee, it is referred back to the full House and Senate for approval and cannot be amended by either chamber. It must be accepted or rejected as a whole by each house. It can only be voted up or down. By manipulating these legislative rules, proponents of outside sections can push legislation through without any deliberation whatsoever.

Critics argue that this kind of lawmaking amounts to shoddy legislative procedure which distorts democracy and makes a mockery of representative government. The problem of outside sections has been of serious concern to good-government reformers, civic-minded activists, and public interest organizations. The Massachusetts Taxpayers Foundation has a long record of opposition to the improper use of outside sections. Its leaders contend that these legislative shortcuts violate Articles 1, 48, and 63 of the state constitution. From time to time, the group has submitted legal briefs to the courts arguing its position, but to no avail. The courts, ever mindful of the doctrine of separation of powers, are extremely reluctant to rule on the constitutionality of the internal rules of the legislative branch.

CENTRALIZED AND AUTOCRATIC LEADERSHIP

Before we continue to examine the budgetary process, we need to take a look at the individuals who control that process. From 1978 to 1995, Senate president William Bulger ran a very tight ship while he presided over the upper chamber. After an unprecedented run of seventeen years, he decided to step down from his position in 1995 to accept the presidency of the University of Massachusetts. The following year, in April 1996, House Speaker Charles Flaherty was forced to resign from his post after pleading guilty to income tax evasion. Senator Thomas F. Birmingham succeeded Bulger, while Thomas M. Finneran took over for Flaherty. Both men were Democrats, and both had chaired the Ways and Means committees of their respective houses. Normally majority leader Richard Voke would have succeeded to the Speaker's office, but Finneran challenged him for the post. The boldness and timing of Finneran's move took most political insiders on Beacon Hill by surprise. In what turned out to be a bitter and contentious fight, Finneran won the Speakership by cutting a deal with Republicans.

In many ways Birmingham and Finneran, the state's top legislative power brokers, exercised highly centralized and autocratic leadership. They consolidated their power by appointing loyalists to committee chairmanships. By no means subtle, Finneran's purges began soon after he took office as Speaker. He punished those Democrats who had voted for Voke by removing them from committee chairs. Among this group was John E. McDonough, whose expertise on health care had earned him a national reputation. Finneran named Paul R. Haley of Weymouth as chairman of the House Ways and Means Committee, which has the primary responsibility for drafting the House version of the state budget and handles all other major legislation. The Speaker uses it to control bills. Finneran came to power as Speaker promising to establish a coherent, orderly, and rational context for the budget debate. In 1997 he imposed a schedule on House members that allowed just one week in April for budget deliberations. He took great pride in delivering that budget to the governor two weeks early.

When the budget process stalled in the summer of 1999, the State House balcony became a meeting place for Birmingham and Finneran, who negotiated how the state would spend $21 billion. The annual budget was due on July 1, the start of the new fiscal year. But July came and went, and then August, and then September. The two leaders worked in shirtsleeves, away from the telephones, the press, and other members of the legislature. By that fall the budget stalemate had become an embarrassment. It dragged on for almost five months before the negotiations were concluded. As David Denison observed, "The long summer of the balcony budget meetings told the public something important about their Legislature: It is being run by two powerful men who will go to extraordinary lengths to get their own way."[3]

Members in both chambers have chafed under the oligarchic control of their presiding officers. In July 2000, a *Boston Globe* Spotlight team painted a picture of a tightly controlled legislature that lacked a climate of openness: "By almost every measure, the state legislature today is an institution in steep decline. Its power, always concentrated among its leadership, has crystallized to a remarkable degree, making House Speaker Thomas M. Finneran and Senate president Thomas F. Birmingham virtual one-man rulers of their respective chambers."[4]

Finneran is a fascinating figure: smart, persuasive, articulate, charming, and tough. That rare combination of talents explains why he is Speaker. Continuing to use his power to reward friends and punish foes, he assembled a new leadership team at the beginning of the legislative session in January 2001. His abrupt reshuffle of committee assignments occurred a week after rank-and-file members had voted to do away with an eight-year term limit that had been imposed on the Speakership in 1985, when Thomas McGee of Lynn was ousted from the post. An autocratic, lunch-bucket Democrat, McGee had been the longest-serving Speaker (1975–85) in the history of the General Court. His vindictive style of leadership had precipitated a revolt by insurgent reformers. For example, when he evicted Representative Edward Markey from his State House office, to dramatize his exile Markey worked from a desk in the hallway. McGee was replaced by George Keverian, a well-liked politician from Everett, who opened the House to genuine debate and gave committee chairmen a free hand to run their own show.

The elimination of the eight-year term limit repealed a House rule that would have forced Finneran to step down in the year 2004. In announcing his new lineup, the Speaker picked Representative John H. Rogers of Norwood, a social conservative and close ally, to succeed Haley as chair of the Ways and Means Committee. Finneran's reshuffling of committee assignments provoked a storm of protest among angry lawmakers. Representative Douglas W. Petersen of Marblehead, a longtime supporter, was removed from his post as chairman of the Natural Resources and Agriculture Committee. Petersen had balked when majority whip Salvatore F. DiMasi asked him how he intended to vote on a scheme to scuttle the Clean Elections law, which had been adopted overwhelmingly by public referendum in 1998. Petersen, who had supported lifting the term limit, told DiMasi to tell Finneran to "shove" the chairmanship if it required him to vote against Clean Elections.[5] In an obvious break with the Speaker, an angry and disillusioned Petersen blasted him publicly, saying, "You disagree with him and you're going to be punished—that's the message. I am confident that he has reached a point where he brooks no dissent and therefore there is no democracy in the House of Representatives."[6]

At the same time, Finneran demoted five of the fifteen Democrats who had voted to maintain the term limit on the Speakership. He transferred Representative Ruth Baiser of Newton from her prized seat on the insurance committee to an obscure panel on personnel and administration. He also removed Ruth Provost of Sandwich from the energy panel, a committee expected to be in the spotlight as fuel costs rose. The Speaker took John Slattery of Peabody off the criminal justice committee and pushed Byron Rushing of Boston's South End off transportation, where his voice was often heard on vital issues such as construction of the MBTA Silver Line. Finally, he stripped Thomas McGee, the son of the former Speaker, of his vice chairmanship of the public service committee. With that, the purge was complete.

But Finneran's moves left him open to attack. Alarmed by such a brazen display of raw power, the *Boston Globe* chastised the Speaker in a blistering editorial. Without mincing words, the editor wrote: "During Finneran's tenure, every year has seen less debate, less dissent, less willingness to fight for the public interest rather than the leadership's desires. Finneran has made the House a very difficult place to work for anyone with half a brain and an ounce of independence, and the result is that very few such people are there now."[7] A few days later, WBZ-TV conducted a public opinion poll, which indicated that only 15 percent of those surveyed believed that there was an open legislature, while a whopping 82 percent felt that it was a closed shop.

Stung by depictions of an "Animal House" atmosphere that prevailed during the budget debates in April 2000, the House enacted a series of internal rules in January 2001 to streamline the budgetary process. For the first time, budget amendments were discussed by subject matter instead of in the random order in which they were filed.[8]

On May 1, 2001, the House voted 96 to 59 to cut off funding for the Clean Elections law, which provided for public financing of campaigns and imposed strict fundraising and spending limits. The budget amendment called for voluntary taxpayer donations instead of public funding to implement the law. Floor debate was heated and at times angry. Several legislators claimed that the voters had not understood the law when they approved it. Others blamed the media for distorting the issue. Representative Douglas Petersen took his fellow legislators to task, calling the House vote "an incredible affront to the citizens of the Commonwealth. This is close to the death knell. The mourners are marching in the streets."[9] Representative

Frank Hynes of Marshfield challenged his colleagues, saying, "This is a defining moment for this Legislature and for each and every one of us."[10]

Meanwhile, supporters of the campaign finance measure attempted to storm the House chamber, but they were blocked by court officers. They stood in the gallery and chanted, "The people voted two to one! We want our election fund." Speaker Finneran did not appear in the House chamber during the lengthy debate, and he voted from his office rather than from the rostrum during the roll call. Acting governor Jane Swift blasted the legislators for subverting the will of the voters. Senate president Birmingham, poised to run for governor in 2002, pledged to provide full funding for the Clean Elections law in the Senate budget.

In retaliation against six members who had voted to preserve the campaign finance law, Finneran's leadership team pushed through budget cuts in programs ranging from homeless shelters to traffic lights in their respective districts. Later, Finneran, who was again noticeably absent, rescinded the cuts, but the punitive message was unmistakable. "It's a message that, 'If you're not with us, we are not with you,'" said Representative Christopher Hodgkin, a Lee Democrat and a vocal Finneran critic.

Like other actors in the political game, the legislature has to concern itself with these realities. For how these actors are perceived by the public is usually a determinant of how they are judged. Despite its shortcomings, the General Court, as a democratic institution, has shown remarkable resiliency over its long 370-year history. Nonetheless, many citizens have an unfavorable view of the legislature. At a time when distrust of politicians and state government runs high, this alienation undermines the legitimacy of state government. And a government without legitimacy is a government in chronic difficulty. Amid an increasingly cynical and fragmented electorate marked by voter apathy and diminished party loyalty, the new skepticism has fueled the drive for term limits and other legislative reforms.

HOW AN APPROPRIATIONS BILL BECOMES A LAW

In order to understand the impact of budgetary outside sections, one must first understand how an appropriations bill becomes a law. The legislature possesses the "power of the purse." Only the legislature can appropriate money. Article 63 of the Massachusetts constitution prescribes the manner in which appropriation measures are passed. Before 1919 there was no single spending and revenue plan for a given fiscal year. Until then, state appropriations were made on an ad hoc basis that required the passage of numerous individual bills. This situation led to what is known as logrolling (i.e., "You support our bill and we will support yours") a practice that usually resulted in the proliferation of many extraneous items. For the most part these were special interest provisions that could not have succeeded if filed separately. The delegates who participated at the constitutional convention of 1917–19 sought to correct this problem. They amended the state constitution by adding Article 63. This amendment, which was eventually ratified by popular vote, contains five sections. Three of those sections are particularly relevant to our discussion.

Section 2 of Article 63 requires that the governor prepare an annual budget to be submitted to the General Court. Section 3 stipulates that the legislature enact a general appropriations bill each year, which contains "all appropriations based upon the budget to be paid from taxes or revenues." In preparing the general appropriations bill, section 3 authorizes the General Court to "increase, decrease, add or omit items in the budget." In accordance with section 5, the general appropriations bill is then submitted to the governor, who may veto "items or parts of items." The executive veto can be overridden by a two-thirds vote of the legislature.[11] These bills as enacted are not subject to referendum or amendment by the people. This last constitutional restriction is mandated by Article 48.

Although Article 63 does not contain language expressly prohibiting the inclusion in general appropriation bills of provisions on subjects other than appropriations, its wording clearly reflects that only items of appropriation are to be included in general appropriations bills. Put another way, there is absolutely no authority for either the governor or the legislature to include general legislation in an appropriations bill. By longstanding practice, and pursuant to the rules of both branches of the legislature, the governor submits the annual state budget in January to the House of Representatives as House Bill number 1. It is assigned to the House Committee on Ways and Means, which then holds hearings on the proposed budget. The committee then reports to the House a recommended appropriations bill. After debate and amendment in the House, the bill is passed and sent to the Senate. It is then assigned to the Senate Committee on Ways and Means, which also holds hearings, drafts its own version of the bill, and reports it to the Senate for consideration and passage. The Senate then returns its version of the bill to the House, which regularly rejects the Senate bill by a single vote. A conference committee then is appointed to resolve the differences between the House and Senate versions of the bill. The bill agreed to by the conference committee is referred back to the full House and Senate for approval. At that point it cannot be amended by either chamber, and must be accepted or rejected as a whole by each.[12] On acceptance, the general appropriations bill is then enacted and sent to the governor for signature, subject to the rights of veto and override.

CONSTITUTIONAL DEBATES AND LEGISLATIVE PRACTICE

One of the main goals of those who participated in the constitutional convention of 1917–19 was to strengthen the hand of the governor as the state's chief financial officer. On this and a series of other issues, they wanted to establish the right of initiative petition, prohibit the use of public funds for parochial schools, and eliminate the excesses of logrolling.[13] In effect, Article 63 gave the chief executive certain powers that enabled him to gain greater control over the bureaucracy. More specifically, this amendment did three things: (1) it established the requirement of a balanced budget; (2) it granted the governor the power of line item veto with respect to items in bills appropriating money; and (3) it excluded from legislative action matters outside the scope of the governor's recommendations.

It behooves us to examine the constitutional convention debates in order to ascertain what the delegates intended at the time. There apparently was little or no discussion during the debates about whether general legislation could be included in the appropriations bill.

The main purpose of Article 63, as articulated by the delegates, was two-fold: first, to consolidate appropriations into one bill to gain greater control and management over expenditures and the means by which they would be defrayed; and second, to define the roles played by the executive and the legislature in this process. In this context, a transcript of the debates shows that the delegates intended that appropriation bills would concern matters relating solely to appropriations. Consider, for instance, the remarks made by Henry Parkman, who introduced Article 63:

> As I understood the question of the gentleman in the fourth division [Mr. Lyman] it is: what is going to happen if this general budget should take up two or three months in discussion. Instead of a multitude of appropriation bills coming in, which undoubtedly do take up a considerable time, there will be this one bill. After that bill is discussed and settled any other appropriation bills can then be taken up, and any other matters can be discussed during the time that this general appropriation bill is perhaps before the Committee on Ways and Means or before any other Committee to which the Legislature chooses to send it. Other matters can be discussed during that period, so that the business of the Legislature need not be hindered.[14]

Parkman's reference to "other matters" clearly indicates that the drafters of Article 63 made a distinction between general appropriation bills, other appropriation bills, and general legislation. In other words, Article 63 was aimed at keeping them separate from one another in the legislative process.

In offering an amendment to Article 63 that would permit the inclusion in the governor's budget of plans that go beyond the fiscal year (which was later adopted), Senator George B. Churchill, a professor at Amherst College, told his fellow delegates, "Now I understand it to be the intent of the committee not by any means to shut out the Governor or the Legislature from considering a plan which may run over a number of years, but it does intend that the appropriation bill shall be confined to the exact expenditures of the fiscal year."[15] Churchill's statement shows the intent of the framers of Article 63 to "confine" general appropriation bills to matters relating to appropriations.

Another clear intent expressed by the delegates was to put a stop to the abuses of logrolling. To quote Churchill again: "We want to prevent waste, we want to prevent logrolling, the special bills, the tit-for-tat kind of work in the Legislature, and we want to center responsibility."[16]

The practice of appending general legislation to appropriation bills no doubt increases the opportunity for logrolling. The passage of appropriation bills is absolutely essential to the operations of state government. Until an appropriations bill becomes law, the Commonwealth is without legal power to spend. Consequently, there is tremendous pressure to enact the bill in a timely fashion. Because of this pressure, there is always the temptation to include legislation that might never be enacted separately. Indeed, as the beginning of a fiscal year approaches, and during the final stages of the process of enacting an appropriations bill, the opportunities for logrolling increase exponentially. This sort of political activity is exactly what the framers of Article 63 sought to eliminate by requiring that annual appropriations bills be enacted separately from other general legislative matters.

Statements made by members of the General Court since the adoption of Article 63 indicate that they intended to focus only on appropriating money when enacting general appropriation bills. These statements tend to support the position that outside sections are prohibited. For instance, on February 11, 1919, Benjamin Loring Young, who chaired the House Committee on Ways and Means, made it perfectly clear to his fellow legislators that he believed general appropriation bills were intended to contain only items of appropriation. Young's remarks are worth quoting because they underscore the legislative intent: "That statute [the Budget Act] and the constitutional amendment taken together make the Governor, so far as finance is concerned, the actual executive head of the state in practice as well as theory. The power of the General Court to add items should obviously be construed as being limited to departmental estimates embodied in the budget, or to other appropriation items properly before the General Court under its rules."[17]

Five years later, in 1924, Henry Shattuck of Boston, who succeeded Young

as Ways and Means chairman, reaffirmed the position taken by his predecessor. Shattuck's comments are insightful:

> The General Court may increase, decrease, or omit items in the General Ap-
> propriation Bill, and may add items relative to matters considered in the bud-
> get. Outside and special matters cannot be added because the General Appro-
> priation Bill, based as it is on the matters considered in the budget, has right
> of way over all other proposals for expenditure of money. That is why your
> Committee on Ways and Means must postpone consideration of such bill until
> after the General Appropriation Bill has been disposed of.[18]

For more than a half-century after the adoption of Article 63, Massachusetts state legislators consistently followed these legislative guidelines. Successive Speakers of the House have dealt with the issue as to the propriety
of amendments to appropriation bills. Many have noted the legislative duty
and authority to provide for "reasonable financial control." The remarks of
Speaker Leverett Saltonstall, made in April 1935, are worth quoting at length:

> Mr. Sawyer of Ware raises the point of order that the amendment recom-
> mended by the committee on Ways and Means which provides "that the in-
> cumbents of said offices on the first day of April in the current year may
> continue to serve in their respective positions without taking a civil service
> examination," is not properly before the House, for the reason that it intro-
> duces subject matter which is not required for reasonable financial control
> and is therefore not germane to an appropriation bill.
>
> The legislation as to which such point of order is raised is the general ap-
> propriation bill which covers the financial requirements of all branches of the
> state government for the current fiscal year.
>
> The issue raised by this point of order is as to whether legislation establish-
> ing the permanent status of persons employed in the Division of Research for
> the Prevention of Crime may properly be included in the general appropriation
> bill. The Chair believes that the subject matter of the amendment is not a
> regulation or restriction required for reasonable financial control.[19]

Not surprisingly, Saltonstall therefore declared the point of order well
taken. Similarly, Speaker Michael F. Skerry in 1955 confronted this same
issue. He recognized that the inclusion of amendments to general appropriation bills that were not related to budget items would violate Article
63. He went on to explain:

> To permit the introduction by amendment of extraneous subjects of legislation
> to general or supplementary appropriation bills, except through the usual me-

dium of introducing legislation, is contrary to the custom that has prevailed in Massachusetts. Such introduction escapes the requirement of the rule regulating the time limit for filing new legislation, the reference of the subject matter to a committee and the benefit the House receives from the report of a committee that has considered the matter, and furthermore this method of introducing legislation denies to the public a proper notice thereof which otherwise they would have received. It could result in entering through the "back door" matters which would be difficult to secure through the usual channels referred to.[20]

Given the events that have since transpired, Skerry's comments made him look prescient. He foresaw the potential abuses that would actually come to pass in the years ahead.

In every appropriation bill since 1919, the first section has set forth the act's purpose, while the second section has contained the line items of appropriation. As we have seen, any additional sections are known on Beacon Hill as "outside sections." The first general appropriation bill, enacted in 1919, contained one outside section, which provided for the reversion of unspent funds to the treasury. As time went on, more outside sections were added to the general appropriations bills. These sections placed conditions or restrictions on or otherwise related directly to the items appropriated, and were therefore appropriately included in these bills. As former representative Mary B. Newman of Cambridge observed to Governor William Weld, "While I was in the legislature, there was unquestioned adherence to these procedures. Rulings of Speakers and Senate Presidents supported the procedures for fifty-five years."[21] Obviously, they saw the danger of logrolling and loading the budget like a Christmas tree with pet projects and pork barrel legislation.

Between 1919 and 1975 outside sections were used sparingly and in a largely responsible manner. During this period, the typical budget contained anywhere from four to twenty-nine outside sections. They did not amend general law, alter existing laws, or add extraneous items to the budget. Rather, they dealt with fund transfers, personnel matters, acceptance of federal grants, and state travel reimbursement rates.

OPENING THE FLOODGATES

In 1975, all that changed. Fresh from the campaign trail, Governor Dukakis found himself saddled with a large fiscal deficit that he had inherited from the outgoing Sargent administration, but he stubbornly refused to raise taxes because of the "no tax" pledge he had made during the campaign. So Speaker Thomas McGee and Senate president Kevin Harrington did it for him. By use of an outside section, they pushed through the largest tax increase in the history of the Commonwealth.[22]

By the same token, they sought to cut unemployment insurance costs by eliminating benefits to workers who left their jobs voluntarily or retired but here they faced stiff opposition from organized labor. So the pressure built within the administration to find a way of changing the law. This pressure built without notable public support or debate. When it became clear that their goal was unattainable by the regular legislative process, Dukakis agreed with Democratic legislative leaders to insert this policy change as an outside section in the budget.[23] This strategy was masterminded by Senator James Kelly, who chaired the Senate Ways and Means Committee, a man well versed in playing the political game even if it meant bending the rules. Such a move was out of character for the reform-minded Dukakis and thus unexpected.

Short-circuiting legislative procedures, these backdoor maneuvers achieved their purpose. The lawmakers had turned the budget process upside down. To quote Mary Newman again, "This was done—the change slipped through and became law—and the floodgates were opened. Since then, the budget has carried an increasing burden of outside sections. And it must be emphasized that this is legislation not submitted by petition, not heard by a committee, not openly debated, and sheltered from the people's right to referendum."[24]

Since then, the number of outside sections has grown dramatically, reaching a record high of 690 in fiscal year 1997. In fiscal year 2001, the budget had 498 outside sections, constituting more than half the pages in the budget document. Since calendar year 1995, between 50 percent and 70 percent of all legislative matters passed were enacted through outside sections.

THE HIGHER EDUCATION REORGANIZATION ACT OF 1980

Perhaps the most Machiavellian use of an outside section was the 1980 reorganization of public higher education. At the time, the political leaders of Massachusetts found it extremely difficult to achieve consensus on this thorny issue. Governor Edward King wanted to create a central governing board but could not break through the stalemate of forces surrounding him. Part of the problem stemmed from the fact that the cluster of state colleges and public universities had been captured by the educational establishment and its powerful labor union, the Massachusetts Teachers Association. These groups wanted to maintain the status quo and staunchly resisted any attempt at restructuring.

Representative James Collins of Amherst, who chaired the House Education Committee, spearheaded the resistance. He saw the move to concentrate power in a state Board of Regents as a threat to the autonomy of the University of Massachusetts at Amherst, which was located in his district. This campus was perceived as the crown jewel in the system. Collins, a UMass/Amherst graduate, was very active in its alumni affairs. In the late 1970s he repeatedly had blocked several reorganization proposals. As the legislative session drew to a close, the lawmakers became deadlocked on the issue. This left them at an intractable impasse.

Under these circumstances, John Finnegan and Chester Atkins, who chaired their respective House and Senate Ways and Means committees, pushed through legislation by outside budget section. They cut the deal in conference committee. There was no floor debate and no opportunity for amending the legislation. The educators were denied any input and were completely shut out. By resorting to these tactics, Finnegan and Atkins outmaneuvered Collins and got the law passed.[25] It was a perfect power play. Governor King signed the bill because it provided a reasonable solution to a vexing problem. Obviously, Collins and the teachers' union were miffed. They realized that they had been outwitted. But Collins and his supporters got even. After a bitter and contentious fight, Collins became the first chancellor of the Board of Regents—a perfect counter–power play.[26]

In state politics, as in other fields of endeavor, nothing succeeds like success. Chester Atkins perfected this backdoor budgetary strategy, which had been invented by his predecessor James Kelly. Indeed, Atkins elevated it to an art form. His successor, Senator Patricia McGovern, simply picked up where he left off. In fact, she used the backdoor maneuver as much as, if not more than, Atkins did. Such political behavior is not hard to explain. The use of outside sections has become an easy, seductive, and almost painless way of legislating. At rock bottom, it is a legislative shortcut that evades the normal procedural safeguards that were designed to prevent hasty legislation.

THE SEDUCTIVENESS OF OUTSIDE SECTIONS

It is natural, then, to ask: For whom do outside sections work and why? In recent decades, governors and the legislative leadership of both political parties have utilized outside sections, at times to accomplish meaningful reforms. They have found the option a convenient way of dealing with complex policy issues without having to jump through all the legislative hoops.

But it is not just governors and legislative leaders who have pulled a fast one by means of outside sections. Rank-and-file legislators who find their bills bottled up in committee push their proposals as outside sections in order to force debate or obtain concessions from the leadership, such as a vow to bring up bills for consideration by a certain date.

"This is not an insignificant option in a highly controlled legislative environment," says former state representative John McDonough.[27] In 1994, state representative Mark Draisen played the outside section card to get his pharmacy freedom-of-choice bill onto the legislative agenda. Similarly, in 1996, John A. Stefanini, a liberal state representative from Framingham, followed the same route with his bill to expand the practice of optometrists. Says McDonough, "In a political environment where stalemate can easily prevent important policy options from getting due consideration, I think this option is preferable to inaction."[28]

Although the use of outside sections as political expedients began under Dukakis and King, their number rising from 99 in 1976 to 158 in 1989, it was during the administrations of Governors William Weld and Paul Cellucci that these budget riders began to stampede. After fifteen years of having a friendly Democrat in the corner office, the Democratic legislative leaders were suddenly forced to cope with the new reality of a Republican governor in the State House.

Ignoring the advice that Mary Newman had given him, Governor Weld saw fit to expand the practice of outside sections. During his first term, this mechanism became the major vehicle for lawmaking. The state budget included 381 outside sections in 1991; 391 in 1992; 597 in 1993; and 389 in 1994. The number soared in 1997 to an all-time high of 690 extraneous provisions. As outside sections increased, the number of bills that were enacted through the traditional process diminished accordingly. In the 1980s, the legislature often enacted more than 700 laws a year: 812 in 1985. In the 1990s, the number of legislative acts drifted down to around 400 per year, reaching a low of 239 in 1997, when the number of outside sections reached its peak. The budget, in effect, became the receptacle for many bills that could not get reported out of committee. Normally these bills would have died there for lack of political support.

The compliant (if not complicit) role played by Weld and Cellucci in this explosion of lawmaking by outside section can be explained in part by the dynamics of Beacon Hill in the 1990s. To get his policies and programs approved, Weld needed to play ball with the Democratic legislative leadership. Basically, he went along to get along. The same was true of Paul Cellucci when he succeeded Weld as governor in 1997. After Weld lost his veto-proof Senate in 1992, he held a much weaker hand politically. Nevertheless, he had been holding weekly meetings with Speaker Charles Flaherty and Senate president William Bulger. There was a spirit of collegiality among these three political leaders. They were reading from the same page, especially with regard to solving the fiscal crisis. This troika embraced wholeheartedly the concept of outside sections. It was a comfortable way for three people to run the state government. All of these factors contributed to the explosive growth of the tactic. The main problem resulted from the fact that "the devil is in the details." And the Boston media missed it completely.

LEGAL STATUS OF OUTSIDE SECTIONS

There have been many gubernatorial vetoes of appropriation items in the years since 1975. Several times the legislature has turned to the Supreme Judicial Court, questioning the validity of these vetoes on the grounds that the governor may not veto separable provisions inserted by the legislature without rejecting the entire budget.

The first of the SJC opinions was handed down in September 1981. This opinion makes clear the court's support of the governor's role with respect to the budget. The "governor's veto" case gave the SJC the opportunity to rule on the constitutionality of outside sections. Following its tradition of strict interpretation, however, it declined to do so.[29] Instead, the court merely reinterpreted its earlier definition of "item." In 1936 the SJC had defined items as "separable fiscal units" and "appropriations of sums of money."[30] It specifically held that "words or phrases are not items or parts of items." Yet, in 1981, the SJC concluded that, to preserve the balance of powers established in Article 63 as well as the separation of powers, the governor's veto power had to extend to separable provisions contained in a general appropriations bill.[31]

In its 1981 decision, the SJC could have stood by its earlier definition of "item" and preserved separation of powers by holding that only items and legitimate conditions attached to the appropriated funds could be included in appropriation bills and vetoed by the governor. It chose not to do so. Nevertheless, it specifically left open the issue of the appropriateness of outside sections, stating, "We need not and do not answer the question whether such separable provisions may properly be included in a budget bill in the first instance." This question had previously been reserved by the SJC.[32]

Governor Edward King had been advised to ask for an opinion from the SJC regarding the legislature's use of his budget as a vehicle for extraneous legislation, but he chose instead to veto sections that he disapproved of, since he thought that many of the other sections were desirable. Presumably this was the same kind of reasoning that led Governor Dukakis to ignore the strictures of Article 63 in 1975.

Curiously enough, the legislature passed a law in 1981 that declared its intent with regard to the improper use of outside sections. This statute,

Chapter 29, section 71, of the Massachusetts General Laws, reads as follows: "A law making appropriations for expenses of the commonwealth shall not contain provisions on any other subject matter. As used in this section, expenses of the commonwealth shall include expenses of the executive, legislative and judicial departments, interest, payments on the public debt, local aid, and other items of expense authorized or required by existing laws." Unfortunately, since its passage in 1981, section 7L had been routinely ignored by the legislature. While the law still remains on the statute books, it merely serves as a paper tiger.

Two years later the SJC cut the legislators some slack. On December 14, 1983, it handed down a decision that dealt with an initiative petition that sought to change the internal rules of the two branches of the legislature. Here the high court was unequivocal. In *Paisner v. Attorney General*, it ruled that "the power to determine their own rules of proceedings is exclusively granted to the Senate and the House respectively."[33] In other words, the SJC recognized that both branches have a constitutional right to determine their own rules, and those rules cannot be changed externally by initiative petition.

In 1987 the SJC found statutes like section 7L to be unenforceable on the grounds that a legislature cannot bind itself or a future legislature simply by passing a law. In the legal case of *Massachusetts Coalition for the Homeless v. Secretary of Human Services*, the high court ruled that this statute "appears to be an impermissible attempt by one legislature to dictate to subsequent ones the way in which constitutionally permissible legislative processes may work." It further noted that section 7L "does not have the force of a constitutional provision restricting particular provisions in a budget, such as exist in some states."[34] Although the SJC's comparison of section 7L with constitutional provisions of other states was dictum, it would seem to indicate that the court did not see a similar prohibition in the Massachusetts constitution.

MASS PIRG LAWSUIT FIZZLES

A large number of public policy questions are brought to the courts by organized interest groups. When it appears to their advantage, interest groups often function as a route for energizing judicial power. Groups whose leaders feel that their interests are being inadequately protected or threatened by other branches of government are very apt to explore avenues of access to the judicial process. In such a situation the group leaders may proceed to institute a test case. If a potential litigant wishes to invoke judicial power, it must also have "standing to sue."

For years, good-government reformers had been searching for a test case.

On July 21, 1993, the Massachusetts Student Public Interest Research Group (Mass PIRG) filed suit in the state's highest court charging that state policymakers had violated the state constitution when they passed a budget rider stripping Mass PIRG of a controversial funding device. This outside section wiped out the group's ability to levy certain fees (known as a negative check-off) on student tuition bills at the twenty-nine state colleges and public university campuses. The distinction between the process (the outside section) and the substance (the negative check-off) was quickly lost by the media. But the issue raised by the Mass PIRG case was not the substance or the desirability of the eliminated provision. Rather, it was the constitutionality of making general law by outside section.[35] In this context, the Mass PIRG challenge seemed a perfect test case.

Given its long-standing opposition to outside budget sections, the Massachusetts Taxpayers Foundation joined in support and filed an amicus curiae brief. Ironically, Mass PIRG had been a thorn in the side of the business community for years, costing companies millions of dollars in fighting what they considered its ill-advised initiative petitions. The business community viewed the negative check-off as bad policy, however, and had actively opposed it.[36] In this particular instance, politics made for strange bedfellows.

The test case was initially heard by a single justice of the Supreme Judicial Court, who then remanded it to superior court. At this juncture, the Mass PIRG attorneys decided to pursue a two-pronged strategy. While continuing to litigate their case in court, they also obtained permission from Attorney General Scott Harshbarger to separate the outside budget section and craft its repeal as a public referendum.[37] They wanted the people to decide the issue, not the legislature. This double-pronged approach removed the immediate legal burden from the courts. After the Mass PIRG organizers had collected the required number of signatures, their question appeared on the ballot the following fall. This referendum, which repealed the outside section, was approved by the voters in November 1994. Consequently, the legal challenge was rendered moot. The superior court judge, who had waited to find out the results of the election, dismissed the case. Regrettably, the constitutional issue was never adjudicated. It was a missed opportunity, but Mass PIRG seemed satisfied with the outcome.[38] It had accomplished what it set out to achieve.

In November 1993, while the Mass PIRG case was pending in court, Attorney General Harshbarger revealed his conflicted role: "This recurring issue needs to be resolved, and while it is my duty to defend the constitutionality of outside sections, I have cooperated and will continue to cooperate with the plaintiffs in various cases raising the issue in order to secure that resolution from the Supreme Judicial Court."[39] Other legal experts were doubtful that such resolution would occur. Clearly, the SJC had already indicated in *Paisner v. Attorney General* that it was reluctant to prescribe internal procedures that other branches must follow. More than this, the high court had declared such internal rules to be beyond judicial scrutiny.

A NEW SECRETARY FOR ADMINISTRATION AND FINANCE

In spring 2000, Stephen P. Crosby joined the Cellucci administration as a new cabinet member, replacing the cerebral Andrew Natsios as secretary for administration and finance. Natsios had been reassigned by Governor Cellucci to manage the Big Dig project and to deal with the cost overrun fiasco. Earlier Natsios had established a research and development unit within his department. Although Crosby had worked in the private sector for many years, he was new to state government. He came aboard with a fresh outlook, but he soon found himself mired in a mountain of bureaucratic red tape and baffled by the byzantine methods of managing the state. Worse yet, he was shocked to discover a plethora of new laws attached to the state budget, which had been passed under the pressure of a fiscal year already begun.

On August 26, Crosby held a press conference to rail against the abuse of outside sections. "Although the legislature is not solely to blame for the proliferation of the budget attachments, I think it is time for the insane system to be halted," he declared. "What I see is a process that is totally screwed up. We just don't know what's in these outside sections. It's a lousy way to make public policy."[40] The new cabinet secretary further noted that the public had little or no chance to influence policy. He had just witnessed the covert way in which the special education law had been changed. But more about that episode in a moment.

Crosby's outburst hit a raw nerve that rankled Senate president Thomas Birmingham, who reacted with a spirited defense of lawmaking by outside sections. "I've never heard this from any secretary of administration and finance before," Birmingham said. "They at least claim to understand the budget. This notion that they [the legislators] only have 10 days, and they have a $21 billion budget that they've never been familiar with before; this excuse is an awful one."[41] Birmingham's staff pointed out that 391 of the 498 outside sections that were approved in fiscal year 2001 were identical to those submitted by the governor and the legislature in the spring. In fact, they claimed that 150 of them had originated in the governor's office.

An unrepentant Crosby fired back, saying that he was less interested in assigning blame than in devising a new system that allowed for more careful consideration and greater public involvement in fashioning those measures that become law. This statement reflected his intent to reduce the number of outside sections. Crosby then asked his research and development unit to prepare a policy brief on the issue.

REVAMPING THE SPECIAL EDUCATION LAW

Almost simultaneously, efforts were under way to change the special education law. Three decades earlier, Massachusetts had passed one of the most progressive special education laws in the country. When it was originally enacted by the legislature in 1974, the program was widely considered to be the most generous in the nation. It required local school districts to provide the "maximum feasible benefit" for their disabled students. This law had proved costly to administer, and the financially strapped school districts were now feeling the pinch. With cities and towns having to pare down their budgets in lean economic times, the future funding of the special-ed law appeared in doubt. Despite questions about the educational value of these efforts, the price tag for the program had mushroomed. As a result, there was a move afoot in the legislature to limit the level of services provided for children with disabilities. Under the rationale of fiscal responsibility, House members, at the behest and arm-twisting of Speaker Finneran, wanted to substitute the less generous federal standard for the state standard currently in place.

A study released at the State House in early March 2000 revealed that tightening the rules of eligibility would mean that some 30,000 of the state's 165,000 special-ed students would no longer qualify. This would result in a savings estimated at $157 million. The study also found that if the federal standard was used instead of the state one, it would save another $8 million to $36 million.[42] Most states had opted for the federal standard.

Although the debate in the legislature focused mainly on eligibility criteria, the intent to lower the standard became abundantly clear. This raised a cry from those parents whose children would be adversely affected. Hundreds of special education advocates descended en masse on the State House in an effort to persuade lawmakers to enhance, not decrease, programs for children. This charge was led by the pro football quarterback Doug Flutie, a resident of Natick, whose young son was autistic. He told the assembled crowd, "In the world of special education, we know no limits, we are going to push for what's right for our children."[43]

Against this backdrop, the legislature dragged its feet and engaged in delaying tactics until mid-July, when the budget was being finalized. With the clock winding down on the legislative session, the lawmakers found themselves deadlocked. Advocates for the disabled warned that the legislature's attempt at narrowing standards would have dire consequences for deaf, autistic, and mentally retarded children. This highly emotional and protracted battle had drawn children in wheelchairs to the State House and brought one legislator to tears. In the end, the proponents opted for an outside section to break the stalemate, and it was hastily approved. Beginning in January 2002, Massachusetts school districts would no longer be required to follow the "maximum benefit" rule.[44]

AGITATION FOR REFORM

The sharp rise in outside sections, along with other failings of the legislature, spawned a movement for reform. One incident that occurred during the 2000 budget debate was particularly noteworthy. On April 17 the House held a raucous late-night budget session. Some members, who apparently had been drinking earlier in the evening, chanted "toga, toga, toga," while others slept off their inebriation and had surrogates cast votes for them. As word of this unsavory episode leaked out, the media lambasted the lawmakers for their boorish behavior and likened their highjinks to those displayed in the movie *Animal House*. Embarrassed by the negative publicity, Speaker Finneran sought to contain the political damage.[45]

Secretary Crosby's outburst against outside sections should have shocked no one familiar with the recent proliferation of these budget tack-ons. More surprising, though, was the push to limit their use which his remarks inspired. Agitation for reform from outside the State House came from advocacy groups such as Common Cause, Mass PIRG, Citizens for Limited Taxation, and the League of Women Voters. Although these groups differ greatly on policy issues, they fundamentally agree that the budget is not the place to rewrite laws.[46]

On the evening of January 17, 2001, Governor Cellucci, in delivering his State of the State address at Mechanics' Hall in Worcester, announced his intentions to reduce the number of outside sections. The budget submitted by the governor included just forty-one outside sections, and the one proposed by the House Committee on Ways and Means contained only thirty-seven. The number of outside sections subsequently mounted as the budget debate in the House and the Senate wore on, but, as of this writing, it seemed likely that there would be fewer extraneous provisions in the fiscal 2002 appropriations law than in any other budget in recent memory. Before leaving office to become U.S. ambassador to Canada, Cellucci filed legislation to amend, clarify, and strengthen the existing legislation restricting the use of outside sections.

Still, ridding the budget of these pesky riders is more difficult than it would appear. That is because, apart from the budget, lawmaking in Massachusetts has practically ground to a halt. As a result, the budget debate— such as it is—has become a substitute for democratic deliberation all session long. Weaning lawmakers from outside sections will be difficult because the budget has turned into the only viable vehicle for all manner of legislative action. And such reform will be no more than cosmetic unless the legislature finds a way to move contentious legislation toward resolution through a process of democratic deliberation, rather than by short-circuiting debate under the pressure of budget writing.

Useful or not, outside sections of the budget have become the crutch of a crippled legislature. Despite the inclusion of some important outside sections each year that are related to the budget, there remain far more outside sections that have no place in the budget document. The reduction of outside sections will contribute to preserving public confidence in the integrity of the legislative process.

It is time for policymakers in Massachusetts to admit that, whether they realize it or not, they have paid a heavy price for outside sections. That price is a crisis of legislative deliberation. In the words of a *Boston Globe* Spotlight report: "Genuine debate on public policy is rare. Roll-call votes are sharply diminishing. Deals cut in secret are quickly rubber-stamped. The committee system, especially in the House, has atrophied. Floor action is infrequent and pro forma. The work product is unremarkable. Dissent is simply not tolerated. Rank-and-file members have seemingly surrendered. And voters have tuned out the legislature in breathtaking numbers."[47] This characterization occurred in the context of an investigation of special interest influence on Beacon Hill. But it could just as easily have described the conditions that make outside sections the legislature's lawmaking method of choice.

A healthy skepticism is warranted when one looks to the courts to resolve the problem. Those who hold power are usually unwilling to allow those they consider to be rivals for power to sit in judgment on their prerogatives. As we have seen, judges are not about to tamper with the internal rules of a coordinate branch of state government. They do not want to touch what amounts to the "third rail" of state politics. Besides, the legislature could always retaliate, as it did when it required the mandatory retirement of judges at age seventy. This leaves the problem essentially in the hands of the governor and the legislature.

To be sure, it is important to address the potential for reform, however remote. The package of legislative changes recommended in January 2001 by the Coalition for Legislative Reform is a positive step in the right direction. To his credit, Governor Cellucci made a good faith effort at reducing outside sections and also proposed amending the existing statute (Chapter 29, section 7L) to clarify the situation. In the final analysis, only legislative self-discipline can put an end to the abuse. That is the crux of the problem. As a policy brief written by the research unit in Stephen Crosby's office notes: "Ultimately, the problem of outside sections is not amenable to a solution imposed on the legislature. Rather, the ability to solve this problem rests with the House and the Senate themselves—through their own internal rulemaking and how they choose to function. The proposed amendment to the Massachusetts General Laws will provide the legislature with an opportunity to clarify the intent of the existing law."[48]

More is at stake here than merely the prestige of the General Court. What is at stake is nothing less than whether the legislature is capable of democratic deliberation. Getting rid of outside sections accomplishes nothing unless the legislature figures out how to take contentious legislation to completion through the conventional process of hearings, committee consideration, floor debate, bicameral compromise, and gubernatorial signature.

Success, however, cannot be measured just in a falling outside section total. Ruling outside sections out of order could simply centralize power in the Speaker and Senate president—taking one more parliamentary maneuver out of the hands of the rank and file. "I would suggest," says one former legislator, "that the harm to citizens would be greater with the loss of this option than any imagined harm from the use of outside sections."[49]

What is needed here is a blueprint—and a demand—for legislative democracy. Stripped of its veneer, lawmaking by outside section is a betrayal of the very essence of democracy. The only way to end that betrayal is to make this fundamental institution of democratic government—the legislature—a democratic institution once again.

NOTES

1. UNDERSTANDING POWER IN MASSACHUSETTS

1. See Greater Boston Chamber of Commerce, "Leading Industries: Drivers of the Regional Economy" (January 2001).

2. See Barry Bluestone and Mary Huff Stevenson, *The Boston Renaissance* (New York: Russell Sage Foundation, 2000).

3. Cindy Rodriguez, "Census Shows a Boston Still Divided," *Boston Globe*, April 20, 2001.

4. David McCullough, *John Adams* (New York: Simon and Schuster, 2001), 220.

5. David Truman, *The Governmental Process, Political Interests, and Public Opinion* (New York: Alfred Knopf, 1951), 33.

6. Robert Dahl, *Who Governs?* (New Haven: Yale University Press, 1961), 192–99.

7. Rick Klein, "Swift Has Spotlight Work in Her Favor," *Boston Globe*, October 7, 2001.

8. Harold Lasswell, *Politics* (New York: McGraw-Hill, 1936), 1.

9. John W. Kingdon, *Agenda, Alternatives, and Public Policy* (Boston: Little, Brown, 1984), 1.

10. In "Quotes of Note," *Boston Globe*, May 27, 2000.

11. Glen Johnson, "Where Moakley Sits, Void Is Seen," *Boston Globe*, February 14, 2001.

12. For a definitive biography of O'Neill, see John A. Farrell, *Tip O'Neill and the Democratic Century* (Boston: Little Brown, 2001).

13. Ibid., 123.

14. Ibid., 541.

15. Adam Clymer, *Edward M. Kennedy: A Biography* (New York: William Morrow, 1999).

16. Joanna Weiss, "No Laughing Matter," *Boston Globe*, June 18, 2000.

17. Quoted in Jack Beatty, *The Rascal King: The Life and Timer of James Michael Curley*, 1874–1958 (Reading, Mass.: Addison-Wesley, 1992), 55–56.

18. Weiss, "No Laughing Matter."

19. Brian C. Mooney, "The New New Yorker," *Boston Globe*, January 28, 2001.

20. In a letter written to David Wilson, a columnist for the *Boston Globe*, dated February 20, 1987, Frank Sargent told the following story: "A few weeks before I became governor, [former governor Foster Furcolo] came out to my house for an evening and told me of mistakes that he made, that I could avoid by knowing them,—things that no one would realize, or even understand, without having sat in the governor's chair. He was hilariously funny telling some of these stories on himself. . . . [H]e's got a great sense of humor and enjoys laughing at himself (as I think I do also). He and I both believe that you should take your job seriously, but not yourself. This is something totally alien to John Volpe or Michael Dukakis!"

21. Thomas C. Palmer Jr., "Cerasoli Charges Big Dig Coverup," *Boston Globe*, March 21, 2001.

22. Beatty, *The Rascal King*, 152.

23. Ibid., 45.

24. Scot Lehigh, "Bulger 101: A Guide to the BMOC," *Boston Globe*, November 26, 1995.

25. Beatty, *The Rascal King*, 52.

26. Daniel J. Elazar, *American Federalism: A View from the States* (New York: Crowell, 1972), 79. See also Gabriel A. Almand and Sidney Verba, *The Civic Culture* (Boston: Little Brown, 1963).

27. Jerome M. Mileur, "Party Politics in the Bay State," in *Party Politics in the New England States*, ed. Jerome M. Mileur (Amherst: Polity Publications, 1997), 89.

28. Edgar Litt, *The Political Cultures of Massachusetts* (Cambridge: MIT Press, 1965), 64.

29. Ibid., 201.

30. Mileur, "Party Politics in the Bay State," 74, 88–89.

31. For a female perspective on women participating in Massachusetts politics, see Betty Taymor, *Running against the Tide* (Boston: Northeastern University Press, 2000).

32. See Thomas J. Whalen, *Kennedy versus Lodge: The 1952 Massachusetts Senate Race* (Boston: Northeastern University Press, 2000).

33. Kathleen Burge, "Quiet Leader Steps Down," *Boston Globe*, December 16, 2000.

34. Michael Rezendes, "Mass. High Court Gains Female Majority," *Boston Globe*, July 27, 2000. See also Lauren Stiller Rikleen, "I'm Learning on the Job as Fast as I Can," *Boston Globe*, December 10, 2000.

35. Jonathan D. Salant, "Cost of Congressional Seat Keeps Going Up," *Boston Globe*, December 27, 2000.

36. Duane Lockard, *New England State Politics* (Princeton: Princeton University Press, 1959), 159.

37. For a good analysis of the development of the office, see Victoria Schuck, "The Massachusetts Governorship: Hamstrung by History?" in *The Role of the Governor in Massachusetts*, ed. Robert R. Robbins (Medford, Mass.: Tufts University, 1961), 11–75. See also Leslie Lipson, *The American Governor from Figurehead to Leader* (Chicago: University of Chicago Press, 1939).

38. Quoted in Cornelius Dalton et. al., *Leading the Way* (Boston: Office of Secretary of State, 1984), 145.

39. Ibid., 145.

40. Ibid., 147.

41. Thomas H. O'Connor, *The Boston Irish: A Political History* (Boston: Northeastern University Press, 1995), 109.

42. See Duane Lockard, *The New Jersey Governor: A Study in Political Power* (Princeton: D. Van Nostrand Company, 1964), 9. I should explain here that the word "modern" is not meant to disparage earlier governors. The word is a convenient way of summing up the newly available resources of leadership that several governors have exploited since the early twentieth century.

43. For a summary of the constitutional amendments resulting from the 1917–19 convention, see Schuck, "The Massachusetts Governorship," 52–62.

44. Quoted in Robert Sobel, *Coolidge: An American Enigma* (Washington, D.C.: Regnery Publishing, 1998), 119.

45. J. Joseph Huthmacher, *Massachusetts People and Politics, 1919–1933* (Cambridge: Harvard University Press, 1959), 222–24.

46. Beatty, *Rascal King*, 350.

47. Garrison Nelson, "Escaping Massachusetts' Gubernatorial Ceiling," *Boston Globe*, February 25, 2001.

48. Litt, *The Political Cultures of Massachusetts*, 43.

49. John P. Mallan and George Blackwood, "The Tax That Beat a Governor: The Ordeal of Massachusetts," in *The Uses of Power*, ed. Alan F. Westin (New York: Harcourt, Brace and World, 1962), 289.

50. For a detailed account of the sales tax battle, see ibid.

51. See Thomas H. Eliot, *Reorganizing the Massachusetts Department of Conservation*, rev. ed., I.C.P. Case Series no. 14 (1960).

52. For an interesting account of Peabody's 1960 gubernatorial campaign, see Murray B. Levin and George Blackwood, *The Compleat Politician: Political Strategy in Massachusetts* (Indianapolis: Bobbs-Merrill, 1962), 83–103, 281–99.

53. Litt, *The Political Cultures of Massachusetts*, 50.

54. Michael Knight, "King Finds Governorship Is No Tea Party," *New York Times*, November 8, 1979.

55. Ibid.

56. Charles Kenney and Robert L. Turner, *Dukakis: An American Odyssey* (Boston: Houghton Mifflin, 1988), 185.

57. Morris Fiorina, *Divided Government* (Boston: Allyn and Bacon, 1996), 66.

58. Frank Phillips, "Rift Seen Growing in State GOP," *Boston Globe*, June 9, 2000.

59. Lockard, *New England State Politics*, 148.

60. Litt, *The Political Cultures of Massachusetts*, 156.

61. Dalton et. al., *Leading the Way*, 145.

62. Ibid., 141–42.

63. Quoted in David Nyhan, "Rep. Haley's Upright Exit," *Boston Globe*, December 22, 2000.

64. See League of Women Voters, *Massachusetts State Government: A Citizen's Handbook* (Cambridge: Harvard University Press, 1956), 91–92.

65. David Armstrong, "Civil Service Panel Criticized as Unprofessional, Pro-union," *Boston Globe*, May 22, 2000.

66. Ibid.

67. Brian C. Mooney, "Agencies Have Grown, Quickly," *Boston Globe*, September 30, 2000.

2. THE SARGENT GOVERNORSHIP

1. For governors who presided in the Bay State during this period, see Robert C. Wood and Bradbury Seasholes, "The Image of the Governor as a Public and Party Leader," in *The Role of the Governor in Massachusetts*, ed. Robert R. Robbins (Medford: Tufts University, 1961), 77–100. The authors interviewed five living former governors: Channing Cox, Leverett Saltonstall, Robert Bradford, Christian Herter, and Foster Furcolo. Their terms in office began in 1921, 1939, 1947, 1953, and 1957, respectively.

2. Interview with William Sargent, December 22, 1998.

3. Quoted in Frank Phillips, "Ex-foes Recall a Man of Charm, Wit," *Boston Globe*, October 23, 1998.

4. Quoted in Jessie F. Sargent, *The Governor's Wife* (Boston: Marlborough House, 1973), vii.

5. John Powers, "Sargent at Ease," *Boston Globe*, October 1, 1998.

6. Quoted in Robert H. Boyle, "Maverick Head of an Odd State," *Sports Illustrated*, April 22, 1974, 51.

7. Sargent, *The Governor's Wife*, 48, 59.

8. William Sargent interview.

9. Douglas Foy told this story at Frank Sargent's memorial service, which was held at Saint Andrew's Episcopal Church in Wellesley, Massachusetts, November 4, 1998.

10. Jay Williams, letter to the editor, *Boston Globe*, November 1, 1998.

11. Interview with Richard Manley, November 5, 1998.

12. Quoted in Boyle, "Maverick Head of an Odd State," 58.

13. Quoted in Powers, "Sargent at Ease."

14. William Sargent interview.

15. Interview with Alan Altshuler, December 10, 1998.

16. Alan Altshuler, "Sarge in Charge," *Journal of State Government*, 63 (July–August 1989): 156.

17. Martha Weinberg, *Managing the State* (Cambridge: MIT Press, 1977), 54–55. This excellent study treats Sargent's governorship in detail; I have relied on it heavily in my treatment of Sargent here. I disagree with Weinberg, however, when it comes to the Department of Mental Health. Sargent exerted significant executive control over DMH, especially with regard to deinstitutionalization and the closing of three state mental hospitals.

18. Boyle, "Maverick Head of an Odd State," 50–58.

19. See Charles Kenny and Robert L. Turner, *Dukakis: An American Odyssey* (Boston: Houghton Mifflin, 1988), 70.

20. Quoted in Powers, "Sargent at Ease."

21. Ken Hartnett, "The Compleat Political Angler—He Lures Voters with Warmth," *Boston Globe*, November 3, 1974.

22. David Nyhan, "An Able Leader and a Great Guy," *Boston Globe*, October 23, 1998.

23. Quoted in Hartnett, "The Compleat Political Angler."

24. Quoted in Powers, "Sargent at Ease."

25. Interview with Al Kramer, December 8, 1998. Kramer contends that Governor Sargent sent in troops more as a defensive measure than as an offensive one.

26. William Sargent interview.

27. Quoted in Boyle, "Maverick Head of an Odd State," 52.

28. Weinberg, *Managing the State*, 46.

29. Quoted in John Powers, "Francis W. Sargent, Ex-governor, Dies," Boston Globe, October 23, 1998.

30. For a useful if highly partisan account of the highway controversy up to 1970, see Alan Lupo et al., *Rites of Way* (Boston: Little, Brown, 1971). This study chronicles the dispute up to the point of the moratorium and leaves off with the question of what should be done next.

31. Altshuler, "Sarge in Charge," 160.

32. Lupo et al., *Rites of Way*, 106.

33. For a good analysis of the BTPR, see Ralph Gakenheimer, *Transportation Planning as Response to Controversy* (Cambridge: MIT Press, 1976).

34. See David Luberoff et al., *Mega-Project: A Political History of Boston's Multibillion-Dollar Artery/Tunnel Project* (Cambridge: Harvard University, 1993), 14.

35. Letter to author from Louis Menand, April 21, 2000.

36. For a detailed account of Sargent's opposition to the Vietnam War and his rationale for supporting the so-called Shea bill, see Francis W. Sargent, "The Issue Is Joined," in John M. Wells, *The People vs. Presidential War* (New York: Dunellen, 1970), 133–35.

37. Al Kramer interview.

38. See the eulogy given by Al Kramer at Sargent's memorial service.

39. See Report of the Modernization Systems Unit, "Management Systems for Massachusetts," June 1971; and Robert Casselman, "State Reorganization: Hoax or Hope," *Boston Globe*, January 14, 1973.

40. Weinberg, *Managing the State*, 141.

41. Robert C. Wood, *Suburbia* (Boston: Houghton Mifflin, 1958), 246–52.

42. Interview with Robert C. Wood, November 18, 1998.

43. For a more detailed account of this episode, see chapter 3 and Richard A. Hogarty, "Downsizing the Massachusetts Mental Health System," *New England Journal of Public Policy* 12, no. 1 (Fall–Winter 1996): 26–27.

44. This account is based primarily on the case study prepared by Stephanie Gould, "Jerome Miller and the Department of Youth Services," pts. A and B (Cambridge: Harvard University, 1976).

45. Michael Jonas, "Outgrowing Juvenile Justice," *Common Wealth* (Winter 2001): 65.

46. See the editorial "Politics and Children," *Boston Globe*, April 12, 1972.

47. The following account relies heavily on a case study prepared by Colin S. Diver, "Park Plaza," Parts A, B, and C (Cambridge: Harvard University, 1975).

48. This discussion follows closely the case study prepared by Alan Konefsky et al., "Massachusetts Department of Correction," pts. 1, 2, and 3 (Cambridge: Harvard University, 1977).

49. Ibid., pt. 2, 4.

50. Ibid., 19.

51. Ibid., pt. 3, 9.

52. Altshuler, "Sarge in Charge," 158.

53. Ibid., 159.

54. Powers, "Francis W. Sargent, Ex-governor, Dies."

55. Letter to author from Kevin Harrington, January 4, 1999.

56. Editorial, *Boston Globe*, October 23, 1998.

3. TRANSFORMING THE MENTAL HEALTH CARE SYSTEM

1. Clea Simon, "Who Has the Right?" *Boston Globe*, April 21, 1996.

2. See Joseph S. Slavet et al., "After the Miracle: A History and Analysis of the Massachusetts Fiscal Crisis," University of Massachusetts at Boston, May 1990.

3. Report of the Governor's Special Commission on Consolidation of Health and Human Services Institutional Facilities, "Actions for Quality Care," June 1991, i.

4. Interview with Carol Upshur, a member of the governor's special commission, July 19, 1995.

5. Report of the Governor's Special Commission, "Actions for Quality Care," iii.

6. Interview with Bernard Carey, September 22, 1995. See also working paper prepared for the Massachusetts Association for Mental Health by Joseph Finnegan and Danna Mauch, "Restructuring the Delivery of Human Services: Focus on Department of Mental Health," November 1990.

7. Interview with Danna Mauch, November 16, 1995.

8. See Eileen Elias and Marc Navon, "Implementing Managed Care in a State Mental Health Authority," mimeographed.

9. For a detailed discussion and analysis of this opposition, see John Laidler, "Storm Calms over Danvers Closure," *Boston Globe*, January 15, 1995. See also Mark Leccese, "Too Much, Too Fast," *Boston Tab*, August 2, 1994.

10. Quoted in Leccese, "Too Much, Too Fast."

11. *Boston Globe*, September 19, 1993. This poll, conducted by KRC Communications Research, which surveyed four hundred registered voters on September 9–10, had a margin of error of 5 percentage points.

12. Letter from mental health commissioner Eileen Elias to DMH central office staff, June 24, 1991.

13. Report of the Senate Committee on Post Audit and Oversight, "A Review of DMH Policy Planning and Implementation during the Closing of Northampton State Hospital," January 1993.

14. Report of Governor's Special Commission, "Actions for Quality Care," 9, 58.

15. Interview with Charles Baker, April 19, 1995.

16. Report of the Governor's Special Commission, "Actions for Quality Care," 58.

17. Here I follow closely the argument developed in Robert C. Wood, *Remedial Law: When Courts Become Administrators* (Amherst: University of Massachusetts Press, 1990), 13–14.

18. See B. Shaw, "Knee Deep in the Big Muddy: A Study of Escalating Commitment to a Chosen Course of Action," *Organization Behavior and Human Performance* 16 (1976): 27–44.

19. Interview with Philip W. Johnston, April 7, 1995.

20. For a detailed criticism of the Weld administration's mental health initiative, see Leccese, "Too Much, Too Fast"; see also the newsletter of AMI of Massachusetts, no. 38 (Summer–Fall 1991): 5.

21. Interview, May 18, 1995, with Katherine Olberg Sternbach, who was employed at DMH from 1979 to 1990 and served as assistant commissioner of mental health under Henry Tomes.

22. Interview with Doris Carreiro, February 16, 1995.

23. Wood, *Remedial Law*, 16.

24. See "Pushing Privatization Too Far," *Boston Globe* editorial, January 27, 1995.

25. For an excellent history of Worcester State Hospital, see Joseph P. Morrissey et al., *The Enduring Asylum: Cycles of Institutional Reform at Worcester State Hospital* (New York: Grune and Stratton, 1980).

26. For an insightful account of the harsh realities and religious bigotry that confronted the Irish in Boston, see Thomas H. O'Connor, *The Boston Irish: A Political History* (Boston: Northeastern University Press, 1995); see also Oscar Handlin, *Boston's Immigrants* (New York: Atheneum, 1970).

27. David J. Rothman, *The Discovery of the Asylum: Social Order and Disorder in the New Republic* (Boston: Little Brown, 1971), 132.

28. Ruth B. Caplan, *Psychiatry and the Community in Nineteenth-Century America* (New York: Basic Books, 1971), 180.

29. J. Michael Moore, *The Life and Death of Northampton State Hospital* (Northampton, Mass.: Historic Society of Northampton, 1995), 3.

30. David Mechanic, *Mental Health and Society Policy* (Englewood Cliffs, N.J.: Prentice-Hall, 1969), 54.

31. Gerald N. Grob, *Mental Illness and American Society, 1875–1940* (Princeton: Princeton University Press, 1983), 74–75.

32. John R. Sutton, "The Political Economy of Madness: The Expansion of the Asylum in Progressive America," *American Sociological Review* 56 (1991): 669. My interpretation relies heavily on Sutton's account.

33. For a chronological evolution of the state mental health care system, see Lizabeth Watson, "Guide to Social Welfare Records," Massachusetts Archives, May 1991, 58–71.

34. John A. Farrell, *Tip O'Neill and the Democratic Century* (Boston: Little, Brown, 2001), 113.

35. Moore, *The Life and Death of Northampton State Hospital*, 12.

36. Watson, "Guide to Social Welfare Records," 23.

37. Quoted in Farrell, *Tip O'Neill and the Democratic Century*, 113.

38. Ibid., 114.

39. For a brief history of mental health services in Massachusetts, see "Comprehensive Plan to Improve Services for Chronically Mentally Ill Persons," vol. 1 (December 1985), 4–7. My interpretation of the development of mental health policy and programs relies substantially on this source.

40. See Paul Lerman, *Deinstitutionalization and the Welfare State* (New Brunswick, N.J.: Rutgers University Press, 1982), 99.

41. Interview with Hubie Jones, August 23, 1995. See also Report of the Task Force on Children Out of School, "Suffer the Children," Boston, 1972, 5–6. In addition, see Peter B. Edelman, "The Massachusetts Task Force Reports: Advocacy for Children," *Harvard Educational Review* (November 1973).

42. Martha W. Weinberg, *Managing the State* (Cambridge: MIT Press, 1977), 192.

43. Ibid., 193.

44. Ibid., 194.

45. Quoted ibid.

46. See Jean Dietz, "Worcester State Hospital Hardly the Worst," *Boston Globe*, February 21, 1985.

47. *Commonwealth v. Wiseman*, Mass. 251 (1969). The court order restricted the showing of the film "only to legislators, judges, lawyers, sociologists, social workers, doctors, psychiatrists, students in these or related fields, and organizations dealing with the social problems of custodial care and mental infirmity."

48. Statement by a former DMH employee who requested anonymity.

49. Interview with Joseph Finnegan, September 20, 1995.

50. Mauch interview.

51. Northampton Consent Decree, Civil Action 76-4423-F (ordered December 7, 1978).

52. Jean Dietz, "Mental Health Chief Defends Personnel," *Boston Globe*, February 19, 1982.

53. Report of the blue-ribbon Commission on the Future of Public Impatient Mental Health Service in Massachusetts, "Mental Health Crossroads," Boston, May 1981.

54. Interview with Catherine Dunham, December 1, 1995.

55. Interview with Rae O'Leary, December 28, 1994.

56. Interview with Barbara Hoffman, August 21, 1995.

57. Laidler, "Storm Calms over Danvers Closure."

58. See Robert L. Okin, "Testing the Limits of Deinstitutionalization," *Psychiatric Services* 46 (June 1995):569.

59. Quoted in Jean Dietz, "Requirements for a Mental Health Chief," *Boston Globe*, February 9, 1983.

60. Ibid.

61. Interview with James Callahan, October 2, 1995. See also Jean Dietz, "Mental Health Chief Fires 10," *Boston Globe*, November 11, 1983; and Ian Menzies, "Revamping Mental Health," *Boston Globe*, June 11, 1984.

62. Interview with Frank Karlon, August 28, 1995.

63. Joseph M. Harvey, "Patients Win Choice on Drugs," *Boston Globe*, November

30, 1983; see also Jean Dietz, "Bay State Ruling Provokes Debate," *Boston Globe*, December 4, 1983.

64. See "First Interim Report of the Special Senate Committee to Study the Impact of Deinstitutionalization of the Mental Health and Retardation Services in the Commonwealth of Massachusetts" (1984), 9.

65. Johnston interview.

66. Ibid.

67. See Michael S. Dukakis, "A Comprehensive Plan to Improve Services for Chronically Mentally Ill Persons," December 1985.

68. Jean Dietz, "Dukakis May Seek Millions for Mental Health Department," *Boston Globe*, December 3, 1985.

69. Governor Michael Dukakis, "Special Message on Mental Health," reprinted in "A Comprehensive Plan to Improve Services for Chronically Mentally Ill Persons," 2–3.

70. Quoted in Jean Dietz, "Reactions Varied on New Mental Health Plan," *Boston Globe*, December 20, 1985.

71. Johnston interview.

72. These data are from the annual reports for Metropolitan State Hospital for the years 1931 and 1932. The reports, which run consecutively until 1969, are available at the Massachusetts Archives.

73. Interview with John MacDougall, August 1, 1995.

74. Chris Black, "State Hospital Had No Water for 2 Days," *Boston Globe*, September 14, 1983.

75. Quoted in Jean Dietz, "Mass. Legislators Tour Troubled State Hospital," *Boston Globe*, April 5, 1984.

76. See Division of Capital Planning and Operations, "Metropolitan State Hospital Final Master Plan Report," vol. 1 (March 1989), 04.02.

77. Peter S. Canellos, "Alleged Sex Abuse of Patients Probed by Middlesex D.A.," *Boston Globe*, November 26, 1990; see also Beverly Ford, "DMH Probes Sex Charges at Met State," *Boston Herald*, April 12, 1990.

78. Sternbach interview.

79. Marylou Sudders memorandum to all staff, November 30, 1990.

80. O'Leary interview.

81. Rae A. O'Leary, Metro-West area director, "Metropolitan State Hospital Phase-Down Project October, 1990 through June, 1991," public document, photocopied, 1.

82. Carreiro interview.

83. O'Leary, "Metropolitan State Hospital Phase-Down Project," 2–3.

84. Interview with Brian Devin, October 26, 1995.

85. Memo from board of trustees to Met State Hospital employees, November 27, 1990.

86. Interview with Alan Greene, October 20, 1995.

87. Memo from Stephen L. Day to all area directors, November 26, 1990.

88. Interviews with Jeff McCue and Maryellen LaSala, January 5, 1995.

89. Memo from Rae O'Leary to Commissioner Eileen Elias, November 14, 1991.

90. Dunham interview.

91. Elias and Navon, "Implementing Managed Care in a State Mental Health Authority," 20.

92. Barbara A. Leadholm and Joan P. Kerzner, "Public Managed Care: Comprehensive Community Support in Massachusetts," *Administration and Policy in Mental Health* 22, no. 5 (May 1995): 551–52.

93. H. Stephen Leff et al., "Consumer Comparisons of Hospital and Community Care Resulting from Department of Mental Health Facility Consolidation: Results of a Follow-Up of Metropolitan State Hospital Consumers," University of Massachusetts, Boston, February 20, 1994.

94. Paul R. Benson, "The Impact of Department of Mental Health Facility Consolidation on Families," University of Massachusetts, Boston, February 20, 1994.

95. Robert A. Dorwart and Sherrie S. Epstein, *Privatization and Mental Health Care* (Westport, Conn.: Auburn House, 1993), 6.

96. Alison Bass, "DMH Sees Increase in Deaths," *Boston Globe*, June 11, 1995; see also Alison Bass, "Patient Deaths Trigger Inquiry," *Boston Globe*, June 13, 1995.

97. Charles D. Baker, "Facts Don't Justify Criticism of Human Services," letter to the editor, *Boston Globe*, June 16, 1995.

98. Michele R. McPhee, "Mental Health Officials Urged to Resign," *Boston Globe*, July 9, 1995.

99. Critical Incident Reporting Task Force, Report on Massachusetts, *Department of Mental Health Service Recipient Mortality, 1991–1993*, Cambridge, Mass., Evaluation Center at HSRI, January 26, 1996.

100. For an update of the reforms that have taken place since Commissioner Mary Lou Sudders took office, see David A. Rocheford, "Mental Health Care in Massachusetts," December 16, 1999. This report was published by the Massachusetts Health Policy Forum.

101. Richard A. Knox and Alice Dembner, "Trapped in Mental Ward," *Boston Globe*, June 4, 2000.

102. Alice Dembner, "Many Children Can't Get Mental Care," *Boston Globe*, April 10, 2001.

103. Quoted in Larry Tye, "Treatment Revolution," *Boston Globe*, April 17, 2001.

104. Ibid.

4. THE SEARCH FOR A CHANCELLOR OF HIGHER EDUCATION

1. Clifton R. Wharton Jr., "Autonomy in Academia: The State's Responsibility to Higher Education," Askwith Lecture, Harvard University, April 14, 1986.

2. For a perceptive analysis of such clashes, see John D. Millett, *Conflict in Higher Education* (San Francisco: Jossey-Bass, 1984), 216.

3. Judith Block McLaughlin and David Riesman, "The Shady Side of Sunshine," *Teachers College Record* 87 (1986): 471.

4. Judith Block McLaughlin, "Plugging Search Committee Leaks," *ACB Reports* (May–June 1985): 24–30.

5. I interviewed the eleven members of the search committee whose names appear in the text, as well as Regents David Beaubien, Gerard Doherty, George Ellison,

Kathleen Harrington, and Edward Lashman, along with former chancellor James Collins, former state secretary of educational affairs Joseph M. Cronin, and Chancellor Franklyn Jenifer. Except where otherwise noted, most of the substantive material for this case study was derived from these interviews. For the record, it should be pointed out that Regent John Fox declined to be interviewed.

6. Robert Wood, "The Public-Private Forum," *New England Journal of Public Policy* 3 (1987): 8.

7. Interview with Joseph Cronin, October 22, 1987. See also Joseph M. Cronin, "Higher Education Policy-Making in Massachusetts," paper prepared for the Alden Seminars, U Mass, April 1987, 6. For a detailed analysis of the weaknesses of the Board of Higher Education, see John A. Stevens, "A Process for Determining the Appropriate Role for the Massachusetts State College System," unpublished qualifying paper, Harvard University, April 1980.

8. Millett, *Conflict in Higher Education*, 104.

9. Cronin, "Higher Education Policy-Making," 7.

10. Board of Regents, "The Massachusetts System of Public Higher Education," mimeographed, 1985, 1–13. See in particular Appendix B.

11. Interview with George Ellison, March 17, 1987.

12. Interviews with Kermit Morrissey, September 8, 1987, and Franklin Patterson, February 25, 1988.

13. Interview with David Beaubien, November 18, 1986.

14. Interview with Paul Ylvisaker, November 11, 1986.

15. Interview with Edward Sullivan, December 9, 1986.

16. Interviews with David Beaubien, November 18, 1986; Gerard Doherty, March 6, 1987; George Ellison, March 17, 1987; Kathleen Harrington, March 10, 1987; James Howell, February 2, 1987; David Knapp, November 26, 1986; Robert Lee, January 16, 1987; and Edward Sullivan, December 9, 1986.

17. Interviews with Mary Lou Anderson, November 25, 1986; Laura Clausen, December 11, 1986; Joyce King, January 27, 1987; Hassan Minor, November 20, 1986; Eileen Parise, December 4, 1986; and Paul Ylvisaker, November 11, 1986.

18. Interview with Hassan Minor, November 20, 1986.

19. Interview with Edward Lashman, May 12, 1988. A native of New Orleans, Lashman attended the University of North Carolina at Chapel Hill and Tulane University, but he never received a degree.

20. Interview with James Howell, February 2, 1987.

21. Steve Carwood, "Dukakis on Higher Education," *Boston Globe*, January 5, 1986.

22. Legislative history of H-5474 and H-5639 is taken from the computer printouts regarding these bills. Speaker Keverian explained his views on the chancellor search controversy at a public policy seminar, which he conducted in the legislative chamber on November 12, 1986 (videocassette). This seminar was sponsored by the John W. McCormack Institute of Public Affairs at UMass/Boston.

23. Letter from Paul Ylvisaker to David Beaubien, June 30, 1986.

24. Minutes of the Board of Regents meeting, February 11, 1986.

25. Interview with Gerard Doherty, March 6, 1987. See also Gerard Doherty, "The Case for Collins," *Boston Globe*, September 9, 1986.

26. Job description of the Massachusetts chancellorship as it appeared in the *Chronicle of Higher Education*, January 29 and February 5, 1986.

27. Board of Regents, "Preliminary Review of Candidates," mimeographed, April 17, 1986.

28. Memorandum from Board of Regents affirmative action officer Bruce Rose to chancellor search committee, April 17, 1986.

29. Interview with Robert Lee, January 15, 1987.

30. Interview with Paul Ylvisaker, November 11, 1986. See also minutes of the Board of Regents meeting, June 9, 1986.

31. Interview with Janet Eisner, December 5, 1986. See also letter from Janet Eisner to search committee, June 12, 1986.

32. Letters to Paul Ylvisaker from Kenneth Lemanski, March 11, 1986, and from Raymond Jordan, March 12, 1986. It should be noted that the letter from the Massachusetts Black Legislative Caucus was submitted three days prior to the March 15 application deadline and well before the candidacy of Franklyn Jenifer became known publicly.

33. Interview with James Howell, February 2, 1987.

34. *Boston Globe*, October 1, 1987.

35. Interview with David Knapp, November 26, 1986.

36. Interview with Franklyn Jenifer, September 3, 1987.

37. Board of Regents, "Candidates' Experience," mimeographed.

38. Board of Regents, "Actions Taken at Final Meeting of the Regents Chancellor Search Committee," June 19, 1986.

39. Interviews with Mary Lou Anderson, November 25, 1986, and Eileen Parise, December 4, 1986.

40. Interview with Joyce King, January 27, 1987.

41. Robert Kuttner, "The Backfires of the Massachusetts Miracle," *Boston Globe*, May 30, 1988.

42. Minutes of the Board of Regents meeting, July 1, 1986.

43. Paul Ylvisaker to Governor Michael Dukakis, July 1, 1986.

44. Janet Eisner to Governor Michael Dukakis, July 7, 1986.

45. Interview with Edward Lashman, May 12, 1988. See also Scot Lehigh, "Indelicato Matters: Dukakis's Untrusted Adviser Moves Up," *Boston Phoenix*, July 15, 1986; and A. A. Michelson, "Politics and Education," *Boston Globe*, July 12, 1986.

46. Interview with Kathleen Harrington, March 10, 1987.

47. Interview with Edward Lashman, May 12, 1988.

48. Quoted in David Nyhan, "Dukakis Takes Aim at Collins," *Boston Globe*, July 13, 1986.

49. Ibid.

50. See Richard Gaines and Michael Segal, *Dukakis and the Reform Impulse* (Boston: Quinlan Press, 1987), 209–18. Curiously, the authors of this adulatory political biography make no mention whatsoever of the Regents controversy. This is a serious omission in light of their emphasis on the traditional politics of the Irish regulars versus the new politics of the Dukakis reformers. The episode is likewise omitted in the biography by Charles Kenney and Robert L. Turner, *Dukakis: An American Odyssey* (Boston: Houghton Mifflin, 1988).

51. Interview with James Collins, February 11, 1987.

52. Scot Lehigh, "Politics," *Boston Phoenix*, August 12, 1986.

53. Bruce Mohl, "Collins Says He Won't Buckle under the Pressure" and "Accounts Differ in Ticket Exchange," *Boston Globe*, July 6 and 29, 1986.

54. Television transcript, "Education in Massachusetts: Opportunity for All," mimeographed, July 10, 1986.

55. Interview with Kathleen Harrington, March 10, 1987.

56. Attorney General Francis X. Bellotti to Gerard F. Doherty, July 25, 1986.

57. Bruce Mohl, "Seven Regents Ask Bellotti to Affirm Collins' Chancellorship," *Boston Globe*, July 25, 1986.

58. Minutes of the Board of Regents special meeting, August 5, 1986.

59. See Muriel Cohen, "Georgia Educator to Head College Board," *Boston Globe*, August 13, 1986, and editorial, *Boston Globe*, August 14, 1986.

60. Interview with Edward Lashman, May 12, 1988.

61. Minutes of the Board of Regents meeting, September 9, 1986.

62. For a defense of Collins's position, see Gerard Doherty, "The Case for Collins," *Boston Globe*, September 9, 1986; and Jerome M. Mileur, "Dukakis: Skilled at Political Writing," *Daily Hampshire Gazette*, July 6, 1986.

63. Interview with former Senate president Maurice A. Donahue, September 6, 1988.

64. Interview with James Collins, February 11, 1987.

65. See Robert Wood, "Three Steps to Improve Board of Regents," *Boston Globe*, September 4, 1986.

66. Millett, *Conflict in Higher Education*, 256.

5. THE HARRINGTONS OF SALEM

1. Diego Ribadeneira and Michael Paulson, "Salem's Ties to Mormons Recalled," *Boston Globe*, May 6, 2000.

2. See John Higham, *Strangers in the Land* (New York: Atheneum, 1978), 6.

3. Paul E. Peterson, *City Limits* (Chicago: University of Chicago Press, 1981), 7.

4. Interview with James McAllister, March 1, 2000. I am indebted to McAllister for his knowledge of Salem history. His familiarity with all the mayors made him an invaluable source of insights and information.

5. See Joan M. Maloney, "John F. Hurley: Salem's First Hurrah," *Essex Institute Historical Collections* (January 1992), 27–58. I am indebted to Joan Maloney for sharing her knowledge and insights about the role of the Irish in Salem politics.

6. Interview with Kevin Harrington, August 11, 1999.

7. Letter from Carol Harrington Mulholland, July 30, 1985.

8. Interview with Francis Burkinshaw, October 19, 1999.

9. For a thumbnail biographical sketch of Joseph B. Harrington, see *Howard's "Who's Who" of the Legislature* (Boston, 1941), 52.

10. Jerome Mileur, "Party Politics in the Bay State," in *Party Politics in the New England States*, ed. Jerome Mileur (Amherst: Polity Publications, 1997), 72.

11. Ibid., 73.

12. *Salem Evening News*, November 6, 1940.

13. Charles H. Trout, *Boston: The Great Depression and the New Deal* (New York: Oxford University Press, 1977), 209.

14. Cornelius Dalton, "When Harrington Spoke, All Listened," *Boston Traveler*, February 4, 1964. Cornelius Dalton was political editor and managing editor of the *Boston Traveler*. He covered local, state, and national politics for over forty years.

15. Jack Beatty, *The Rascal King* (Reading, Mass.: Addison-Wesley, 1992), 197. See also Joseph Huthmacher, *Massachusetts People and Politics, 1919–1933* (New York: Atheneum, 1973), 55.

16. *Record of the Impeachment of Daniel H. Coakley* (Boston, 1945). See in particular "Statement of Senator Harrington and Other Senators," 106–20. See also *Massachusetts Legislative Documents* (1941), vol. 8, House Document no. 2588 (June 9, 1941), and House Document no. 2617 (June 20, 1941).

17. Doris Kearns Goodwin, *No Ordinary Time* (New York: Simon and Schuster, 1994), 65.

18. A. Scott Berg, *Lindbergh* (New York: Berkley Books, 1998), 425–30. See also Reeve Lindbergh, *Under a Wing: A Memoir* (New York: Simon and Schuster, 1998), 201–3.

19. James F. King, "Major Test of Foreign Policy of F.D.R. Due in 7th District Congressional Fight," *Salem Evening News*, December 4, 1941.

20. Ibid.

21. Ibid.

22. Ibid.

23. John P. Mallen and George Blackwood, "The Tax That Beat a Governor: The Ordeal of Massachusetts," in *The Uses of Power*, ed. Alan F. Westin (New York: Harcourt, Brace and World, 1962), 307.

24. Berg, *Lindbergh*, 413.

25. Interview with Carol Mulholland, July 11, 2000.

26. "Lane Is Democratic and Pratt Republican Nominee for Congress," *Salem Evening News*, December 17, 1941.

27. "Sen. Thomas J. Lane Wins Congressional Seat," *Salem Evening News*, December 31, 1941.

28. Quoted in Cornelius Dalton, "When Harrington Spoke, All Listened," *Boston Traveler*, February 4, 1964.

29. *Salem Evening News*, November 4, 1942.

30. *Salem Evening News*, November 8, 1944.

31. Interview with Francis Burkinshaw, October 19, 1999.

32. Interview with George and Eleanor Berry, March 16, 2000.

33. Editorial, *Salem Evening News*, February 4, 1964.

34. Interview with Kevin Harrington, August 11, 1999.

35. Cornelius Dalton et al., *Leading the Way* (Boston: Office of the Massachusetts Secretary of State, 1984), 316.

36. Interview with George and Eleanor Berry, March 16, 2000. For an obituary of Joseph B. Harrington, see *Salem Evening News*, December 4, 1967. I am indebted to George Berry, who allowed access to the files of extensive newspaper clippings and campaign memorabilia that he had collected on the Harringtons.

37. For a more detailed account of Kevin Harrington's career, see Robert D.

Gaudet, "The Willis-Harrington Commission: The Politics of Education Reform," *New England Journal of Public Policy* 3, no. 2 (Summer–Fall 1987): 66–87.

38. Mike Barnicle, "Harrington: I Ran This Place My Way...," *Boston Globe*, August 16, 1977.

39. Charles Kenney and Robert L. Turner, *Dukakis: An American Odyssey* (Boston: Houghton Mifflin, 1988), 122.

40. Walter V. Robinson, "It's President Bulger Now," *Boston Globe*, August 1, 1978.

41. Interview with Carol Mulholland, July 11, 2000.

42. Interview with Donald Flynn, May 27, 2000.

43. Interview with Richard Delande, August 26, 1999.

44. For a good analysis of these perceptions, see Charles Kenney, "The Transformation of Michael Harrington," *The Free Paper*, February 12, 1977.

45. Interview with Robert Baker, February 22, 2000.

46. Interview with Michael Harrington, August 11, 1999. In a letter to Robert Baker dated October 29, 1969, Michael Harrington wrote, "I liked the ad then as I like it now and have felt, in addition to being very flattering from a personal point of view, was the best piece of work from all reports during the campaign on the part of all the candidates involved."

47. Carl Johnson, "Two Candidates Blast Saltonstall at Debate," *Salem Evening News*, August 13, 1969.

48. "Mayor Backs Harrington Bid for 6th Congressional Post," *Salem Evening News*, August 6, 1969.

49. Roland A. Corneau, "Candidates Hit Harrison Backing," *Salem Evening News*, August 18, 1969.

50. Roland A. Corneau, "Saltonstall, Harrington Get Set for the Big One," *Salem Evening News*, August 27, 1999.

51. David Johnson, "Salty: Forthright Leadership," *Salem Evening News*, August 27, 1969.

52. Interview with Michael Harrington, August 11, 1999.

53. Foster T. Chandler, "It's Mike's Day!" *Salem Evening News*, October 1, 1969.

54. Crocker Snow Jr., "McGovern, Kennedy Ask Groundtroop Pullout within a Year," *Boston Globe*, October 16, 1969.

55. Michael Schudson, *The Good Citizen: A History of American Life* (New York: Free Press, 1998), 273.

56. Mileur, "Party Politics in the Bay State," 74.

57. Adam Clymer, *Edward M. Kennedy: A Biography* (New York: William Morrow and Company, 1999), 196.

58. Stephen Wermiel, "Harrington Faces Hearing Nov. 3 for CIA Leaks," *Boston Globe*, October 22, 1975.

59. For valuable insights into the controversy surrounding Congressman Michael Harrington, I am indebted to my faculty colleague Garrison Nelson, who is professor of political science at the University of Vermont and a senior fellow at the McCormack Institute at the University of Massachusetts, Boston. He teaches American politics and specializes in Congress.

60. David Farrell, "Bid for State-Run Electricity Is Doomed," *Boston Globe*, October 20, 1967.

61. Kenney, "The Transformation of Michael Harrington," 18.

62. Julie Maganis, "Feds Charge Harrington," *Salem Evening News*, January 15, 2000.

63. Tom Dalton, "Harrington Pleads Guilty to Misusing Money," *Salem Evening News*, September 21, 2001; and Shelley Murphy, "Harrington Reaches Plea Deal," *Boston Globe*, September 21, 2001.

6. FROM MBM SCANDAL TO STATE ETHICS REFORM

1. This essay was originally written as a case study for use by the Citizens' Legislative Seminar during the spring of 1978. At the time the essay was titled"The Dilemma of Financial Disclosure in Massachusetts." It focused solely on the controversy surrounding the adoption of Senate Rule 10-B. For purposes of this book, I have substantially revised and updated the essay to reflect the events that have transpired in Massachusetts since 1978. This revised version reconstructs the story surrounding the creation of the state ethics commission and the work that it has done in enforcing the public integrity laws.

2. Quoted in David Nyhan, "Under Tom's Thumb," *Boston Globe*, July 19, 2000.

3. Robert C. Wood, *Whatever Possessed the President* (Amherst: University of Massachusetts Press, 1993), 18.

4. See Robert C. Wood, "In the Service of the Commonwealth," commencement speech, University of Massachusetts, Boston, June 4, 1994.

5. Ray Richard, "First to Blow the Whistle on MBM Contract," *Boston Globe*, March 26, 1978.

6. See Senate Committee on Ethics, Senate Document no. 1483 (April 1, 1977), 10.

7. Jeremiah V. Murphy, "The Tip of the Iceberg," *Boston Globe*, April 9, 1977.

8. Robert J. Rosenthal, "$11,000 MBM 'Obligation' Alleged," *Boston Globe*, May 26, 1978.

9. Louis D. Brandeis, "What Publicity Can Do," *Harpers Weekly*, December 20, 1913, 10–13.

10. Robert L. Turner, "Crooked Hill, Cabbies Call It, as MBM Churns On," *Boston Globe*, March 26, 1978.

11. Ibid.

12. Letter from Harry Greenwald, June 28, 1978.

13. Interview with Chester Atkins, June 12, 1978.

14. Adapted from Chester Atkins to employees of the Senate, November 8, 1977.

15. Senate Committee on Ethics, Senate Document no. 1859 (August 16, 1977).

16. Initiative petition of Albert P. Riloff and others, House Document no. 5151 (January 4, 1978).

17. Norman Lockman, "Tough Ethics Bill Sent on to House," *Boston Globe*, April 26, 1978.

18. Norman Lockman, "A Battle of Bills on Ethics," *Boston Globe*, April 27, 1978.

19. Ibid.

20. Ibid.

21. Ibid.

22. See Senate Document no. 1434 (March 23, 1978).

23. See Senate Document no. 1859, 375 Mass. 795.

24. Norman Lockman, "Court Gives Common Cause Ethics Bill a Lift," *Boston Globe*, April 28, 1978. See also editorial, *Boston Globe*, April 29, 1978.

25. Norman Lockman, "Ethics Bill Passes Late Legislative Test," *Boston Globe*, June 1, 1978.

26. Norman Lockman, "Mass. Ethics Code Is Signed into Law," *Boston Globe*, June 6, 1978.

27. Ibid.

28. Ibid.

29. Nick King, "For Many, It's Goodbye to Legislature," *Boston Globe*, June 19, 1978.

30. Ibid.

31. Norman Lockman, "Disclosure Law: No Joy on the Hill," *Boston Globe*, December 26, 1978.

32. King, "For Many, It's Goodbye to Legislature."

33. Keverian was later cited by the state ethics commission in 1990 for hiring House employees to do private work for pay at his residence and for accepting ten oriental rugs "on consignment" from a friend who did significant business with the State House.

34. Ibid.

35. Lockman, "Disclosure Law: No Joy on the Hill."

36. Ibid.

37. Norman Lockman, "Atkins Quits as Chairman of Senate's Ethics Panel," *Boston Globe*, July 27, 1978.

38. Interview with John L. Callahan, former general secretary of Amherst College, June 12, 2000.

39. Scot Lehigh, "Turning the Corner on a Crooked Road," *Boston Globe*, January 21, 2001.

40. Ibid.

41. Ibid.

42. Ibid.

43. Ibid.

44. Interview with Joseph Barresi, June 23, 2000.

45. Scot Lehigh, "Cellucci-Cerasoli Feud Good News for Reilly," *Boston Globe*, March 23, 2001.

46. Ibid.

47. Lehigh, "Turning the Corner on a Crooked Road."

48. Wayne Woodlief, "The Guv is 1-for-2 on IG, Campaigns," *Boston Herald*, January 23, 2001.

49. Thomas C. Palmer Jr., "Report Says $83 Million in Big Dig Errors Have Slipped Away," *Boston Globe*, January 25, 2001.

50. Frank Phillips, "Outside Finalist for IG Departs," *Boston Globe*, June 5, 2001.

51. Ibid.

52. Ibid.

53. Frank Phillips and Ralph Ranalli, "New Inspector Candidates Sought," *Boston Globe*, June 8, 2001.

54. *Boston Globe*, May 23, 1993.

55. Ibid.

56. *Boston Globe*, May 30, 1993.

57. See *Final Report of Special Commission on Ethics*, June 12, 1995.

58. Sawyer's conviction was vacated on November 15, 1999, after he filed a writ of *error coram nobis* based on the U.S. Supreme Court decision in *United States v. Sun-Diamond Almond Growers* (119 S. Ct., 143 L. Ed. 2d 576, 1999).

59. Michael Rezendes and Sacha Pheiffer, "Court Limits Scaccia Rulings," *Boston Globe*, May 6, 2000.

60. Ibid.

61. Ibid.

62. Michael Rezendes, "Ethics Panel Makeup May Be a Conflict," *Boston Globe*, May 17, 2000. The conflict law, G.L. c. 268A, was enacted in 1962 and gave criminal enforcement power to the attorney general.

63. Ibid.

64. Ibid.

65. Michael Rezendes, "Ethics Panel Member Quits to End Mix-up," *Boston Globe*, May, 18, 2000.

66. Ibid.

67. Ibid.

68. Frank Phillips, "Panel Drops Most Charges against Swift," *Boston Globe*, August 24, 2000.

69. Frank Phillips, "Panel Rejects Deal, Fines Swift $1,250," *Boston Globe*, September 20, 2000.

70. Robert Keough, "Hanging Tough," *CommonWealth* (Winter 2001): 45.

7. THE USES AND ABUSES OF OUTSIDE SECTIONS

1. In September 1993 I co-authored a public policy research paper titled "Circumventing Democracy: Lawmaking by Outside Budget Section" with the late Richard Manley, who was a senior fellow at the McCormack Institute and former president of the Massachusetts Taxpayers Foundation. I owe him a large debt of gratitude for educating me in the intricacies of the state's budgetary process. This revised version of that paper partially reformulates and greatly expands my earlier views on the subject and takes up many new considerations that were not contemplated earlier.

2. Quoted in Ian Menzies, "Outside Section Bills Evade Scrutiny," *Quincy Patriot Ledger*, November 17, 1993.

3. Dave Denison, "State Budget Stalemate," *CommonWealth* (Spring 2001): 57.

4. Thomas Farragher et al., "Lobbyists' Power Grows in Tightly Controlled Legislature," *Boston Globe*, July 16, 2000.

5. Frank Phillips, "House Mulls Weakening of Election Law," *Boston Globe*, February 1, 2001. See also George Derringer, "Petersen Falls from Favor with Finneran," *Marblehead Reporter*, February 1, 2001.

6. Frank Phillips, "Finneran Gives Loyalists Leadership Roles," *Boston Globe*, January 30, 2001.

7. "Finneran's Grip," *Boston Globe*, January 31, 2001.

8. Rich Klein, "Budget Debate Praised, Blamed," *Boston Globe*, May 9, 2001.

9. Rick Klein, "Clean Elections Dealt Blow," *Boston Globe*, May 2, 2001.

10. Quoted in editorial, "A Defining Vote," *Boston Globe*, May 3, 2001.

11. See Joseph R. Barresi, *The Massachusetts Constitution: A Citizen's Edition* (Boston: John W. McCormack Institute, 1997), 21–22.

12. See Joint Rules of the Senate and House of Representatives, Rule 11.

13. For a detailed account of the 1917–19 constitutional convention, see John P. Whittaker, "The Impact of the State Constitutional Convention of 1917 on State Aid to Higher Education in Massachusetts," *New England Journal of Public Policy* 7 (Spring–Summer 1991): 39–54. See also Cornelius Dalton et al., *Leading the Way* (Boston: Office of the Secretary of State, 1984), 222–23.

14. *Debates in the Massachusetts Constitutional Convention, 1917–1919* (Boston: Wright & Potter, 1918–1920), 1146–47.

15. Ibid., 1184.

16. Ibid., 1165.

17. Statement of Representative Benjamin Loring Young of Weston, chairman of the House Committee on Ways and Means, relative to the general appropriation bill for 1919 (H-1370), February 11, 1919.

18. Statement of Representative Henry Shattuck of Boston, chairman of the House Committee on Ways and Means, relative to the general appropriation bill for 1924 (H-1312), February 1924.

19. *House Journal*, April 25, 1935, 889.

20. *House Journal*, September 11, 1955, 2: 2377.

21. Mary B. Newman to Governor William F. Weld, December 15, 1992.

22. Interview with Kevin Harrington, May 8, 2001.

23. See General Laws of Massachusetts, Chap. 684 of the Acts of 1975.

24. Newman to Governor Weld.

25. See Chap. 329 of the Acts of 1980, sec. 112.

26. For a detailed account of this controversy, see chap. 4 and Richard A. Hogarty, "The Search for a Massachusetts Chancellor: Autonomy and Politics in Higher Education," *New England Journal of Public Policy* 4 (Summer–Fall 1988): 7–38.

27. Letter from John E. McDonough, December 29, 2000.

28. Ibid.

29. *Opinions of the Justices*, 384 Mass. 820, 826 (1981).

30. *Opinions of the Justices*, 294 Mass. 616, 620 (1936).

31. 384 Mass. 820, 826; 425 N.E. 2nd 750, 754 (1981).

32. *Opinions of the Justices*, 373 Mass. 911, 915; 370 N.E. 2nd 1350, 1352 (1977).

33. *Paisner v. Attorney General*, 390 Mass. 593, 602 (1983).

34. 400 Mass. 806, 816 (1987).

35. Peter J. Howe, "Stripped of Funding Device, Mass PIRG Files Suit," *Boston Globe*, July 22, 1993.

36. Interview with Michael J. Widmer, director of the Massachusetts Taxpayers Foundation, February 6, 2001.

37. Interview with Reed Witherby, the attorney who represented Mass PIRG, February 2, 2001.

38. Interview with Janet Domenitz, director of Mass PIRG, February 5, 2001.

39. Attorney General Scott Harshbarger to Raymond Torto, director of the John W. McCormack Institute of Public Affairs, November 29, 1993.

40. Brian MacQuarrie, "Official Hits State Budget Scramble," *Boston Globe*, August 27, 2000.

41. Ibid.

42. Jordana Hart, "Study Eyes Savings with Tighter Special-Ed Rules," *Boston Globe*, March 3, 2000.

43. Doreen Iudica Vigue, "Flutie Leads Charge for Special Ed," *Boston Globe*, March 16, 2000.

44. Michael Crowley, "Special Education Law Change Approved," *Boston Globe*, July 18, 2000.

45. Michael Crowley, "Angry Finneran Yields on Late-Night Sessions," *Boston Globe*, May 17, 2000.

46. Interview with Ken White, director of Common Cause, September 7, 2000.

47. Thomas Farragher et al., "Lobbyists' Power Grows in Tightly Controlled Legislature," *Boston Globe*, July 16, 2000.

48. Executive Office for Administration and Finance, "Outside Sections: Misuse and Reform," Policy Brief Series no. 8 (April 2001), 8–9. The research and analysis for this policy brief was prepared mainly by James T. Gass.

49. Letter from John E. McDonough, December 29, 2000.

INDEX

RICHARD A. HOGARTY was born and raised in New Jersey. He received his bachelor's degree from Dartmouth College, his master's from the University of Pennsylvania, and his doctorate in political science from Princeton University, where he studied with Duane Lockard. He served on active duty as an officer in the United States Marine Corps from 1955 to 1957. Professor Hogarty taught at the University of Massachusetts Boston, in the political science department and the College of Public and Community Service (CPCS), from 1968 until his retirement in 1998. He was a member of the planning faculty group that led to the creation of CPCS in the early 1970s and directed the UMass/Boston graduate program in public affairs for many years. He is currently professor emeritus of political science and a senior fellow at the John W. McCormack Institute of Public Affairs at UMass/Boston and serves as a member of the Massachusetts Mental Health Planning Council. Professor Hogarty has written and published numerous articles, position papers, and research reports on public policy issues and is the author of *Leon Abbett's New Jersey: The Emergence of the Modern Governor* (American Philosophical Society). The father of six children, he lives in Marblehead, Massachusetts, with his wife, Ann.